Graeme Baber

International Law Changes in Light of the Invasion of Ukraine

nova
science publishers
www.novapublishers.com

DOI: https://doi.org/10.52305/DBAN6487

NOTICE TO THE READER

Library of Congress Cataloging-in-Publication Data

Names: Baber, Graeme author
Title: International law changes in light of the invasion of Ukraine / Graeme Baber.
Description: Hauppauge : Nova Science Publishers, 2025. | Series: Laws and legislation | Includes bibliographical references and index. |
Identifiers: LCCN 2025004929 (print) | LCCN 2025004930 (ebook) | ISBN 9798895303849 hardcover | ISBN 9798895304532 adobe pdf
Subjects: LCSH: Russo-Ukrainian War, 2014---Law and legislation | Russian Invasion of Ukraine, 2022 | Crimea (Ukraine)--History--Russian occupation, 2014- | War (International law) | United Nations. Security Council | Permanent Court of International Justice | International Court of Justice
Classification: LCC KZ6795.U46 B33 2025 (print) | LCC KZ6795.U46 (ebook) | DDC 341.6--dc23/eng/20250219
LC record available at https://lccn.loc.gov/2025004929
LC ebook record available at https://lccn.loc.gov/2025004930

Published by Nova Science Publishers, Inc. † New York

To my Mum, to the memories of my Dad and grandparents,
and to the memory of our cat Lux (2007-2024)

Contents

Preface xi

List of Abbreviations xiii

Chapter 1 **Introduction** 1

Abstract 1

The Background 1

The Problem 3

The UN Charter *3*

What Is Done When a Member State of the UN Breaches the UN Charter? *4*

The Russian Veto *4*

Under What Circumstances Does the UN Charter Require a Permanent Member of the UNSC to Abstain from Voting? *6*

Do Any of the Above-Listed Circumstances Apply to Russia Regarding Its Invasion of Ukraine? What Conclusions Can Be Drawn? *6*

What Other Action May Be Taken After a Breach of the UN Charter? *7*

Comment *10*

Conclusion 11

Chapter 2 **The First World War, the League of Nations, and the Permanent Court of International Justice** 13

Abstract 13

Introduction 14

The First World War and the Peace Treaties 15

The First World War *15*

The Peace Treaties *16*

Comment *16*

The League of Nations 16

Introduction *16*

The Foundation of the League of Nations *17*

The Covenant of the League of Nations *20*

The Dissolution of the League of Nations *23*

Comment *24*

The Permanent Court of International Justice 24

Introduction *24*

The Foundation of the PCIJ *25*

The Covenant of the League of Nations and the PCIJ......26
The Statute of the PCIJ......28
The Dissolution of the PCIJ......32
Comment......33
Conclusion......33

Chapter 3 **The Second World War, the United Nations, and the International Court of Justice**......35
Abstract......35
Introduction......36
The Second World War and Its Settlements......36
The Second World War......36
Settlements Following the Second World War......38
Comment......40
The United Nations......40
Introduction......40
The Foundation of the UN......40
The UN Charter......47
Comment......56
The International Court of Justice......56
Introduction......56
The Foundation of the ICJ......57
The Statute of the ICJ......57
Comment......63
Conclusion......63

Chapter 4 **The Charter of the United Nations and the Development of International Law to the Present**......65
Abstract......65
Introduction......66
The First Occurrence of 'International Law': Sources......66
The Second Occurrence of 'International Law': Principles......66
The Third Occurrence of 'International Law': Progressive Development and Codification......66
The Workings and Output of the ILC......68
Membership......68
Progressive Development of International Law......68
Codification of International Law......69
Summaries of Work of the ILC......70
Comment......72
Primary Sources: International Conventions......73
Introduction......73
Defining the Terms 'Convention' and 'Treaty'......73
Work of the ILC......75
Vienna Convention on the Law of Treaties (1969)......98
Vienna Convention on the Law of Treaties Between States and International Organizations or Between International Organizations (1986)......105

Comment ... *105*
Primary Sources: International Custom ... 107
Introduction ... *107*
Work of the ILC ... *107*
Conclusions on Identification of Customary International Law ... *111*
Comment ... *120*
Primary Sources: *Jus Cogens* ... 120
Introduction ... *120*
Work of the ILC ... *121*
Draft Conclusions on Identification and Legal Consequences of Peremptory Norms of General International Law (Jus Cogens) ... *121*
Comment ... *143*
Primary Sources: General Principles of Law ... 143
Introduction ... *143*
Work of the ILC ... *144*
Draft Conclusions on General Principles of Law Adopted by the ILC on First Reading ... *144*
Comment ... *154*
Secondary Sources ... 154
Introduction ... *154*
Work of the ILC ... *156*
Draft Conclusions on Subsidiary Means for the Determination of Rules of International Law Provisionally Adopted Thus Far by the ILC ... *156*
Comment ... *158*
Conclusion ... 159

Chapter 5 **The Legality of the Invasion of Ukraine** ... 161
Abstract ... 161
Introduction ... 161
Applying the Law to the Facts ... 162
Conclusion ... 171

Chapter 6 **Why Changes Are Needed to the United Nations and to International Law** ... 173
Abstract ... 173
Introduction ... 174
Permanent Membership of the UNSC ... 175
The Veto ... 176
Use of the Veto May Disable the UNSC ... *176*
Exercise of the Veto May Prevent Implementation of Amendments to the UN Charter That Have Been Adopted by the General Assembly ... *176*
Practice of the Permanent Members of the UNSC in Their Use of the Veto ... *177*
Suggestions That Have Been Made for the Use of the Veto ... *177*
Comment ... *182*

Dispute Settlement for Territorial Disagreements 183
The Statute of the ICJ 184
Declarations Made under Article 36(2) of the Statute of the ICJ..184
Article 38(2) of the Statute of the ICJ..187
Article 59 of the Statute of the ICJ 187
Comment..187
Reservations to Multilateral Conventions.. 188
The Direction of International Law 196
From the 1920s to the 2020s: Revisiting the Case of the S.S. "Lotus"..196
Does Such Development in International Law Indicate a Wider Trend?...198
Comment..199
Conclusion 200

Chapter 7 **Suggested Changes to the United Nations and to International Law**.. 201
Abstract.. 201
Introduction.. 201
Amendments to the UN Charter... 202
Paragraph 1 of Article 2 of the UN Charter......................................202
Article 27 of the UN Charter...202
The First Sentence of Paragraph 2 of Article 47 of the UN Charter..203
Chapter VIII of the UN Charter: Regional Arrangements.................203
Article 94 of the UN Charter...204
Chapter XVIII of the UN Charter: Amendments...............................205
Paragraph 1 of Article 7 of the UN Charter.......................................205
Statute of the Parliament of the United Nations...................................... 206
Amendments to the Statute of the ICJ 213
Article 36 of the Statute of the ICJ...213
Article 38 of the Statute of the ICJ...214
Article 59 of the Statute of the ICJ...214
Amendment to the Draft Conclusions of the ILC 214
Conclusion 214

Chapter 8 **Conclusion** 215
Abstract.. 215
Introduction.. 216
Good Government: St. Augustine of Hippo.. 216
Good Government: Applying the Augustinian Method........................... 218
Heads and Senior Members of the National Governments of States 218
Officials of the UN...219
International Judges, Advocates and Scholars...................................219
Comment...220
The Future: What Issues Are Still to Be Addressed?............................... 220

Introduction *220*
The ILC *220*
The ICJ *221*
The ITLOS *222*
Comment *223*
Conclusion 223

About the Author 225

References 227

Bibliography 259

Index 273

Preface

The thoughts that led to the writing of *International Law Changes in the Light of the Invasion of Ukraine* were crystallized in 2014, when Russia occupied Crimea and little was done in response. The UNSC was unable to act because Russia's Permanent Representative to the UN would veto – and did veto – any proposals for resolutions of the UNSC on this matter. Of course, the USSR had a history of invading its neighbours – most recently Afghanistan in 1979 in respect of which I can remember the announcement on the BBC News, but the fact that Russia has continued a similar trend in the post-Soviet era has appeared shocking. I addressed the matter of the UNSC veto in Essay Ten of *Essays on International Law*, but nothing was done regarding this – nor could, in practice, be done because of the restrictions that the UN Charter imposes on its amendment. When Russia followed its activities of 2014 with the main invasion of Ukraine in 2022, it was clear that a further publication had to be presented. Initially, I did not take this on – retiring from writing early in 2023 after the submission to the publisher of *An Overview of Corporate Securities Law in Four English-Language Jurisdictions*. But, by the end of that year, it became clear that I had to do something. This book is the outcome.

The monograph introduces the problem in its first chapter. It follows this with a chronological development of institutional international law in Chapters 2 and 3, and describes the work that the ILC has done regarding sources of international law in Chapter 4. Chapter 5 applies this law to the invasion of Ukraine. Chapter 6 addresses the need for changes to the international legal framework. My recommended alterations are set out in Chapter 7. The final chapter concludes.

Given the gravity of the situation concerning the stasis of the UN Charter, I hope that the need for modifications to it is taken as seriously as the current circumstances merit. This book may provide impetus for the process of appropriate change to begin. I also hope that you enjoy your reading.

Graeme Baber
December 2024

List of Abbreviations

BBC	British Broadcasting Corporation
ECOSOC	Economic and Social Council of the United Nations
EU	European Union
EUR	Euros
ICC	International Criminal Court
ICJ	International Court of Justice
ILC	International Law Commission
ITLOS	International Tribunal for the Law of the Sea
NATO	North Atlantic Treaty Organization
PCIJ	Permanent Court of International Justice
UK	United Kingdom of Great Britain and Northern Ireland
UN	United Nations
UN Charter	Charter of the United Nations
UNCLOS	United Nations Convention on the Law of the Sea 1982
UNSC	United Nations Security Council
USA	United States of America
USD	United States Dollars
USSR	Union of Soviet Socialist Republics

Chapter 1

Introduction

Abstract

President Boris Yeltsin was respected for attempting political and market reform in Russia along Western lines, i.e., working towards democracy and a free market economic system. When Vladimir Putin succeeded Mr. Yeltsin as President of the Russian Federation, I considered that relations between Russia and the West would regress – but not to the same extent as after the Second World War. Russian troops occupied Crimea in February 2014 and proceeded to invade further Ukrainian territory in February 2022. As Russia and Ukraine are Member States of the UN, both are bound by the terms of the UN Charter. By invading Ukraine, Russia contravened paragraphs 2(3) and 2(4) of the UN Charter. On the dissolution of the USSR in December 1991, Russia assumed all of its obligations under the UN Charter. As the UN accepted Russia's position, the latter is the successor to the USSR as permanent member of the UNSC – with accompanying veto (i.e., 'the Russian veto'). The Russian veto takes the form of the absence of a concurring vote by Russia to non-procedural decisions of that body, as the first clause of paragraph 3 of Article 27 of the UN Charter requires. To veto a submission that is put before the UNSC, the permanent member must vote against it. As the second clause of paragraph 3 of Article 27 of the UN Charter makes clear by omission, permanent members (including Russia) are not required thereunder to abstain when participating in a vote on a proposed decision under a provision of Chapter VII of the UN Charter. Thus, Russia is legally able to veto any compulsory measures that the UNSC might propose concerning its invasion of Ukraine. A representation by a senior official of the UN to a party regarding the latter's conduct towards the UN Charter in a situation in which the UNSC cannot act reflects the position of the UN on the matter concerned. The UN Secretary-General stressed to leaders of Russia that its invasion of Ukraine was in breach of the UN Charter. In doing this, His Excellency Mr. Guterres left no room for those leaders to later claim with any legitimacy that they were unaware of the fact that the activities of Russian armed forces in Ukraine were inconsistent with any of the prevailing rules of international law. The remainder of the monograph is devoted to attempting to satisfactorily address the problem of a permanent member of the UNSC being free to veto proposals put before the UNSC which may compromise its national, governmental or leaders' interests, even if such a member has committed one or more contraventions of provisions of the UN Charter.

Keywords: charter, member, permanent, Russia, Ukraine, UN, UNSC, veto, vote

The Background

My connection with Russia and with the Russian language dates back to my schooling. On being presented with options for middle-school study, many pupils wished to study German. Parents were invited to hear talks from the various subject teachers. The Russian master, the late Mr. Ian Leverton, introduced several catchy phrases – one of which would be politically-unacceptable today but which remains in my memory – in English, 'the harder you beat the wife the better the cabbage soup.' I have long forgotten the Russian for this phrase, but do remember the Russian word for 'cabbage soup.' Anyroad, his presentation caught my mother's interest, and she convinced me that I could learn German later and that I should study Russian – which I duly did.

Having missed the school trip to Moscow and Leningrad (as it then was), I did not think about the matter again until I received a notification in the booklet of the Oxford Society (as it then was) offering a canal and river trip to Russia in May and June 1996 under the direction of the late Dr. Tony Hurran. I telephoned him; he said to me: "Graeme, if you can get yourself a Russian visa, you would be welcome to join us." I went to the Russian Embassy with no luck, and returned to the office of the travel agent. The agent, a very kind gentleman, said to me: "I will get the visa for you." And he duly did. So, I joined The Oxford Society for the two-week visit, which was a thoroughly enjoyable experience.

The three days in Moscow on the trip included a visit to the city's Kremlin, where we saw many treasures in good order. We were offered the chance to stay on there for a few hours, and one of my travel companions invited me to see the tombs of the rulers of Muscovy in the Cathedral of the Archangel with him – which I wished to do but had unfortunately left my camera on the riverboat. I went to collect it. A little later, I managed to re-enter the Kremlin with the aid of a yellow ticket which was sold to me at the gate. Unknown to me, this ticket was a pass for a political rally that was being held in the State Kremlin Palace – it was approaching the date of the 1996 Russian presential election. When I arrived, the rally had started and the main hall in the Palace had been shut. I entered the basement, and picked up a booklet with various photographs of the then-President, Boris Yeltsin, including one of him playing tennis. He was seeking re-election as President of the Russian Federation. Returning to the ground floor, I was ushered onto the gallery, where I had a view of the hall in darkness other than a few torchlights on the stage and some talking – but packed with people. I thought to myself: "If they find out that I am an Englishman, then I will be suspected of spying and may be arrested. I wouldn't like to ask Dr. Hurran to help to get me out of a Russian jail." The people on the stage had spotted me on the gallery, and one of the torchlights was shone onto me. I had to go. But I knew that I shouldn't run out of the building. I did one of the bravest things that I have ever done. I walked slowly and in a dignified manner down to the ground floor, said 'thank you' and 'goodbye' in Russian to the staff there, and left the building quietly. I walked steadily to the nearest exit of the Kremlin. No-one followed me. I told nobody of this experience until I had returned home.

1996 was the zenith of cordiality between Russia and the West, and President Yeltsin was a gentleman who was respected for attempting political and market reform of his country along Western lines, i.e., working towards democracy and a free market economic system. It was an ideal time to visit Russia, to see what it really had to offer the non-Russian and what the Russian people were like. When Vladimir Putin succeeded Mr. Yeltsin as President of the Russian Federation on the last day of 1999, I felt that relations would regress – but not to the same extent as in the bitter years after the Second World War. Notwithstanding a fairly military approach from the Russian Government in the early years of the Putin administrations[1], it was a surprise to me, therefore, when a Ukrainian LL.M. student – an intelligent lady and the daughter of a law professor in Kyiv, wanted to talk to me (as a lecturer whom she seemed to

[1] Dmitry Medvedev was President of the Russian Federation between 2008 and 2012. But he was – and remains – an ally of Mr. Putin's. Mr. Putin was Prime Minister of Russia during that time.

know had some knowledge of Russia) about the risk that she and they were under, during her time at BPP University. She was very kind to me, and I met her father, a delightful, educated gentleman. But I couldn't at the time see the reason for so much urgency. Unfortunately, it soon became clear. In February 2014, Russian troops housed in the Sevastopol naval base under an agreement between Russia and Ukraine, started to take over Crimea. Shortly afterwards, the peninsular was in Russian hands. There was further Russian activity in Donbas. I knew that the UN could do little, due to the Russian permanent seat on the UNSC with its accompanying veto. But I thought that the then President of the United States, Barack Obama, might send an American warship or two to the Black Sea – without firing – in order to attempt to stop the Russian invasion of Crimea, which was Ukrainian territory. He did not. Crimea remained under the control of the Russian Government, and fighting continued between Ukrainian and pro-Russian groups in Donbas.

After a scare in the spring of 2021[2], Russia invaded Ukraine on three fronts (north, east and south) in February 2022. The Russo-Ukraine war continues today, i.e., at the time of writing.

The Problem

The UN Charter

Russia and Ukraine are both Member States of the UN[3] [1]. Consequently, both countries are bound by the terms of the UN Charter[4]. These include paragraphs 3 and 4 of Article 2 of the

---

[2] While the Ukrainian Government considered that the number of Russian troops along the border between Ukraine and Russia had risen by 100,000 to 120,000 by the middle of April 2021, most of these troops had already been located at the borders of Ukraine as a result of their presence there from previous incursions into Ukrainian territory (Bielieskov, M. (2021), "The Russian and Ukrainian Spring 2021 War Scare," published September 21, 2021, accessed June 8, 2024, <https://www.csis.org/analysis/russian-and-ukrainian-spring-2021-war-scare>).

[3] The USSR joined the UN as an original Member State on 24th October 1945 (United Nations (2024), "Russian Federation," accessed June 8, 2024, <https://www.un.org/en/about-us/member-states/russian-federation>). Both Russia and Ukraine were part of the USSR from its foundation on 30th December 1922 until its dissolution on 26th December 1991, continuing as Member States of the UN thereafter (Conquest, R., Dewdney, J., McCauley, M., Pipes, R., and Dobrianskyi, Y. (1999), "Soviet Union," published July 26, 1999, last updated June 7, 2024, accessed June 8, 2024, <https://www.britannica.com/place/Soviet-Union>; Salenko, A. (2015), Legal Aspects of the Dissolution of the Soviet Union in 1991 and Its Implications for the Reunification of Crimea with Russia in 2014, *Heidelberg Journal of International Law*, Volume 15, 141-166, 145; United Nations (2024), "Russian Federation," accessed June 8, 2024, <https://www.un.org/en/about-us/member-states/russian-federation>; United Nations (2024), "Ukraine," accessed June 8, 2024, <https://www.un.org/en/about-us/member-states/ukraine>). In addition to the USSR, the Ukrainian Soviet Socialist Republic was a founding Member State of the UN – joining the last-mentioned on 24th October 1945 and changing its name to 'Ukraine' on 24th August 1991 (United Nations (2024), "Member States," accessed November 19, 2024, <https://www.un.org/en/about-us/member-states>; United Nations (2024), "Ukraine," accessed November 19, 2024, <https://www.un.org/en/about-us/member-states/ukraine>).

[4] The UN and its Member States "in pursuit of the Purposes [of the UN] stated in Article 1 [of the UN Charter], shall act in accordance with the following Principles[:] *All Members*, in order to ensure to all of them the rights and benefits resulting from membership, *shall fulfill in good faith the obligations assumed by them in accordance with the present Charter*" (United Nations (1945), "Charter of the United Nations," *United Nations Treaty Series* Registration Number N/A, Article 2(2); emphasis added). The text to fns 129-144 lays down Article 1 of the UN Charter.

aforementioned, which respectively require Member States to settle their disputes peacefully[5] and to refrain from using, or threatening to employ, force against the political independence or territorial integrity of any state[6]. It is submitted that Russia, by invading Ukraine on 24th February 2022, breached both of these provisions.

What Is Done When a Member State of the UN Breaches the UN Charter?

A Member State of UN that has persistently contravened the Principles that the UN Charter contains may be expelled by the UN General Assembly, if the UNSC recommends this[7]. These Principles include the seven that Article 2 of the UN Charter sets out – of which those contained in its paragraphs 3 and 4 are a part[8].

In the case of Russia's actions towards Ukraine, it would need to be determined whether Russia had *persistently* infracted paragraph 3 and/or paragraph 4 of the UN Charter. However, even if the majority of Member States on the UNSC considered that Russia had so violated these provisions, they would in practice be unable to secure a recommendation of the UNSC to expel Russia from the UN, because Russia would be free to use its veto in the UNSC to prevent this.

The Russian Veto

The UN General Assembly does not have power to pass resolutions that bind Member States[9]. By contrast, these countries are required to implement decisions of the UNSC[10]. With regard to maintaining international peace and security, the UNSC determines which Member States are required to carry out its decisions[11].

The UN Charter provides for the UNSC to comprise a representative of each of 15 Member States, five of which are permanent members – France, the Republic of China, the UK, the USA and the USSR [2]. In 1949, the Kuomintang – which ruled the Republic of China – was defeated

[5] All Member States of the UN "shall settle their international disputes by peaceful means in such a manner that international peace and security, and justice, are not endangered" (United Nations (1945), "Charter of the United Nations," Article 2(3)).

[6] All Member States of the UN "shall refrain in their international relations from the threat or use of force against the territorial integrity or political independence of any state, or in any other manner inconsistent with the Purposes of the United Nations" (United Nations (1945), "Charter of the United Nations," Article 2(4)). The text to fns 129-144 sets out the Purposes of the UN.

[7] A Member State of UN "which has persistently violated the Principles contained in the present Charter may be expelled from the Organization by the General Assembly upon the recommendation of the Security Council" (United Nations (1945), "Charter of the United Nations," Article 6).

[8] Fn 5 lays down Article 2(3) of the UN Charter (i.e., the third Principle). The first sentence of fn 6 states Article 2(4) of the UN Charter (i.e., the fourth Principle). The first sentence of fn 4 comprises the second Principle, i.e., Article 2(2) of the UN Charter. The paragraph headed 'I: Purposes and Principles', in the subsection entitled 'The UN Charter' in the section titled 'The United Nations' in Chapter 2, includes the first, fifth, sixth and seventh Principles.

[9] A careful read of Articles 10 to 17 of the UN Charter show this to be the case.

[10] The Member States of the UN "agree to accept and carry out the decisions of the Security Council in accordance with the present Charter" (United Nations (1945), "Charter of the United Nations," Article 25).

[11] The steps that are "required to carry out the decisions of the Security Council for the maintenance of international peace and security shall be taken by all the Members of the United Nations or by some of them, as the Security Council may determine" (United Nations (1945), "Charter of the United Nations," Article 48(1)).

by the Chinese Communist Party, which established the People's Republic of China, and, in 1971, the UN General Assembly passed Resolution 2758 (XXVI), which replaced the former with the latter as the representatives of China to the UN [3]; thus, the current Chinese permanent member of the UNSC – with attached veto – is the People's Republic of China. In December 1991, Russia assumed all the rights and obligations of the USSR under the UN Charter[12]; as the UN accepted Russia's position [4], the latter is the successor to the USSR as permanent member of the UNSC – with accompanying veto (hereinafter referred to as 'the Russian veto').

The Russian veto takes the form of the absence of a concurring vote by Russia – as one of the permanent members of the UNSC – to non-procedural[13] decisions of that body, as the first clause of paragraph 3 of Article 27 of the UN Charter requires.

> Decisions of the Security Council on all other [(i.e., all non-procedural)] matters shall be made by an affirmative vote of nine members including the concurring votes of the permanent members[14]; ... [5].

It is opined that the wording of the second clause of paragraph 3 of Article 27 of the UN Charter indicates that an abstention by a permanent member to the UNSC on a vote does not amount to the use of its veto regarding the proposed decision that is based on this vote; to veto a submission which is put before the UNSC, the permanent member must vote against it[15].

---

[12] The UNSC notes: "By a letter dated 24 December 1991, the Secretary-General [of the UN] requested the President of the Security Council to bring to the attention of the members of the Council the text of a letter of the same date from the Permanent Representative [to the UN] of the Union of Soviet Socialist Republics, transmitting to the Secretary-General a letter, also of the same date, from Mr. Boris Yeltsin, President of the Russian Federation, in which he informed the Secretary-General that the membership of the Union of Soviet Socialist Republics in the United Nations ... was being continued by the Russian Federation with the support of the countries of the Commonwealth of Independent States. He requested that the name "Russian Federation" should be used in the United Nations in place of the name "Union of Soviet Socialist Republics" and stated that the Russian Federation maintained full responsibility for all the rights and obligations of the Union of Soviet Socialist Republics under the Charter of the United Nations ...". (United Nations (1995), General Assembly Official Records Forty-seventh Session Supplement No.2 (A/47/2): Report of the Security Council 16 June 1991-15 June 1992 (New York: United Nations), 277).

[13] The UN Charter does not empower the permanent members of the UNSC to veto that entity's decisions on procedural matters (United Nations (1945), "Charter of the United Nations," Article 27(2)).

[14] It is submitted that the wording of this clause, i.e., the first clause of paragraph 3 of Article 27 of the UN Charter, is ambiguous. The clause does not make clear whether the nine affirmative votes must include concurring votes of all five permanent members of the UNSC, or, alternatively, whether any concurring votes of the permanent members – in contrast to abstentions by permanent members – are merely to be included in the total number of concurring votes. If the first interpretation is the correct one, then the clause needs a comma to be inserted after the word 'members' and a subsequent rewording; it should read: 'Decisions of the Security Council on all other matters shall be made by an affirmative vote of nine members[,] which shall include the concurring votes of the permanent members;'. If the second interpretation is the right one, then, another phrase must be added to the clause in order to exclude dissenting votes by permanent members; the adjusted clause might read as follows: 'Decisions of the Security Council on all other matters shall be made by an affirmative vote of nine members – including the concurring votes of the permanent members, as long as none of the permanent members casts a dissenting vote;'. The phrase 'as long as' is used rather than the phrase 'provided that', because the latter phrase follows at the start of the second clause of paragraph 3 of Article 27 of the UN Charter.

[15] In the ICJ's Advisory Opinion in *Legal Consequences for States of the Continued Presence of South Africa in Namibia (South West Africa) notwithstanding Security Council Resolution 276 (1970)*, the Government of South Africa contended that Security Council Resolution 276 (1970) was not adopted by an affirmative vote of nine members of the UNSC including the permanent members' concurring votes – as the first clause of paragraph 3 of Article 27 of the UN Charter requires, because two of the permanent members abstained (Advisory Opinion of 21 June 1971, *I.C.J. Reports 1971*, 16-66, 22). The ICJ stated: "[T]he proceedings of the Security Council extending over a long period supply abundant evidence that presidential rulings and the positions taken by members of the Council, in particular its permanent members, have consistently and uniformly interpreted the

> ... provided that, in decisions under Chapter VI [of the UN Charter[16]], and under paragraph 3 of Article 52 [of the UN Charter], a party to a dispute shall abstain from voting [5].

Thus, the Russian veto amounts to a dissenting vote by the Russian representative to the UNSC on a non-procedural matter concerning which the latter intends to take a decision.

Under What Circumstances Does the UN Charter Require a Permanent Member of the UNSC to Abstain from Voting?

A member – including a permanent member – of the UNSC must abstain from voting if it is a party to a dispute with which a decision under Chapter VI of the UN Charter or paragraph 3 of Article 52 of the UN Chapter is concerned [5]. These decisions include any on the following matters: one that: 1. calls on parties to a dispute to settle it by a method of dispute resolution [6] – which the UNSC may make if the continuance of the dispute "is likely to endanger the maintenance of international peace and security" [7], 2. "recommend[s] appropriate procedures or methods of adjustment" to a dispute of this description or a situation of similar nature [8], 3. "recommend[s] such terms of settlement as [the UNSC] may consider appropriate" to a dispute of this description [9], 4. "make[s] recommendations to the parties with a view to a pacific settlement of [any] dispute" if all of those parties request this [10], or 5. encourages the advancement of peaceful resolution of local disputes through regional arrangements or agencies [11] that consider issues concerning "the maintenance of international peace and security as are appropriate for regional action" [12].

Do Any of the Above-Listed Circumstances Apply to Russia Regarding Its Invasion of Ukraine? What Conclusions Can Be Drawn?

It is submitted that 1. does not apply because the Russian invasion already endangers the maintenance of international peace and security, and that 4. probably does not apply because Russia is unlikely to request the UNSC to make recommendations for pacific settlement of its dispute with Ukraine. Furthermore, all of the abovelisted decisions of the UNSC involve non-compulsory actions for the recipient(s) – which results from the use of the words 'call upon,' 'recommend,' 'make recommendations,' and 'encourage' in the UN Charter, so Russia, if a recipient of such a decision, is able to sidestep its implementation in an instance in which it does not exercise the Russian veto. Rather, the UNSC must take action under Chapter VII of

---

practice of voluntary abstention by a permanent member as not constituting a bar to the adoption of resolutions. By abstaining, a member does not signify its objection to the approval of what is being proposed; in order to prevent the adoption of a resolution requiring unanimity of the permanent members, a permanent member has only to cast a negative vote. This procedure followed by the Security Council ... has been generally accepted by Members of the United Nations and evidences a general practice of that Organization." (*Legal Consequences for States of the Continued Presence of South Africa in Namibia (South West Africa) notwithstanding Security Council Resolution 276 (1970)*, Advisory Opinion of 21 June 1971, *I.C.J. Reports 1971*, 16-66, 22).

[16] Chapter VI of the UN Charter is entitled 'Pacific Settlement of Disputes', and comprises Articles 33 to 38 inclusive. The paragraph headed 'VI: Pacific Settlement of Disputes', in the subsection titled 'The UN Charter' in the section entitled 'The UN Charter' in Chapter 3, lays down provisions from Chapter VI of the UN Charter.

the UN Charter[17] in order to address the situation – and, as the second clause of paragraph 3 of Article 27 of the UN Charter makes clear by omission[18], permanent members of the UNSC (including Russia) are not required thereunder to abstain when participating in a vote on a proposed decision under a provision of that Chapter. Thus, it is opined that, as the UN Charter reads at present, Russia is legally able to veto any compulsory measures that the UNSC might propose concerning its invasion of Ukraine.

What Other Action May Be Taken After a Breach of the UN Charter?

A non-exclusive list includes measures taken under Article 51 of the UN Charter, the passing of a non-binding resolution of the UN General Assembly, action specified in the operative part of a judgment or order of the ICJ, and the making of a statement by a senior official of the UN. In this subsection, a paragraph is devoted to each of these course of action – together with a comment on its application to the case at hand.

Measures Taken under Article 51 of the UN Charter

A Member State of UN may exercise a right of self-defence, alone or with other countries, if it is subject to an armed attack – until the UNSC has taken measures to continue international peace and security[19] [13]. An 'armed attack' includes action across an international border by regular armed forces, and the sending – by or on behalf of a state – of non-regular armed groups which conduct acts of such gravity as to constitute an actual armed attack by regular armed forces[20] [14]. For the right to collective self-defence to apply, the Member State for whose benefit this is used must have declared itself to have been the victim of an armed attack [15], and that country must have requested assistance [16]. Both individual and collective self-defence only justify measures that are proportional to the armed attack and which are necessary in order to respond to it [17]. It is submitted that, in the wake of the Russian invasion of Ukraine, Ukraine has exercised its right to collective self-defence under Article 51 of the UN Charter with NATO – although this is within the context of an already-established relationship between Ukraine and NATO[21].

---

[17] Chapter VII of the UN Charter is entitled 'Action with Respect to Threats to the Peace, Breaches of the Peace, and Acts of Aggression', and consists of Articles 39 to 51 inclusive. The paragraph headed 'VII: Action with Respect to Threats to the Peace, Breaches of the Peace, and Acts of Aggression', in the subsection titled 'The UN Charter' in the section entitled 'The UN Charter' in Chapter 3, sets out provisions from Chapter VII of the UN Charter.

[18] The text to fn 16 comprises the second clause of paragraph 3 of Article 27 of the UN Charter.

[19] Nothing in the UN Charter "shall impair the inherent right of individual or collective self-defence if an armed attack occurs against a Member of the United Nations, until the Security Council has taken measures necessary to maintain international peace and security. Measures taken by Members in the exercise of this right of self-defence shall be immediately reported to the Security Council and shall not in any way affect the authority and responsibility of the Security Council under the present Charter to take at any time such action as it deems necessary in order to maintain or restore international peace and security." (United Nations (1945), "Charter of the United Nations," Article 51).

[20] But an 'armed attack' does not include "assistance to rebels in the form of the provision or weapons or logistical or other support" (*Case concerning Military and Paramilitary Activities in and against Nicaragua (Nicaragua v. United States of America), The Merits*, Judgment of 27 June 1986, *I.C.J. Reports 1986*, 14-150, 104).

[21] NATO "fully supports Ukraine's inherent right to self-defence, and its right to choose its own security arrangements"; Ukraine's cooperation with NATO commenced when the newly-independence Ukraine joined the North Atlantic Cooperation Council in 1991 and the Partnership for Peace Programme in 1994, and were intensified with the signing of the Charter on a Distinctive Partnership in 1997 – which founded the NATO-Ukraine Commission (replaced by the NATO-Ukraine Council in 2023) as the main entity for developing the

The Passing of a Non-Binding Resolution of the UN General Assembly

While the resolutions of the General Assembly are not legally binding upon Member States of the UN[22], they may be persuasive. On 2nd March 2022, the General Assembly passed Resolution ES-11/1 (LXXVI), which among other things, demands that Russia immediately cease to use force against Ukraine and refrain from further illegal threat or use of force against any UN Member State [18]. On 24th March 2022, the General Assembly approved Resolution ES-11/2 (LXXVI), which reiterates the need for Resolution ES-11/1 (LXXVI) to be fully implemented [19] and repeats its request from the earlier resolution for hostilities by Russia against Ukraine to immediately stop [20]. It is opined that these resolutions were insufficiently persuasive to convince Russia to terminate its activities in Ukraine.

Action Specified in the Operative Part of a Judgment or Order of the ICJ

If a relevant case comes before the ICJ, then the Court may issue a judgment or advisory opinion (as appropriate[23]) – or, prior to such issuance, an order, which, in respect of a contentious case, may be one that introduces provisional measures. An operative clause in a judgment, or in an order made before the latter, may instruct one of the parties to cease its, or both of them to terminate their, illegal activities. The ICJ included two such instructions in the operative clause of *Allegations of Genocide under the Convention on the Prevention and Punishment of the Crime of Genocide (Ukraine v. Russian Federation), Provisional Measures*[24]. These were that Russia must immediately suspend the military actions which it started on 24th February 2022 on Ukrainian territory, and ensure that any military armed units which it directs or supports – in addition to any persons and organizations that it manages or controls – take no steps to advance those military activities [21]. While Russia (and Ukraine) are required to abide by these instructions from the ICJ [22, 23], Russia has not done so. In this situation, the UN Charter permits the other party, i.e., Ukraine, to refer the matter to the UNSC[25], which would be unable

---

relationship between NATO and Ukraine (North Atlantic Treaty Organization (2024), "Relations with Ukraine," last updated May 10, 2024, accessed June 12, 2024, <https://www.nato.int/cps/en/natohq/topics_37750.htm>). The purpose of NATO is "to guarantee the freedom and security of its members through political and military means"; these members are Albania, Belgium, Bulgaria, Canada, Croatia, Czechia, Denmark, Estonia, Finland, France, Germany, Greece, Hungary, Iceland, Italy, Latvia, Lithuania, Luxembourg, Montenegro, the Netherlands, North Macedonia, Norway, Poland, Portugal, Romania, Slovakia, Slovenia, Spain, Sweden, Türkiye, the UK and the USA (North Atlantic Treaty Organization (2024), "What is NATO?," accessed June 12, 2024, <https://www.nato.int/nato-welcome/>).

[22] Fn 9 and accompanying text.

[23] Contentious cases are brought before the ICJ either by notification of a special agreement between the parties or by a written application that is to be addressed to the Registrar of the Court (United Nations (1945), "Statute of the International Court of Justice," *United Nations Treaty Series* Registration Number N/A, Article 40(1)). The ICJ may provide an advisory opinion on any question of law at the request of a body that is authorized by, or in accordance with, the UN Charter to make this call (United Nations (1945), "Statute of the International Court of Justice," Article 40(1)). The bodies that are authorized *by* the UN Charter to request the ICJ to furnish an advisory opinion are the UNSC and the General Assembly (United Nations (1945), "Charter of the United Nations," Article 96(1)). Those that are authorized *in accordance with* the UN Charter to make such a request are other UN organs and UN specialized agencies, but only on legal questions that arise within the ambit of their activities and subject to the permission of the General Assembly (United Nations (1945), "Charter of the United Nations," Article 96(2)).

[24] Order of 16 March 2002, *I.C.J. Reports 2022*, 211-231.

[25] If a party to a case before the ICJ does not undertake the obligations that are incumbent upon it under a judgment (or order) made by the Court, then the other party may call upon the UNSC, which, may, if it considers it to be necessary, make recommendations or determine measures to be taken to effect the judgment (or the operative part of the order) (United Nations (1945), "Charter of the United Nations," Article 94(2)).

to introduce measures requiring Russia to implement the operative provisions of the ICJ's order because the Russian representative to the UNSC would be likely to exercise the Russian veto.

A Statement by a Senior Official of the UN

In a situation in which the UNSC is unable to act in response to a breach of the UN Charter, and in which the party or parties that have contravened one of more provisions of the UN Charter refuse to accept that it or they have done so, then it is submitted that responsibility rests with one of the senior officials of the UN to inform that party or those parties that it is, or they are, in violation of the UN Charter and that this is a contravention of international law – of which the UN Charter is a fundamental part. In private law, an officer of a company or other concern often has the power to bind this entity to a course of action that (s)he specifies; in many instances, the business may not subsequently retract on the obligation(s) to which the officer has committed it to. Analogously, a representation by a senior official of the UN to a party regarding the latter's conduct towards the UN Charter in a situation in which the UNSC cannot act reflects the position of the UN on the matter concerned. It was therefore a source of much relief when – with a little prior help from his friends – the UN Secretary-General squared up to the task of visiting Moscow in order to stress to the leaders of Russia that its invasion of Ukraine was in breach of the UN Charter[26], combining this responsibility with discussions with them on the evacuation of civilians who were trapped in the Ukrainian city of Mariupol which was then under intense attack from the armed forces of Russia[27]. In doing this, His Excellency Mr.

[26] The readout from the Secretary-General's meeting with the President of the Russian Federation on 26th April 2022 is as follows: "The Secretary-General met with the President of the Russian Federation, H.E. Mr. Vladimir Putin, in Moscow this afternoon. During the tête-a-tête meeting, the Secretary-General reiterated the United Nations' position on Ukraine, and they discussed the proposals for humanitarian assistance and evacuation of civilians from conflict zones, namely in relation to the situation in Mariupol. The President agreed, in principle, to the involvement of the United Nations and the International Committee for the Red Cross in the evacuation of civilians from the Azovstal plant in Mariupol. Follow-on discussions will be had with the United Nations Office for the Coordination of Humanitarian Affairs and the Russian Defence Ministry." (Guterres, A. (2022), "Readout of the Secretary-General's meeting with H.E. Mr. Vladimir Putin, President of the Russian Federation," published April 26, 2022, accessed June 13, 2024, <https://www.un.org/sg/en/content/sg/readout/2022-04-26/readout-of-the-secretary-general%E2%80%99s-meeting-he-mr-vladimir-putin-president-of-the-russian-federation?_gl=1*1fmukpc*_ga*MzI1NTMwMjU0LjE3MTgyMTA0OTc.*_ga_TK9BQL5X7Z*MTcxODI3NzU3MC40LjAuMTcxODI3NzU3MC4wLjAuMA..>). Earlier during 26th April 2022, the Secretary-General had met the Russian Foreign Minister, Mr. Sergey Lavrov (United Nations (2022), "Activities of Secretary-General in Russian Federation, 25-26 April: SG/T/3309," published May 6 2022, accessed June 13, 2024, <https://press.un.org/en/2022/sgt3309.doc.htm>). It was in this meeting that the Secretary-General set out the UN position on the Russian invasion of Ukraine; his comments after the meeting on the matter were as follows: "I had a very frank discussion with the Foreign Minister, Sergey Lavrov, and it is clear that there are two different positions on what is happening in Ukraine. According to the Russian Federation, what is taking place is a special military operation with the objectives that were announced. According to the UN, in line with the resolutions passed by the General Assembly, Russia's invasion of Ukraine is a violation of its territorial integrity and against the Charter of the United Nations." (Guterres, A. (2022), "Secretary-General's remarks at press encounter with Russian Foreign Minister, Sergey V. Lavrov," published April 26, 2022, accessed June 13, 2024, <https://www.un.org/sg/en/content/sg/press-encounter/2022-04-26/secretary-generals-remarks-press-encounter-russian-foreign-minister-sergey-v-lavrov?_gl=1*26o48x*_ga*MzI1NTMwMjU0LjE3MTgyMTA0OTc.*_ga_TK9BQL5X7Z*MTcxODI4MTk1My41LjEuMTcxODI4MjIzNC4wLjAuMA..>).

[27] Fn 26 summarizes the Secretary-General's meeting with the President of the Russian Federation on 26th April 2022, during which the evacuation of civilians from Mariupol was discussed. This matter was also addressed in the Secretary-General's meeting with the Russian Foreign Minister (Guterres, A. (2022), "Secretary-General's remarks at press encounter with Russian Foreign Minister, Sergey V. Lavrov," published April 26, 2022, accessed June 13, 2024, <https://www.un.org/sg/en/content/sg/press-encounter/2022-04-26/secretary-generals-remarks-press-encounter-russian-foreign-minister-sergey-v-lavrov?_gl=1*26o48x*_ga*MzI1NTMwMjU0LjE3MTgyMTA0OTc.*_ga_TK9BQL5X7Z*MTcxODI4MTk1My41LjEuMTcxODI4MjIzNC4wLjAuMA..>).

Guterres left no room for those leaders to later claim with any legitimacy that they were unaware of the fact that the activities of Russian armed forces in Ukraine were inconsistent with any of the prevailing rules of international law.

Comment

All that is reasonably possible has been done by the UN – especially the Secretary-General – and by NATO to contain the effects of the Russian invasion of Ukraine on 24th February 2022, given the UNSC's inability to impose compulsory measures under Chapter VII of the UN Charter on Russia due the wielding of the Russian veto. The Secretary-General's intervention of 26th April 2022, together with NATO's proportionate policy of reasonable financial and military aid to Ukraine in collective self-defence in accordance with Article 51 of the UN Charter, has made it inevitable that, one day, the boundaries of the states of Ukraine and Russia will be restored to their positions on 26th December 1991 – in accordance with international law[28]. While this is the good news, there remain multiple issues of concern.

First, there is the status of Crimea – legally an autonomous region within the borders of Ukraine. But Crimea has traditionally been the homeland of its own peoples, many of whom have been displaced. There are Russians in Crimea – but this does not make it a province of Russia by right. Furthermore, the security arrangements that applied to Crimea in the period prior to 27th February 2014[29] have been rendered obsolete by subsequent events. New security arrangements for Crimea will need to be established. All this is ground for future discussion.

Second, there is the issue of Russian populations in Ukraine, especially in Donbas. This is part of a wider matter according to which, during the period in which the USSR was the sovereign state comprising republics, people from different republics moved within the USSR, sometimes crossing boundaries between republics. Thus, Ukraine is not the only ex-Soviet republic to have sizeable Russian minorities in some of its provinces. These are subjects for future discussion – after the borders of Ukraine and Russia that existed on 26th December 1991 have been reinstated[30].

Third, there is the Convention on the Prevention and Punishment of the Crime of Genocide, to which both Russia and Ukraine are parties. According to the Convention, genocide is a crime under international law even in time of war [24]. Genocide is also covered by the Rome Statute of the ICC [25], as are crimes against humanity [26], war crimes [27] and the crime of aggression [28]. Both Ukraine and Russia have signed the Rome Statute of the ICC, but neither have ratified it as yet [29]. While the Rome Statute of the ICC has been ratified by 124 States Parties, there are significant omissions regarding its ratification – which include not only Russia and Ukraine (which have signed it) but also China, India, Indonesia, Pakistan, Saudi Arabia

---

[28] The USSR was officially dissolved on 26th December 1991 (fn 3), at which point the former Soviet republics – including Russia and Ukraine – became independent states and Member States of the UN. It is opined that the borders which existed between these then newly-independent states on that date are the boundaries which are currently recognized as being valid under international law.

[29] This was the day upon which armed Russian troops without insignia seized control of the Crimean parliament building in Simferopol, raising the Russian flag (Reuters (2014), Timeline: Political crisis in Ukraine and Russia's occupation of Crimea, *Reuters*, Saturday 8 March 2014; Encyclopaedia Britannica (1998), "History of Crimea," published July 20, 1998, last updated June 14, 2024, accessed June 14, 2024, <https://www.britannica.com/place/Crimea/History>).

[30] Fn 28.

and Türkiye (which have not signed it), and Iran and the USA (which have signed it) [29]. Thus, there is a way to go before the standards set out therein are universally and wholly accepted as being part of customary international law.

Fourth, there is the need for Ukrainian villages, towns and cities whose buildings have been damaged or destroyed during the conflict with Russia to be rebuilt – which will require funding that amounts to billions of USD (or equivalent in other currencies). Discussions are already taking place as to the sources for this finance and as to the arrangements for its provision and repayment[31].

Fifth, there is the issue of the paralysis of the UNSC in the face of the Russian invasion of Ukraine. Although Russia is in breach of the UN Charter, the UNSC has been unable to introduce any measures under Chapter VII of the UN Charter that address the Russian occupation of Ukraine, consequent to the Russian veto. This has been an avoidable problem, as reform of this aspect of the UN Charter should have taken place before now. I have been one of those who previously identified the difficulty. I suggested the addition of a new paragraph to Article 27 of the UN Charter, in order to eliminate the blockage in the UNSC caused its by permanent members vetoing proposals for decisions that may adversely affect their territorial interests[32].

In essence, therefore, 'the problem' as ascertained in this section is the freedom of a permanent member of the UNSC to veto proposals put before the UNSC which may compromise its national, governmental or leaders' interests, even if such a member has committed one or more contraventions of provisions of the UN Charter. This matter is intensified by the UNSC being the only part of the UN that can pass resolutions which legally bind the latter's Member States. The lack of response from the UNSC to illegal activities of Russian armed forces in Ukraine demonstrates this difficulty.

The remainder of this monograph is devoted to attempting to satisfactorily address this problem. Rather than attending to it in a narrow fashion, i.e., suggesting and/or reiterating from *Essays on International Law* alterations to Article 27 of the UN Charter as the sole remedy, subsequent chapters of the current book look at aspects of the history of the UN and the ICJ and attempt to generate a wider range of recommendations for changes to the UN and to international law on the basis of the experience of the unlawful Russian occupation of territory within Ukraine.

Conclusion

This chapter sets out the background from a personal perspective to the problem of the lack of response from the UNSC to the Russian invasion of Ukraine, and then identifies this difficulty. The next chapter describes institutional developments in international law consequential to the First World War.

---

[31] At the G7 summit in Italy in June 2024, the leaders of the seven constituent states (Canada, France, Germany, Italy, Japan, the UK and the USA), together with the Presidents of the European Council and the European Commission, agreed to use future interest payments from Russia's frozen central bank assets – most of which are held in the EU – as security for the issuance of a loan to Ukraine to be used to pay for the reparation of damage caused there by the Russian invasion of Ukraine (Watling, T. (2024), G7 leaders strike deal on $50bn funding for Ukraine using Russian assets, *The Independent*, Thursday 13 June 2024).

[32] See Baber, G. (2017), *Essays on International Law* (Newcastle-upon-Tyne: Cambridge Scholars Publishing), at pages 346-348.

Chapter 2

The First World War, the League of Nations, and the Permanent Court of International Justice

Abstract

The PCIJ was established without compulsory jurisdiction, and its successor the ICJ was not granted it either. This may have been because international arbitration had proved to be powerless to stop the First World War from spiralling out of control. About ten million troops were killed in the First World War and more than twenty million were wounded. Millions of civilians died in that war, which resulted in about ten million refugees across Europe. The Paris Peace Conference of 1919 and 1920 set the terms for the Peace Treaties that officially ended the First World War. The Covenant of the League of Nations was the foremost common attribute of the settlement following the First World War; it was included, as Part I, in the Treaties of Versailles, Saint-Germain, Neuilly, Trianon and Sèvres. The Peace Treaties redrew international boundaries and limited the number of permissible troops in defeated countries. The creation of the League of Nations introduced a global institution to moderate relations among states, and between states and other territories. President Woodrow Wilson mentioned a 'League for Peace' in his speech to the Senate on 22nd January 1917. On 8th January 2018, he put forward a 14-point plan for global peace. While Dr. Wilson did not succeed in carrying out his post-war programme in full at the Paris Peace Conference, he did secure adoption of the Covenant of the League of Nations on 28th April 1919 – which entered into force on 10th January 1920, at which point the League of Nations came into being. Except where expressly provided otherwise, non-procedural decisions at any meeting of the Council of the League of Nations or the Assembly of the League of Nations required the agreement of all the Members of the League of Nations that were represented there. On 20th April 1946, the League of Nations was dissolved. The League of Nations was insufficiently resourced to be able to contain the military rise of Germany, Italy and Japan during the 1930s. The Protocol of Signature of the Statute for the Permanent Court of International Justice, to which the Statute of the PCIJ was adjoined, was opened for signature on 16th December 1920. By September 1921, a majority of the Members of the League of Nations had ratified the Protocol – which occasioned the immediate establishment of the PCIJ. The jurisdiction of the PCIJ comprises all cases that the disputants refer to it and all issues that are specifically provided for in conventions and treaties in force. A decision of the PCIJ has no binding force except between the parties and in respect of the particular case. The PCIJ convened for the final time in October 1945, and was dissolved on 17th April 1946 by a resolution of the League of Nations. The replacement of the PCIJ by a new court – the ICJ – had nothing to do with perceptions of the PCIJ as a functional court, which worked well and published respected judgments and advisory opinions. The ICJ continued, and built on, this activity.

Keywords: Assembly, case, Council, Covenant, League, PCIJ, peace, Statute, war

Introduction

While international law's origins predate the twentieth century[33], this description starts early within that century – as the foundation of the League of Nations begins the institutional phase of this topic. Some jurists writing in the late nineteenth century, and attending the Hague Conferences of 1899 and 1907 had wished to establish an international court which possessed compulsory jurisdiction, i.e., all states that were parties to the statute of this court would be required to submit all their cross-border disputes to it[34] [30]. But the PCIJ was founded without compulsory jurisdiction, and its successor the ICJ was not granted it either. A possible reason for this was that international arbitration had proved to be powerless to stop the First World War from spiralling out of control – even though it had helped to resolve small and medium conflicts prior to 1914[35] [31]. The main institution of the post-war order – the League of Nations – centred on collective decision-making rather than on arbitration and adjudication, and the PCIJ was designed to function on its margins [32].

[33] Hugo Grotius (1583-1645) is widely acknowledged to be the father of international law, in particular pursuant to the writing of his monograph entitled *De Jure Belli at Pacis* (On the Law of War and Peace). But the beginnings of the subject can be traced much earlier – to Roman law and before.

[34] One of the output documents from the Hague Conference of 1899 was the 1899 Convention for the Pacific Settlement of International Disputes, which established the Permanent Court of Arbitration: "With the object of facilitating an immediate recourse to arbitration for international differences, which it has not been possible to settle by diplomacy, the Signatory Powers undertake to organize a Permanent Court of Arbitration, accessible at all times and operating, unless otherwise stipulated by the parties, in accordance with the Rules of Procedure inserted in the present Convention. ... The Permanent Court shall be competent for all arbitration cases, unless the parties agree to institute a special Tribunal." (Permanent Court of Arbitration (2016), 1899 Convention for the Pacific Settlement of International Disputes (The Hague: Permanent Court of Arbitration), 7, Articles 19 and 20). The 1907 Convention for the Pacific Settlement of International Disputes – an output document from the Hague Conference of 1907 – has replaced the 1899 Convention for the Pacific Settlement of International Disputes (Permanent Court of Arbitration (2016), 1907 Convention for the Pacific Settlement of International Disputes (The Hague: Permanent Court of Arbitration), 37, Article 91). Like the 1899 Convention, the 1907 Convention provides for the Permanent Court of Arbitration: "With the object of facilitating an immediate recourse to arbitration for international differences, which it has not been possible to settle by diplomacy, the Contracting Powers undertake to maintain the Permanent Court of Arbitration, as established by the First Peace Conference [(i.e., the Hague Conference of 1899)], accessible at all times, and operating, unless otherwise stipulated by the parties, in accordance with the rules of procedure inserted in the present Convention. ... The Permanent Court is competent for all arbitration cases, unless the parties agree to institute a special Tribunal." (Permanent Court of Arbitration (2016), 1907 Convention for the Pacific Settlement of International Disputes, 27, Articles 41 and 42).

[35] A landmark in the successful use of arbitration for the settlement of international disputes is the *Alabama Claims* arbitration, in which Great Britain was ordered by a tribunal comprising five arbitrators – one from each of Brazil, Great Britain, Italy, Switzerland and the USA – to pay 15.5 million USD to the USA in gold, for its breach of provisions of the treaty between Great Britain and the USA concluded and signed at Washington D.C. of 8th May 1871 which provided for all claims under this treaty to be settled by an arbitral tribunal of such composition (United Nations (2012), Alabama claims of the United States of America against Great Britain: Award rendered on 14 September 1872 by the tribunal of arbitration established by Article I of the Treaty of Washington of 8 May 1871, *Reports of International Arbitral Awards*, Volume XXIX, 125-134, 128 and 133-134).

The First World War and the Peace Treaties

The First World War

The Start of the First World War

On 28th June 1914, Austrian Archduke Franz Ferdinand and his wife, Sophie, were shot by Gavrilo Princip of the Young Bosnia movement, while touring Sarajevo after they had inspected the imperial armed forces in Bosnia and Herzegovina[36] [33]. In response to a letter from Austrian Emperor Franz Josef I to German Kaiser Wilhelm II requesting the latter's support, on 6th July 1914, German Chancellor Theobald von Bethmann Hollweg informed representatives of the Austrian regime that it had the German government's full backing [33]. On 23rd July 1914, the Austro-Hungarian ambassador to Serbia informed the Serbian government that it must suppress anti-Austrian propaganda, eliminate terrorist organizations within Serbia, and accept an independent investigation by the Austro-Hungarian government into the abovementioned assassination; if it did not so act, then – said the ambassador – it would be subject to military action [33]. The Serbian regime appealed to the Russian government for help, following which the latter began to mobilize its army in the belief that the German government would use the crisis as an excuse to begin a war in the Balkans [33]. On 28th July 1914, Austria-Hungary declared war on Serbia [33]. On 1st August 1914, Germany announced that it was at war with Russia [33]. Germany attacked France – allied to Russia – via neutral Belgium, thereby bringing the UK into the war on the Serbian-Russian-French side [33].

The Scale of the First World War. 1. Populations of the Belligerents

Including the those of the states that entered the war after 1914, the constituent populations of the belligerents totalled more than eight hundred million people [34]. *2. Military casualties and injuries.* About ten million troops were killed in the war; more than twenty million were wounded [34]. *3. Civilian casualties.* This totalled millions of people – the precise figure depends upon how wide one draws the definition beyond those who died in the actual fighting [34]. *4. Refugees.* The war resulted in about ten million refugees across Europe [34].

The End of the First World War

On 11th November 1918 an armistice was signed – entering into force later that day [35], which terminated the war in Western Europe as its conditions precluded Germany from continuing the conflict; Bulgaria, the Ottoman Empire and Austria-Hungary had signed similar agreements on 29th September 1918 [36], 30th October 1918 [37] and 3rd November 1918, respectively [38, 39]. Fighting continued elsewhere [38]. The Paris Peace Conference of 1919 and 1920 set the terms for the Peace Treaties that officially ended the First World War [38, 39]. The entry into

---

[36] At this time, Bosnia and Herzegovina was under Austro-Hungarian rule, having been occupied by Austro-Hungarian forces since 1878 and formally annexed to Austria-Hungary in 1908, causing resentment among Serb and South Slav nationalists in Bosnia and Herzegovina and leading to the growth of revolutionary groups and secret societies – including Young Bosnia – that were devoted to the overthrow of Austro-Hungarian rule there (Lampe, J., Malcolm, N., and Pickering P. (1999), "Bosnia and Herzegovina under Austro-Hungarian rule," published June 1, 1999, last updated June 23, 2024, accessed June 24, 2024, <https://www.britannica.com/place/Bosnia-and-Herzegovina/Bosnia-and-Herzegovina-under-Austro-Hungarian-rule>; Carroll, E., and Hepler, R. (2024), "Bosnian Crisis of 1908: Overview, History & Effect," accessed June 24, <https://study.com/academy/lesson/the-bosnian-crisis-of-1908-annexation-by-austria-hungary.html>).

force of the Treaty of Lausanne on 6th August 1924 marked the conclusion of the First World War[37] [40, 41].

The Peace Treaties

These comprised agreements between the Allied and Associated Powers, i.e., the victors in the First World War, and defeated states individually, namely the Treaty of Versailles with Germany – which was signed on 28th June 1919, the Treaty of Saint-Germain with Austria – signed on 10th September 1919, the Treaty of Neuilly with Bulgaria – signed on 27th November 1919, the Treaty of Trianon with Hungary – signed on 4th June 1920, and the Treaty of Sèvres with the Ottoman Empire – signed on 10th August 1920 – which went unratified and was replaced by the Treaty of Lausanne (signed on 24th July 1923) recognizing the boundaries of the Ottoman Empire's successor state Turkey (or Türkiye as it is now called[38]) [39, 41, 42]. The Treaty of Versailles formed the template for the Treaties of Saint-Germain, Neuilly, Trianon and Sèvres, which followed its principles, namely, that the defeated states were required to disarm, pay reparations, and surrender territory to other countries [42]. The Covenant of the League of Nations was the foremost common attribute of the settlement following the First World War; it was included, as Part I, in the Treaties of Versailles, Saint-Germain, Neuilly, Trianon and Sèvres [43].

Comment

The First World War was dreadful, and, with the benefit of hindsight, appears to have been, in part, mindless. Its severity necessitated supranational action to try to limit the possibility and the scale of future conflicts. The Paris Peace Conference, its main output – the Peace Treaties, and the establishment of the League of Nations, were the attempts of the Allied and Associated Powers to address this matter. The Peace Treaties redrew international boundaries and limited the number of permissible troops in defeated countries. The creation of the League of Nations introduced a global institution to moderate relations among states, and between states and other territories.

The League of Nations

Introduction

The League of Nations was the moderator of international relations between states in the period between the First and Second World Wars. The original parties to the Covenant of the League of Nations agreed to it "[i]n order to promote international co-operation and to achieve

[37] The Treaty of Lausanne replaced the unratified Treaty of Sèvres (text to fn 38).

[38] In a request submitted to the Secretary-General of the UN by the state's Minister of Foreign Affairs on 26th May 2022, the Republic of Türkiye changed its official name from the Republic of Turkey to the Republic of Türkiye (United Nations (2024), "Türkiye," accessed June 25, 2024, <https://www.un.org/en/about-us/member-states/turkiye>).

international peace and security by" four means stated therein[39] [44]. The Covenant provided for the establishment of a Council, an Assembly, a PCIJ via the Council, and a system of mandates for colonies and territories that were no longer under the sovereignty of states which were defeated in the First World War – as well as for other lands specified therein.

The Foundation of the League of Nations

The Presidents of the USA in the early twentieth century, namely Messrs. Theodore Roosevelt (1901-1909) and William Taft (1909-1913) and Dr.[40] Woodrow Wilson (1913-1921), were interested in promoting international peace. Mr. Roosevelt was awarded the Nobel Peace Prize for his negotiation of peace between Russia and Japan in 1905 and for having employed arbitration in a dispute of the USA with Mexico – and his former Secretary of State Mr. Elihu Root was also a winner of the Nobel Peace Prize [45]. Messrs. Taft and Root had been among the originators of the *League to Enforce Peace*[41] [43], which, under the presidency of Mr. Taft, pushed for and supported the establishment of the League of Nations, of which Dr. Wilson was the main architect and in respect of which – for his role as its founder – Dr. Wilson won the Nobel Peace Prize [46, 47].

As President of the USA, Dr. Wilson maintained the neutrality of the USA in the First World War until 2nd April 2017, when, in response to the sinking of four of the USA's ships by German submarines on 27th March 2017 – which was part of the unrestricted submarine warfare policy that Germany had announced on 31st January 2017, he asked the Congress for a declaration of war – which it granted on 6th April 2017 [48]. Dr. Wilson mentioned a 'League for Peace' before he took the USA to war with Germany and its allies, as in the following abridged version of his 'Peace Without Victory' speech to the Senate on 22nd January 1917.

> ... I have sought this opportunity to address you because I thought that I owed it to you, as the council associated with me in the final determination of our international obligations, to disclose to you without reserve the thought and purpose that have been taking form in my mind in regard to the duty of our government in the days to come, when it will be necessary to lay afresh and upon a new plan the foundation of peace among the nations. ... To take part in such a service will be the opportunity for which [the people of the USA] have sought to prepare themselves by the very principles and purposes of their polity and the approved practices of their government ... . That service is ... to add their authority

---

[39] These four means are "the acceptance of obligations not to resort to war", "the prescription of open, just and honourable relations between nations", "the firm establishment of the understandings of international law as the actual rule of conduct among Governments", and "the maintenance of justice and a scrupulous respect for all treaty obligations in the dealings of organised peoples with one another" (League of Nations – Official Journal (1920), The Covenant of the League of Nations, *League of Nations – Official Journal*, February 2020, 3-11, 3, Article 1).

[40] Dr. Woodrow Wilson (1856-1924) held a Doctor of Philosophy degree in political science from Johns Hopkins University for a dissertation titled '*Congressional Government: A Study in American Politics*'; he was later appointed Professor of Jurisprudence and Political Economy, and, subsequently, President, of Princeton University (Wilson Center (2024), "About Woodrow Wilson," accessed June 26, 2024, <https://www.wilsoncenter.org/about-woodrow-wilson>).

[41] The *League to Enforce Peace* was an international organization that was established in 1915, with the aim of promoting a global body for world peace; it ceased its operations in 1923 (Tennessee Virtual Archive (2024), "League to Enforce Peace convention invitation to Governor Rye," accessed June 26, 2024, <https://teva.contentdm.oclc.org/digital/collection/p15138coll18/id/2590/>).

> and their power to the authority and force of other nations to guarantee peace and justice throughout the world. Such a settlement cannot now be long postponed. It is right that[,] before it comes, this government should frankly formulate the conditions upon which it would feel justified in asking our people to approve its formal and solemn adherence to a League for Peace. I am here to attempt to state those conditions. The present war must first be ended ... . The treaties and agreements which bring it to an end must embody terms which will create a peace that is worth guaranteeing and preserving ... . If the peace presently to be made is to endure, it must be a peace made secure by the organized major force of mankind. The terms of the immediate peace agreed upon will determine whether it is a peace for which such a guarantee can be secured. ... There must be, not a balance of power but a community power; not organized rivalries but an organized, common peace. ... [I]t must be a peace without victory. ... Victory would mean peace forced upon the loser, a victor's terms imposed upon the vanquished. ... Only a peace between equals can last. ... The equality of nations upon which peace must be founded if it is to last must be an equality of rights ... . No peace can last ... which does not recognize and accept the principle that governments derive all their just powers from the consent of the governed, and that no right anywhere exists to hand peoples about from sovereignty to sovereignty as if they were property. ... So far as practicable, moreover, every great people now struggling toward a full development of its resources and of its powers should be assured a direct outlet to the great highways of the sea. ... And the paths of the sea must alike in law and in fact be free. ... I am proposing government by the consent of the governed; ... freedom of the seas ... ; and that moderation of armaments which makes of armies and navies a power for order merely, not an instrument of aggression or of selfish violence. ... [49].

It credits Dr. Wilson that his 'Peace Without Victory' speech to the Senate, which was given before there was a question of the USA changing its neutral position in the First World War, is consistent with his address to the Congress of 8th January 1918 – in which he put forward a 14-point plan for global peace, a condensation of which comprises the following quote.

> ... The programme of the world's peace ... is our programme; and that programme ... is this: I. Open covenants of peace, openly arrived at, after which there shall be no private international understandings of any kind but diplomacy shall proceed always frankly and in the public view. II. Absolute freedom of navigation upon the seas, outside territorial waters, alike in peace and in war, except as the seas may be closed in whole or in part by international action for the enforcement of international covenants. III. The removal, so far as possible, of all economic barriers and the establishment of an equality of trade conditions among all the nations consenting to the peace and associating themselves for its maintenance. IV. Adequate guarantees given and taken that national armaments will be reduced to the lowest point consistent with domestic safety. V. A free, open-minded, and absolutely impartial adjustment of all colonial claims, based upon a strict observance of the principle that in determining all such questions of sovereignty the interests of the populations concerned must have equal weight with the equitable claims of the government whose title is to be determined. VI. The evacuation of all Russian territory and such a settlement of all questions affecting Russia as will secure the best and freest cooperation of the other nations of the world in obtaining for her an unhampered and unembarrassed opportunity for the independent determination of her own political development and national policy ... . VII. Belgium ... must be evacuated and restored, without any attempt

> to limit the sovereignty which she enjoys in common with all other free nations. ... VIII. All French territory should be freed and the invaded portions restored ... . IX. A readjustment of the frontiers of Italy should be effected along clearly recognizable lines of nationality. X. The peoples of Austria-Hungary ... should be accorded the freest opportunity to autonomous development. XI. Rumania, Serbia, and Montenegro should be evacuated; occupied territories restored; Serbia accorded free and secure access to the sea; and the relations of the several Balkan states to one another determined by friendly counsel along historically established lines of allegiance and nationality; and international guarantees of the political and economic independence and territorial integrity of the several Balkan states should be entered into. XII. The Turkish portion of the present Ottoman Empire should be assured a secure sovereignty, but the other nationalities which are now under Turkish rule should be assured an undoubted security of life and an absolutely unmolested opportunity of autonomous development, and the Dardanelles should be permanently opened as a free passage to the ships and commerce of all nations under international guarantees. XIII. An independent Polish state should be erected which should include the territories inhabited by indisputably Polish populations, which should be assured a free and secure access to the sea, and whose political and economic independence and territorial integrity should be guaranteed by international covenant. XIV. A general association of nations must be formed under specific covenants for the purpose of affording mutual guarantees of political independence and territorial integrity to great and small states alike [50].

Restoration of territories, access for all states to the sea, freedom of navigation on the seas, international guarantees of political independence and territorial integrity of states, autonomous development of non-state national areas, equality of trade conditions and open covenants of peace: this is a fair, forward-looking agenda. While Dr. Wilson did not manage to carry out his post-war program in full at the Paris Peace Conference, he did secure adoption of the Covenant of the League of Nations [48].

The Covenant of the League of Nations was adopted at the Paris Peace Conference on 28th April 1919, and entered into force on 10th January 1920 [51] – at which point the League of Nations officially came into being[42] [52]. Amendments to Article 6[43], Articles 12, 13 and 15[44],

---

[42] On 15th November 1920, 41 Members of the League of Nations gathered in Geneva for the opening session of its Assembly (United Nations (2024). "The League of Nations," accessed June 29, 2024, <https://www.ungeneva.org/en/about/league-of-nations/overview>).

[43] The last paragraph of Article 6 of the Covenant of the League of Nations was amended from: "The expenses of the Secretariat shall be borne by the Members of the League in accordance with the apportionment of the expenses of the International Bureau of the Universal Postal Union.", to: "The expenses of the League shall be borne by the Members of the League in the proportion decided by the Assembly." (League of Nations – Official Journal (1920), The Covenant of the League of Nations, *League of Nations – Official Journal*, February 2020, 3-11, 4, Article 6; International Criminal Court (ICC) Legal Tools Database (2008), "Covenant of the League of Nations," published November 10, 2008, accessed July 2, 2024, <https://legal-tools.org/doc/106a5f>; International Criminal Court (ICC) Legal Tools Database (2024), Covenant of the League of Nations, 1919, as amended (The Hague: International Criminal Court), Article 6).

[44] The text to fn 71 explains why Articles 12, 13 and 15 of the Covenant of the League of Nations were amended. The next quoted passage after the text to fn 71 lays down the original version of Article 12 of the Covenant of the League of Nations. The text to fns 72-77 sets out the amended version of Article 12 of the Covenant of the League of Nations. Fns 72-77 specify the amendments to Article 12 of the Covenant of the League of Nations. The paragraph that includes the text to fns 78 and 79 discusses Article 13 of the Covenant of the League of Nations. The paragraph whose last sentence is the text to fn 80 considers Article 15 of the Covenant of the League of Nations.

and Article 4[45], came into effect on 13th August 1924, 26th September 1924, and 19th July 1926, respectively [51].

The Covenant of the League of Nations

Article 1

The original Members of the League of Nations are the signatories that the Annex to the Covenant names[46], and such of the other states that the Annex names as shall accede to the Covenant without reservation[47] [53]. A fully self-governing state, dominion or colony that the Annex does not name may become a Member of the League of Nations, if two-thirds of the Assembly agree to its admission to the League[48] [53].

Articles 2-7

The League of Nations shall act by means of an Assembly and a Council, having a permanent Secretariat [54]. At its meetings, the Assembly may consider any issue within the League's purview or which affects global peace; each Member of the League has one vote and may present no more than three representatives [55]. The Council shall comprise representatives of the Principal Allied and Associated Powers – which are its permanent members, and representatives of four other Members of the League of Nations; with the approval a majority of the Assembly, the Council may name additional Members of the League whose representatives shall always be its members [56], i.e., it may introduce one or more further

---

[45] Fn 49 states this amendment to Article 4 of the Covenant of the League of Nations.

[46] The Annex to the Covenant of the League of Nations lists "Original Members of the League of Nations Signatories of the Treaty of Peace" thus: the USA, Belgium, Bolivia, British Empire – Canada, Australia, South Africa, New Zealand and India, China, Cuba, Ecuador, France, Greece, Guatemala, Haiti, Hedjaz (now part of Saudi Arabia), Honduras, Italy, Japan, Liberia, Nicaragua, Panama, Peru, Poland, Portugal, Roumania (now Romania), Serb-Croat-Slovene State, Siam (now Thailand), Czecho-Slovakia and Uruguay (League of Nations – Official Journal (1920), The Covenant of the League of Nations, *League of Nations – Official Journal*, February 2020, 3-11, 11, Annex). The USA did not become a Member of the League of Nations, because the Senate, on 19th November 1919, failed to ratify the Treaty of Versailles (of which Part I comprised The Covenant of the League of Nations) – which the Senate Foreign Relations Committee had not amended but to which it had added 14 reservations (United States Senate (2024), "Senate Rejects the Treaty of Versailles," accessed June 29, 2024, <https://www.senate.gov/about/powers-procedures/treaties/senate-rejects-treaty-of-versailles.htm>).

[47] The Annex to the Covenant of the League of Nations lists "States Invited to Accede to the Covenant" so: Argentine Republic, Chili (now Chile), Colombia, Denmark, the Netherlands, Norway, Paraguay, Persia (now Iran), Salvador (i.e., El Salvador), Spain, Sweden, Switzerland and Venezuela (League of Nations – Official Journal (1920), The Covenant of the League of Nations, *League of Nations – Official Journal*, February 2020, 3-11, 11, Annex).

[48] To be admitted as a Member of the League of Nations, the state, dominion or colony must "give effective guarantees of its sincere intention to observe its international obligations" and "accept such regulations as may be prescribed by the League in regard to its military, naval and air forces and armaments" (League of Nations – Official Journal (1920), The Covenant of the League of Nations, *League of Nations – Official Journal*, February 2020, 3-11, 3, Article 1). Ireland was the only dominion to have been admitted as a Member to the League of Nations under this second paragraph of Article 1 of the Covenant of the League of Nations; states which the Assembly of the League of Nations admitted to membership of the League of Nations under that paragraph include Afghanistan and Ethiopia, but exclude Armenia, Georgia and Ukraine (Grant, T. (2019), 'Chapter 2 – The League of Nations as a Universal Organization' *in* Erpelding, M., Hess, B., and Ruiz Fabri, H. (eds.) (2019), *Peace Through Law: The Versailles Peace Treaty and Dispute Settlement After World War I*, First edition (Baden-Baden: Nomos Verlagsgesellschaft), 76-77).

permanent members thereof[49]. At its meetings, the Council may address any matter within the League's compass or which affects world peace; each Member of the League that is represented on the Council has one vote and may have only one representative[50] [56]. Except where expressly provided otherwise, non-procedural[51] decisions at any meeting of the Council or of the Assembly shall require the agreement of all the Members of the League of Nations that are represented there [57]. The permanent Secretariat shall be established at the Seat of the League of Nations [58], which is in Geneva [59]. The Secretariat shall consist of a Secretary-General and such secretaries and staff as may be needed [58]. All positions that are associated with the League of Nations – including the Secretariat – shall be open equally to female and male applicants[52] [59].

Article 8

The Members of the League of Nations recognize that the preservation of peace requires national armaments to be reduced to the lowest point which is compatible with state safety and the enforcement of international obligations by common action [60]. Taking account of the geography of each state, the Council shall make plans for this reduction – for governments to consider and act upon [60]. After governments have adopted these plans, any instance of exceeding the limits of armaments set therein requires the Council's authorization [60]. The Members of the League of Nations agree to exchange full and honest information as to the quantity of their armaments, their air, naval and military programmes, and the war-readiness of their industries [60].

Articles 10 and 11

The Members of the League of Nations undertake to respect and preserve the territorial integrity and political independence of all Members as against external aggression [61]. Any war or threat of war is a concern to the whole League of Nations, and the League shall take any action that may be considered to be wise and effectual to protect international peace[53] [62].

---

[49] In an amendment that took effect on 19th July 1926 (text to fn 45), the following paragraph was added to Article 4 of the Covenant of the League of Nations: "The Assembly shall fix by a two-thirds majority the rules dealing with the election of the non-permanent Members of the Council, and particularly such regulations as relate to their term of office and the conditions of re-eligibility." (International Criminal Court (ICC) Legal Tools Database (2008), "Covenant of the League of Nations," published November 10, 2008, accessed July 2, 2024, <https://legal-tools.org/doc/106a5f>; International Criminal Court (ICC) Legal Tools Database (2024), Covenant of the League of Nations, 1919, as amended (The Hague: International Criminal Court), Article 4).

[50] A Member of the League of Nations that is not represented on the Council may send a representative to sit as a member at any meeting of the Council while issues which specifically affect the interest of that Member of the League are being considered there (League of Nations – Official Journal (1920), The Covenant of the League of Nations, *League of Nations – Official Journal*, February 2020, 3-11, 4, Article 4).

[51] All issues of procedure at meetings of the Assembly or of the Council may be decided by a majority of the Members of the League of Nations that are represented there (League of Nations – Official Journal (1920), The Covenant of the League of Nations, *League of Nations – Official Journal*, February 2020, 3-11, 4, Article 5).

[52] This provision shows a theme of participation and openness, which marked a step towards a different attitude to that prevailing before the First World War (Grant, T. (2019), 'Chapter 2 – The League of Nations as a Universal Organization' in Erpelding, M., Hess, B., and Ruiz Fabri, H. (eds.) (2019), *Peace Through Law: The Versailles Peace Treaty and Dispute Settlement After World War I*, First edition, 80).

[53] Each Member of the League of Nations may bring to the attention of the Council or of the Assembly any circumstance affecting international relations that threatens to disturb global peace or the good understanding between nations upon which peace rests (League of Nations – Official Journal (1920), The Covenant of the League of Nations, *League of Nations – Official Journal*, February 2020, 3-11, 6, Article 11).

Article 18

Every international agreement or treaty that any Member of the League of Nations enters into shall be immediately be registered with the Secretariat and promptly published by it [63]. This registration is necessary prior to the instrument taking effect [63].

Article 22

This article concerns the appointment of mandatories to specified non-state territories, including those that were under the sovereignty of the states defeated in the First World War[54], those within the Ottoman Empire[55] and those in Central Africa[56], South-West Africa (later renamed Namibia), and islands of the South Pacific[57] [64]. For each mandate, the mandatory shall provide the Council of the League of Nations with an annual report in respect of the territory that has been committed to its charge; the Council is to define the extent of authority, control or administration that the mandatory is to exercise – if the Members of the League of Nations have not already agreed upon this [64].

Article 23

Paragraph (a) lays down the authority for the establishment of the International Labour Organization[58] [65]. Paragraphs (b) to (f) set out responsibilities for Members of the League

---

[54] The Covenant reads: "To those colonies and territories which as a consequence of the late war have ceased to be under the sovereignty of the States which formerly governed them and which are inhabited by peoples not yet able to stand by themselves under the strenuous conditions of the modern world, there should be applied the principle that the well-being and development of such peoples form a sacred trust of civilization and that securities for the performance of this trust should be embodied in this Covenant. The best method of giving practical effect to this principle is that the tutelage of such peoples should be entrusted to advanced nations who by reason of their resources, their experience or their geographical position can best undertake this responsibility, and who are willing to accept it, and that this tutelage should be exercised by them as Mandatories on behalf of the League." (League of Nations – Official Journal (1920), The Covenant of the League of Nations, *League of Nations – Official Journal*, February 2020, 3-11, 9, Article 22).

[55] The Covenant states: "Certain communities formerly belonging to the Turkish Empire have reached a stage of development where their existence as independent nations can be provisionally recognised subject to the rendering of administrative advice and assistance by a Mandatory until such time as they are able to stand alone. The wishes of these communities must be a principal consideration in the selection of the Mandatory." (League of Nations – Official Journal (1920), The Covenant of the League of Nations, *League of Nations – Official Journal*, February 2020, 3-11, 9, Article 22).

[56] The Covenant reads: "Other peoples, especially those of Central Africa, are at such a stage that the Mandatory must be responsible for the administration of the territory under conditions which will guarantee freedom of conscience and religion, subject only to the maintenance of public order and morals, the prohibition of abuses such as the slave trade, the arms traffic and the liquor traffic, and the prevention of the establishment of fortifications or military and naval bases and of military training of the natives for other than police purposes and the defence of territory, and will also secure equal opportunities for the trade and commerce of other Members of the League." (League of Nations – Official Journal (1920), The Covenant of the League of Nations, *League of Nations – Official Journal*, February 2020, 3-11, 9, Article 22).

[57] The Covenant states: "There are territories, such as South-West Africa and certain of the South Pacific Islands, which, owing to the sparseness of their population, or their small size, or their remoteness from the centres of civilisation, or their geographical contiguity to the territory of the Mandatory, and other circumstances, can be best administered under the laws of the Mandatory as integral portions of its territory, subject to the safeguards above mentioned in the interests of the indigenous population." (League of Nations – Official Journal (1920), The Covenant of the League of Nations, *League of Nations – Official Journal*, February 2020, 3-11, 9, Article 22).

[58] The Covenant reads: "[T]he Members of the League: (*a*) will endeavour to secure and maintain fair and humane conditions of labour for men, women and children, both in their own countries and in all countries to which their commercial and industrial relations extend, and for that purpose will establish and maintain the necessary international organisations;" (League of Nations – Official Journal (1920), The Covenant of the League of Nations, *League of Nations – Official Journal*, February 2020, 3-11, 10, Article 23(a); emphasis original).

regarding indigenous people[59], supervision of trafficking[60] and of cross-border trade in arms[61], freedom of communications, movement and commerce[62], and the prevention and control of disease[63] [65].

The Dissolution of the League of Nations

When the UN Charter entered into force on 24th October 1945, the League of Nations was active – as it had been during the Second World War [66]. On 20th April 1946, the League of Nations was dissolved [67]. Some of the League's assets – including its headquarters in Geneva (i.e., the Palais des Nations) were transferred to the UN [66].

Article 387 of the Treaty of Versailles established the International Labour Organization, as follows: "A permanent organisation is hereby established for the promotion of the objects set forth in the Preamble. The original Members of the League of Nations shall be the original Members of this organisation, and hereafter membership of the League of Nations shall carry with it membership of the said organisation." (International Labour Office – Official Bulletin (1923), Chapter VI: Part XIII of the Treaty of Peace of Versailles. *International Labour Office – Official Bulletin*, Volume I, April 1919 – August 1920, 332-345, 333, Article 387). The objects that the Preamble to Section I (which is entitled 'Organisation of Labour') of Part XIII (which is titled 'Labour') of the Treaty of Peace of Versailles lays down are threefold: "Whereas the League of Nations has for its object the establishment of universal peace, and such a peace can be established only if it is based upon social justice; And whereas conditions of labour exist involving such injustice, hardship and privation to large numbers of people as to produce unrest so great that the peace and harmony of the world are imperilled; and an improvement of those conditions is urgently required: as, for example, by the regulation of the hours of work, including the establishment of a maximum working day and week, the regulation of the labour supply, the prevention of unemployment, the provision of an adequate living wage, the protection of the worker against sickness, disease and injury arising out of his employment, the protection of children, young persons and women, provision for old age and injury, protection of the interests of workers when employed in countries other than their own, recognition of the principle of freedom of association, the organisation of vocational and technical education and other measures; Whereas also the failure of any nation to adopt humane conditions of labour is an obstacle in the way of other nations which desire to improve the conditions in their own countries:" (International Labour Office – Official Bulletin (1923), Chapter VI: Part XIII of the Treaty of Peace of Versailles, *International Labour Office – Official Bulletin*, Volume I, April 1919 – August 1920, 332-345, 332-333, Preamble).

[59] The Covenant states: "[T]he Members of the League: ... (*b*) undertake to secure just treatment of the native inhabitants of territories under their control;" (League of Nations – Official Journal (1920), The Covenant of the League of Nations, *League of Nations – Official Journal*, February 2020, 3-11, 10, Article 23(b); emphasis original).

[60] The Covenant reads: "[T]he Members of the League: ... (*c*) will entrust the League with the general supervision over the execution of agreements with regard to the traffic in women and children, and the traffic in opium and other dangerous drugs;" (League of Nations – Official Journal (1920), The Covenant of the League of Nations, *League of Nations – Official Journal*, February 2020, 3-11, 10, Article 23(c); emphasis original).

[61] The Covenant states: "[T]he Members of the League ... (*d*) will entrust the League with the general supervision of the trade in arms and ammunition with the countries in which the control of this traffic is necessary in the common interest;" (League of Nations – Official Journal (1920), The Covenant of the League of Nations, *League of Nations – Official Journal*, February 2020, 3-11, 10, Article 23(d); emphasis original).

[62] The Covenant reads: "[T]he Members of the League ... (*e*) will make provision to secure and maintain freedom of communications and of transit and equitable treatment for the commerce of all Members of the League ... ;" (League of Nations – Official Journal (1920), The Covenant of the League of Nations, *League of Nations – Official Journal*, February 2020, 3-11, 10, Article 23(e); emphasis original).

[63] The Covenant states: "[T]he Members of the League ... (*f*) will endeavour to take steps in matters of international concern for the prevention and control of disease." (League of Nations – Official Journal (1920), The Covenant of the League of Nations, *League of Nations – Official Journal*, February 2020, 3-11, 10, Article 23(f); emphasis original).

Comment

The fact that the Second World War took place notwithstanding the presence and work of the League of Nations does not mean that the League was a failure. Rather, it means that the League was insufficiently resourced to be able to contain the military rise of Germany, Italy, and Japan during the 1930s. Part of the reason for this was the absence of the USA among the participants in the League. Traditionally, the leaders of the USA have stood for justice and peace – and, by the twentieth century, the USA was a prosperous state with widespread international influence. Another part of the reason was the global economic depression (the 'Great Depression') of the early 1930s, during which countries participating in the League would have suffered dwindling finances and, consequently, shown reduced commitment to the accomplishment of international peace through the League. It is more accurate to say that the Second World War was inevitable given the economic and political mix of the mid-1930s, than that the League of Nations was inherently ineffective in preventing that war – although the requirement of the Covenant of the League of Nations for unanimity in the Assembly and in the Council on decisions regarding non-procedural matters[64] may have been an inhibitory factor to the Members of the League being able to take co-ordinated, decisive, preventative action to effectively address the slide towards a global war. On the contrary, it is to the credit of the architects of the League that its Covenant provided a good initial blueprint – which was appropriate for its time – for how a major international organization devoted to achieving and maintaining peace should be constituted.

The Permanent Court of International Justice

Introduction

Notwithstanding the consensus immediately after the First World War that the new international court – the PCIJ – should not be granted compulsory jurisdiction over the disputes of states parties to its statute, it would be arbiter of several disputes in the interwar years by virtue of its nomination as such in compromissory clauses or in the optional clause of Article 36 of the Statute of the PCIJ[65]. This, together with the advisory jurisdiction that Article 14 of the Covenant of the League of Nations[66] and – after its introduction into the Statute of the PCIJ

[64] Text to fn 51.

[65] Members of the League of Nations and states that the Annex to the Covenant names (fns 46 and 47) may "declare that they recognize as compulsory *ipso facto* and without special agreement, in relation to any other Member or State accepting the same obligation, the jurisdiction of the Court in all or any of the classes of legal disputes concerning: (*a*) the interpretation of a treaty; (*b*) any question of international law; (*c*) the existence of any fact which, if established, would constitute a breach of an international obligation; (*d*) the nature of extent of the reparation to be made for the breach of an international obligation. The declaration referred to above may be made unconditionally or on condition of reciprocity on the part of several or certain Members or States, or for a certain time." (Permanent Court of International Justice (1926), Statute of the Court, *P.C.I.J. Series D No.1*, 7-27, 19-20, Article 36; emphasis original).

[66] The PCIJ may "give an advisory opinion upon any dispute or question referred to it by the Council or by the Assembly" of the League of Nations (League of Nations – Official Journal (1920), The Covenant of the League of Nations, *League of Nations – Official Journal*, February 2020, 3-11, 6, Article 14).

– Chapter IV of the Statute[67] conferred upon the Court, such jurisdiction also being exercised fairly frequently during the interwar period, enabled the PCIJ to build up a case law which tended to be respected in its subsequent judgments and advisory opinions and in those of the ICJ.

The Foundation of the PCIJ

Article 14 of the Covenant of the League of Nations required the Council of the League of Nations to draw up and submit to the Members of the League proposals to set up a PCIJ[68]. At its second session, the Council appointed an Advisory Committee of Jurists, which met frequently in The Hague between 16th June 1920 and 24th July 1920 – on which date it adopted a report which was submitted to the Council and which included draft articles of the Statute of the PCIJ [68]. At its eighth (30th July 1920 to 5th August 1920) and tenth (20th October 1920 to 28th October 1920) sessions, the Council of the League of Nations examined and amended the draft Statute of the PCIJ, which it presented in a report to the First Assembly of the League of Nations in November 1920 [68].

The Assembly of the League of Nations referred the draft articles to its Third Committee, which appointed a sub-committee for the purpose of considering the matter in detail [68]. The sub-committee held ten meetings at which the draft articles were discussed [68]. On 7th December 1920, the sub-committee adopted a report that contained the results of its work; it submitted this to the Third Committee of the Assembly, which unanimously adopted the draft Statute of the PCIJ on 11th December 1920 and presented it to the Assembly [68]. At its twenty-first plenary meeting on 13th December 1920, the First Assembly unanimously adopted the draft Statute of the PCIJ – having made amendments to it [68]; the Assembly's resolution included the following text.

RESOLUTION
concerning the establishment of a
PERMANENT COURT OF INTERNATIONAL JUSTICE
Passed by the assembly of the League of Nations, Geneva, December 13th, 1920.

1. The Assembly unanimously declares its approval of the draft Statute of the Permanent Court of International Justice – as amended by the Assembly – which was prepared by

[67] Chapter IV of the Statute of the PCIJ, which was introduced into the Statute by the Protocol concerning the Revision of the Statute of the Permanent Court of International Justice of 14th September 1929, comprises Articles 65-68 of the Statute. The first of these articles states: "Questions upon which the advisory opinion of the Court is asked shall be laid before the Court by means of a written request, signed either by the President of the Assembly or the President of the Council of the League of Nations, or by the Secretary-General of the League under instructions from the Assembly or the Council. The request shall contain an exact statement of the question upon which an opinion is required, and shall be accompanied by all documents likely to throw light upon the question." (Permanent Court of International Justice (1940), Statute of the Court, as amended, *P.C.I.J. Series D No.1*, 13-28, 27, Article 65). Fn 98 contains Article 68 of the revised Statute of the PCIJ.

[68] The Council of the League of Nations "shall formulate and submit to the Members of the League for adoption plans for the establishment of a Permanent Court of International Justice. The Court shall be competent to hear and determine any dispute of an international character which the parties thereto submit to it. ..." (League of Nations – Official Journal (1920), The Covenant of the League of Nations, *League of Nations – Official Journal*, February 2020, 3-11, 6, Article 14). Fn 66 lays down the final sentence of Article 14 of the Covenant of the League of Nations.

> the Council under Article 14 of the Covenant[69] and submitted to the Assembly for its approval.
>
> 2. In view of the special wording of Article 14, the Statute of the Court shall be submitted within the shortest possible time to the Members of the League of Nations for adoption in the form of a Protocol duly ratified and declaring their recognition of this Statute. It shall be the duty of the Council to submit the Statute to the Members.
> 3. As soon as this Protocol has been ratified by the majority of the Members of the League, the Statute of the Court shall come into force ... [69].

The Protocol of Signature of the Statute for the Permanent Court of International Justice, to which the Statute of the PCIJ was adjoined, was opened for signature on 16th December 1920 [68, 70]. By September 1921, a majority of Members of the League of Nations had ratified the Protocol [68]. Thus, at this time the Statute of the PCIJ came into force [71], which, by virtue of Article 1 of the Statute[70], occasioned the immediate establishment of the PCIJ.

The Covenant of the League of Nations and the PCIJ

Articles 12, 13, 15 and 16 of the Covenant of the League of Nations concern disputes between Members of the League of Nations. Article 17 of the Covenant addresses disputes between a Member of the League and a state that is not a Member of the League, and those between two states that are not Members. Amendments to Articles 12, 13 and 15 of the Covenant came into effect on 26th September 1924, which adapted these provisions in the light of the fact that the PCIJ had become operational in 1922[71]. For example, in the original version of the Covenant of the League of Nations, its Article 12 reads as follows.

> The Members of the League agree that if there should arise between them any dispute likely to lead to a rupture, they will submit the matter either to arbitration or to inquiry by the Council, and they agree in no case to resort to war until three months after the award by the arbitrators or the report by the Council. In any case under this Article the award of the arbitrators shall be made within a reasonable time, and the report of the Council shall be made within six months after the submission of the dispute [72].

The amended version of Article 12 of the Covenant of the League of Nations reads thus.

---

[69] Fn 68.

[70] This first sentence of this article states: "A Permanent Court of International Justice is hereby established, in accordance with Article 14 of the Covenant of the League of Nations." (Permanent Court of International Justice (1926), Statute of the Court, *P.C.I.J. Series D No.1*, 7-27, 7, Article 1). Fns 68 and 66 set out Article 14 of the Covenant of the League of Nations.

[71] The PCIJ held its inaugural session in 1922 (International Court of Justice (2024), "Permanent Court of International Justice," accessed July 4, 2024, <https://www.icj-cij.org/pcij>). Its first judgment was *Case of the S.S. "Wimbledon," Question of Intervention by Poland*, Judgment of 28 June 1923, *P.C.I.J. Series A No.1 (1923)*, 11-14. The PCIJ's main judgment in *Case of the S.S. "Wimbledon"* followed a few weeks later, i.e., Judgment of 17 August 1923, *P.C.I.J. Series A No.1 (1923)*, 15-34. The first advisory opinion of the PCIJ was earlier than its first judgment, i.e., *Designation of the Workers' Delegate for the Netherlands at the Third Session of the International Labour Conference*, Advisory Opinion of 31 July 1922, *P.C.I.J. Series B No.1 (1922)*, 9-27.

> The Members of the League agree that[72], if there should arise between them any dispute likely to lead to a rupture[73] they will submit the matter either to arbitration *or judicial settlement*[74] or to enquiry[75] by the Council, and they agree in no case to resort to war until three months after the award by the arbitrators *or the judicial decision*[76]*,* or the report by the Council. In any case under this Article the award of the arbitrators *or the judicial decision*[77] shall be made within a reasonable time, and the report of the Council shall be made within six months after the submission of the dispute [73].

The amended version of Article 13 of the Covenant of the League of Nations requires Members of the League to submit to arbitration or to judicial settlement before the PCIJ the entire subject-matter of disputes that cannot be satisfactorily resolved by diplomacy [74]. Disputes that "are generally suitable for submission to arbitration or judicial settlement" include those "as to the interpretation of a treaty, as to any question of international law, as to the existence of any fact which if established would constitute a breach of any international obligation, or as to the extent and nature of the reparation to be made for any such breach" [74]. These four categories of dispute that Article 13 of the Covenant lists are the same as the four classes of legal dispute that the optional clause of Article 36 of the Statute of the PCIJ[78] sets down. As these are listed in the original version of Article 13 of the Covenant of the League of Nations – as well as in the amended version – but in the former in relation to arbitration only[79], their inclusion in the optional clause of Article 36 of the Statute of the PCIJ in 1920 must have been the result of them being copied from the original (i.e., 1919) version of Article 13 of the Covenant.

Article 15 of the Covenant of the League of Nations requires Members of the League to submit to the Council of the League of Nations a dispute between them that they did not submit to either arbitration or judicial settlement in compliance with Article 13 of the Covenant – which it must attempt to resolve [75]. If the Council does not settle the dispute, then it is to write and publish a report comprising a factual statement and recommendations [75, 76]. If the members of the Council unanimously agree this report, then the Members of the League agree not to declare war on any party to the dispute that complies with its recommendations [75, 76]. If they do not so agree, then Members of the League "reserve to themselves the right to take such action as they shall consider necessary for the maintenance of right and justice" [75, 76]. This last provision opens the way for Members of the League to declare war on one or more of the parties to the dispute – the condition is subjective, i.e., that *the Member itself* considers its action to be necessary for the maintenance of right and justice. Article 16 of the Covenant,

---

[72] Emphasis added. The amendment inserts a comma after the word 'that'.

[73] The amendment deletes the comma after the word 'rupture'.

[74] Emphasis added. The amendment adds the phrase 'or judicial settlement' after the word 'arbitration'.

[75] Emphasis added. The amendment changes the word 'inquiry' to the word 'enquiry'.

[76] Emphasis added. The amendment adds the phrase 'or the judicial decision,' – including the comma, after the phrase 'the award by the arbitrators'.

[77] Emphasis added. The amendment adds the phrase 'or the judicial decision' after the phrase 'the award of the arbitrators'.

[78] Fn 65 comprises the optional clause of Article 36 of the Statute of the PCIJ.

[79] Paragraph 2 of the original version of Article 13 of the Covenant of the League of Nations states: "Disputes as to the interpretation of a treaty, as to any question of international law, as to the existence of any fact which if established would constitute a breach of any international obligation, or as to the extent and nature of the reparation to be made for any such breach, are declared to be among those which are generally suitable for submission to arbitration." (League of Nations – Official Journal (1920), The Covenant of the League of Nations, *League of Nations – Official Journal*, February 2020, 3-11, 6, Article 13).

however, discourages any Member of the League from starting a war rashly – for its first paragraph declares that any such Member which resorts to war "in disregard of its covenants in Articles 12, 13 or 15" of the Covenant of the League of Nations is "deemed to have committed an act of war against all other Members of the League" [77] – for which that article provides remedies[80].

Article 17 of the Covenant of the League of Nations attempts to apply Articles 12 to 16 of the Covenant to disputes involving at least one state that is not a Member of the League[81]. If this cannot be done, then the Council of the League of Nations may act accordingly[82].

The Statute of the PCIJ

The Statute of the PCIJ was amended once, in September 1929[83] [68]. As the Protocol concerning the Revision of the Statute of the Permanent Court of Justice came into effect on 1st

[80] All Members of the League "undertake immediately to subject it [(i.e., the covenant-disregarding Member)] to the severance of all trade or financial relations, the prohibition of all intercourse between their nationals and the nationals of the covenant-breaking State, and the prevention of all financial[,] commercial or personal intercourse between the nationals of the covenant-breaking State and the nationals of any other State, whether a Member of the League or not"; moreover, "It shall be the duty of the Council in such case to recommend to the several Governments concerned what effective military, naval or air force the Members of the League shall severally contribute to the armed forces to be used to protect the covenants of the League. The Members of the League agree, further, that they will mutually support one another in the financial and economic measures which are taken under this Article, in order to minimize the loss and inconvenience resulting from the above measures, and that they will mutually support one another in resisting any special measures aimed at one of their number by covenant-breaking State, and that they will take the necessary steps to afford passage through their territory to the forces of any of the Members of the League which are co-operating to protect the covenants of the League. Any Member of the League which has violated any covenant of the League may be declared to be no longer a Member of the League by a vote of the Council concurred in by the Representatives of all the other Members of the League represented thereon." (League of Nations – Official Journal (1920), The Covenant of the League of Nations, *League of Nations – Official Journal*, February 2020, 3-11, 7-8, Article 16).

[81] The first three paragraphs of Article 17 of the Covenant of the League of Nations read as follows: "In the event of a dispute between a Member of the League and a State which is not a Member of the League, or between States not Members of the League, the State or States not Members of the League shall be invited to accept the obligations of Membership in the League for the purposes of such dispute, upon such conditions as the Council may deem just. If such invitation is accepted, the provisions of Articles 12 to 16 inclusive shall be applied with such modifications as may be deemed necessary by the Council. Upon such invitation being given the Council shall immediately institute an inquiry into the circumstances of the dispute and recommend such action as may seem best and most effectual in the circumstances. If a State so invited shall refuse to accept the obligations of the Membership in the League for the purposes of such dispute, and shall resort to war against a Member of the League, the provisions of Article 16 shall be applicable as against the State taking such action." (League of Nations – Official Journal (1920), The Covenant of the League of Nations, *League of Nations – Official Journal*, February 2020, 3-11, 8, Article 17).

[82] The final paragraph of Article 17 of the Covenant of the League of Nations states: "If both parties to the dispute when so invited refuse to accept the obligations of Membership in the League for the purposes of such dispute, the Council may take such measures and make such recommendations as will prevent hostilities and will result in the settlement of the dispute."(League of Nations – Official Journal (1920), The Covenant of the League of Nations, *League of Nations – Official Journal*, February 2020, 3-11, 8, Article 17).

[83] The Resolution concerning the Revision of the Statute of the Permanent Court of International Justice adopted by the Assembly of the League of Nations, which is dated 14th September 1929, and the Protocol concerning the Revision of the Statute of the Permanent Court of International Justice, also of 14th September 1929, introduce the amendments to the Statute of the PCIJ. Fn 67 sets out one of these amendments, i.e., the addition of Article 65 to the Statute of the PCIJ. Fn 98 includes another of these amendments, i.e., the addition of Article 68 to the Statute of the PCIJ.

February 1936 – by which time most of the judgments[84], and all of the advisory opinions[85], of the PCIJ had been delivered, the original version of the Statute of the PCIJ is used to share an essence of the contents of this document[86] [78].

Organization of the PCIJ

The Court is to comprise fifteen members – eleven judges and four deputy judges[87] – who are elected from among individuals of high moral character, and who are qualified for appointment to the most senior judicial posts or are competent juriconsults in international law [79]. The members of the PCIJ shall be elected by the Council and by the Assembly from a list of persons that the national groups in the Permanent Court of Arbitration nominate[88] [80]. These members shall be elected for nine years, and may be re-elected [81]. A member of the PCIJ who is elected to replace a member whose period of appointment has not come to an end will hold this position for the remainder of the latter's term [82]. The judges – and the deputy judges[89] when undertaking their duties on the PCIJ – may not perform any administrative or political function[90] [83]. A member[91] of the PCIJ may neither act as advocate, counsel or agent in any international[92] case, nor partake in the decision of any case in which the member has previously been involved [84]. The PCIJ shall elect, and may re-elect, its President and Vice-President for

---

[84] The PCIJ delivered eight judgments after 1st February 1936. These are as follows: (i) *The Pajzs, Czáky, Esterházy Case*, Judgment of 16 December 1936, *P.C.I.J. Series A/B No.68 (1936)*, 30-66; (ii) *The Diversion of Water from the Meuse*, Judgment of 28 June 1937, *P.C.I.J. Series A/B No.70 (1937)*, 4-33; (iii) *Lighthouses in Crete and Samos*, Judgment of 8 October 1937, *P.C.I.J. Series A/B No.71 (1937)*, 94-106; (iv) *The Borchgrave Case, Preliminary Objections*, Judgment of 6 November 1937, *P.C.I.J. Series A/B No.72 (1937)*, 158-171; (v) *Phosphates in Morocco, Preliminary Objections*, Judgment of 14 June 1938, *P.C.I.J. Series A/B No.74 (1938)*, 10-30; (vi) *The Panevezys-Saldutiskis Railway Case*, Judgment of 28 February 1939, *P.C.I.J. Series A/B No.76 (1939)*, 4-23; (vii) *The Electricity Company of Sofia and Bulgaria, Preliminary Objection*, Judgment of 4 April 1939, *P.C.I.J. Series A/B No.77 (1939)*, 64-85; (viii) *The "Société Commerciale de Belgique"*, Judgment of 15 June 1939, *P.C.I.J. Series A/B No.78 (1939)*, 160-179.

[85] The last advisory opinion of the PCIJ was given on 4th December 1935, i.e., *Consistency of Certain Danzig Legislative Decrees with the Constitution of the Free City*, Advisory Opinion of 4 December 1935, *P.C.I.J. Series A/B No.65 (1935)*, 41-58.

[86] If the revised version of the Statute of the PCIJ differs from the original version regarding a provision to which the text refers, then the revised version of that provision is mentioned in a footnote.

[87] The revised version of the Statute of the PCIJ does not provide for deputy judges (Permanent Court of International Justice (1940), Statute of the Court, as amended, *P.C.I.J. Series D No.1*, 13-28, 13, Article 3).

[88] If a Member of the League of Nations is not represented in the Permanent Court of Arbitration, then its list of candidates for judicial appointment to the PCIJ is prepared by its government "under the same conditions as those prescribed for members of the Permanent Court of Arbitration by Article 44 of the Convention of The Hague of 1907 for the pacific settlement of international disputes" (Permanent Court of International Justice (1926), Statute of the Court, *P.C.I.J. Series D No.1*, 7-27, 7, Article 4). The first two sentences of Article 44 of the 1907 Convention for the Pacific Settlement of International Disputes state: "Each Contracting Power selects four persons at the most, of known competency in questions of international law, of the highest moral reputation, and disposed to accept the duties of Arbitrator. The persons thus elected are inscribed, as Members of the Court, in a list which shall be notified to all the Contracting Powers by the [International] Bureau [of the Permanent Court of Arbitration]." (National University of Singapore (2021), 1907 Convention for the Pacific Settlement of International Disputes, 18 October 1907, UKTS 6 (1971) Cmnd. 4575, 1 Bevans 577, 2 AJIL Supp. 43 (1908), 1-18, 10, Article 44).

[89] Fn 87.

[90] Nor, according to the revised version of the Statute of the PCIJ, may members of the Court "engage in any other occupation of a professional nature" (Permanent Court of International Justice (1940), Statute of the Court, as amended, *P.C.I.J. Series D No.1*, 13-28, 16, Article 16).

[91] A deputy judge may not act as advocate, counsel or agent only in "cases in which they are called upon to exercise their functions on the Court" (Permanent Court of International Justice (1926), Statute of the Court, *P.C.I.J. Series D No.1*, 7-27, 12, Article 17).

[92] The revised version of the Statute of the PCIJ omits the word 'international' (Permanent Court of International Justice (1940), Statute of the Court, as amended, *P.C.I.J. Series D No.1*, 13-28, 16, Article 17).

three years, and shall appoint its Registrar [85]. The seat of the Court – where its President and Registrar shall reside – shall be in the Hague [86]. If, for a special reason, a member of the PCIJ does not wish to participate in the decision, or the President of the Court considers that a member should not so partake, then the one must inform the other of this [87]. Bar when it is expressly stated, the full Court shall sit [88]. With a view to the swift dispatch of business, each year the PCIJ shall form a chamber composed of three[93] judges who, at the request of the disputants, may hear and decide upon cases by summary procedure [89]. The PCIJ shall frame rules for regulating its procedure[94] [90]. Judges of the nationality of each party to a case shall retain their right to sit before the PCIJ, and each disputant shall choose a judge of its nationality if there should not be one – selecting first from among the deputy judges[95]; if there are two or more parties in the same interest, then they shall be regarded as one party only [91].

Competence of the PCIJ

The jurisdiction of the PCIJ consists of all cases that the disputants refer to it and all issues that are specifically provided for in conventions and treaties in force [92]. Article 36 of the Statute of the PCIJ contains an optional clause, which empowers a state to choose to accept the jurisdiction of the PCIJ as compulsory over up to four specified classes of international law dispute and in a selection of circumstances specified therein[96]. If there is disagreement as to whether the PCIJ has jurisdiction over a particular case, then the PCIJ resolves the matter [93]. Article 38 of the Statute of the PCIJ specifies sources of international law that the PCIJ shall apply, which are as follows.

> 1. International conventions, whether general or particular, establishing rules expressly recognized by the contesting States; 2. International custom, as evidence of a general practice accepted as law; 3. The general principles of law recognized by civilized nations; 4. Subject to the provisions of Article 59 [of the Statute of the PCIJ], judicial decisions and the teachings of the most highly qualified publicists of the various nations, as subsidiary means for the determination of rules of law [94].

Article 59 of the Statute of the PCIJ reads as follows.

> The decision of the Court has no binding force except between the parties and in respect of that particular case [95].

---

[93] The revised version of the Statute of the PCIJ increase the number of judges in the summary chamber to five, and provides for the selection of a further two judges in order to replace a judge that is unable to hear a case there (Permanent Court of International Justice (1940), Statute of the Court, as amended, *P.C.I.J. Series D No.1*, 13-28, 19, Article 29).

[94] These are the Rules of Court of the PCIJ, which the PCIJ drew up in 1922 and revised in 1926, 1931 and 1936 (International Court of Justice (2024), "History," accessed July 9, 2024, <https://www.icj-cij.org/history>). The Rules of Court of the PCIJ are found on the ICJ's website at <https://www.icj-cij.org/pcij-series-d>.

[95] The revised version of the Statute of the PCIJ does not refer to selection from among deputy judges (Permanent Court of International Justice (1940), Statute of the Court, as amended, *P.C.I.J. Series D No.1*, 13-28, 20, Article 31).

[96] Fn 65 lays down the optional clause of Article 36 of the Statute of the PCIJ.

Article 38 of the Statute of the PCIJ also permits the Court to determine a case *ex aequo et bono*[97], if the disputants agree to this [94].

Procedure in Cases Before the PCIJ[98]

The PCIJ's official languages shall be English and French; if the disputants agree in which of these the case should be conducted, then the PCIJ will deliver the judgment in that language[99] [96]. Cases are brought before the PCIJ either by a notification of a special agreement between the parties or by a written application addressed to the Registrar of the Court[100], indicating in each case the subject of the dispute and the identity of the disputants [97]. The PCIJ shall be empowered to lay down any provisional measures that ought to be taken in order to preserve either party's respective rights [98]. The procedure shall comprise written and oral proceedings; the written proceedings shall consist of communication through the Registrar to the parties and to the judges, of Cases, Countercases and, if necessary, Replies, together with all supporting documents, in the order and within the time that the PCIJ specifies; the oral proceedings shall comprise the hearing before the Court of advocates, counsel, agents, witnesses and experts [99]. The President of the PCIJ, or, if absent[101], the Vice-President of the PCIJ, or, if also absent, the senior judge, shall preside at the hearing [100]. At any time, the PCIJ may select an individual or organization to conduct an enquiry or give an expert opinion [101]. During the hearing, pertinent questions are to be put to the witnesses and experts according to the Rules of Court of the PCIJ[102] [102]. Whenever one of the disputants shall not appear before the Court or shall fail to defend its case, the other party may ask the PCIJ to decide in its favour; prior to doing this, the Court must satisfy itself that it has jurisdiction and that the claim is well-founded legally and factually [103]. A majority of the judges present at the hearing shall decide all

---

[97] The notion of '*ex aequo et bono*' "is based upon the idea of 'fundamental fairness' as a guideline principle in arbitration and other dispute settlement processes. Provided that the parties expressly agree, it enables judges and arbitrators to decide a case according to what – in literal translation of the original phrase – 'is fair (or equitable) and good' (Fair and Equitable Treatment). That is also to say 'in good conscience' and notwithstanding the written law. ..." (Kotzur, M. (2009), "Ex aequo et bono," last updated July 2009, accessed July 10, 2024, <https://opil.ouplaw.com/display/10.1093/law:epil/9780199231690/law-9780199231690-e1402>).

[98] This procedure applies to contentious cases. Provisions relating to the PCIJ's advisory jurisdiction – including those on procedural matters – were introduced into the Statute of the PCIJ by the Protocol concerning the Revision of the Statute of the Permanent Court of International Justice of 14th September 1929 (fn 67 and accompanying text). Article 68 of the revised Statute of the PCIJ is noteworthy: "In the exercise of its advisory functions, the Court shall further be guided by the provisions of the Statute which apply in contentious cases to the extent to which it recognizes them to be applicable." (Permanent Court of International Justice (1940), Statute of the Court, as amended, *P.C.I.J. Series D No.1*, 13-28, 28, Article 68).

[99] If there is no such agreement, then "each party may, in the pleadings, use the language which it prefers; the decision of the Court will be given in French and English. In this case the Court will at the same time determine which of the two texts shall be considered as authoritative. The Court may, at the request of the parties, authorize a language other than French or English to be used." (Permanent Court of International Justice (1926), Statute of the Court, *P.C.I.J. Series D No.1*, 7-27, 21, Article 39).

[100] The Registrar of the PCIJ shall immediately convey the application to everyone concerned, and shall notify the Members of the League of Nations via the Secretary-General of the League and (in the revised version of the Statute of the PCIJ only) any states that are entitled to appear before the Court (Permanent Court of International Justice (1926), Statute of the Court, *P.C.I.J. Series D No.1*, 7-27, 21, Article 40; Permanent Court of International Justice (1940), Statute of the Court, as amended, *P.C.I.J. Series D No.1*, 13-28, 23, Article 40).

[101] The revised version of the Statute of the PCIJ uses the phrase "if he is unable to preside" in place of the phrase "in his absence" in the original version of the Statute of the PCIJ (Permanent Court of International Justice (1940), Statute of the Court, as amended, *P.C.I.J. Series D No.1*, 13-28, 24, Article 45; Permanent Court of International Justice (1926), Statute of the Court, *P.C.I.J. Series D No.1*, 7-27, 23, Article 45).

[102] Fn 94 and accompanying text.

questions; if there is an equality of votes, then the President of the PCIJ (or the deputy) shall have a casting vote [104]. The judgment shall state the reasons upon which it is founded, and shall include the names of the judges who have participated in the decision [105]. If the judgment does not represent the unanimous opinion of the judges, in whole or in part, then any judge may furnish a separate opinion [106]. The judgment is final; there is no appeal against it[103] [107]. In limited circumstances[104], a party can apply for revision of a judgment; if the PCIJ accepts this application, then it will commence proceedings for revision[105] [108]. If a state deems that it possesses "an interest of a legal nature which may be affected the decision in the case", then it may petition the PCIJ for it to be allowed to intervene as a third party; the Court will determine this request [109]. States parties to a convention have the right to intervene in proceedings of the PCIJ which concern the interpretation of provisions of that convention[106] [110].

The Dissolution of the PCIJ

On 9th October 1944, delegates still present at the Dumbarton Oaks Conference[107] adopted the "Proposals for the Establishment of a General International Organization", which included provisions concerning the foundation of an international court of justice within the framework of that future entity [78]. The United Nations Committee of Jurists, meeting in Washington in April 1945 to June 1945, left unresolved the question of whether a new court should be established [71, 78]. This was submitted to the United Nations Conference on International Organization, which convened on 25th April 1945 in San Francisco [78], and which decided to establish a new court [71, 78] – the future ICJ. The main reasons for this decision were: (i) as the court was to be the main judicial organ of the UN, it was considered to be inappropriate that

[103] If there is disagreement about the scope or meaning of the judgment, then the PCIJ shall construe it if any party so requests (Permanent Court of International Justice (1926), Statute of the Court, *P.C.I.J. Series D No.1*, 7-27, 26, Article 60).

[104] A disputant may make an application for a judgment of the PCIJ to be revised "only when it is based upon the discovery of some fact of such a nature as to be a decisive factor, which fact was, when the judgment was given, unknown to the Court and also to the party claiming revision, always provided that such ignorance was not due to negligence"; the disputant must make the application for revision of a judgment of the PCIJ within six months of the discovery of that new fact, and within ten years of the date of the judgment (Permanent Court of International Justice (1926), Statute of the Court, *P.C.I.J. Series D No.1*, 7-27, 26, Article 61).

[105] These proceedings "will be opened by a judgment of the Court expressly recording the existence of the new fact, recognizing that it has such a character as to lay the case open to revision, and declaring the application admissible on this ground" (Permanent Court of International Justice (1926), Statute of the Court, *P.C.I.J. Series D No.1*, 7-27, 26, Article 61).

[106] Article 63 of the Statute of the PCIJ reads: "Whenever the construction of a convention to which States other than those concerned in the case are parties is in question, the Registrar shall notify all such States forthwith. Every State so notified has the right to intervene in the proceedings: but if it uses this right, the construction given by the judgment will be equally binding upon it." (Permanent Court of International Justice (1926), Statute of the Court, *P.C.I.J. Series D No.1*, 7-27, 27, Article 63).

[107] The Dumbarton Oaks Conference was a meeting held at Dumbarton Oaks, between representatives of the UK, the USA and the USSR (from 21st August 1944 to 28th September 1944) and between representatives of China, the UK and the USA (from 29th September 1944 to 7th October 1944) to draw up proposals for a global organization that became the basis for the UN (Encyclopaedia Britannica (1998), "Dumbarton Oaks Conference," published July 20, 1998, last updated August 14, 2023, accessed July 11, 2024, <https://www.britannica.com/event/Dumbarton-Oaks-Conference>; Dumbarton Oaks Archives (2015), "The Dumbarton Oaks Conversations, 1944," published June 15, 2017, accessed July 11, 2024, <https://www.doaks.org/newsletter/news-archives/2015/the-dumbarton-oaks-conversations-1944>).

the PCIJ should perform this role with its link to the League of Nations, (ii) the foundation of a new court was more consistent (than the continuation of the PCIJ) with the provision in the UN Charter that all Member States of the UN would be parties to the statute of the court[108], (iii) several states which were parties to the Statute of the PCIJ were absent from the San Francisco Conference, and some states that were represented at the San Francisco Conference were not parties to the Statute of the PCIJ, and (iv) the PCIJ was considered by some to form part of an older order in which states in Europe had dominated the legal and political affairs of the international community [71].

The PCIJ convened for the final time in October 1945 [71, 78]. Its judges resigned on 31st January 1946 [71, 78]. On 17th April 1946, the PCIJ was dissolved by a resolution of the League of Nations [78].

Comment

The PCIJ rose and fell with the League of Nations. The advent of a new international organization – the UN – brought with it the advent of a new court, the ICJ. This was nothing to do with perceptions of the PCIJ as a functional court, which worked well and published respected judgments and advisory opinions. The wish for continuity in the settlement of international disputes was shown by the establishment of the ICJ at the Peace Palace in the Hague simultaneously with the dissolution of the PCIJ, which had also been located there. The ICJ was to keep on with the PCIJ's work, and to build on it.

The International Labour Organization survived the dissolution of the League of Nations, and became a specialized agency of the UN. Why did this fare better than the PCIJ? It may have been because there was perceived to be a need for institutional stability regarding the production of International Labour Conventions, and also because labour law was a discrete area with little connection with the primary global organization, i.e., the League of Nations or the UN. But these points could be put forward analogously regarding the work of the international court. Therefore, the fact that the International Labour Organization and the PCIJ found themselves to be on different sides of the preservation line may been due to perceptions regarding the global legal and political order to which labour law seemed to be of less relevance than dispute settlement, i.e., a development of point (iv) in the immediately-preceding subsection. Whatever the reason or reasons for the differing treatment of the PCIJ and the International Labour Organization, it is welcome that the latter has been maintained from its foundation in 1919.

Conclusion

This chapter describes the First World War, the League of Nations and the PCIJ, including provisions of the agreements on which the latter two were based. The next chapter introduces

---

[108] This provision is paragraph 1 of Article 93 of the UN Charter, which states: "All Members of the United Nations are *ipso facto* parties to the Statute of the International Court of Justice." (United Nations (1945), "Charter of the United Nations," Article 93(1); emphasis original).

a similar combination of entities over the next chronological period, i.e., the Second World War, the UN and the ICJ.

Chapter 3

The Second World War, the United Nations, and the International Court of Justice

Abstract

The German invasion of Poland on 1st September 1939 gave rise to several declarations of war on Germany, causing the Second World War to begin. The attack by Japan on the USA at Pearl Habor, Hawaii, on 7th December 1941 rendered the Second World War a global conflict. Casualties of that war comprised fifty million to sixty million deaths – three-quarters of these civilians, twenty-five million injured military personnel, and tens of millions of displaced people. The Second World War officially ceased on 2nd September 1945. There was no peace treaty with Germany after the war. The Treaties of Peace with Bulgaria, Finland, Hungary, Italy and Romania were signed in Paris on 10th February 1947. They included terms of surrender and disarmament, territorial adjustments, war reparations, the recognition of human rights and the punishment of war criminals. The UN Charter was signed in San Francisco on 26th June 1945 and entered into force on 24th October 1945, thereby establishing the UN on the latter day. The UN is founded on the principle of sovereign equality of all its Member States. It is not wholly based on this principle – there is a higher class of membership for the five Member States of the UN that are permanent members of the UNSC, and a standard class of membership for all other Member States. Any change to the UN Charter that a two-thirds majority in a vote at conference recommends is to take effect when this alteration is ratified by a two-thirds majority of the Member States – including all five permanent members of the UNSC. Thus, each of the permanent members of the UNSC is empowered by the UN Charter to block amendments to it by failing to ratify those changes. This puts these five countries in a strong position relative to the other Member States. While this was an understandable basis on which to create the UN Charter in the 1940s, it is not appropriate as a long-lasting arrangement. The ICJ held its inaugural meeting on 3rd April 1946. It is to operate in accordance with the Statute of the ICJ, which is grounded upon the Statute of the PCIJ. The jurisdiction of the ICJ comprises all cases that the disputants refer to it, and all issues that the UN Charter – or effective treaties and conventions – provide for. A decision of the ICJ has no binding force except between the parties and in respect of the particular case. As amendments to the Statute of the ICJ are to be carried out by the same procedure that the UN Charter gives for its amendments, and as these only take effect when ratified by two-thirds of the Member States of the UN – including all five permanent members of the UNSC, each permanent member is empowered by the Statute of the ICJ to prevent any amendment from entering into force by omitting to ratify it. Hence, in this aspect, not all states parties to the Statute of the ICJ are equal before the Court.

Keywords: Assembly, Conference, ICJ, peace, Principle, Statute, UN, UNSC, war

Introduction

The onset of the Second World War induced the dissolution of the League of Nations and the conceptualization of the UN, which became the League's replacement after the war. The ICJ superseded the PCIJ, continuing the latter's work with the same President of the Court[109]. Only a few articles of the UN Charter have been amended. The Statute of the ICJ has not, as yet, been revised. Do these two documents remain entirely sufficient to support the challenges in international relations and law that are taking place eighty years after their creation? An attempt to answer this question can only be made with the aid of familiarity with their articles, to which much of this chapter is devoted. Before this, the Second World War and its settlements, and the establishment of the UN, are considered.

The Second World War and Its Settlements

The Second World War

The Commencement of the Second World War

Germany occupied the Rhineland in March 1936 without response from France[110], conquered Austria in March 1938 without reprisals from France or Great Britain, annexed the Sudentenland in October 1938 by prior agreement with Czechoslovakia, France, Great Britain and Italy – part of the policy of known as 'appeasement' towards Germany, and invaded the remainder of Czechoslovakia in March 1939 without retaliation – at which point Great Britain ended that policy [111, 112]. In the early morning of 1st September 1939, Germany invaded Poland [113, 114]. On 25th August 1939, Great Britain and Poland had signed a mutual assistance agreement [113, 115], the German knowledge of which had precipitated a brief delay in Germany's planned invasion of Poland from 26th August 1939 until 1st September 1939 [113]. Later in the day of 1st September 1939, France and Great Britain informed Germany that, unless it suspended all of its aggressive action against Poland and withdrew its armed forces from Polish territory, they would carry out their obligations to Poland [116]. Norway, Switzerland, Finland and Italy proclaimed neutrality [117]. At 9 a.m. on 3rd September 1939, Great Britain sent an ultimatum to Germany regarding the above suspension and withdrawal – the German Government was required to provide acceptable assurances of these to the British

---

[109] Dr. José Gustavo Guerrero (1876-1958) was Minister for Foreign Affairs of El Salvador (1927-1928), President of the Assembly of the League of Nations (1929-1930), Judge (1931-1946) and President (1936-1946) of the PCIJ, and Judge (1946-1958) and President (1946-1949) of the ICJ (International Court of Justice (2018), "Tribute to José Gustavo Guerrero, first President of the International Court of Justice," published October, 23, 2018, accessed July 15, 2024, <https://www.icj-cij.org/node/105726>; International Court of Justice (2024), "History," accessed July 15, 2024, <https://www.icj-cij.org/history>).

[110] Under the Versailles Treaty, Germany was required to demilitarize the Rhineland: "Germany is forbidden to maintain or construct any fortifications either on the left bank of the Rhine or on the right bank to the west of a line drawn 50 kilometres to the East of the Rhine. ... In the area defined above the maintenance and the assembly of armed forces, either permanently or temporarily, and military manoeuvres of any kind, as well as the upkeep of all permanent works for mobilization, are in the same way forbidden." (Government of the United States of America (1919), *Treaty of Peace with Germany (Treaty of Versailles)*, Treaty and protocol signed at Versailles June 28, 1919, protocol signed by Germany at Paris January 10, 1920, entered into force January 10, 1920, 4.15 p.m., as between contracting parties (the United States was not a party), 1919 For. Rel. (Paris Peace Conference, XIII) 55, 740, 743; 66th Congress, 1st Session, Senate Document 51, 43-240, 65, Articles 42 and 43).

Government in London by 11 a.m., British Summer Time, on that day, in order to avoid a declaration of war by Great Britain on Germany from taking effect [118]. As no such assurances were received, thenceforth Great Britain was at war with Germany [118]. France delivered a similar ultimatum to Germany but for 5 p.m. on 3rd September 1939, which the latter disregarded [119]. Consequently, at 5.p.m on that day, France declared war on Germany [119]. Also on 3rd September 1939, Australia, India and New Zealand declared war on Germany, and Belgium announced its neutrality [119]. On 5th September 1939, the USA proclaimed its neutrality [120]. On 6th September 1939, South Africa declared war on Germany [120]. On 10th September 1939, Canada declared war on Germany [121]. Thus, the Second World War had begun. On 27th September 1940, Germany, Italy and Japan signed a ten-year defence alliance, which is known as the Tripartite Pact, and which was aimed at keeping the USA out of the Second World War – as it referred to mutual assistance when any one of those states was attacked by a country that was involved in neither the European war nor the Sino-Japanese conflict[111] [122, 123]. On 7th December 1941, Japan attacked the USA at Pearl Harbor, Hawaii, and occupied the International Settlement at Shanghai [124]. At Pearl Harbor, several ships were sunk and hundreds of aeroplanes destroyed [125]. On the following day, the USA declared war on Japan – as did Australia, Canada, Costa Rica, Dominican Republic, El Salvador, Free France, Great Britain, Guatemala, Haiti, Honduras, the Netherlands, Netherlands East Indies (now Indonesia), New Zealand, Panama and South Africa, and Japan invaded Thailand – which surrendered [126]. China and Cuba declared war on Japan on 9th December 1941 [127]. On 11th December 1941, Germany and Italy declared a state of war with the USA – and *vice versa*, Nicaragua and Poland declared war on Japan, and Costa Rica, Cuba, Dominican Republic, Guatemala and Nicaragua declared war on Germany and Italy [128]. There followed a flurry of declarations of war: Haiti, Honduras and Panama on Germany and Italy (12th December 1941), Rumania (now Romania) on the USA (12th December 1941), El Salvador on Germany and Italy (13th December 1941), Bulgaria on the USA (13th December 1941), Czechoslovakia on all countries at war with Great Britain, Russia or the USA (16th December 1941), Albania on the USA (17th December 1941), and Nicaragua on Bulgaria, Hungary and Rumania (20th December 1941) [129]. The attack at Pearl Habor had truly rendered the Second World War a global conflict.

Casualties of the Second World War

While estimates vary, an educated guess is fifty million to sixty million deaths, with three quarters of these civilians [130, 131, 132, 133]. Twenty-five million military personnel were wounded [132]. Tens of millions of people were displaced [131].

The End of the Second World War

On 6th June 1944, American, British, and Canadian troops landed on five beachheads in Normandy; by the end of August 1944, all of northern France had been freed from the invading

---

[111] In the late evening of 18th September 1931, Japan dynamited a section of the South Manchurian railway, which was followed during the night with fighting between Chinese and Japanese troops – signifying the start of the Sino-Japanese conflict (Government of the United States of America (1944), *Events leading up to World War II: Chronological history of certain major international events leading up to and during World War II with the ostensible reasons advanced for their occurrence, 1931-1944*, 78th Congress, 2nd Session, House Document No. 541 (Washington: United States Government Printing Office), 4). By 1937, Japan controlled large parts of China (Harry S. Truman Presidential Library and Museum (2024), "Invasion of Manchuria," accessed July 18, 2024, <https://www.trumanlibrary.gov/education/presidential-inquiries/invasion-manchuria>).

German forces [134]. These troops reorganized and advanced into Germany from the west, while the forces of the USSR entered Germany from the east; both armies converged on Berlin, causing the European part of the Second World War to terminate on 8th May 1945[112] [134, 135]. The Act of Military Surrender was signed by the Chief of Staff of the German Army in the early morning hours of 7th May 1945 at Supreme Headquarters, Allied Expeditionary Force, in Reims[113] [136, 137]. The Pacific part of the Second World War was officially ended on 10th August 1945, when the Government of Japan issued a statement agreeing to accept the terms of surrender that had been dictated in the Potsdam Declaration[114] – consequent to the atomic bombs that the USA dropped on Hiroshima on 6th August 1945 and Nagasaki on 9th August 1945[115] [135, 138]. The Second World War officially ceased on 2nd September 1945, when Japan signed formal surrender documents aboard the USS *Missouri*[116] [139, 140].

Settlements Following the Second World War

Germany: The Act of Military Surrender and the Potsdam Conference

The Act of Military Surrender[117] included an unconditional surrender of all forces under German control to the Supreme Commander of Allied Expeditionary Forces and the Soviet High Command, and an instruction to the German High Command to immediately order those

[112] German troops in north-west Europe surrendered to British forces at Lüneburg Heath on 4th May 1945 (Lowe, K. (2020), "How and when did WW2 end?" published September 1, 2020, accessed July 19, 2024, <https://www.historyextra.com/period/second-world-war/how-when-ww2-end-ve-day-vj-day-fighting-atomic-bombs-japan-world-europe/>; The British Army (2020), "Marking the 75 Anniversary of the Luneberg Surrender," published May 4, 2020, accessed July 19, 2024, <https://www.army.mod.uk/news-and-events/news/2020/05/veday-lueneberg-surrender/>).

[113] As the USSR did not recognize the signing of the Act of Military Surrender in Reims on 7th May 1945, another copy of the Act was signed in Berlin at 11.01 p.m. the following day – which is called 'Victory in Europe' Day, VE Day or V-E Day; at that moment, it was 9th May 1945 in Moscow – hence the Russian celebration of 'Victory Day' on 9th May (Lowe, K. (2020), "How and when did WW2 end?" published September 1, 2020, accessed July 19, 2024, <https://www.historyextra.com/period/second-world-war/how-when-ww2-end-ve-day-vj-day-fighting-atomic-bombs-japan-world-europe/>; Lowe, K. (2021), "A brief guide to VE Day," published May 8, 2021, accessed July 19, 2024, <https://www.historyextra.com/period/second-world-war/brief-guide-ve-day-victory-europe-ww2/>; The National WWII Museum New Orleans (2024), "The End of World War II 1945," accessed July 19, 2024, <https://www.nationalww2museum.org/war/topics/end-world-war-ii-1945>).

[114] The Potsdam Declaration was an ultimatum that China, Great Britain and the USA issued on 26th July 1945 at the Potsdam Conference, which called for the unconditional surrender of Japan (Encyclopaedia Britannica (2018), "Potsdam Declaration," published January 31, 2018, last updated July 19, 2024, accessed July 19, 2024, <https://www.britannica.com/topic/Potsdam-Declaration>).

[115] Keith Lowe writes: "Understanding that his armed forces had no response to this terrifying new weapon, Japanese emperor Hirohito prepared a speech, which he broadcast to the nation on 15 August. Although he never used the word 'surrender', he announced that he had told his government to accept the demands of the Allies. The alternative, he made clear, was the complete "collapse and obliteration of the Japanese nation". All over Asia and the Pacific, Japanese troops began to lay down their weapons. As a consequence of this speech, 15 August 1945 is officially commemorated as the anniversary of VJ Day in Britain and Korea, and unofficially so across much of Asia. However, a formal surrender document was not signed until 2 September aboard the American battleship, *USS Missouri*. This later date is considered the anniversary of VJ Day in the USA." (Lowe, K. (2020), "How and when did WW2 end?" published September 1, 2020, accessed July 19, 2024, <https://www.historyextra.com/period/second-world-war/how-when-ww2-end-ve-day-vj-day-fighting-atomic-bombs-japan-world-europe/>; emphasis original). VJ Day (or V-J Day) stands for 'Victory over Japan' Day (Government of the United States of America (2021), "U.S. Department of Defense: Victory over Japan Day End of WWII," accessed July 19, 2024, <https://www.defense.gov/Multimedia/Experience/VJ-Day/>).

[116] Fn 115.

[117] Fn 113 and accompanying text.

troops to cease their active operations at 11.01 p.m. (Central European time) on 8th May 1945 and to stay in the positions that they occupied at that moment [137]. The Potsdam Conference was a meeting between the Prime Minister of the UK – Mr. Winston Churchill (as he then was), the President of the USA, Mr. Harry Truman, and the General Secretary of the Communist Party of the USSR, Mr. Joseph Stalin, from 17th July 1945 to 2nd August 1945, which was held to negotiate terms for the end of the Second World War [141]. There was no peace treaty with Germany after the war[118]. The reconstitution of a national Government of Germany was postponed indefinitely – the Allied Control Commission, which was constituted by France, the UK, the USA and the USSR, would run the country during the interregnum [141]; Germany would be divided into four zones of occupation, each to be controlled by one of those states [130]. It would also be demilitarized and disarmed[119] [141]. Poland lost territory in its east to the USSR and gained territory in its west from Germany [141]. China, the UK and the USA published the Potsdam Declaration[120] [141].

The Paris Peace Treaties

The Paris Peace Conference after the Second World War was held from 29th July 1946 to 15th October 1946 [142]. Its output was recommendations for changes to draft peace treaties between the Allied powers and each of the following Axis powers: Bulgaria, Finland, Hungary, Italy and Romania – which had been prepared by the Council of Foreign Ministers[121] during its sessions at London and Paris earlier in 1946 [142, 143, 144]. The Council of Foreign Ministers adopted a majority of these recommendations in its final drafting of those treaties in New York from 4th November 1946 to 12th December 1946 [142]. The treaties – i.e., the Treaty of Peace with Bulgaria, the Treaty of Peace with Finland, the Treaty of Peace with Hungary, the Treaty of Peace with Italy and the Treaty of Peace with Romania – were signed in Paris on 10th February 1947; they included terms of surrender and disarmament, territorial adjustments, sums payable in respect of damage caused by the activities of these states in the war, the recognition of human rights and the punishment of war criminals [143].

---

[118] Bitter disputes between the Allies over the division of Germany during the Cold War precluded the conclusion of a peace treaty with Germany until its reunification in 1990 (Oxford Reference (2024), "Overview: Paris Peace Treaties," accessed July 20, 2024, <https://www.oxfordreference.com/display/10.1093/oi/authority.20110803100306594>).

[119] All parts of German industry that could be used for military purposes were to be disassembled, all German military and paramilitary forces were to be abolished, and the production of military hardware in Germany was to be prohibited (Government of the United States of America (2009), "U.S. Department of State Archive: The Potsdam Conference, 1945," published January 20, 2009, accessed July 20, 2024, <https://2001-2009.state.gov/r/pa/ho/time/wwii/93275.htm>).

[120] Fn 114 and accompanying text. The USSR did not sign the Potsdam Declaration, as it had not declared war on Japan (Government of the United States of America (2009), "U.S. Department of State Archive: The Potsdam Conference, 1945," published January 20, 2009, accessed July 20, 2024, <https://2001-2009.state.gov/r/pa/ho/time/wwii/93275.htm>).

[121] The Council of Foreign Ministers was the organization of the foreign ministers of France, the UK, the USA and the USSR which, in meetings between 1945 and 1972, attempted to reach political agreements following the Second World War (Encyclopaedia Britannica (2009), "Council of Foreign Ministers," published March 18, 2009, last updated September 25, 2013, accessed July 21, 2024, <https://www.britannica.com/topic/Council-of-Foreign-Ministers>).

Comment

The Second World War was a huge catastrophe that caused multiple casualties and led to a changed map of the world, and especially of Europe. It caused or contributed to other subsequent major events, including the Cold War, the foundation of Israel and the Korean War. One positive that emerged from it was the establishment of the UN and of other international organizations – such as the International Monetary Fund and the International Bank for Reconstruction and Development, which were created in principle at the Bretton Woods Conference of July 1944. The world was changing – mainly in a positive way; there was a universal wish to prevent or avoid the occurrence of such horrors again.

The United Nations

Introduction

The UN is the most significant entity that emerged from the tragedy of the Second World War. Its areas of work include not only the pursuit and maintenance of global peace and security and the furtherance of international law, but also the promotion of sustainable development, the protection of human rights, and the co-ordination of international responses to humanitarian disasters. It operates within a co-ordinated structure of funds, programmes and specialized agencies, which, together, are referred to as the UN System – the topic of another book by the author of this one[122].

The Foundation of the UN

Inter-Allied Meeting and Resolution: 12th June 1941

On that day, the Governments of Australia, Canada, South Africa and the UK, the exiled Governments of Belgium, Czechoslovakia, Greece, Luxembourg, the Netherlands, Norway, Poland and Yugoslavia, and the Representatives of General de Gaulle – the leader of Free Frenchmen, met at St. James's Palace, London [145]. Their Resolution declared "[t]hat the only true basis of enduring peace is the willing co-operation of free peoples in a world in which, relieved of the menace of aggression, all may enjoy economic and social security; and that it is their intention to work together, and with other free peoples, both in war and peace to this end" [146].

Atlantic Charter: 14th August 1941

The Prime Minister of the UK, Mr. Winston Churchill, and the President of the USA, Mr. Franklin Roosevelt, issued this joint declaration following four days of conferences between the UK and the USA aboard warships anchored in Placentia Bay – adjacent to Newfoundland [147]. The Atlantic Charter set out eight principles, the essence of which are as follows: (i) the UK and the USA seek no territorial or other aggrandizement [148]; (ii) they only wish to

---

[122] Baber, G. (2019), *The United Nations System* (Newcastle-upon-Tyne: Cambridge Scholars Publishing).

witness territorial changes that accord with the freely-expressed wishes of the relevant people [149]; (iii) they observe the right of all peoples to choose the form of government that applies to the latter [150]; (iv) they will attempt to advance the enjoyment by all states of equal access to the worldwide trade and raw materials which those countries need for their economic prosperity [151]; (v) they wish to achieve optimum economic collaboration between all states in order to secure development, social security and better labour standards, [152]; (vi) they hope to see an assured and freedom-giving peace [153]; (vii) this peace should enable all people to cross the oceans and high seas unhindered [154]; (viii) they believe that all nations must come to renounce the use of force [155].

Declaration by United Nations: 1st January 1942

This document was signed by Messrs. Winston Churchill, Frankin Roosevelt, Maxim Litvinov – the Ambassador of the USSR to the USA, and T.V. Soong – the Minister of Foreign Affairs of China, on 1st January 1942, and by representatives of twenty-two other countries the next day[123] [156]. By signing the Declaration by United Nations, each government subscribed to the Atlantic Charter [157], agreed to utilize its whole resources against the Axis Powers [158], and pledged to co-operate with the other governments which signed this joint declaration and not to make a separate armistice or peace with the aforementioned adversaries [159]. The Declaration by United Nations is the first official use of the term 'United Nations' [156].

Declaration of Four Nations on General Security (Moscow Declaration): 30th October 1943

Article 7 of this document refers to 'members of the United Nations'[124], which, it is submitted, refers to the countries that signed the Declaration by United Nations – which Recital 1 thereof mentions[125]. Article 4 of the Declaration of Four Nations on General Security prepares the ground for the establishment of the UN, as soon as the Second World War is over[126]; it is opined

[123] These countries are Australia, Belgium, Canada, Costa Rica, Cuba, Czechoslovakia, Dominican Republic, El Salvador, Greece, Guatemala, Haiti, Honduras, India, Luxembourg, the Netherlands, New Zealand, Nicaragua, Norway, Panama, Poland, South Africa and Yugoslavia; there were the following later adherents to the Declaration by United Nations, which, by date of communication of their compliance, are Mexico (5th June 1942), the Philippines (10th June 1942), Ethiopia (28th July 1942), Iran (16th January 1943), Brazil (8th February 1943), Bolivia (27th April 1943), Iran (10th September 1943), Colombia (22nd December 1943), Liberia (26th February 1944), France (26th December 1944), Ecuador (7th February 1945), Peru (11th February 1945), Chile (12th February 1945), Paraguay (12th February 1945), Venezuela (16th February 1945), Uruguay (23rd February 1945), Turkey (24th February 1945), Egypt (27th February 1945), Lebanon (1st March 1945), Saudi Arabia (1st March 1945) and Syria (1st March 1945) (Yale University (2008), Yale Law School Lillian Goldman Law Library The Avalon Project – Declaration by the United Nations: January 1, 1942).

[124] The governments of China, the UK, the USA and the USSR "Jointly declare: ... *7.* That they will confer and cooperate with one another and with other members of the United Nations to bring about a practicable general agreement with respect to the regulation of armaments in the post-war period" (Yale University (2008), Yale Law School Lillian Goldman Law Library The Avalon Project – The Moscow Conference Joint Four-Nation Declaration: October, 1943, Article 7; emphasis original).

[125] The governments of China, the UK, the USA and the USSR "United in their determination, in accordance with the declaration by the United Nations of January, 1942, and subsequent declarations, to continue hostilities against those Axis powers with which they respectively are at war until such powers have laid down their arms on the basis of unconditional surrender;" (Yale University (2008), Yale Law School Lillian Goldman Law Library The Avalon Project – The Moscow Conference Joint Four-Nation Declaration: October, 1943, Recital 1).

[126] The governments of China, the UK, the USA and the USSR "Jointly declare: ... *4.* That they recognize the necessity of establishing at the earliest practicable date a general international organization, based on the principle of the sovereign equality of all peace-loving states, and open to membership by all such states, large and small, for the maintenance of international peace and security" (Yale University (2008), Yale Law School Lillian Goldman

that it was a simple matter of connective continuity for the leaders of the Allied Powers to transmute the term 'United Nations' from the countries that signed the Declaration by United Nations to the name of the planned new international organization.

Tehran Conference: 28th November 1943 to 1st December 1943

This was a meeting between Messrs. Winston Churchill, Franklin Roosevelt and Joseph Stalin, in which they co-ordinated their military strategy against Germany and Japan, and discussed territorial adjustments that might be made after the Second World War [160]. At the meeting, Mr. Roosevelt summarized his vision of the proposed international organization in which the future UN would be dominated by China, the UK, the USA and the USSR, which would have power to instantly address any threat to the peace and any unanticipated emergency requiring action [160].

Dumbarton Oaks Conference: 21st August 1944 to 7th October 1944[127]; Proposals for the Establishment of a General International Organization[128]

As the following two comparative extracts, which are respectively from the Proposals for the Establishment of a General International Organization and the UN Charter, demonstrate, the former truly constituted a precursor document to the latter. However, the Proposals for the Establishment of a General International Organization did not provide an agreed arrangement on a few issues – such as the voting system of the UNSC and the membership provisions for the USSR's constituent republics; these were settled at the Yalta Conference [161].

> The purposes of the [General International] Organization should be: 1. To maintain international peace and security; and to that end to take effective collective measures for the prevention and removal of threats to the peace and the suppression of acts of aggression or other breaches of the peace, and to bring about by peaceful means adjustment or settlement of international disputes which may lead to a breach of the peace; 2. To develop friendly relations among nations and to take other appropriate measures to strengthen universal peace; 3. To achieve international cooperation in the solution of international economic, social and other humanitarian problems; and 4. To afford a center for harmonizing the actions of nations in the achievement of these common ends [162].

> The *Purposes*[129] of the *United Nations are*[130]: 1. To maintain international peace and security[131], and to that end*:*[132] to take effective collective measures for the prevention and

Law Library The Avalon Project – The Moscow Conference Joint Four-Nation Declaration: October, 1943, Article 4; emphasis original).

[127] Fn 107.

[128] Text to fn 107.

[129] Emphasis added. Article 1 of the UN Charter capitalizes the 'p' in the word 'purposes' in Chapter 1 of the Proposals for the Establishment of a General International Organization.

[130] Emphasis added. Article 1 of the UN Charter replaces the phrase 'Organization should be' in Chapter 1 of the Proposals for the Establishment of a General International Organization with the phrase 'United Nations are'.

[131] Emphasis added. Article 1 of the UN Charter replaces the semicolon after the word 'security' in Chapter 1 of the Proposals for the Establishment of a General International Organization with a comma.

[132] Emphasis added. Article 1 of the UN Charter places a semicolon between the words 'end' and 'to' in Chapter 1 of the Proposals for the Establishment of a General International Organization.

> removal of threats to the peace[133], and *for*[134] the suppression of acts of aggression or other breaches of the peace, and to bring about by peaceful means, *and in conformity with the principles of justice and international law*[135], adjustment or settlement of international disputes *or situations*[136] which *might*[137] lead to a breach of the peace; 2. To develop friendly relations among nations *based on respect for the principle of equal rights and self-determination of peoples*[138], and to take other appropriate measures to strengthen universal peace; 3. To achieve international co-operation[139] in *solving*[140] international *problems of an economic, social, cultural or humanitarian character*[141], *and in promoting and encouraging respect for human rights and for fundamental freedoms for all without distinction as to race, sex, language, or religion*[142]; and 4. To *be*[143] a center for harmonizing the actions of nations in the *attainment*[144] of these common ends [163].

The following provisions from Chapter VI of the Proposals for the Establishment of a General International Organization, which is entitled 'The Security Council,' show that the problem described in Chapter 1 concerning the veto of each of the permanent members of the UNSC, which has materialized in respect of Russia regarding its voting on proposals put forward there for decision concerning its actions in Ukraine[145], was created inadvertently before

---

[133] Emphasis added. Article 1 of the UN Charter inserts a comma after the phrase 'to the peace' in Chapter 1 of the Proposals for the Establishment of a General International Organization.

[134] Emphasis added. Article 1 of the UN Charter adds the word 'for' before the phrase 'the suppression of acts of aggression' in Chapter 1 of the Proposals for the Establishment of a General International Organization.

[135] Emphasis added. Article 1 of the UN Charter adds the phrase ', and in conformity with the principles of justice and international law,' – including a comma at the start of this expression and another at the end of it, after the phrase 'by peaceful means' in Chapter 1 of the Proposals for the Establishment of a General International Organization.

[136] Emphasis added. Article 1 of the UN Charter adds the phrase 'or situations' after the phrase 'adjustment or settlement of international disputes' in Chapter 1 of the Proposals for the Establishment of a General International Organization.

[137] Emphasis added. Article 1 of the UN Charter changes the word 'may' in Chapter 1 of the Proposals for the Establishment of a General International Organization to the word 'might'.

[138] Emphasis added. Article 1 of the UN Charter adds the phrase 'based on respect for the principle of equal rights and self-determination of peoples,' – including the comma, after the phrase 'friendly relations among nations' in Chapter 1 of the Proposals for the Establishment of a General International Organization.

[139] Emphasis added. Article 1 of the UN Charter inserts a hyphen between the consecutive letter 'o's in the word 'cooperation' in Chapter 1 of the Proposals for the Establishment of a General International Organization.

[140] Emphasis added. Article 1 of the UN Charter replaces the phrase 'the solution of' with the word 'solving', before the last instance of the word 'international' in Chapter 1 of the Proposals for the Establishment of a General International Organization.

[141] Emphasis added. Article 1 of the UN Charter recasts the phrase 'economic, social and other humanitarian problems' after the final instance of the word 'international' in Chapter 1 of the Proposals for the Establishment of a General International Organization, as the phrase 'problems of an economic, social, cultural, or humanitarian character.'

[142] Emphasis added. Article 1 of the UN Charter adds the phrase ', and in promoting and encouraging respect for human rights and for fundamental freedoms for all without distinction as to race, sex, language, or religion' – including the initial comma, before the characters '; and 4. To' in Chapter 1 of the Proposals for the Establishment of a General International Organization.

[143] Emphasis added. Article 1 of the UN Charter replaces the word 'afford' in Chapter 1 of the Proposals for the Establishment of a General International Organization with the word 'be.'

[144] Emphasis added. Article 1 of the UN Charter replaces the word 'achievement' in Chapter 1 of the Proposals for the Establishment of a General International Organization with the word 'attainment.'

[145] The subsections entitled 'The Russian veto', 'Under what circumstances does the UN Charter require a permanent member of the UNSC to abstain from voting?' and 'Do any of the abovelisted circumstances apply to Russia regarding its invasion of Ukraine? What conclusions can be drawn?', in the section titled 'The Problem' in Chapter 1, together explain that the veto takes the form of a dissenting vote by a permanent member to the UNSC on a non-procedural matter concerning which the latter intends to take a decision – in particular the negative

the UN came into existence, i.e., in the construction of this preliminary document at the Dumbarton Oaks Conference and in the section on voting in the UNSC that was added to it at the Yalta Conference.

> *Section A. Composition*[146]. The Security Council should consist of one representative of each of eleven members of the Organization. Representatives of the United States of America, the United Kingdom of Great Britain and Northern Ireland, the Union of Soviet Socialist Republics, the Republic of China, and, in due course, France, should have permanent seats. The General Assembly should elect six states to fill the non-permanent seats. ... [164].
>
> *Section B. Principle Functions and Powers*[147]. 1. In order to ensure prompt and effective action by the Organization, members of the Organization should by the Charter confer on the Security Council primary responsibility for the maintenance of international peace and security and should agree that in carrying out these duties under this responsibility it should act on their behalf [165]. ... 3. The specific powers conferred on the Security Council in order to carry out these duties are laid down in Chapter VIII [166]. 4. All members of the Organization should obligate themselves to accept the decisions of the Security Council and to carry them out in accordance with the provisions of the Charter [167]. ...
>
> [Agreed upon at the Yalta conference.] *Section C: Voting*[148]. 1. Each member of the Security Council should have one vote [168]. 2. Decisions of the Security Council on procedural matters should be made by an affirmative vote of seven members [169]. 3. Decisions of the Security Council on all other matters should be made by an affirmative vote of seven members including the concurring votes of the permanent members; provided that, in decisions under Chapter VIII, Section A, and under the second sentence of Paragraph 1 of Chapter VIII, Section C, a party to a dispute should abstain from voting [170].

It is submitted that Chapter VIII Section A of the Proposals for the Establishment of a General International Organization, which is titled 'Pacific Settlement of Disputes,' is a preliminary version of Chapter VI of the UN Charter – which has the same title[149], and that the

vote of Russia (i.e., the Russian veto) on proposals before the UNSC for a determination regarding illegal activities of Russian armed forces in Ukraine, which are outside the circumstances under which the UN Charter requires a member of the UNSC to abstain from voting.

[146] Emphasis original.

[147] Emphasis original.

[148] Emphasis original.

[149] For example, Paragraph 3 of Chapter VIII Section A of the Proposals for the Establishment of a General International Organization reads: "The parties to any dispute the continuance of which is likely to endanger the maintenance of international peace and security should obligate themselves, first of all, to seek a solution by negotiation, mediation, conciliation, arbitration or judicial settlement, or other peaceful means of their own choice. The Security Council should call upon the parties to settle their dispute by such means." (Derecho Internacional Público (2024), Dumbarton Oaks – Washington Conversations on International Peace and Security Organization, October 7, 1944: Proposals for the Establishment of a General International Organization, Chapter VIII, Section A, Paragraph 3). This corresponds to Article 33 of the UN Charter – the first article within Chapter VI of that document, which states: "1. The parties to any dispute, the continuance of which is likely to endanger the maintenance of international peace and security, shall, first of all, seek a solution by negotiation, enquiry, mediation, conciliation, arbitration, judicial settlement, resort to regional agencies or arrangements, or other peaceful means of their own choice. 2. The Security Council shall, when it deems necessary, call upon the parties to settle their dispute by such means." (United Nations (1945), "Charter of the United Nations," Article 33). The

second sentence of Paragraph 1 of Chapter VIII Section C is a precursory version of paragraph 3 of Article 52 of the UN Charter[150]. Thus, the second clause of Paragraph 3 of Chapter VI Section C of the Proposals for the Establishment of a General International Organization offers, in essence, the same circumstances under which a member of the UNSC is to be expected to abstain from voting as its successor provision – the second clause of paragraph 3 of Article 27 of the UN Charter[151] – does. Hence, just as the UNSC has been unable to take action under Chapter VII of the UN Charter in order to attempt to stop the Russian invasion of Ukraine because Russia was legally able to veto proposals for these measures put before the UNSC[152], so it would be unable to take action under the preliminary version of Chapter VII of the UN Charter, which, it is opined, is Chapter VIII Section B of the Proposals for the Establishment of a General International Organization – which is entitled 'Determination of Threats to the Peace or Acts of Aggression and Action With Respect Thereto'[153].

Yalta Conference: 4th February 1945 to 11th February 1945

This was a meeting of the leaders of the UK, the USA and the USSR – respectively Messrs. Winston Churchill, Franklin Roosevelt and Joseph Stalin, in which the USSR was promised

---

Office of the Historian in the USA equates Chapter VIII Section A of the Proposals for the Establishment of a General International Organization with Chapter VI of the UN Charter (Government of the United States of America (2024), "Department of State – Office of the Historian: Foreign Relations of the United States, Diplomatic Papers, 1945, General – The United Nations, Volume I: Guide to discussions of Dumbarton Oaks proposals and corresponding articles of the Charter of the United Nations, 1944-1945," accessed July 25, 2024, <https://history.state.gov/historicaldocuments/frus1945v01/guide>).

150 The second sentence of Paragraph 1 of Chapter VIII Section C reads: "The Security Council should encourage settlement of local disputes through such regional arrangements or by such regional agencies, either on the initiative of the states concerned or by reference from the Security Council." (Derecho Internacional Público (2024), Dumbarton Oaks – Washington Conversations on International Peace and Security Organization, October 7, 1944: Proposals for the Establishment of a General International Organization, Chapter VIII, Section C, Paragraph 1). Paragraph 3 of Article 52 of the UN Charter states: "The Security Council shall encourage the development of pacific settlement of local disputes through such regional arrangements or by such regional agencies either on the initiative of the states concerned or by reference from the Security Council." (United Nations (1945), "Charter of the United Nations," Article 52(3)).

151 The quoted passage immediately following fn 15 lays down the second clause of paragraph 3 of Article 27 of the UN Charter.

152 This is explained in the subsection entitled 'Do any of the abovelisted circumstances apply to Russia regarding its invasion of Ukraine? What conclusions can be drawn?', in the section titled 'The Problem' in Chapter 1.

153 For example, Paragraph 3 of Chapter VIII Section B of the Proposals for the Establishment of a General International Organization reads: "The Security Council should be empowered to determine what diplomatic, economic, or other measures not involving the use of armed force should be employed to give effect to its decisions, and to call upon members of the Organization to apply such measures. Such measures may include complete or partial interruption of rail, sea, air, postal, telegraphic, radio and other means of communication and the severance of diplomatic and economic relations." (Derecho Internacional Público (2024), Dumbarton Oaks – Washington Conversations on International Peace and Security Organization, October 7, 1944: Proposals for the Establishment of a General International Organization, Chapter VIII, Section A, Paragraph 3). This corresponds to Article 41 of the UN Charter – the third article within Chapter VII of that document, which states: "The Security Council may decide what measures not involving the use of armed force are to be employed to give effect to its decisions, and it may call upon the Members of the United Nations to apply such measures. These may include complete or partial interruption of economic relations and of rail, sea, air, postal, telegraphic, radio, and other means of communication, and the severance of diplomatic relations." (United Nations (1945), "Charter of the United Nations," Article 41). The Office of the Historian in the USA equates Chapter VIII Section B of the Proposals for the Establishment of a General International Organization with Chapter VII of the UN Charter (Government of the United States of America (2024), "Department of State – Office of the Historian: Foreign Relations of the United States, Diplomatic Papers, 1945, General – The United Nations, Volume I: Guide to discussions of Dumbarton Oaks proposals and corresponding articles of the Charter of the United Nations, 1944-1945," accessed July 26, 2024, <https://history.state.gov/historicaldocuments/frus1945v01/guide>).

that it would regain control of territory that it had lost to Japan in the Russo-Japanese War of 1904 to 1905, including the Kuril Islands and southern Sakhalin, in return for its support in opposition to Japan towards the end of the Second World War [171]. All three gentlemen agreed upon a voting plan, which was subsequently inserted into the Proposals for the Establishment of a General International Organization as its Chapter VI Section C[154], and Mr. Stalin agreed to Soviet participation in the UN[155] [171].

San Francisco Conference: 25th April 1945 to 26th June 1945; UN Charter

Delegates from fifty nations, representing more than 80% of the global population, gathered in San Francisco for the United Nations Conference on International Organization [156]. The highest body was the Conference in Plenary Session[156], which was in charge of the voting and adoption of the text [172]. The process of writing the UN Charter lasted two months – every part of it had to be voted upon and accepted by a majority of two-thirds [156]. In the context of the current monograph, the following passage from the website of the UN is noteworthy.

> One issue that provoked long and heated debate was the right of each permanent member of the SC[157] to veto any resolution passed by the SC[.] (The permanent members were China, the USSR, the United States, the United Kingdom, and France.) The smaller powers feared that when one of the "Big Five" menaced the peace, the SC would be powerless to act. They wanted to reduce the power of the SC veto. But the great powers insisted on the veto. They stated the main responsibility for world peace would fall most heavily on them. Eventually, the smaller powers conceded the point in the interest of setting up the world organization [156].

It is submitted that the 'smaller powers' were prospicient in this view, and should perhaps have done more at the San Francisco Conference to reduce the scope of this veto – even if they were then in too weak a position politically to ensure its omission from the UN Charter. In particular, these countries should have argued that the veto must not be able to be exercised by a particular permanent member in an instance in which the UNSC proposed to take a decision under Chapter VII of the UN Charter – in a situation in which the interests of that permanent member were affected more than those of the majority of Member States of the UN by the success or failure of this proposal at the UNSC. The UN Charter entered into force on 24th October 1945, thereby establishing the UN on that day [156, 172, 173].

---

[154] The text to fn 148 sets out Chapter VI Section C of the Proposals for the Establishment of a General International Organization.

[155] The USSR withdrew its claim that every Soviet republic should have membership of the UN General Assembly (Encyclopaedia Britannica (1999), "Yalta Conference," published May 4, 1999, last updated July 24, 2024, accessed July 26, 2024, <https://www.britannica.com/event/Yalta-Conference>).

[156] Below the plenary there were established a Steering Committee, which considered significant issues of policy and procedure, an Executive Committee, which served the Steering Committee by preparing recommendations for it to consider, a Coordination Committee, which assisted the Executive Committee and was helped by an Advisory Committee of Jurists, and a Credentials Committee, which verified the credentials of delegates; beneath this level, the scrutiny of the key issues to be resolved was divided among four general commissions – Commissions I (General Provisions), II (General Assembly), III (Security Council) and IV (Judicial Organization), which co-ordinated the work of twelve technical committees that were entrusted to prepare draft proposals (United Nations (2024), "The San Francisco Conference," accessed July 26, 2024, <https://www.un.org/en/about-us/history-of-the-un/san-francisco-conference>).

[157] 'SC' is an abbreviation for 'Security Council' – which is referred to as 'UNSC' in the present book.

The UN Charter

Preamble

The fourfold goals are to prevent war, reaffirm faith in human rights, establish conditions for the maintenance of justice and of respect for international legal obligations, and further social progress and improved living standards [174]. To achieve these, the peoples of the UN have decided to unite their efforts to practice tolerance and neighbourliness, maintain worldwide peace and security, ensure that armed force may only be used in the public interest, and utilize global systems to advance the social and economic development of every nation [174].

Table 3.1. The structure of the UN Charter

Number of the Chapter	Title of the Chapter	Articles in the Chapter
-	Preamble	-
I	Purposes and Principles	1-2
II	Membership	3-6
III	Organs	7-8
IV	The General Assembly	9-22
V	The Security Council	23-32
VI	Pacific Settlement of Disputes	33-38
VII	Action with Respect to Threats to the Peace, Breaches of the Peace, and Acts of Aggression	39-51
VIII	Regional Arrangements	52-54
IX	International Economic and Social Cooperation	55-60
X	The Economic and Social Council	61-72
XI	Declaration Regarding Non-Self-Governing Territories	73-74
XII	International Trusteeship System	75-85
XIII	The Trusteeship Council	86-91
XIV	The International Court of Justice	92-96
XV	The Secretariat	97-101
XVI	Miscellaneous Provisions	102-105
XVII	Transitional Security Arrangements	106-107
XVIII	Amendments	108-109
XIX	Ratification and Signature	110-111

I: Purposes and Principles

The Purposes of the UN have been stated[158]. In pursuit of those, the UN and its Member States must act in compliance with seven Principles. The first is that the UN is founded on the principle of sovereign equality of all its Member States [175]. It is submitted that UN is not *wholly* based on this principle, as five Member States have permanent seats on the UNSC[159], and each of these is authorized by the first clause of Article 27(3) of the UN Charter[160] to block non-procedural motions before the UNSC by voting against them (i.e., each is permitted to veto these proposals), subject to the restriction in the second clause of Article 27(3) of the UN Charter[161]. Following George Orwell's famous quote from Chapter 10 of the novel *Animal*

[158] The text to fns 129-144 lays down the Purposes of the UN.

[159] These are China (i.e., the People's Republic of China), France, Russia, the UK and the USA (second paragraph of the subsection entitled 'The Russian veto', in the section titled 'The Problem' in Chapter 1).

[160] The text to fn 14 lays down the first clause of Article 27(3) of the UN Charter.

[161] The text to fn 16 sets out the second clause of Article 27(3) of the UN Charter.

Farm[162], taken together Articles 2(1), 23(1) and 27(3) of the UN Charter create the condition that 'All Member States are equal, but some are more equal than others,' i.e., there is a higher class of membership for the five Member States of the UN that are permanent members of the UNSC, and a standard class of membership for all other Member States. Thus, the calibre of leadership in, and the integrity of the leaders of, each of the Member States of the UN that are also permanent members of the UNSC are determinants of the quality and quantity (as UNSC decisions may be vetoed) of the decisions taken by the UNSC. The second, third and fourth Principles are stated in Chapter 1[163]. The fifth Principle requires all Member States of the UN to give the latter all possible help in any action that it performs in observance of the UN Charter – and to refrain from assisting any state against which the UN is taking measures [176]. The sixth Principle obliges the UN to ensure that countries which are not Member States of the UN act in consonance with the Principles to the extent that is necessary to maintain worldwide peace and security [177]. The seventh Principle declares that nothing in the UN Charter empowers the UN to intervene in internal matters of any state [178].

II: Membership

The admission of new Member States is carried out through a decision of the UN General Assembly, upon a recommendation of the UNSC [179]. If the UNSC so advocates, then the General Assembly may suspend a Member State, against which the first-mentioned has taken action, from the last-mentioned's exercise of the privileges and rights of membership of the UN[164] [180]. A Member State may be expelled from the UN for persistently contravening the Principles that the UN Charter contains[165].

III: Organs

The UN General Assembly, the UNSC, the ECOSOC, the ICJ, the Trusteeship Council and the Secretariat are established as principal organs of the UN [181]. There are to be no restrictions on eligibility for participation of men and women on equal terms in the UN's principal and subsidiary organs [182].

IV: The General Assembly

The UN General Assembly may discuss any issue that is within the ambit of the UN Charter or which concerns the functions and powers of an organ of the UN, and may make recommendations thereon to the Member States, the UNSC or both [183]. However, the General Assembly shall not make any recommendation regarding a situation or dispute in respect of which the UNSC is discharging the functions that the UN Charter assigns to it [184]. It may consider, and make recommendations to the Member States, the UNSC or both about, the overall principles of co-operation in maintaining global peace and security [185]. The General Assembly may discuss any matter that relates to this maintenance which the UNSC, any Member State, or any country that is not a Member State, has brought before it, and may

---

[162] 'All animals are equal but some are more equal than others'.

[163] The first sentence of fn 4 contains the second Principle, i.e., Article 2(2) of the UN Charter. Fn 5 lays down the third Principle, i.e., Article 2(3) of the UN Charter. The first sentence of fn 6 sets out the fourth Principle, i.e., Article 2(4) of the UN Charter.

[164] The UNSC may restore the abovementioned Member State's pre-suspension status (United Nations (1945), "Charter of the United Nations," Article 5).

[165] Fn 7 and accompanying text.

make recommendations thereon to the state(s) concerned, the UNSC, or both; it shall refer any action which is needed to the UNSC [186]. The General Assembly may draw the UNSC's attention to situations that are likely to threaten worldwide peace and security [187]. The General Assembly shall instigate studies and make recommendations in order to further global political, cultural, economic, educational, health and social co-operation, encourage gradual development of international law and its codification, and aid in the actualization of human rights and fundamental freedoms [188]. It may recommend measures for the peaceful modification of any situation [189]. The General Assembly receives and scrutinizes annual and special reports from the UNSC [190] and reports from other organs of the UN [191]. It looks at, and approves, the UN's budget [192]. Decisions of the General Assembly are made by a majority of its members that are present and voting [193], other than those on important matters[166]– which require a two-thirds majority of such members [194]; each member has one vote [195]. The General Assembly meets regularly every year and in special sessions that the Secretary-General of the UN convokes at the request of the UNSC or of a majority of the Member States [196]. It adopts its rules of procedure, elects a president for each session, and establishes such subsidiary organs as it considers to be necessary for the fulfilment of its functions [197].

V: The Security Council

The UNSC comprises fifteen Member States of the UN – ten non-permanent members that are elected by the UN General Assembly and five permanent members[167] [198]. The non-permanent members of the UNSC are elected for a two-year term, and cannot be re-elected immediately [199]. The Member States are obligated to accept and implement the UNSC's decisions[168]. Each member of the UNSC has one vote [200]. Decisions of the UNSC are made by an affirmative vote of at least nine of its fifteen members[169]. The UNSC adopts its rules of procedure [201], and establishes such subsidiary organs as it deems to be requisite for undertaking its functions [202].

VI: Pacific Settlement of Disputes

If the continuance of a dispute is likely to imperil the maintenance of worldwide peace and security, then the disputants must look for a solution by peaceful means of their choice [7]. When the UNSC considers it to be required, then the aforementioned may look to the parties to resolve their dispute by such means [203]. The UNSC may inquire into any dispute, or any situation that might result in global friction or bring about a dispute, in order to ascertain whether the continuation of the dispute or situation is likely to jeopardize the perpetuation of international peace and security [204]. Any Member State of the UN may bring such a dispute or situation to the attention of the UNSC or of the UN General Assembly [205]. A country that

[166] These matters include (among other things) recommendations concerning the maintenance of international peace and security, the election of the UNSC's non-permanent members, the election of the members of the ECOSOC, the admission of new Member States to the UN, the expulsion of Member States from the UN, the suspension of the privileges and rights of UN membership, and questions relating to the UN's budget (United Nations (1945), "Charter of the United Nations," Article 18(2)).

[167] The second paragraph of the subsection entitled 'The Russian veto', in the section titled 'The Problem' in Chapter 1, describes the permanent members of the UNSC.

[168] Fn 10.

[169] Fn 13, fns 14 and 15 and accompanying text, and the text to fn 16, lay down information concerning voting in the UNSC.

is not a Member State of the UN may draw to the attention of the UNSC or of the General Assembly any dispute to which it is a party, if it accepts beforehand – with regard to the dispute – the obligations of pacific resolution for which the UN Charter provides [206]. At any point in a dispute that is likely to put the continuance of international peace and security at risk, or of a situation of similar nature, the UNSC may recommend[170] suitable procedures or means of adjustment [8]. If the parties to such a dispute do not settle it by peaceful methods of their choice, then they are to refer it to the UNSC [207], which, if it considers that the prolongation of the dispute is likely to threaten worldwide peace and security, decides whether to recommend either as mentioned above[171] or terms of resolution that it deems to be appropriate [9]. If all the disputants so request, the UNSC may make recommendations to them, with the aim of peacefully resolving their dispute [10].

VII: Action with Respect to Threats to the Peace, Breaches of the Peace, and Acts of Aggression

The UNSC shall decide whether there exists a threat to, or transgression of, the peace, or a deed of aggression, and either make recommendations, or determine what measures are to be taken, to maintain or restore global peace and security [208]. Before making these recommendations or deciding upon those measures, the UNSC may look to the parties to observe such provisional measures as it considers to be necessary or advisable – in order to stop the situation from worsening [209]. The UNSC may determine what measures that do not necessitate the use of armed force are to be utilized to effect its decisions, and may turn to the Member States of the UN to apply these[172] [210]. Should the UNSC deem that the aforementioned measures would be insufficient or have proved to be deficient, it may use such air personnel, sailors or soldiers as may be needed to maintain or re-establish worldwide peace and security [211]. In order to contribute to the continuation of global peace and security, all Member States of the UN promise to make available to the UNSC – on the last-mentioned's call and in compliance with one or more special agreements – armed forces, facilities and help that are indispensable for the purpose of maintaining worldwide peace and security [212]. The agreement(s) shall govern the numbers and types of armed forces, their general location and state of readiness, and the nature of the facilities and assistance to be supplied[173] [213]. Before calling upon a Member State which is not represented on the UNSC to furnish armed forces in satisfaction of the abovementioned obligations, the UNSC shall invite this Member State to partake in those of its decisions that concern the use of contingents of the latter's armed forces [214]. To enable the UN to take military measures urgently, Member States shall hold national air-force contingents instantly available for joint international enforcement action [215]. Aided by the Military Staff Committee[174], the UNSC shall make plans for the employment of armed force [216]. The

---

[170] The UNSC should heed any procedures for resolving the dispute that the parties have already adopted, and bear in mind that the disputants should, in general, refer legal disputes to the ICJ in keeping with the last-mentioned's statute budget (United Nations (1945), "Charter of the United Nations," Article 36(2)-(3)).

[171] Fn 170 and accompanying text.

[172] The measures may include total or partial interruption of economic relations, and of air, postal, radio, rail, sea, telegraphic and other ways of communication, and the discontinuance of diplomatic relations (United Nations (1945), "Charter of the United Nations," Article 41).

[173] The agreement(s) shall be made between the UNSC and Member States of the UN, or between the UNSC and groups of Member States, and are to be ratified by the signatory states in conformity with their respective constitutional processes (United Nations (1945), "Charter of the United Nations," Article 43(3)).

[174] The Military Staff Committee is a permanent-member-manned campaign advisory board: "1. There shall be established a Military Staff Committee to advise and assist the Security Council on all questions relating to the

decisions of the UNSC for the continuance of international peace and security are implemented by the Member States, both directly and by means of their action in apposite global agencies [217]; the UNSC determines which Member States are obliged to effect its decisions[175]. The Member States shall help each other to carry out the measures that the UNSC prescribes [218]. If any state is faced with specific economic difficulties arising from the application of measures that the UNSC is taking against another country, then it may consult the UNSC regarding the solution of these problems [219]. Chapter 1 discusses the right of self-defence – which is the subject of Article 51 of the UN Charter[176].

VIII: Regional Arrangements

Regional arrangements or agencies for addressing issues that relate to the maintenance of worldwide peace and security must be compatible with the Purposes and Principles of the UN[177] [12]. The Member States of the UN which become parties to these arrangements or which constitute those agencies must attempt to attain peaceful resolution of local disputes through the arrangements or by means of the agencies, before referring them to the UNSC [220]. The UNSC shall encourage the furtherance of pacific resolution of local disputes via the aforementioned arrangements or by the abovementioned agencies [11]. Where suitable, the UNSC shall use such regional arrangements or agencies to carry out enforcement measures under its authority and with its permission[178] [221]. The UNSC must always be kept totally informed of activities that are undertaken or being considered within the framework of regional arrangements, or by regional agencies, for the continuation of international peace and security [222].

Security Council's military requirements for the maintenance of international peace and security, the employment and command of forces placed at its disposal, the regulation of armaments, and possible disarmament. 2. The Military Committee shall consist of the Chiefs of Staff of the permanent members of the Security Council or their representatives. Any Member of the United Nations not permanently represented on the Committee shall be invited by the Committee to be associated with it when the efficient discharge of the Committee's responsibilities requires the participation of that Member in its work. 3. The Military Staff Committee shall be responsible under the Security Council for the strategic direction of any armed forces placed at the disposal of the Security Council. Questions relating to the command of such forces shall be worked out subsequently. 4. The Military Staff Committee, with the authorization of the Security Council and after consultation with appropriate regional agencies, may establish regional sub-committees." (United Nations (1945), "Charter of the United Nations," Article 47).

[175] Fn 11 and accompanying text.

[176] Fn 19 sets out Article 51 of the UN Charter. The scope of the right of self-defence contained therein is described in the paragraph containing the text to that footnote, i.e., the paragraph headed 'Measures taken under Article 51 of the UN Charter, in the subsection entitled 'What other action may be taken after a breach of the UN Charter?' in the section titled 'The Problem' in Chapter 1.

[177] The text to fns 129-144 lays down the Purposes of the UN. The third, antepenultimate, penultimate and final sentences of the paragraph headed 'I: Purposes and Principles', above in the current subsection (i.e., the subsection entitled 'The UN Charter', in the section titled 'The United Nations' – above in the present chapter (i.e., Chapter 3)), respectively comprise the first, fifth, sixth and seventh Principles of the UN, i.e., correspondingly paragraphs 1, 5, 6 and 7 of Article 2 of the UN Charter. The first sentence of fn 4 contains the second Principle, i.e., Article 2(2) of the UN Charter. Fn 5 consists of the third Principle, i.e., Article 2(3) of the UN Charter. The first sentence of fn 6 sets out the fourth Principle, i.e., Article 2(4) of the UN Charter.

[178] It is submitted that the remainder of Article 53 of the UN Charter, i.e., the clauses referring to an 'enemy state', should be deleted from the UN Charter, as they are no longer applicable. The text to fn 643 recommends this erasure, as part of a suggestion for modification to Chapter VIII of the UN Charter. Chapter VIII of the UN Charter is entitled 'Regional Arrangements' and comprises Articles 52-54.

IX: International Economic and Social Cooperation

With the intention of creating conditions of stability and well-being that are needed for pacific, friendly relations between nations which are founded on regard for the principle of equal rights and free choice of peoples, the UN shall further improved standards of living, full employment and conditions of economic and social advancement and development [223], solutions for global economic, health, social and related difficulties, and worldwide cultural and educational collaboration [224], and general respect for, and adherence to, human rights and fundamental freedoms for everyone [225]. All Member States of the UN promise to take shared and separate action in co-operation with the latter, for the attainment of the aforementioned goals [226]. The specialized agencies shall be brought into relationship with the UN [227]; the ECOSOC may enter into, with any of the specialized agencies, agreements that define the terms upon which the relevant agency shall be brought into relationship with the UN[179] [228]. The UN shall make recommendations as to how to co-ordinate the specialized agencies' policies and activities [229]. Where appropriate, the UN shall initiate negotiations among the relevant states for the establishment of any new specialized agencies that are required to achieve the abovementioned goals [230]. Responsibility for carrying out the functions of the UN that are set out in this chapter (i.e., Chapter IX of the UN Charter) is entrusted to the General Assembly, and – under the last-mentioned's authority – to the ECOSOC, which shall, for this purpose, have the powers that Chapter X of the UN Charter confers upon it [231].

X: The Economic and Social Council

The ECOSOC comprises fifty-four Member States of the UN, which the General Assembly elects [232]. Eighteen members of the ECOSOC are chosen each year for a triennial term [233]. Each member has one representative at the ECOSOC [234]. The ECOSOC may initiate or compile studies and reports regarding international cultural, economic, educational, health, social and related issues, and may make recommendations on any of these matters to the General Assembly, the Member States, and relevant specialized agencies [235]. It may formulate suggestions in order to promote respect for, and compliance with, universal human rights and fundamental freedoms [236]. The ECOSOC may convene global conferences over subjects that are within its competence [237], and prepare draft conventions on such topics for submission to the General Assembly [238]. It may co-ordinate the specialized agencies' activities by means of consultation with and recommendations to them, and through suggestions to the General Assembly and to the Member States [239]. The ECOSOC may provide information to the UNSC, and assists the latter upon its request [240]. It shall discharge such functions as are within its competence, in association with the implementation of the General Assembly's recommendations [241]. With the General Assembly's approval, the ECOSOC may undertake services at the request of the Member States of the UN or the specialized agencies [242]. It may conduct such other activities as are specified elsewhere in the UN Charter or as may be allocated to it by the General Assembly [243]. Decisions of the ECOSOC are made by a majority of its members present and voting [244]; each member has one vote [245]. The ECOSOC shall found commissions in economic and social spheres and for the furtherance of human rights, and such other commissions as may be necessary for undertaking its functions [246]. It shall invite any Member State of the UN to take part, without

[179] These agreements are conditional upon approval by the UN General Assembly (United Nations (1945), "Charter of the United Nations," Article 63(1)).

voting, in its deliberations on any issue of specific concern to that Member State [247]. The ECOSOC may arrange for representatives of the specialized agencies to engage, without voting, with its discussions, and with those of the commissions which it has established, and for its representatives to partake in the conversations of those agencies [248]. The ECOSOC may make appropriate arrangements for consultation with non-governmental organizations that are affected by matters within its competence [249]. The ECOSOC adopts its rules of procedure [250]. It meets as needed in line with these rules, which include provision for the convoking of meetings when requested by a majority of its members [251].

XI: Declaration Regarding Non-Self-Governing Territories

Member States of the UN that have, or assume, duties for the administration of territories whose peoples have not yet gained a full amount of self-government, recognize the principle that the interests of the residents of these places are of the greatest importance, and accept as an inviolable trust the obligation to fully promote the welfare of these inhabitants – within the structure for global peace and security which the UN Charter provides, and, with this objective in mind, to (a) ensure due regard for the culture of the relevant peoples, their economic, educational, political and social advancement, their fair treatment, and their safeguarding from abuses, (b) evolve self-government, take into due consideration the political aspirations of these peoples, and help them to progressively develop their own political organizations, (c) further worldwide peace and security, (d) promote useful measures of development, support research, and co-operate with each other and with specialized international entities with the aim of meeting the purposes that this article[180] sets out, and (e) communicate regularly to the Secretary-General technical information concerning economic, educational and social conditions in the non-trust territories[181] for which they are responsible [252]. Member States of the UN agree that their policy with reference to the aforementioned territories is to be grounded on the general principle of good-neighbourliness in commercial, economic and social matters [253]. The current list of territories to which Chapter XI of the UN Charter applies – which are called Non-Self-Governing Territories – comprises the following: American Samoa, Anguilla, Bermuda, the British Virgin Islands, the Cayman Islands, the Falkland Islands, French Polynesia, Gibraltar, Guam, Montserrat, New Caledonia, Pitcairn, Saint Helena, Tokelau, the Turks and Caicos Islands, the United States Virgin Islands, and Western Sahara [254].

XII: International Trusteeship System

The UN shall launch an international trusteeship system for the administration and superintendence of those territories as may be placed thereunder by forthcoming international agreements [255]; these are called trust territories [255, 256]. All eleven trust territories have either become independent states or voluntarily joined neighbouring jurisdictions[182] [256].

---

[180] 'This article' is Article 73 of the UN Charter.

[181] 'Trust territories' are territories that are administered under the UN's international trusteeship system (first sentence of the next paragraph, which is headed 'XII: International Trusteeship System).

[182] The trust territories, with the administering authority in brackets, were the Cameroons under British administration (UK), the Cameroons under French administration (France), Italian Somaliland (Italy), Nauru (Australia, New Zealand and the UK), New Guinea (Australia), Rwanda-Urundi (Belgium), Tanganyika (UK), Togoland under British administration (UK), Togoland under French administration (France), Trust territory of the Pacific Islands (USA), and Western Samoa (New Zealand) (United Nations (2023), "Dag Hammarskjöld Library: Ask DAG – UN Trusteeship Council Documentation: Trust Territories Introduction," last updated December 29, 2023, accessed August 7, 2024, <https://research.un.org/en/docs/tc/territories>).

XIII: The Trusteeship Council

The Trusteeship Council shall draw up a questionnaire on the economic, educational, political and social advancement of the residents of each trust territory [257]. For every trust territory, its administering authority shall create an annual report for the UN General Assembly on the basis of this questionnaire [257]. With no trust territories remaining, the Trusteeship Council suspended its workings on 1st November 1994 [256].

XIV: The International Court of Justice

The ICJ is the main judicial organ of the UN [258]. All Member States of the UN are parties to the Statute of the ICJ, by virtue of their membership of the former[183] [259]. A non-Member State of the UN may become a party to the Statute of the ICJ, on conditions to be decided in each instance by the General Assembly upon the UNSC's recommendation[184] [260]. Each Member State of the UN promises to abide by the determination of the ICJ, in any case to which the first-mentioned is a party [261]. If it does not fulfil this promise, then the other party may seek recourse from the UNSC[185]. The ICJ may, upon request by organs of the UN and specialized agencies, provide an advisory opinion on a question of law[186].

XV: The Secretariat

The Secretariat comprises a Secretary-General and such staff as the UN may require [262]. The Secretary-General is appointed by the General Assembly upon the UNSC's recommendation, and is the chief administrative officer of the UN [262]. The Secretary-General may bring to the UNSC's attention any issue that (s)he considers may endanger the maintenance of global peace and security [263], and is required to construct an annual report for the General Assembly on the UN's work [264]. In performing their obligations, the Secretary-General and the staff shall neither look for, nor receive, instructions from any authority outside the UN, and shall forbear from taking any action that might discredit their position as international officials who are responsible to the UN only [265]. Each Member State of the UN undertakes to observe the purely international character of the obligations of the Secretary-General and staff, and not to attempt to influence them in the performance of their duties [266]. The Secretary-General is to appoint the staff under regulations that the General Assembly has established[187] [267]. Suitable employees are to be permanently assigned to each organ of the UN, and constitute a part of the Secretariat [268].

---

[183] Fn 108 lays down Article 93(1) of the UN Charter.

[184] Switzerland, Liechtenstein, San Marino, Japan and Nauru were parties to the Statute of the ICJ prior to becoming Member States of the UN; the conditions imposed were the same in each instance (International Court of Justice (2024), "States not members of the United Nations parties to the Statute," accessed August 17, 2024, <https://www.icj-cij.org/states-not-members>).

[185] Fn 25 sets out this right of access to the UNSC.

[186] The antepenultimate, penultimate and last sentences of fn 23 supply details on this matter.

[187] The most important consideration in the employment of staff and in the specification of the conditions of service is the need to secure the highest levels of competence, efficiency and integrity; staff should be recruited from as broad a geographical area as possible (United Nations (1945), "Charter of the United Nations," Article 101(3)).

XVI: Miscellaneous Provisions

All treaties and international agreements which any Member State enters into after the UN Charter comes into force[188] shall be promptly registered with the Secretariat and published by it [269]. No party to any such treaty or agreement that has not be so registered may invoke it in front of any organ of the UN [270]. If there is a conflict between the duties of Member States under the UN Charter and their responsibilities under any other international instrument, then their obligations under the UN Charter will prevail [271]. The UN shall possess, in the territory of each of its Member States, such legal capacity as may be required for the discharge of its functions and the realization of its purposes [272], and such immunities and privileges as are necessary for the accomplishment of its purposes[189] [273].

XVII: Transitional Security Arrangements

These rules no longer apply, and could therefore be deleted from the UN Charter without this having negative effect.

XVIII: Amendments to the UN Charter

In order to facilitate revision of the UN Charter, a general conference of the Member States of the UN may be held on a date and at a place to be decided by a two-thirds majority of the members of the General Assembly and by a vote of any nine members of the UNSC [274]. At this conference, each Member State will have one vote [274]. Any change to the UN Charter that a two-thirds majority in a vote at conference recommends is to take effect when this alteration is ratified by two-thirds of the Member States of the UN – including all five permanent members of the UNSC – in compliance with their respective constitutional processes [275]. Amendments to the UN Charter enter into force for all Member States when these have been adopted by a two-thirds majority of the members of the General Assembly and ratified by two-thirds of the Member States – including all five permanent members of the UNSC – in observance of their respective constitutional processes [276]. Table 3.2 specifies the amendments to the UN Charter that have been made to date.

Table 3.2. Amendments to the UN Charter [277]

Article (Paragraph)	Amendment detail	Date that the UN General Assembly adopted the amendment	Date that the amendment entered into force
23	The membership of the UNSC was enlarged from eleven members to fifteen members.	17th December 1963	31st August 1965
27	The number of members of the UNSC that are required to vote affirmatively for a decision to pass there was increased from seven members to nine members	17th December 1963	31st August 1965
61	The membership of the ECOSOC was expanded from eighteen members to twenty-seven members.	17th December 1963	31st August 1965
	The membership of the ECOSOC was further raised from twenty-seven members to fifty-four members.	20th December 1971	24th September 1973

[188] The UN Charter became effective on 24th October 1945 (final sentence of the subsection entitled 'The Foundation of the UN', in the section titled 'The United Nations' – above in the current chapter (i.e., Chapter 3)).

[189] Representatives of the Member States of the UN, and officials of the UN, shall similarly possess such immunities and privileges as are requisite for the independent fulfilment of its functions in association with the UN (United Nations (1945), "Charter of the United Nations," Article 105(2)).

Table 3.2. Continued

Article (Paragraph)	Amendment detail	Date that the UN General Assembly adopted the amendment	Date that the amendment entered into force
109(1)	The number of members of the UNSC that are required to determine the date and the place to hold a general conference of the Member States of the UN in order to facilitate revision of the UN Charter was lifted from seven members to nine members.	20th December 1965	12th June 1968

XIX: Ratification and Signature

The UN Charter was to be ratified by its signatory states in conformity with their respective constitutional processes [278]. The ratifications were to be deposited with the Government of the USA [279]. The UN Charter was to come into effect upon the deposit of ratifications by China, France, the UK, the USA and the USSR and by a majority of the remaining signatory states [280]. The Chinese, English, French, Russian and Spanish versions of the UN Charter are equally authentic [281].

Comment

The UN is based on the holding power and integrity of five states, i.e., China, France, Russia, the UK and the USA, who are victors from the Second World War (or, in the case of Russia, a successor state from the USSR which was a victor from that conflict). These are the permanent members of the UNSC, each of which has a veto in votes on proposals before the UNSC. Each of these states is empowered by the UN Charter to block amendments to it by failing to ratify those changes. This puts these five countries in a strong position relative to the other Member States of the UN, whose rights are equal with one another under the UN Charter but are lesser than those of the permanent members – whose rights are equal with those of the other permanent members. This was an understandable basis on which the UN Charter was created in the 1940s. However, it is not appropriate as a long-lasting arrangement for the UN or any successor body to the UN. Notwithstanding this, the UN has been an influence for good in the world over the eighty years of its existence – saving lives in conflicts and other catastrophes, tackling poverty, empowering women and minority groups, furthering independence for – and supporting projects in – developing and less-developed states, and providing a forum for international debate. Thus, proposals on any substantial changes to this organization need to be approached with both wisdom and care.

The International Court of Justice

Introduction

The ICJ is the successor court to the PCIJ. It has heard many contentious cases and provided a substantial number of advisory opinions. A sizeable proportion of the contentious cases before the ICJ have concerned its determination of whether it has jurisdiction to hear the case – a plea that the subject-matter of the case is outside the jurisdiction of the ICJ by the defendant state is a common argument, which has sometimes been successful. This is an outcome of the ICJ having optional, rather than compulsory, jurisdiction. As a considerable amount of the judges' time has been spent entertaining jurisdictional matters and other issues of admissibility, there has perhaps been a less than optimal amount of judicial deliberation at the ICJ on issues relating to the merits of the cases on which it is asked to adjudicate.

The next subsection describes the establishment of the ICJ. This is succeeded by consideration of the Statute of the ICJ, followed by a comment.

The Foundation of the ICJ

In 1942, the Secretary of State of the USA and the Foreign Secretary of the UK proclaimed that they were in favour of the foundation or re-establishment of an international court after the Second World War, and the Inter-American Juridical Committee recommended that the PCIJ's jurisdiction be continued [71, 78]. Early in 1943, the Government of the UK invited jurists to London to comprise an informal Inter-Allied Committee on the Future of the Permanent Court of International Justice to look into the matter of the prolongation of the international court [71, 78]. This committee published its report on 10th February 1944, in which it recommended that: (i) the statute of any new international court should be grounded on that of the PCIJ, (ii) the new court should continue to exercise an advisory jurisdiction, (iii) it should not be obligatory for parties to the statute to accept the jurisdiction of the new court, and (iv) the new court should not possess jurisdiction to address issues that are fundamentally political [71].

The United Nations Conference on International Organization – which convened on 25th April 1945 in San Francisco [78] – decided to found a new court [71 78], which would be a principal organ of the UN [71]. Paragraph 1 of Article 7 of the UN Charter provides for this[190]. The first members of the ICJ were elected at the ninth meeting of the UNSC and at the twenty-third, twenty-fourth and twenty-fifth meetings of the UN General Assembly, on 6th February 1946, in agreement with Articles 2 to 15 of the Statute of the ICJ [78]. The ICJ held its inaugural meeting on 3rd April 1946 in the Peace Palace at the Hague, and elected its President, Vice-President and Registrar on 6th April 1946 [78].

The Statute of the ICJ

The ICJ is to operate in accordance with the Statute of the ICJ, which is grounded upon the Statute of the PCIJ and which is an integral part of the UN Charter [258]. In Chapter 2, the original version of the Statute of the PCIJ is covered[191]. Unlike the Statute of the PCIJ[192], the

---

[190] The first sentence of the paragraph headed 'III: Organs', in the subsection entitled 'The UN Charter' in the section titled 'The United Nations' – above in the present chapter (i.e., Chapter 3), lays down Article 7(1) of the UN Charter.

[191] Fn 86 and accompanying text. The subsection entitled 'The Statute of the PCIJ', in the section titled 'The Permanent Court of International Justice' in Chapter 2, describes provisions of the Statute of the PCIJ.

[192] Text to fn 83.

Statute of the ICJ has not been amended [282]. The same structure and paragraph headings are used in the current subsection as in its equivalent[193] in Chapter 2.

Organization of the ICJ

The Court is to consist of fifteen members from different states[194] who are elected from among individuals of high moral character, and who are qualified for appointment to the most senior judicial positions or are competent juriconsults in international law [283]. The members of the ICJ shall be elected by the UN General Assembly and the UNSC from a list of persons that the national groups in the Permanent Court of Arbitration nominate[195] [284]. These members are to be elected for nine years, and may be re-elected [285]. A member of the ICJ who is elected to replace a member whose period of appointment has not concluded will remain in office for the rest of the latter's term [286]. Such a member may neither undertake any political or administrative function, nor engage in any other professional line of work[196] [287]. A member of the ICJ may neither act as advocate, counsel or agent in any case [288], nor take part in the decision of any case in which the member has previously been involved[197] [289]. The ICJ shall elect its President and Vice-President for three years[198] [290]. It shall appoint its Registrar, and may make provision for the appointment of other officers as could be required [291]. The seat of the Court – where the President and Registrar shall reside – shall be in the Hague [292]. If, for a specific reason, a member of the ICJ does not wish to partake in the decision, or the President of the Court considers that a member should not so participate, then the one must inform the other of this[199] [293]. Except where the Statute of the ICJ expressly specifies otherwise, the full Court shall sit [294]. Occasionally, the ICJ may set up one or more chambers – constituted by at least three judges – for addressing particular classes of cases, such as those relating to labour and those concerning conveyance and communications [295]. At any time, the ICJ may found a chamber for handling a specific case; with the disputants' approval, it shall determine the number of judges to form this chamber [296]. Cases shall be heard and decided upon by the abovementioned chambers, if the parties ask for this [297]. With a view to the quick dispatch of business, each year the ICJ shall establish a chamber composed of five judges who, at the request of the disputants, may hear and settle cases by summary procedure[200] [298]. A judgment that any of the aforementioned chambers renders shall be considered as delivered

---

[193] Second sentence of fn 191.

[194] A person who could be considered to be a national of more than one state shall be deemed to be a national of the state in which (s)he usually implements civil and political rights (United Nations (1945), "Statute of the International Court of Justice," Article 3(2)).

[195] If a Member State of the United Nations is not represented in the Permanent Court of Arbitration, then its list of candidates for judicial appointment to the ICJ is prepared by its government "under the same conditions as those prescribed for members of the Permanent Court of Arbitration by Article 44 of the Convention of The Hague of 1907 for the pacific settlement of international disputes" (United Nations (1945), "Statute of the International Court of Justice," Article 4(2)). The second and third sentences of fn 88 set out the first and second sentences, respectively, of Article 44 of the 1907 Hague Convention for the Pacific Settlement of International Disputes.

[196] The ICJ is to resolve any doubt on this issue (United Nations (1945), "Statute of the International Court of Justice," Article 16(2)).

[197] The ICJ is to settle any uncertainty regarding this matter (United Nations (1945), "Statute of the International Court of Justice," Article 17(3)).

[198] The President and Vice-President of the ICJ may be re-elected (United Nations (1945), "Statute of the International Court of Justice," Article 21(1)).

[199] If the President and the member disagree, then the ICJ shall resolve the problem (United Nations (1945), "Statute of the International Court of Justice," Article 24(3)).

[200] The ICJ shall select two further judges in order to replace those who are unable to sit (United Nations (1945), "Statute of the International Court of Justice," Article 29).

by the ICJ [299]. The ICJ shall draw up rules for performing its functions; in particular, it shall set out rules of procedure[201] [300]. Judges of the nationality of each party to a case shall retain their right to sit before the ICJ [301]. Each disputant shall choose a judge of its nationality, if there should not be one [302]. If there are at least two parties in the same interest, then they shall be considered to be one party only[202] [303].

Competence of the ICJ

Only states may be parties to cases before the ICJ [304]. The ICJ is open to the states parties to the Statute of the ICJ[203] [305]. The jurisdiction of the ICJ consists of all cases that the disputants refer to it, and all issues which the UN Charter – or effective treaties and conventions – provide for [306]. Next there is the optional clause, i.e., paragraph 2 of Article 36 of the Statute of the ICJ.

> The states parties to the present Statute may at any time declare that they recognize as compulsory *ipso facto*[204] and without special agreement, in relation to any other state accepting the same obligation, the jurisdiction of the Court in all legal disputes concerning: a. the interpretation of a treaty; b. any question of international law; c. the existence of any fact which, if established, would constitute a breach of an international obligation; d. the nature or extent of the reparation to be made for the breach of an international obligation[205] [307].

These declarations by states parties to the Statute of the ICJ[206] may be made either unconditionally or on condition of reciprocity, or for a definite time [308]. Declarations that are in force shall be considered, as between the states parties to the Statute, to be acceptances of the compulsory jurisdiction of the ICJ for the time that they remain to run and in keeping with their terms [309]. The use of the phrase 'compulsory jurisdiction of the ICJ' is interesting, both because the ICJ only has compulsory jurisdiction in this very limited sense – its jurisdiction is optional in two ways, i.e., a state must be a party to the Statute of the ICJ and, unless the relevant reference to the ICJ's jurisdiction is within a treaty to which the state is a party, it needs to have 'opted in' to the jurisdiction of the Court by making a declaration under

---

[201] These are the Rules of Court of the ICJ, which the ICJ composed in 1946, amended in 1972, revised in 1978 and amended this revised version in 2001, 2005, 2019, 2020 and 2024 (McIntyre, J. (2019), "The International Court of Justice Releases New Rules of Court," published November 4, 2019, accessed August 13, 2024, <https://www.ejiltalk.org/the-international-court-of-justice-releases-new-rules-of-court/>; Honniball, A. (2020), "ICJ Amendments to the Rules of Court," published June 29, 2020, accessed August 13, 2024, <https://demaribus.net/2020/06/29/icj-amendments-to-the-rules-of-court-2/>; McIntyre J. (2024), "The ICJ Changes the Rules for Intervention," published March 11, 2024, accessed August 13, 2024, <https://www.ejiltalk.org/the-icj-changes-the-rules-for-intervention/>). The Rules of Court of the ICJ are available on the ICJ's website at <https://www.icj-cij.org/rules>.

[202] The ICJ shall resolve this matter, if there is any doubt concerning it (United Nations (1945), "Statute of the International Court of Justice," Article 31(5)).

[203] The conditions under which the ICJ shall be available to other states shall – subject to special provisions that treaties in force contain – be drawn up by the UNSC; these conditions must grant the parties equality before the Court (United Nations (1945), "Statute of the International Court of Justice," Article 35(2)).

[204] Emphasis added.

[205] If there is a dispute as to whether the ICJ has jurisdiction to entertain the case, then the ICJ shall settle the matter (United Nations (1945), "Statute of the International Court of Justice," Article 36(6)).

[206] The declarations are to be deposited with the Secretary-General of the UN, who shall convey copies thereof to the states parties to the Statute of the ICJ and to the Registrar of the Court (United Nations (1945), "Statute of the International Court of Justice," Article 36(4)).

Article 36(2) of the ICJ Statute – whose scope it is permitted to limit by the wording that it uses in its declaration. But this 'compulsory jurisdiction' provision is absent from both the original and the amended version of Article 36 of the Statute of the PCIJ. Does this indicate that momentum is moving in the direction of providing compulsory jurisdiction to the ICJ over interstate disputes that are of a legal nature? Regarding references to jurisdiction in treaties, the Statute of the ICJ provides for a seamless continuity between the 'old order' described in Chapter 2 and the current one.

> Whenever a treaty or convention in force provides for reference of a matter to a tribunal to have been instituted by the League of Nations, or to the Permanent Court of International Justice, the matter shall, as between the parties to the present Statute, be referred to the International Court of Justice [310].

Paragraph 1 of Article 38 of the Statute of the ICJ identifies sources of international law that the ICJ is to apply, which are the same as those that the PCIJ applied[207] and are as follows.

> a. international conventions, whether general or particular, establishing rules expressly recognized by the contesting states; b. international custom, as evidence of a general practice accepted as law; c. the general principles of law recognized by civilized nations; d. subject to the provisions of Article 59 [of the Statute of the ICJ], judicial decisions and the teachings of the most highly qualified publicists of the various nations, as subsidiary means for the determination of rules of law [311].

Article 59 of the Statute of the ICJ is identical to Article 59 of the PCIJ[208].

> The decision of the Court has no binding force except between the parties and in respect of that particular case [23].

Paragraph 2 of Article 38 of the Statute of the ICJ – like the final sentence of Article 38 of the Statute of the PCIJ[209], allows the Court to resolve a case *ex aequo et bono*[210], if the disputants agree thereto [312].

Procedure in Cases Before the ICJ[211]

The official languages of the ICJ shall be English and French; if the disputants agree in which of these the case should be conducted, then the ICJ will be deliver its judgment in that language[212] [313]. At any party's request, the ICJ shall authorize that party to use a language

---

[207] The first quoted passage in the paragraph headed 'Competence of the PCIJ', in the subsection entitled 'The Statute of the PCIJ' in the section titled 'The Permanent Court of International Justice' in Chapter 2, lists these sources.

[208] The second quoted passage in the paragraph headed 'Competence of the PCIJ', in the subsection entitled 'The Statute of the PCIJ' in the section titled 'The Permanent Court of International Justice' in Chapter 2, lays down Article 59 of the Statute of the PCIJ.

[209] The text to fn 97 sets out the last sentence of Article 38 of the Statute of the PCIJ.

[210] Fn 97 defines the term '*ex aequo et bono*'.

[211] The procedure that this paragraph describes applies to contentious cases. The ICJ may apply aspects of it in exercising its advisory jurisdiction: "In the exercise of its advisory functions[,] the Court shall further be guided by the provisions of the present Statute which apply in contentious cases to the extent to which it recognizes them to be applicable." (United Nations (1945), "Statute of the International Court of Justice," Article 68).

[212] If the parties do not agree as to the language in which their case should proceed, then "each party may, in the pleadings, use the language which it prefers; the decision of the Court shall be given in French and English. In

other than English or French [314]. Cases are brought before the ICJ either by a notification of a special agreement between the disputants or by a written application addressed to the Registrar of the Court[213], indicating the identity of the parties and the subject of their dispute [315]. The ICJ shall be empowered to set out any provisional measures that need to be taken in order to protect the respective rights of either disputant [316]. The procedure shall comprise written and oral proceedings [317]. The written proceedings shall involve communication through the Registrar to the parties and to the Court, of memorials, counter-memorials and, if necessary, replies, as well as all supporting documents, in the order and within the time that the ICJ determines [318]. The oral proceedings shall comprise the hearing before the Court of advocates, counsel, agents, witnesses and experts [319]. The President of the ICJ, or, if unable to preside, the Vice-President of the ICJ, or, if also unable to preside, the senior judge present, shall preside at the hearing [320]. At any time, the ICJ may choose an individual or organization to carry out an enquiry or furnish an expert opinion [321]. During the hearing, apposite questions are to be put to the witnesses and experts in accordance with the Rules of Court of the ICJ[214] [322]. Whenever one of the disputants omits to appear before the Court or does not defend its case, the other party may request the ICJ to decide in its favour [323]. Prior to doing this, the Court must satisfy itself that it has jurisdiction and that the claim is well-founded – both in law and in fact [324]. A majority of the judges who are present at the hearing shall determine all questions [325]. If there is an equality of votes, then the President of the ICJ or his surrogate will have a casting vote [326]. The judgment shall state the reasons upon which it is grounded [327]. It shall include the names of the judges who have partaken in the decision [328]. If the judgment does not represent the judges' unanimous opinion, in whole or in part, then any judge may supply a separate opinion [329]. The judgment is final; it is not subject to appeal[215] [330]. In limited circumstances, a party may apply for revision of a judgment[216]. If the ICJ accepts this application, then it will begin proceedings for revision[217]. If a state deems that it possesses "an interest of a legal nature which may be affected by the decision in the case", then it may request the ICJ for it to be allowed to intervene [331]. The Court will determine this request [332]. States parties to a convention have the right to intervene in proceedings of the ICJ that concern the interpretation of provisions of this convention[218].

---

this case the Court shall at the same time determine which of the two texts shall be considered as authoritative." (United Nations (1945), "Statute of the International Court of Justice," Article 39(2)).

[213] The Registrar of the PCIJ shall immediately circulate the application to everyone concerned (United Nations (1945), "Statute of the International Court of Justice," Article 40(2)). The Registrar shall notify the Member States of the UN via the Secretary-General, and also any other states that are entitled to participate in the hearing (United Nations (1945), "Statute of the International Court of Justice," Article 40(3)).

[214] Fn 201 and accompanying text.

[215] If there is disagreement regarding the compass or meaning of the judgment, then the ICJ shall interpret it if any party requests this (United Nations (1945), "Statute of the International Court of Justice," Article 60).

[216] A disputant may make an application for a judgment of the ICJ to be revised "only when it is based upon the discovery of some fact of such a nature as to be a decisive factor, which fact was, when the judgment was given, unknown to the Court and also to the party claiming revision, always provided that such ignorance was not due to negligence" (United Nations (1945), "Statute of the International Court of Justice," Article 61(1)). The disputant must make the application for revision of a judgment of the ICJ within six months of the discovery of this fact, and within ten years of the date of the judgment (United Nations (1945), "Statute of the International Court of Justice," Article 61(4)-(5)).

[217] These proceedings "shall be opened by a judgment of the Court expressly recording the existence of the new fact, recognizing that it has such a character as to lay the case open to revision, and declaring the application admissible on this ground" (United Nations (1945), "Statute of the International Court of Justice," Article 61(2)).

[218] Article 63 of the Statute of the ICJ declares: "1. Whenever the construction of a convention[,] to which states other than those concerned in the case are parties[,] is in question, the Registrar shall notify all such states forthwith.

Advisory Opinions[219]

The ICJ may furnish an advisory opinion on any legal question at the request of a body that is authorized by, or in compliance with, the Charter of the UN to make this call [333]. The abovementioned body shall lay before the Court a written request that contains a precise statement of the question upon which it requires an opinion, accompanied by all documents that are likely to elucidate the question [334]. The Registrar of the ICJ shall immediately provide notice of the request for an advisory opinion to all states that are entitled to appear before the Court [335]. The Registrar shall notify any such state, or an international organization, which the Court (or, if not sitting, the President of the ICJ) deems likely to able to supply information about the question, that the ICJ will be ready to receive, within a time limit which the President is to determine, written statements – or to hear, at a purposely-held public sitting, oral statements – that concern the question[220] [336]. States and worldwide organizations which have submitted written or oral statements, or both, shall be allowed to comment on the statements that other states or global organizations have made – to the extent, in the form, and within the time-limits, which the Court (or, if not sitting, the President of the ICJ) shall decide in each specific case; accordingly, the Registrar of the Court shall, at the appropriate time, convey any such written statements to states and organizations that have presented similar statements [337].

Amendment of the Statute of the ICJ[221]

Amendments to the Statute of the ICJ are to be realized by the same procedure that the UN Charter provides for amendments to the last-mentioned[222], subject to any provisions which the General Assembly adopts upon recommendation of the UNSC regarding the participation of states that are parties to the Statute but are not Member States of the UN[223] [338]. The ICJ shall

---

2. Every state so notified has the right to intervene in the proceedings; but if it uses this right, the construction given by the judgment will be equally binding upon it." (United Nations (1945), "Statute of the International Court of Justice," Article 63).

[219] Regarding the application of procedure in contentious cases before the ICJ to procedure concerning its advisory opinions, see fn 211.

[220] Should any such state have not received this notification, it may express a wish to submit a written statement to, or to be heard by, the ICJ; the Court may grant or refuse that request (United Nations (1945), "Statute of the International Court of Justice," Article 66(3)).

[221] The Statute of the ICJ has not been amended (text to fn 192).

[222] The paragraph headed 'XVIII: Amendments to the UN Charter', in the subsection entitled 'The UN Charter' in the section titled 'The United Nations' – above in the current chapter (i.e., Chapter 3), sets out the procedure for amendments to be made to the UN Charter.

[223] These provisions comprise Resolution 2520 (XXIV) of the General Assembly, which reads as follows: "*The General Assembly*, *Recalling* that, under Article 69 of the Statute of the International Court of Justice, the Security Council may recommend to the General Assembly for adoption provisions concerning the participation of States which are parties to the Statute, but are not members of the United Nations, in the procedure for effecting amendments to the Statute, *Having* received the recommendations of the Security Council in this regard, contained in Council resolution 272 (1969) of 23 October 1969, *Decides* that: (a) A State which is a party to the Statute of the International Court of Justice, but is not a member of the United Nations, may participate in the General Assembly in regard to amendments to the Statute in the same manner as the Members of the United Nations; (b) Amendments to the Statute of the International Court of Justice shall come into force for all States which are parties to the Statute when they have been adopted by a vote of two-thirds of the States which are parties to the Statute and ratified in accordance with their respective constitutional processes by two-thirds of the States which are parties to the Statute and in accordance with the provisions of Article 69 of the Statute and Article 108 of the Charter of the United Nations." (United Nations (1969), Resolution 2520 (XXIV) adopted by the General Assembly on 4th December 1969; emphasis original). The text to fns 222 and 223 lays down Article 69 of the Statute of the ICJ. The fourth sentence of the paragraph headed 'XVIII: Amendments to

be empowered to propose amendments to the Statute of the ICJ which it considers may be necessary, by means of written messages to the Secretary-General [339].

Comment

The Statute of the ICJ is similar in both its substance and its form[224], to the Statute of the PCIJ. This is clear from an inspection of the three headed paragraphs in the subsection entitled 'The Statute of the PCIJ' in the section titled 'The Permanent Court of International Justice' and their corresponding headed paragraphs in the subsection entitled 'The Statute of the ICJ' above in the current section (i.e., that titled 'The International Court of Justice'). This observation comes as no surprise, as Article 92 of the UN Charter states that the Statute of the ICJ is founded upon the Statute of the PCIJ [258] – and some of the provisions of the former are identical, or very alike, to the corresponding provisions by article number in the latter – especially in its amended version[225]. Bearing this similarity in mind, and given the choice of the drafters of the Statute of the ICJ to maintain the optional jurisdiction of the Court that had applied to it under the Statute of the PCIJ, the addition of paragraph 5 to Article 36 of the Statute of the ICJ referring to 'compulsory jurisdiction' under the circumstances specified therein[226] may indicate that the wish for the Court to exercise compulsory jurisdiction over all interstate legal disputes remains present in the minds of some statesmen and professionals.

As amendments to the Statute of the ICJ are to be carried out by the same procedure that the UN Charter provides for its amendments, and as these only take effect when ratified by two-thirds of the Member States of the UN – including all five permanent members of the UNSC, each permanent member of the UNSC is empowered by the Statute of the ICJ to prevent any amendment from entering into force by omitting to ratify it. This means that, in this aspect, not all states parties to the Statute of the ICJ are equal before the Court.

Conclusion

This chapter details the Second World War, the UN and the ICJ, including much of the agreements upon which the latter two are grounded. The next chapter considers the development of international law to the current time, within the framework of the UN Charter and paragraph 1 of Article 38 of the Statute of the ICJ, looking at sources of the subject with reference to work of the ILC.

---

the UN Charter', in the subsection entitled 'The UN Charter' in the section titled 'The United Nations' – above in the present chapter (i.e., Chapter 3), consists of Article 108 of the Charter of the UN.

[224] The Statute of the PCIJ does not contain numbered paragraphs within any of its articles. The Statute of the ICJ divides its longer articles into paragraphs.

[225] In the Statute of the ICJ, some of these corresponding provisions are divided into paragraphs (fn 224).

[226] See the sentence immediately following the text to fn 206.

Chapter 4

The Charter of the United Nations and the Development of International Law to the Present

Abstract

The UN Charter mentions 'international law' thrice. These references are to 'sources of international law,' 'principles of international law' and 'progressive development of international law and its codification.' The UN Charter defines neither 'sources' nor 'principles,' and so Article 38(1) of the Statute of the ICJ is applied. On 21st November 1947, the UN General Assembly adopted Resolution 174 (II), which established the ILC and approved its statute. Article 1(1) of the Statute of the ILC states that its object is "the promotion of the progressive development of international law and its codification" – terms that Article 15 of the last-mentioned statute defines. Article 38(1) of the Statute of the ICJ refers to 'international conventions,' 'international custom,' 'general principles of law' and 'subsidiary means,' each of which merits a section regarding the ILC's work; a further section is dedicated to *jus cogens*, given its crucial importance. The generic meaning of the terms 'convention' and 'treaty' are synomymous; the specific meaning of each differs from that of the other. The ILC's research regarding conventional international law has led to the conclusion of the Vienna Convention on the Law of Treaties 1969, the Vienna Convention on the Succession of States in respect of Treaties 1978, and the Vienna Convention on the Law of Treaties between States and International Organizations or between International Organizations 1986, as well as several standards and accompanying commentaries. This work is gradually building a comprehensive system of conventional international law. The ILC has thoroughly investigated, and provided guidance on, the formation of customary international law, resulting in the publication of the conclusions on identification of customary international law, in 2018. It took the ILC until 2011 to identify this fundamental, substantial area of international law for further study – and the precise rules that currently comprise the body of customary international law need to be collated and the resulting volumes regularly updated. A peremptory norm of general international law – *jus cogens* – prevails over other sources of international law, and may be modified solely by a subsequent peremptory norm of general international law. The commentaries on the draft conclusions on identification and legal consequences of peremptory norms of general international law (*jus cogens*) give a thorough account of matters concerning *jus cogens*. The ILC could expand its list of *jus cogens*, frequently update this list, publish a list of principles of international law that generate *erga omnes* obligations, and regularly update that list, too. The ILC has adopted drafted conclusions on general principles of law on first reading. While the ILC's work on conventional international law has fulfilled both of the ILC's goals, its work on other sources of international law is more preliminary – bringing a degree of order to important elements of the subject that have not been structured. A regularly-updated, comprehensive manual of the rules is needed. Much progress has been made in developing the content of international law during this topic's institutional phase. The research and publications of the ILC are a major part of this advancement.

Keywords: convention, customary, ILC, international, *jus*, law, peremptory, treaty

Introduction

'International law' is a phrase that would be familiar to students of the UN Charter. It occurs three times therein. The first of these is in the Preamble of the UN Charter, in which the "peoples of the United Nations" wish "to establish conditions under which justice and respect for the obligations arising from treaties and other sources of international law can be maintained" [174]. The second instance is in paragraph 1 of Article 1 of the UN Charter.

> The Purposes of the United Nations are: 1. To maintain international peace and security, and to that end: ... to bring about by peaceful means, and in conformity with the principles of justice and international law, adjustment or settlement of international disputes or situations which might lead to a breach of the peace [340].

The third occurrence of the abovementioned phrase is in subparagraph 1(a) of Article 13 of the UN Charter, in which the General Assembly of the UN is to "initiate studies and make recommendations for the purpose of: a. ... encouraging the progressive development of international law and its codification" [341].

The First Occurrence of 'International Law': Sources

While the UN Charter does not describe 'sources of international law,' these are referred to in paragraph 1 of Article 38 of the Statute of the ICJ as international conventions [342], international custom [343], "the general principles of law recognized by civilized nations" [344] and "judicial decisions and the teachings of the most highly qualified publicists" – which are "subsidiary means for determination of rules of law" [345].

The Second Occurrence of 'International Law': Principles

Neither the UN Charter nor the Statute of the ICJ define 'principles of international law.' The latter refers to "the general principles of law recognized by civilized nations" [344].

The Third Occurrence of 'International Law': Progressive Development and Codification

On 11th December 1946, the UN General Assembly adopted Resolution 94 (I), which established the Committee on the Progressive Development of International Law and its Codification, which was directed to study ways that the General Assembly could carry out its responsibilities under subparagraph 1(a) of Article 13 of the UN Charter [346, 347]. An abridged version of this resolution is as follows.

> *The General Assembly, Recognizes* the obligation laid upon it by Article 13, paragraph 1, sub-paragraph a, of the Charter to initiate studies and make recommendations for the purpose of encouraging the progressive development of international law and its

> codification; *Realizes the need* ... for a report on the methods whereby the General Assembly may most effectively discharge its obligations under the above-mentioned provision: *Therefore, Resolves* to establish a Committee of seventeen Members of the United Nations to be appointed by the General Assembly on the recommendation of the President ... ; *Directs* the Committee to study: (*a*) The methods by which the General Assembly should encourage the progressive development of international law and its eventual codification; (*b*) Methods of securing the co-operation of the several organs of the United Nations to this end; (*c*) Methods of enlisting the assistance of such national or international bodies as might aid in the attainment of this objective; and to report to the General Assembly at its next regular session. ...[227] [348].

The Committee on the Progressive Development of International Law and its Codification held thirty meetings between 12th May 1947 and 17th June 1947, adopting a report recommending the launch of an international law commission and setting out provisions intending to supply the basis for its statute [346]. Most of the committee considered that members of the future ILC should serve in their individual capacities as professionals of acknowledged competence in international law [346]. The greater part of the committee considered that the commission's work should always be conducted in close co-operation with the political authorities of states, and that the UN General Assembly should determine measures to be taken regarding the drafts the commission prepares [346].

Although some members of the Committee on Progressive Development of International Law and its Codification considered there to be no distinct difference between the progressive development of international law and the codification of this subject, the majority deemed there to be substantive dissimilarities between them [346]. The committee recognized 'progressive development' as the drafting of a convention on a topic that had international law had not yet regulated or in respect of which the law had not yet been considerably-developed – or framed in the practice of states [349]. It accepted 'codification' as the more-precise preparation and systematization of the law in spheres in which there had been copious state practice, precent and doctrine [349].

A large majority of the Sixth Committee of the General Assembly– entrusted with the consideration of legal matters[228] – wished to establish an international law commission [346]. On 21st November 1947, the General Assembly adopted Resolution 174 (II), which founded the ILC and approved its statute [346]. The first elections to the ILC took place on 3rd November 1948 [346]. The ILC convoked the first of its yearly sessions on 12th April 1949 [346]. Its object is "the promotion of the progressive development of international law and its codification" [350].

---

[227] Emphasis original. At the same plenary meeting that the UN General Assembly adopted Resolution 94 (I), on the President's recommendation it appointed the following Member States to serve on the Committee on the Progressive Development of International Law and its Codification: Argentina, Australia, Brazil, China, Colombia, Egypt, France, India, the Netherlands, Panama, Poland, Sweden, the UK, the USA, the USSR, Venezuela and Yugoslavia (United Nations (1946), Resolution 94 (I) adopted by the General Assembly on 11th December 1946, Postscript).

[228] The Sixth Committee is the main forum in the General Assembly for discussion of legal matters (last sentence of fn 256).

The Workings and Output of the ILC

Membership

The ILC comprises thirty-four members, who are each a national of a different state [351]. The UN General Assembly elects these members from a list composed of nominations of up to four candidates[229] which each of the governments of the Member States of the UN provides[230] [352]. The electors are to consider that the successful candidates should be of accepted competence in international law and that, in the ILC as a whole, the leading forms of civilization and the foremost legal systems of the globe should be represented[231] [353]. The members of the ILC are elected for five years[232], and may be re-elected [354].

Progressive Development of International Law

If the UN General Assembly refers a proposal for the progressive development of international law to the ILC, then, in general, the latter: (a) appoints one of its members to be Rapporteur, (b) draws up a plan of work, (c) sends a questionnaire to the governments of Member States of the UN, and invites them to furnish – within a set period of time – information that is, and data which are, relevant to items within the scheme of work, (d) appoints some of its members to assist the Rapporteur with the preparation of drafts pending receipt of replies to the questionnaire, (e) consults with experts and scientific institutions, (f) considers the drafts that the Rapporteur supplies, (g) when considering a draft to be acceptable, requests the Secretary-General to issue it as an ILC document, (h) invites the governments to advance their comments

[229] Two of the candidates are nationals of the nominating Member State, and the other two are nationals of other Member States (United Nations (1947), "Statute of the International Law Commission," Adopted by the General Assembly in Resolution 174 (II) of 21st November 1947, as amended by Resolutions 485 (V) of 12th December 1950, 984 (X) of 3rd December 1955, 985 (X) of 3rd December 1955 and 36/39 of 18th November 1981, Article 4).

[230] The Secretary-General prepares this list, which comprises the names of all the nominees, and submits it to the General Assembly in order to facilitate the election of members of the ILC (United Nations (1947), "Statute of the International Law Commission," Article 7).

[231] Candidates – up to the maximum number that are specified for each regional group – who secure the highest number of votes and a majority of the votes of the Member States of the UN which are represented at the election and thereby voting, are elected (United Nations (1947), "Statute of the International Law Commission," Article 9(1)). Regarding regional groups, the thirty-four members of the ILC are elected thus: (a) eight nationals from African states, (b) seven nationals from Asian states, (c) three nationals from Eastern European states, (d) six nationals from Latin American states, (e) eight nationals from Western European or other states, (f) one national from African states or Eastern European states in rotation, and (g) one national from Asian states or Latin American states in rotation (United Nations (1981), Resolution 36/39 adopted by the General Assembly on 18th November 1981, Operative Paragraph 3). Accordingly, the allocation of seats on the ILC for the five-year term commencing on 1st January 2023 is nine nationals from African states (i.e., (a) + (f)), eight nationals from Asia-Pacific states (i.e., (b) + (g)), three nationals from Eastern European states (i.e., (c)), six nationals from Latin American states (i.e., (d)), and eight nationals from Western European or other states (i.e., (e)) (International Law Commission (2023), "Membership: 2021 Election of the International Law Commission," last updated August 4, 2023, accessed August 23, 2024, <https://legal.un.org/ilc/elections/2021election_outcome.shtml>).

[232] The election of the members of the ILC for a five-year term running from 1st January 2023 until 31st December 2027 took place on 12th November 2021, at the 32nd meeting of the UN General Assembly at its seventy-sixth session (International Law Commission (2023), "Membership: 2021 Election of the International Law Commission," last updated August 4, 2023, accessed August 23, 2024, <https://legal.un.org/ilc/elections/2021election_outcome.shtml>).

on that document within a reasonable time, (i) expects the Rapporteur and members appointed specially to reconsider the draft, taking into account those comments, and to formulate a closing draft and explanatory report to submit to the ILC for consideration and adoption, and (j) presents the draft thus adopted, with its recommendations, to the General Assembly via the Secretary-General [355]. The ILC also considers proposals and draft multilateral conventions which are put forward by Member States of the UN, the UNSC, the ECOSOC, the ICJ, the Trusteeship Council, the Secretariat, specialized agencies, or official bodies that have been established by intergovernmental agreement to further the progressive development of international law and its codification, and conveyed to it for this purpose by the Secretary-General[233] [181, 356].

Codification of International Law[234]

The ILC surveys the entire field of international law with the aim of selecting topics to be codified, while being recognizant of existing drafts [357]. If it considers that the codification of a specific topic is needed and beneficial, then it submits its recommendations to the UN General Assembly[235] [358].

The ILC assumes a plan of work which is suitable for each case [359]. Through the Secretary-General, it addresses to governments a detailed request to provide the texts of documents that are relevant to the subject being studied and which it deems necessary [360].

The ILC prepares its drafts as articles, and introduces them to the General Assembly together with a commentary that contains ample presentation of precedents and other pertinent information – including doctrine, judicial decisions and treaties, and whose conclusions mark out the degree of agreement on each point regarding doctrine and concerning the practice of states, and delineate divergencies and disagreements which exist – as well as arguments that are called upon in favour of one solution or another [361]. When the ILC considers a draft to be adequate, it asks the Secretary-General to publish it as an ILC document [362]. The ILC entreats governments to submit comments on that document within a reasonable time [363].

[233] If, in these cases, the ILC deems it suitable to proceed with the examination of the proposals or draft multilateral conventions, then it: (a) constructs a plan of work, studies the proposals or draft multilateral conventions, and compares them with other proposals and draft multilateral conventions, if any, on the same topics, (b) transmits a questionnaire to all Member States of the UN and to the principal organs of the UN, specialized agencies and official bodies mentioned above (i.e., in the text to the current footnote (fn 233)) that are affected by the question, and invites them to impart their comments within a reasonable time, (c) submits a report and its recommendations to the UN General Assembly, and (d) proceeds according to Article 16 of the Statute of the ILC, if the General Assembly should bid the ILC proceed – although the questionnaire referred to therein may be unnecessary (United Nations (1947), "Statute of the International Law Commission," Article 17(2)). The sentence immediately preceding the text to the present footnote (i.e., fn 233) lays down Article 16 of the Statute of the ILC.

[234] In addition to the procedure described in the text of the current subsection (i.e., the subsection entitled 'Codification of international law'), Section B (Codification of international law) of Chapter II (Functions of the International Law Commission) of the Statute of the ILC contains a provision on collecting materials that attest to items of customary international law: "The Commission shall consider ways and means for making the evidence of customary international law more readily available, such as the collection and publication of documents concerning State practice and of the decisions of national and international courts on questions of international law, and shall make a report to the General Assembly on this matter." (United Nations (1947), "Statute of the International Law Commission," Article 24).

[235] The ILC prioritizes requests of the UN General Assembly to tackle any question (United Nations (1947), "Statute of the International Law Commission," Article 18(3)).

Taking these remarks into consideration, the ILC prepares a final draft and an explanatory report, which it sends – with its recommendations – to the UN General Assembly by way of the Secretary-General [364].

The ILC may recommend to the UN General Assembly to take no action, make note of or adopt the report by resolution, recommend the draft to Member States of the UN with the intention of reaching terms on a convention, or convene a conference in order to hammer out a treaty [365]. Whenever the General Assembly considers it to be advantageous, it may refer a draft back to the ILC for the latter to reconsider or redraft this document [366].

Summaries of Work of the ILC

Table 4.1. Summaries of the work of the ILC [367]

Broad area	Topic	Progress
Sources of international law	Law of treaties	Completed
	Treaties concluded between states and international organizations or between two or more international organizations	
	Most-favoured-nation clause (Part One)	
	Most-favoured-nation clause (Part Two)	
	Ways and means for making the evidence of customary international law more readily available	
	Extended participation in general multilateral treaties concluded under the auspices of the League of Nations	
	Reservations to multilateral conventions	
	Review of the multilateral treaty-making process	
	Reservations to treaties	
	Fragmentation of international law: difficulties arising from the diversification and expansion of international law	
	Effects of armed conflicts on treaties	
	Subsequent agreements and subsequent practice in relation to interpretation of treaties	
	Provisional application of treaties	
	Identification of customary international law	
	Peremptory norms of general international law (*jus cogens*[236])	
	General principles of law	Under consideration
	Subsidiary means for the determination of rules of international law	
	Non-legally binding international agreements	
Subjects of international law	Fundamental rights and duties of states	Discontinued
Succession of states	Succession of states and governments	Commenced and sub-divided into topics (i) and (ii)
	Succession of states in respect of treaties (i)	Completed
	Succession of states in respect of matters other than treaties (ii)	
	Nationality in relation to the succession of states	
	Succession of states in respect of state responsibility	Under consideration

[236] The term '*jus cogens*' "is a latin phrase that literally means "compelling law." It designates norms from which no derogation is permitted by way of particular agreements. It stems from the idea already known in Roman law that certain legal rules cannot be contracted out, given the fundamental values they uphold." (Lagerwall, A. (2015), "*Jus Cogens*," last updated May 29, 2015, accessed August 27, 2024, <https://www.oxfordbibliographies.com/display/document/obo-9780199796953/obo-9780199796953-0124.xml>).

Broad area	Topic	Progress
State jurisdiction/ immunity from jurisdiction	Jurisdictional immunities of states and their property	Completed
	Immunity of state officials from foreign criminal jurisdiction	Under consideration
Law of international organizations	Representation of states in their relations with international organizations	Completed
	Status, privileges and immunities of international organizations, their officials, experts, etc.	Discontinued
Position of the individual in international law	Nationality, including statelessness	Completed
	Protection of persons in the event of disasters	
	Right of asylum	Not pursued further
International criminal law	Formulation of the Nürnberg Principles	Completed
	Question of international criminal jurisdiction	
	Draft code of crimes against the peace and security of mankind (Part I) (iii)	
	Draft code on crimes against the peace and security of mankind (Part II) – including the draft Statute of the ICC	
	Obligation to extradite or prosecute (*aut dedere aut judicare*[237])	
	Crimes against humanity	
	Prevention and repression of piracy and armed robbery at sea	Under consideration
	Question of defining aggression	Commenced and incorporated into topic (iii)
Law of international spaces	Law of the sea – régime of the high seas	Completed
	Law of the sea – régime of the territorial sea	
	Law of the non-navigational uses of international watercourses	
	Shared national resources (Law of Transboundary Aquifers)	
	Protection of the environment in relation to armed conflicts	
	Protection of the atmosphere	
	Juridical régime of historic waters, including historic bays	Discontinued
	Shared natural resources (oil and gas)	
	Sea-level rise in relation to international law	Under consideration
Law of international relations	International liability for injurious consequences arising out of acts not prohibited by international law	Commenced and sub-divided into topics (iv) and (v)
	Diplomatic intercourse and immunities	Completed
	Consular intercourse and immunities	
	Special missions	
	Question of the protection and inviolability of diplomatic agents and other persons entitled to special protection under international law	
	Status of the diplomatic courier and the diplomatic bag not accompanied by the diplomatic courier	
	State responsibility	

[237] The word '*dedere*' is the present infinitive of the verb '*dedo*'; it means "to give up, to give in, to surrender[;] to abandon, to consign, to devote (to)[;] to yield, to hand, to deliver over"; the word '*judicare*' is an alternative spelling of the word '*iudicare*', which is the present infinitive of the verb '*iudico*'; it means "to judge, to give judgment; to sentence; to conclude, to decide; to declare, to appraise"; the word '*aut*', means "or, or rather or else", and, when repeated, i.e., '*aut ... aut*', means "either ... or" (Latin Dictionary (2024), "*Latin – English Dictionary,*" accessed August 27, 2024, <https://www.online-latin-dictionary.com/>). An appropriate translation for the phrase "*aut dedere aut judicare*" from these words is "either to deliver over or to sentence". An "*aut dedere aut judicare system* consists of two core elements: an obligation to extradite or prosecute any alleged offender found in the state's territory and an obligation to establish a title of conditional universal jurisdiction" (Colorio, M. (2024), "The *Aut Dedere Aut Judicare* System for Crimes Against Humanity: A Critical but Missing Tool in the Fight Against Impunity," *Journal of International Criminal Justice*, 22(1), 1-17, 1).

Table 4.1. (Continued)

Broad area	Topic	Progress
	International liability for injurious consequences arising out of acts not prohibited by international law (prevention of transboundary damage from hazardous activities) (iv)	
	Diplomatic protection	
	Unilateral acts of states	
	International liability for injurious consequences arising out of acts not prohibited by international law (international liability in case of loss from transboundary harm arising out of hazardous activities) (v)	
	Responsibility of international organizations	
	Expulsion of aliens	
Settlement of disputes	Arbitral procedure	Completed
	Settlement of disputes to which international organizations are parties	Under consideration
Long-term programme of work	Future topics	

As Table 4.1 shows, the ILC has embarked upon a comprehensive programme of progressive development and codification of international law, and has completed its work on most of the topics listed therein. Over a difficult, diverse subject, it is steadily creating an order from the proven elements of the topic and uncertain ground towards their periphery and that falling between them. This constructive movement is largely due to the clever, diligent professionals of the subject appointed to the ILC who have energetically researched and edited these areas, with the support of the UN General Assembly and Secretariat, and the leadership of the majority of UN Member States. But this activity must continue. That of concern in the present book is work of the ILC on sources of international law, in particular, those which paragraph 1 of Article 38 of the Statute of the ICJ sets out[238].

Comment

In the text that follows, a section is devoted to each of the three primary sources of international law that paragraph 1 of Article 38 of the Statute of the ICJ identifies, namely, international conventions, international custom, and general principles of law, together with one on *jus cogens*[239] – which is included for its crucial importance. Reference is made to work of the ILC over these areas – including that of general principles of law, which has not been finalized. A section is also dedicated to secondary sources of international law as envisaged by the aforementioned paragraph of the Statute. Then, the current chapter concludes.

[238] The quoted passage immediately following the text to fn 207 specifies the sources of international law that the ICJ is to apply, which Article 38(1) of the Statute of the ICJ lays down.

[239] Fn 236 defines the term '*jus cogens*'.

Primary Sources: International Conventions

Introduction

This part of international law is fundamental. There were co-operative agreements between peoples in the Middle East, even before the founding of Rome in 753 BC/BCE[240]. But systemization of the law of treaties took place much later, with work of the ILC – leading to the publication of the Vienna Convention on the Law of Treaties 1969 and the Vienna Convention on the Law of Treaties between States and International Organizations or between International Organizations 1986. The latter instrument has not yet entered into force. A subsection is devoted to each of these treaties, preceded by a subsection concerning work of the ILC on, or relating to, the law of international conventions.

The UN Charter contains the words ‘conventions,’ ‘treaty’ and ‘treaties.’ The Statute of the ICJ refers to ‘convention,’ ‘conventions,’ ‘treaty’ and ‘treaties.’ Article 38(1)(a) of the Statute of the ICJ includes the term ‘international conventions’[241]. For clarity, the next subsection is dedicated to defining the words ‘convention’ and ‘treaty.’

Defining the Terms ‘Convention’ and ‘Treaty’

The generic meaning of the terms ‘convention’ and ‘treaty.’ The Vienna Convention on the Law of Treaties 1969 provides a broad definition of the word ‘treaty,’ in which the keywords are ‘international’ and ‘states.’

> For the purposes of the present Convention: (*a*[242]) “treaty” means an international agreement concluded between States in written form and governed by international law, whether embodied in a single instrument or in two or more related instruments and whatever its particular designation [368];

This definition of the word ‘treaty’ differs from that in the Vienna Convention on the Law of Treaties between States and International Organizations or between International Organizations 1986, insofar as the subject-matter of the latter is not the same as that of the former.

---

240 Shaw, M. (1999), “International law: Historical development,” published July 26, 1999, last updated July 30, 2024, accessed August 27, 2024, <https://www.britannica.com/topic/international-law/Historical-development>; Carozza, P., Glendon, M., Hazard, J., Jolowicz, H., Kiralfy, A., Millner, M., Powell, R., Rheinstein, M., and Stein, P. (1998), “Roman law,” published July 24, 1998, last updated February 16, 2024, accessed August 27, 2024, <https://www.britannica.com/topic/Roman-law>). The abbreviation ‘BC’ stands for ‘Before Christ’; it is used in the Christian calendar to refer to a year before the birth of Jesus Christ (Cambridge Dictionary (2024), “BC adverb,” accessed August 27, 2024, <https://dictionary.cambridge.org/dictionary/english/bc>). The abbreviation ‘BCE’ stands for ‘Before Common Era’, ‘Before Current Era’ or ‘Before Christian Era’; it is used to refer to a year before the birth of Jesus Christ, at which point the Christian calendar starts to count years (Cambridge Dictionary (2024), “BCE adverb,” accessed August 27, 2024, <https://dictionary.cambridge.org/dictionary/english/bce>).

241 The quoted passage immediately following the text to fn 207 commences with Article 38(1)(a) of the Statute of the ICJ.

242 Emphasis original.

> For the purposes of the present Convention: (*a*[243]) "treaty" means an international agreement governed by international law and concluded in written form: (i) between one or more States and one or more international organizations; or (ii) between international organizations, whether that agreement is embodied in a single instrument or in two or more related instruments and whatever its particular designation [369];

The generic definition of the word 'treaty' in the UN Treaty Collection's definition of key terms refers to, and incorporates, both of the definitions quoted above.

> The term "treaty" has regularly been used as a generic term embracing all instruments binding at international law concluded by international entities, regardless of their formal designation. Both the 1969 Vienna Convention and the 1986 Vienna Convention confirm this generic use of the term "treaty". ... In order to speak of a "treaty" in the generic sense, an instrument has to meet various criteria. First of all, it has to be a binding instrument, which means that the contracting parties intended to create legal rights and duties. Secondly, the instrument must be concluded by states or international organizations with treaty-making power. Thirdly, it has to be governed by international law, Finally the engagement has to be in writing. ... [370].

The UN Treaty Collection's definition of key terms provides the following generic definition of the word 'convention.'

> Art.38(1)(a) of the Statute of the International Court of Justice refers to "international conventions, whether general or particular" as a source of law, apart from international customary rules and general principles of international law and – as a secondary source – judicial decisions and the teachings of the most highly qualified publicists[244]. This generic use of the term "convention" embraces all international agreements, in the same way as does the generic term "treaty." Black letter law is also regularly referred to as "conventional law," in order to distinguish it from the other sources of international law. The generic term "convention" is thus synonymous with the generic term "treaty" [370].

The specific meaning of the terms 'convention' and 'treaty.' Unlike the generic meaning of these two terms, the specific meaning of each – i.e., the type of international instrument which contains the word 'convention' or the word 'treaty' – differs from that of the other. The UN Treaty Collection explains.

> Whereas in the last century the term "convention" was regularly employed for bilateral agreements, it now is generally used for formal multilateral treaties with a broad number of parties. Conventions are normally open for participation by the international community as a whole, or by a large number of states. Usually the instruments negotiated under the auspices of an international organization are entitled conventions (e.g., Convention on Biological Diversity of 1992, United Nations Convention on the Law of the Sea of 1982, Vienna Convention on the Law of Treaties of 1969). The same holds true for instruments adopted by an organ of an international organization (e.g., the 1951 ILO Convention

[243] Emphasis original.

[244] The quoted passage immediately following the text to fn 207 identifies the sources of international law that the ICJ is to apply, which Article 38(1) of the Statute of the ICJ lays down.

concerning Equal Remuneration for Men and Women Workers for Work of Equal Value, adopted by the International Labour Conference or the 1989 Convention on the Rights of the Child, adopted by the General Assembly of the UN) [370].

... Usually the term "treaty" is reserved for matters of some gravity that require more solemn agreements. Their signatures are usually sealed and they normally require ratification. Typical examples of international instruments designated as "treaties" are Peace Treaties, Border Treaties, Delimitation Treaties, Extradition Treaties and Treaties of Friendship, Commerce and Cooperation. The use of the term "treaty" for international instruments had considerably declined in the last decade in favor of other terms [370].

Work of the ILC

Law of Treaties

At its first session, in 1949, the ILC chose the law of treaties as a topic for codification [371]. It appointed Professor James Brierly, Sir Hersch Lauterpacht, Sir Gerald Fitzmaurice and Sir Humphrey Waldock as the successive Special Rapporteurs for the subject at its first, fourth, seventh and thirteenth sessions in 1949, 1952, 1955 and 1961, respectively [371]. Having considered describing the law of treaties as an expository code, at its thirteenth session, in 1961, the ILC altered the plan of its work to the preparation of draft articles which might form the basis for an international convention [371]. The set of draft articles that the ILC adopted was reviewed by the Committee of the Whole and the Drafting Committee at the first session of the United Nations Conference on the Law of Treaties – which was held in Vienna from 26th March 1968 to 24th May 1968, and at the first part of the second session of the United Nations Conference on the Law of Treaties – which took place in Vienna from 9th April 1969 to 22nd May 1969 [371]. The remainder of the latter session was devoted to thirty plenary meetings, at which the articles that the Committee of the Whole and the Drafting Committee had prepared were examined [371]. The Conference adopted the Vienna Convention on the Law of Treaties on 22nd May 1969[245] [371]. The Convention entered into force on 27th January 1980 [371].

Treaties Concluded Between States and International Organizations or Between Two or More International Organizations

The aforementioned second session of the United Nations Conference on the Law of Treaties adopted a resolution which recommended that the UN General Assembly should refer to the ILC the study of the issue of treaties made between states and international organizations or betwixt at least two of the latter [372]. Acting on this recommendation, the General Assembly, in Resolution 2501 (XXIV) of 12th November 1969[246], advised that the ILC should address the

[245] The subsection titled 'Vienna Convention on the Law of Treaties 1969', below in the current section (i.e., that entitled 'Primary Sources: International Conventions'), describes provisions of the Vienna Convention on the Law of Treaties 1969.

[246] Its Operative Paragraph 5 states: "*The General Assembly*, ... 5. *Recommends* that the International Law Commission should study, in consultation with the principal international organizations, as it may consider appropriate in accordance with its practice, the question of treaties concluded between States and international organizations or between two or more international organizations, as an important question;" (United Nations (1969), Resolution 2501 (XXIV) adopted by the General Assembly on 12th November 1969, Operative Paragraph 5; emphasis original).

matter, in consultation with the main international organizations [372]. At its twenty-second session, in 1970, the ILC included the question in its programme of work, and established a subcommittee to assess the preliminary problems involved in the investigation of this topic [372]. The subcommittee recommended the appointment of a Special Rapporteur for the subject, which the ILC did – designating Dr. Paul Reuter as such at its twenty-third session, in 1971 [372]. At its twenty-fifth session, in 1973, the ILC asked the Special Rapporteur to commence the preparation of a set of draft articles, based upon his first two reports and the comments made during this session [372]. At its twenty-sixth session, in 1974, the ILC started the first reading of these draft articles [372]. It adopted the final text of the draft articles – together with commentaries – at its thirty-fourth session, in 1982 [372], and submitted these items to the General Assembly with a recommendation that the latter convoke a conference to agree a convention on this theme [372]. The General Assembly, by means of Resolution 39/86 of 13th December 1984[247], announced that the United Nations Conference on the Law of Treaties between States and International Organizations or between International Organizations would be held in Vienna from 18th February 1986 to 21st March 1986 [372]. The Conference allotted to the Committee of the Whole those draft articles adopted by the ILC and submitted to the General Assembly in 1982 that required substantive deliberation, as well as the preparation of the preamble and the closing provisions of the forthcoming convention [372]. It referred the other draft articles from this set directly to the Drafting Committee, which was also responsible for attending to the draft articles that the Committee of the Whole referred to it, co-ordinating and reviewing the drafting of all the texts adopted, and preparing the final document [372]. The Conference adopted the Vienna Convention on the Law of Treaties between States and International Organizations or between International Organizations on 20th March 1986[248] [372]. This Convention requires thirty-five states parties to deposit instruments of ratification or accession with the Secretary-General of the UN, in order to enter into force [373]. At the time of writing, the Secretary-General has received thirty-three such depositions[249], which is almost enough for the Vienna Convention on the Law of Treaties between States and International Organizations or between International Organizations 1986 to operate[250] [374].

---

[247] Its Operative Paragraph 1 declares: "*The General Assembly*, ... 1. *Decides* that the United Nations Conference on the Law of Treaties between States and International Organizations or between International Organizations shall be held at Vienna from 18 February to 21 March 1986;" (United Nations (1984), Resolution 39/86 adopted by the General Assembly on 13th December 1984, Operative Paragraph 1; emphasis original).

[248] The subsection titled 'Vienna Convention on the Law of Treaties between States and International Organizations or between International Organizations 1986', below in the present section (i.e., that entitled 'Primary Sources: International Conventions), sets out provisions of the Vienna Convention on the Law of Treaties between States and International Organizations or between International Organizations 1986.

[249] The following states parties have deposited instruments with the Secretary-General: Albania, Argentina, Australia, Austria, Belarus, Belgium, Bulgaria, Colombia, Croatia, Cyprus, Czech Republic, Denmark, Estonia, Gabon, Germany, Greece, Hungary, Italy, Liberia, Liechtenstein, Malta, Mexico, Moldova, the Netherlands, Portugal, Senegal, Slovakia, Spain, State of Palestine, Sweden, Switzerland, the UK and Uruguay (United Nations (2024), "United Nations Treaty Collection: Chapter XXIII Law of Treaties – 3. Vienna Convention on the Law of Treaties between States and International Organizations or between International Organizations," last updated August 29, 2024, accessed August 29, 2024, <https://treaties.un.org/Pages/ViewDetails.aspx?src=TREATY &mtdsg_no=XXIII-3&chapter=23&clang=_en>).

[250] The following international organizations are also parties to the Vienna Convention on the Law of Treaties between States and International Organizations or between International Organizations 1986: the International Atomic Energy Agency, the International Civil Aviation Organization, the International Criminal Police Organization, the International Labour Organization, the International Maritime Organization, the Organisation for the Prohibition of Chemical Weapons, the Preparatory Commission for the Comprehensive Nuclear-Test-Ban Treaty Organization, the UN, the United Nations Industrial Development Organization, the Universal Postal Union, the World Health Organization and the World Intellectual Property Organization (United Nations (2024),

Extended Participation in General Multilateral Treaties Conducted under the Auspices of the League of Nations

After the ILC had brought the matter to the attention of the UN General Assembly at its fourteenth session, in 1942, the latter requested the ILC to examine the question of participation of new states in multilateral treaties agreed under the League of Nations[251], which, in their provisions, authorized the Council of the League to invite more states to become parties – but to which states that had not been so invited by the Council before the League's dissolution were unable to accede to the treaty for want of an invitation [375]. In line with General Assembly Resolution 1766 (XVII), the ILC resumed its consideration of the issue at its fifteenth session[252]. The ILC concluded that the General Assembly seemed to be entitled to designate an organ of the UN to assume and discharge the powers that, according to the participation clauses of the relevant treaties, were previously exercisable by the Council of the League[253] [375]. The General Assembly designated itself as the organ of the UN to exercise the power that twenty-one multilateral treaties conferred on the Council of the League to invite states to accede to them[254] [375].

"United Nations Treaty Collection: Chapter XXIII Law of Treaties – 3. Vienna Convention on the Law of Treaties between States and International Organizations or between International Organizations," last updated August 29, 2024, accessed August 29, 2024, <https://treaties.un.org/Pages/ViewDetails.aspx?src=TREATY&mtdsg_no=XXIII-3&chapter=23&clang=en>).

[251] The relevant resolution records: "*The General Assembly*, ... 1. *Requests* the International Law Commission to study further the question of extended participation in general multilateral treaties concluded under the auspices of the League of Nations, giving due consideration to the views expressed during the discussions at the seventeenth session of the General Assembly, and to include the results of the study in the report of the Commission covering the work of its fifteenth session;" (United Nations (1962), Resolution 1766 (XVII) adopted by the General Assembly on 20th November 1962, Operative Paragraph 1; emphasis original).

[252] Fn 251 lays down the pertinent operative paragraph of Resolution 1766 (XVII).

[253] The report of the ILC concludes: "50. ... (*c*) [I]n the light of the arrangements which were made on the occasion of the dissolution of the League of Nations and the assumption by the United Nations of some of its functions and powers in relation to treaties concluded under the auspices of the League, the General Assembly appears to be entitled, if it so desires, to designate an organ of the United Nations to assume and fulfil the powers which, under the participation clauses of the treaties in question, were formerly exercisable by the Council of the League. This would provide ... a simplified and expeditious procedure for achieving the object of extending the participation in general multilateral treaties concluded under the auspices of the League. ..." (International Law Commission (1963), Report of the International Law Commission 1963: Questions of extended participation in general multilateral treaties concluded under the auspices of the League of Nations, *Yearbook of the International Law Commission*, 1963, Volume II, 217-223, 223).

[254] The pertinent resolution notes: "*The General Assembly*, *Having considered* the question of extended participation in general multilateral treaties concluded under the auspices of the League of Nations, and the report of the International Law Commission thereon, *Noting* that there are twenty-one such treaties of a technical and non-political character which by their terms authorized the Council of the League of Nations to invite additional States to become parties, and thus were not intended to be closed to new States, *Further noting* that since the Council of the League ceased to exist a large number of new States have come into being and that many of them have been unable to become parties to the treaties in question for lack of an invitation to accede, ... 1. *Decides* that the General Assembly is the appropriate organ of the United Nations to exercise the power conferred by multilateral treaties of a technical and non-political character on the Council of the League of Nations to invite States to accede to those treaties; ... 4. *Further requests* the Secretary-General to invite each State which is a Member of the United Nations or member of a specialized agency or a party to the Statute of the International Court of Justice, or has been designated for this purpose by the General Assembly, and which otherwise is not eligible to become a party to the treaties in question, to accede thereto by depositing an instrument of accession with the Secretary-General of the United Nations; ... ." (United Nations (1963), Resolution 1903 (XVIII) adopted by the General Assembly on 18th November 1963, Recitals 1-3, and Operative Paragraphs 1 and 4; emphasis original).

Reservations to Multilateral Conventions

In Resolution 478 (V) of 16th November 1950, the UN General Assembly requested the ICJ to give an advisory opinion on reservations to the Convention on the Prevention and Punishment of the Crime of Genocide 1948 [376], which it duly did in *Reservations to the Convention on the Prevention and Punishment of the Crime of Genocide*[255]. Also in Resolution 478 (V), the General Assembly invited the ILC to study the issue of reservations to multilateral conventions in general, and to report to the former at its sixth session, in 1951[256] [376]. In its report to the General Assembly, the ILC declared that the criterion of compatibility of a reservation with the object and purpose of a convention, which the ICJ applied in *Reservations to the Convention on the Prevention and Punishment of the Crime of Genocide*[257], would, in the main, be unsuitable for application to multilateral conventions[258] [376]. Having concluded that provisions concerning the admissibility of reservations should be placed in multilateral conventions[259], the ILC's report proceeded to outline good practice in the handling of

[255] Advisory Opinion of 28 May 1951, *I.C.J. Reports 1951*, 15-30.

[256] Its Operative Paragraph 2 states: "*The General Assembly*, ... 2. *Invites* the International Law Commission: (*a*) In the course of its work on the codification of the law of treaties, to study the question of reservations to multilateral conventions both from the point of view of codification and from that of the progressive development of international law; to give priority to this study and to report thereon, especially as regards multilateral conventions of which the Secretary-General is the depositary, this report to be considered by the General Assembly at its sixth session; (*b*) In connexion with this study, to take account of all the views expressed during the fifth session of the General Assembly, and particularly in the Sixth Committee;" (United Nations (1950), Resolution 478 (V) adopted by the General Assembly on 16th November 1950, Operative Paragraph 2; emphasis original). The Sixth Committee of the UN General Assembly is the main forum in the General Assembly for consideration of legal questions (United Nations (2024), "General Assembly of the United Nations: Sixth Committee (Legal)," accessed August 31, 2024, <https://www.un.org/en/ga/sixth/>).

[257] In the operative part of its advisory opinion, the ICJ held "that a State which has made and maintained a reservation which has been objected to by one or more of the parties to the Convention [on the Prevention and Punishment of the Crime of Genocide 1948] but not by others, can be regarded as being a party to the Convention if the reservation is compatible with the object and purpose of the Convention; otherwise that State cannot be regarded as being a party to the Convention", "that if a party to the Convention [on the Preservation and Punishment of the Crime of Genocide 1948] objects to a reservation which it considers to be incompatible with the object and purpose of the Convention, it can in fact consider that the reserving State is not a party to the Convention", and "that if, on the other hand, a party accepts the reservation as being compatible with the object and purpose of the Convention, it can in fact consider that the reserving State is a party to the Convention" (*Reservations to the Convention on the Prevention and Punishment of the Crime of Genocide*, Advisory Opinion of 28 May 1951, *I.C.J. Reports 1951*, 15-30, 29-30).

[258] Paragraph 24 of the report applies the following reasoning: "The Commission believes that the criterion of the compatibility of a reservation with the object and purpose of a multilateral convention, applied by the International Court of Justice to the Convention on Genocide [(fn 257)], is not suitable for application to multilateral conventions in general. It involves a classification of the provisions of a convention into two categories, those which do and those which do not form part of its object and purpose. It seems reasonable to assume that, ordinarily at least, the parties regard the provisions of a convention as an integral whole, and that a reservation to any of them may be deemed to impair its object and purpose. Even if the distinction between provisions which do and those which do not form part of the object and purpose of a convention be regarded as one that it is intrinsically possible to draw, the Commission does not see how the distinction can be made otherwise than subjectively. If State A tenders a reservation which State B regards as compatible and State C regards as incompatible with the object and purpose of the convention, [then] there is no objective test by which the difference may be resolved; ... . So long as the application of the criterion of compatibility remains a matter of subjective direction, some of the parties being willing to accept a reservation and others not, the status of a reserving State in relation to the convention must remain uncertain. ..." (International Law Commission (1951), Report of the International Law Commission 1951: Reservations to Multilateral Conventions, *Yearbook of the International Law Commission*, 1951, Volume II, 125-131, 128).

[259] Paragraph 33 of the report states: "The Commission suggests that organs of the United Nations, specialized agencies and States should, in the course of preparing multilateral conventions, consider the insertion therein of provisions relating to the admissibility or non-admissibility of reservations and to the effect to be attributed to

reservations[260]. In Resolution 598 (VI) of 12th January 1952, the General Assembly endorsed the ILC's recommendation to insert clauses on reservations in future conventions[261], advised that the ICJ's advisory opinion in *Reservations to the Convention on the Prevention and Punishment of the Crime of Genocide* should be followed regarding the Convention on the Prevention and Punishment of the Crime of Genocide 1948[262], and asked the Secretary-General to act as depositary for documents including reservations or objections without passing on the legal effect of those papers[263] [376]. The ILC addressed the theme of reservations again in the

---

them." (International Law Commission (1951), Report of the International Law Commission 1951: Reservations to Multilateral Conventions, *Yearbook of the International Law Commission*, 1951, Volume II, 125-131, 130).

[260] Paragraph 34 of the report declares: "The Commission suggests that, in the absence of contrary provisions in any multilateral convention and of any organizational procedure applicable, the following practice should be adopted with regard to reservations to multilateral conventions ... : (1) The depositary of a multilateral convention should, upon receipt of each reservation, communicate it to all States which are or which are entitled to become parties to the convention. (2) The depositary of a multilateral convention, in communicating a reservation to a State which is entitled to object, should at the same time request that State to express its attitude towards the reservation within a specified period, and such period may be extended if this is deemed to be necessary. If, within the period so specified or extended, a State fails to make its attitude towards the reservation known to the depositary, or if, without expressing an objection to the reservation, it signs, ratifies, or otherwise accepts the convention within the period, it should be deemed to have consented to the reservation. (3) The depositary of a multilateral convention should communicate all replies to its communications, in respect of any reservation to the convention, to all States which are or which are entitled to become parties to the convention. (4) If a multilateral convention is intended to enter into force as a consequence of signature only, [then] a State which offers a reservation at the time of signature may become a party to the convention only in the absence of objection by any State which has previously signed the convention; ... . (5) If ratification or acceptance in some other form, after signature, is requisite to bring a multilateral convention into force, [then] (*a*) A reservation made by a State at the time of signature should have no effect unless it is repeated or incorporated by reference in the later ratification or acceptance by that State; (*b*) A State which tenders a ratification or acceptance with a reservation may become a party to the convention only in the absence of objection by any other State which, at the time the tender is made, has signed, or ratified or otherwise accepted the convention; ... provided, however, that an objection by a State which has merely signed the convention should cease to have the effect of excluding the reserving State from becoming a party, if within a period of twelve months from the time of the making of its objection, the objecting State has not ratified or otherwise accepted the convention." (International Law Commission (1951), Report of the International Law Commission 1951: Reservations to Multilateral Conventions, *Yearbook of the International Law Commission*, 1951, Volume II, 125-131, 130-131; emphasis original).

[261] Operative Paragraph 1 of the resolution reads: "*The General Assembly*, ... 1. *Recommends* that organs of the United Nations, specialized agencies and States should, in the course of preparing multilateral conventions, consider the insertion therein of provisions relating to the admissibility or non-admissibility of reservations and to the effect to be attributed to them;" (United Nations (1952), Resolution 598 (VI) adopted by the General Assembly on 12th January 1952, Operative Paragraph 1; emphasis original).

[262] Operative Paragraph 2 of the resolution states: "*The General Assembly*, ... 2. *Recommends* to all States that they be guided in regard to the Convention on the Prevention and Punishment of the Crime of Genocide by the advisory opinion of the International Court of Justice of 28 May 1951; (United Nations (1952), Resolution 598 (VI) adopted by the General Assembly on 12th January 1952, Operative Paragraph 2; emphasis original). This advisory opinion is *Reservations to the Convention on the Prevention and Punishment of the Crime of Genocide*, Advisory Opinion of 28 May 1951, *I.C.J. Reports 1951*, 15-30.

[263] Operative Paragraph 3 of the resolution declares: "*The General Assembly*, ... 3. *Requests* the Secretary-General: (*a*) In relation to reservations to the Convention on the Prevention and Punishment of the Crime of Genocide to conform his practice to the advisory opinion of the Court of 28 May 1951; (*b*) In respect of future conventions concluded under the auspices of the United Nations of which he is the depositary: (i) To continue to act as depositary in connexion with the deposit of documents containing reservations or objections, without passing upon the legal effect of such documents; and (ii) To communicate the text of such documents relating to reservations or objections to all States concerned, leaving it to each State to draw legal consequences from such communications." (United Nations (1952), Resolution 598 (VI) adopted by the General Assembly on 12th January 1952, Operative Paragraph 3; emphasis original). This advisory opinion is *Reservations to the Convention on the Prevention and Punishment of the Crime of Genocide*, Advisory Opinion of 28 May 1951, *I.C.J. Reports 1951*, 15-30. In Operative Paragraph 1 of Part B of Resolution 1452 (XIV) of 7th December 1959, the UN General Assembly amends Operative Subparagraph 3(*b*) of Resolution 598 (VI) of 12th January 1952 to

draft articles on the law of treaties and on the matter of treaties concluded between states and international organizations or between two or more international organizations [376]. These provisions became Articles 19 to 23 of the Vienna Convention on the Law of Treaties 1969, and – with slight modifications in the light of the change in contracting parties – Articles 19 to 23 of the Vienna Convention on the Law of Treaties between States and International Organizations or between International Organizations 1986 [376]. The former clauses – with footnotes to the latter articles that emphasize differences from the former – are reproduced in the following passage. The ILC further pursued the topic of reservations in subsequent work [376], to which the next headed paragraph (i.e., that named 'Reservations to treaties') in the present subsection is dedicated.

PART II. CONCLUSION AND ENTRY INTO FORCE OF TREATIES[264]

SECTION 2. RESERVATIONS

Article 19. FORMULATION OF RESERVATIONS

A State may, when signing, ratifying, accepting, approving or acceding to a treaty, formulate a reservation unless:

(*a*) The reservation is prohibited by the treaty;
(*b*) The treaty provides that only specified reservations, which do not include the reservation in question, may be made; or
(*c*) In cases not falling under sub-paragraphs (*a*) and (*b*), the reservation is incompatible with the object and purpose of the treaty[265].

Article 20. ACCEPTANCE OF AND OBJECTION TO RESERVATIONS

1. A reservation expressly authorized by a treaty does not require any subsequent acceptance by the other contracting States unless the treaty so provides.
2. When it appears from the limited number of the negotiating States and the object and purpose of a treaty that the application of the treaty in its entirety between all the parties is an essential condition of the consent of each one to be bound by the treaty, a reservation requires acceptance by all the parties.

asking the Secretary-General to extend the practice requested of him therein regarding future conventions concluded under the auspices of the UN, to all conventions negotiated under the auspices of the UN that do not contain clauses to the contrary (United Nations (1959), Resolution 1452 (XIV) adopted by the General Assembly on 7th December 1959, Part B, Operative Paragraph 1). Clause (*b*) in the first sentence of the current footnote (i.e., fn 263) is Operative Subparagraph 3(*b*) of Resolution 598 (VI) of 12th January 1952.

264 All capitalized and italicized words, letters and numbers in this quoted passage are in the original document.

265 Article 19 of the Vienna Convention on the Law of Treaties between States and International Organizations or between International Organizations 1986 reads as follows: "A State OR AN INTERNATIONAL ORGANIZATION may, when signing, ratifying, FORMALLY CONFIRMING, accepting, approving or acceding to a treaty, formulate a reservation unless: (*a*) the reservation is prohibited by the treaty; (*b*) the treaty provides that only specified reservations, which do not include the reservation in question, may be made; or (*c*) in cases not falling under subparagraphs (*a*) and (*b*), the reservation is incompatible with the object and purpose of the treaty." (United Nations (1986), "Vienna Convention on the Law of Treaties between States and International Organizations or between International Organizations," A/CONF.129/15, Official Records of the United Nations Conference on the Law of Treaties between States and International Organizations or between International Organizations, Volume II, 93-109, 98, Article 19; capital emphasis added; italic emphasis original).

3. When a treaty is a constituent instrument of an international organization and unless it otherwise provides, a reservation requires the acceptance of the competent organ of that organization.
4. In cases not falling under the preceding paragraphs and unless the treaty otherwise provides:
(*a*) Acceptance by another contracting State of a reservation constitutes the reserving State a party to the treaty in relation to that other State if or when the treaty is in force for those States;
(*b*) An objection by another contracting State to a reservation does not preclude the entry into force of the treaty as between the objecting and reserving States unless a contrary intention is definitely expressed by the objecting State;
(*c*) An act expressing a State's consent to be bound by the treaty and containing a reservation is effective as soon as at least one other contracting State has accepted the reservation.
5. For the purposes of paragraphs 2 and 4 and unless the treaty otherwise provides, a reservation is considered to have been accepted by a State if it shall have raised no objection to the reservation by the end of a period of twelve months after it was notified of the reservation or by the date on which it expressed its consent to be bound by the treaty, whichever is later[266].

Article 21. LEGAL EFFECTS OF RESERVATIONS AND OF OBJECTIONS TO RESERVATIONS

1. A reservation established with regard to another party in accordance with articles 19, 20 and 23:
(*a*) Modifies for the reserving State in its relations with that other party the provisions of the treaty to which the reservation relates to the extent of the reservation; and

[266] Article 20 of the Vienna Convention on the Law of Treaties between States and International Organizations or between International Organizations 1986 reads as follows: "1. A reservation expressly authorized by a treaty does not require any subsequent acceptance by the CONTRACTING STATES AND CONTRACTING ORGANIZATIONS OR, AS THE CASE MAY BE, BY THE CONTRACTING ORGANIZATIONS unless the treaty so provides. 2. When it appears from the limited number of the negotiating States AND NEGOTIATING ORGANIZATIONS OR, AS THE CASE MAY BE, OF THE NEGOTIATING ORGANIZATIONS and the object and purpose of a treaty that the application of the treaty in its entirety between all the parties is an essential condition of the consent of each one to be bound by the treaty, a reservation requires acceptance by all the parties. 3. When a treaty is a constituent instrument of an international organization and unless it otherwise provides, a reservation requires the acceptance of the competent organ of that organization. 4. In cases not falling under the preceding paragraphs and unless the treaty otherwise provides: (*a*) acceptance of a reservation by A CONTRACTING STATE OR BY A CONTRACTING ORGANIZATION constitutes the reserving State OR INTERNATIONAL ORGANIZATION a party to the treaty in relation to THE ACCEPTING STATE OR ORGANIZATION if or when the treaty is in force for THE RESERVING STATE OR ORGANIZATION AND FOR THE ACCEPTING STATE OR ORGANIZATION; (*b*) an objection by A CONTRACTING STATE OR BY A CONTRACTING ORGANIZATION to a reservation does not preclude the entry into force of the treaty as between the OBJECTING STATE OR INTERNATIONAL ORGANIZATION AND THE RESERVING STATE OR ORGANIZATION unless a contrary intention is definitely expressed by the objecting State OR ORGANIZATION; (*c*) an act expressing the consent of a State OR OF AN INTERNATIONAL ORGANIZATION to be bound by the treaty and containing a reservation is effective as soon as at least one contracting State OR ONE CONTRACTING ORGANIZATION has accepted the reservation. 5. For the purposes of paragraphs 2 and 4, and unless the treaty otherwise provides, a reservation is considered to have been accepted by a State OR BY AN INTERNATIONAL ORGANIZATION if it shall have raised no objection to the reservation by the end of a period of twelve months after it was notified of the reservation or by the date on which it expressed its consent to be bound by the treaty, whichever is later." (United Nations (1986), "Vienna Convention on the Law of Treaties between States and International Organizations or between International Organizations," Article 20; capital emphasis added; italic emphasis original).

(*b*) Modifies those provisions to the same extent for that other party in its relations with the reserving State.

2. The reservation does not modify the provisions of the treaty for the other parties to the treaty *inter se*[267].
3. When a State objecting to a reservation has not opposed the entry into force of the treaty between itself and the reserving State, the provisions to which the reservation relates do not apply as between the two States to the extent of the reservation[268].

Article 22. WITHDRAWAL OF RESERVATIONS AND OF OBJECTIONS TO RESERVATIONS

1. Unless the treaty otherwise provides, a reservation may be withdrawn at any time and the consent of a State which has accepted the reservation is not required for its withdrawal.
2. Unless the treaty otherwise provides, an objection to a reservation may be withdrawn at any time.
3. Unless the treaty otherwise provides, or it is otherwise agreed:
   (*a*) The withdrawal of a reservation becomes operative in relation to another contracting State only when notice of it has been received by that State;
   (*b*) The withdrawal of an objection to a reservation becomes operative only when notice of it has been received by the State which formulated the reservation[269].

---

[267] The expression '*inter se*' "is a Latin phrase meaning "between or amongst themselves." It describes the rights and obligations that arise only within a particular group or between individuals, who, in a specific set of circumstances, have similar legal status. Sometimes, it is also used to distinguish between those who have the rights or obligations and those who do not." (Cornell University (2022), "Cornell Law School: Legal Information Institute – *inter se*," last updated in April 2022, accessed September 3, 2024, <https://www.law.cornell.edu/wex/inter_se>). In this usage of the phrase '*inter se*', it applies to states parties to a treaty, rather than within a group – unless this is the group of states that are parties to the treaty – or to individuals.

[268] Article 21 of the Vienna Convention on the Law of Treaties between States and International Organizations or between International Organizations 1986 reads as follows: "A reservation established with regard to another party in accordance with articles 19, 20 and 23: (*a*) modifies for the reserving State OR INTERNATIONAL ORGANIZATION in its relations with that other party the provisions of the treaty to which the reservation relates to the extent of the reservation; and (*b*) modifies those provisions to the same extent for that other party in its relations with the reserving State OR INTERNATIONAL ORGANIZATION. 2. The reservation does not modify the provisions of the treaty for the other parties to the treaty *inter se*. 3. When a State OR AN INTERNATIONAL ORGANIZATION objecting to a reservation has not opposed the entry into force of the treaty between itself and the reserving State OR ORGANIZATION, the provisions to which the reservation relates do not apply as between the RESERVING STATE OR ORGANIZATION AND THE OBJECTING STATE OR ORGANIZATION to the extent of the reservation." (United Nations (1986), "Vienna Convention on the Law of Treaties between States and International Organizations or between International Organizations," Article 21; capital emphasis added; italic emphasis original). Fn 267 defines the term '*inter se*'.

[269] Article 22 of the Vienna Convention on the Law of Treaties between States and International Organizations or between International Organizations 1986 reads as follows: "1. Unless the treaty otherwise provides, a reservation may be withdrawn at any time and the consent of a State OR OF AN INTERNATIONAL ORGANIZATION which has accepted the reservation is not required for its withdrawal. 2. Unless the treaty otherwise provides, an objection to a reservation may be withdrawn at any time. 3. Unless the treaty otherwise provides, or it is otherwise agreed: (*a*) the withdrawal of a reservation becomes operative in relation to A CONTRACTING STATE OR A CONTRACTING ORGANIZATION only when notice of it has been received by that State OR THAT ORGANIZATION; (*b*) the withdrawal of an objection to a reservation becomes operative only when notice of it has been received by the State OR INTERNATIONAL ORGANIZATION which formulated the reservation." (United Nations (1986), "Vienna Convention on the Law of Treaties between States and International Organizations or between International Organizations," Article 22; capital emphasis added; italic emphasis original).

Article 23. PROCEDURE REGARDING RESERVATIONS

1. A reservation, an express acceptance of a reservation and an objection to a reservation must be formulated in writing and communicated to the contracting States and other States entitled to become parties to the Treaty.
2. If formulated when signing the treaty subject to ratification, acceptance or approval, a reservation must be formally confirmed by the reserving State when expressing its consent to be bound by the treaty. In such a case the reservation shall be considered as having been made on the date of its confirmation.
3. An express acceptance of, or an objection to, a reservation made previously to confirmation of the reservation does not itself require confirmation.
4. The withdrawal of a reservation or of an objection to a reservation must be formulated in writing[270] [377].

A newly-independent state retains any reservation to a treaty that was in place regarding the territory over which it has gained sovereignty, unless it repudiates this reservation or formulates a new one on the same topic [378]. The abovementioned state must not make a new reservation that falls within paragraphs (*a*), (*b*) or (*c*) of Article 19 of the Vienna Convention on the Law of Treaties 1969[271] [379]. The rules which Articles 20 to 23 of the Vienna Convention on the Law of Treaties 1969 set out[272], apply to that reservation [380]. It is submitted that the treatment which Article 21 of the Vienna Convention on the Law of Treaties 1969 and Article 21 of the Vienna Convention on the Law of Treaties between States and International Organizations or between International Organizations 1986 specify, creates a bilateral treaty between a reserving and accepting state or international organization which differs from the main multilateral convention to the extent of the reservation that applies, or the reservations which apply, between them. This is unsatisfactory from the perspective of certainty of international law, especially in cases in which there are many reservations to a multilateral treaty. From the viewpoint of certainty of the law, it is advisable to permit as few objections and reservations by contracting states and international organizations as possible – which necessitates a broad definition of the term 'object and purpose of the treaty.'

[270] Article 23 of the Vienna Convention on the Law of Treaties between States and International Organizations or between International Organizations 1986 reads as follows: "1. A reservation, an express acceptance of a reservation and an objection to a reservation must be formulated in writing and communicated to the contracting States AND CONTRACTING ORGANIZATIONS and other States AND INTERNATIONAL ORGANIZATIONS entitled to become parties to the treaty. 2. If formulated when signing the treaty subject to ratification, ACT OF FORMAL CONFIRMATION, acceptance or approval, a reservation must be formally confirmed by the reserving State OR INTERNATIONAL ORGANIZATION when expressing its consent to be bound by the treaty. In such a case the reservation shall be considered as having been made on the date of its confirmation. 3. An express acceptance of, or an objection to, a reservation made previously to confirmation of the reservation does not itself require confirmation. 4. The withdrawal of a reservation or of an objection to a reservation must be formulated in writing." (United Nations (1986), "Vienna Convention on the Law of Treaties between States and International Organizations or between International Organizations," Article 23; capital emphasis added; italic emphasis original).

[271] The text to fn 265 comprises Article 19 of the Vienna Convention on the Law of Treaties 1969.

[272] The text to fns 266, 267-268, 269 and 270 lays down Articles 20, 21, 22 and 23 of the Vienna Convention on the Law of Treaties 1969, respectively.

Reservations to Treaties

At its forty-fifth session, in 1993, the ILC decided to study the topic titled 'The law and practice relating to reservations to treaties'[273], subject to the UN General Assembly's approval [381]. The ILC noted that the Vienna Convention on the Law of Treaties 1969, the Vienna Convention on the Succession of States in respect of Treaties 1978 and the Vienna Convention on the Law of Treaties between States and International Organizations or between International Organizations 1986 contained principles on reservations to treaties, but that these principles were too general to be a guide for the practice of states[274] [381]. In Resolution 48/31 of 9th December 1993[275], the General Assembly endorsed the ILC's decision on this matter, on the understanding that the final form of the work would be determined after a preliminary study had been presented to it [381]. At its forty-sixth session, in 1994, the ILC appointed Dr. Alain Pellet as Special Rapporteur for the subject [381]. At its forty-seventh session, in 1995, the ILC had before it the Special Rapporteur's first report, which outlined the ambit and form of the ILC's future work and proposed the form that its results might take [381]. After the ILC had considered the report, the Special Rapporteur synopsized the conclusions that he had reached regarding the title of the topic – which should read 'Reservations to treaties'[276], the form of the study's results – which should be a guide to practice concerning reservations that comprises draft articles with commentaries, the flexible manner in which the ILC's work on this subject should be conducted, and the consensus of the ILC that the relevant provisions of the Vienna Conventions should not be changed [381]. At its sixty-third session, in 2011 – after the ILC had received and examined several reports of the Special Rapporteur, it had in front of it Dr. Pellet's seventeenth report, as well as observations and comments received from governments on the provisional version of the Guide to Practice on Reservations to Treaties which it has adopted at its sixty-second session, in 2010 [381]. The ILC founded a working group, in order to progress with the finalization of the text of the guidelines that constituted the Guide to Practice [381]. On the basis of the working group's recommendations, the ILC adopted the Guide to Practice on Reservations to Treaties [381]. In Resolution 66/98 of 9th December

---

[273] The ILC modified this title to 'Reservations to treaties' at its forty-seventh session, in 1995 (International Law Commission (2023), "Summaries of the Work of the International Law Commission: Reservations to treaties," last updated June 29, 2023, accessed September 4, 2024, <https://legal.un.org/ilc/summaries/1_8.shtml>).

[274] The aforementioned conventions furnish "ambiguous answers to the questions of differentiating between reservations and declarations of interpretation, the scope of declarations of interpretation, the validity of reservations (the conditions for the lawfulness of reservations and their applicability to another State) and the regime of objections to reservations (in particular, the admissibility and scope of objections to a reservation which is neither prohibited by the treaty nor contrary to its object or purpose). These conventions are also silent on the effect of reservations on the entry into force of treaties, problems pertaining to the particular object of some treaties (in particular[,] the constituent instruments of international organizations and human rights treaties), reservations to codification treaties and problems resulting from particular treaty techniques (elaboration of additional protocols, bilateralization techniques)." (International Law Commission (2023), "Summaries of the Work of the International Law Commission: Reservations to treaties," last updated June 29, 2023, accessed September 4, 2024, <https://legal.un.org/ilc/summaries/1_8.shtml>).

[275] Its Operative Paragraph 7 states: "*The General Assembly*, ... 7. *Endorses* the decision of the International Law Commission to include in its agenda the topics "The law and practice relating to reservations to treaties" and "State succession and its impact on the nationality of natural and legal persons", on the understanding that the final form to be given to the work on these topics shall be decided after a preliminary study is presented to the General Assembly;" (United Nations (1993), Resolution 48/31 adopted by the General Assembly on 9th December 1993, Operative Paragraph 7; emphasis original). It is the first of these two titles with which the current headed paragraph (i.e., that named 'Reservations to treaties') is concerned; the ILC subsequently altered this title from 'The law and practice relating to reservations to treaties' to 'Reservations to treaties' (fn 273).

[276] Fn 273 and accompanying text.

2011[277], the General Assembly commended the ILC for completing its work on the Guide to Practice on Reservations to Treaties [381]. In Resolution 68/111 of 16th December 2013[278], the General Assembly welcomed the successful completion of the ILC's work on reservations to treaties, noted the Guide to Practice on Reservations to Treaties 2011[279], and encouraged the maximum dissemination of the Guide to Practice [381].

Review of the Multilateral Treaty-Making Process

In Resolution 32/48 of 8th December 1977[280], the UN General Assembly asked the Secretary-General of the UN to prepare a report concerning the techniques and procedures used to elaborate multinational conventions [382]. Therein it invited the ILC to submit its observations on the topic for inclusion in this report[281], which the ILC duly did in July 1979[282] [382].

---

[277] Its Operative Paragraph 4 notes: "*The General Assembly*, ... 4. *Commends* the International Law Commission for the completion of its work on the draft articles on the responsibility of international organizations, the draft articles on the effects of armed conflicts on treaties, and the Guide to Practice on Reservations to Treaties;" (United Nations (2011), Resolution 66/98 adopted by the General Assembly on 9th December 2011, Operative Paragraph 4; emphasis original).

[278] Its Operative Paragraphs declare: "*The General Assembly*, ... 1. *Welcomes* the successful completion of the work of the International Law Commission on the subject of reservations to treaties and its adoption of the Guide to Practice on Reservations to Treaties, including the guidelines and a detailed commentary thereto; 2. *Expresses its appreciation* to the Commission for its continuing contribution to the codification and progressive development of international law; 3. *Takes note* of the Guide to Practice, presented by the Commission, including the guidelines, the text of which is annexed to the present resolution, and encourages its widest possible dissemination." (United Nations (2013), Resolution 68/111 adopted by the General Assembly on 16th December 2013, Operative Paragraphs 1-3; emphasis original).

[279] The Guide to Practice on Reservations to Treaties 2011 is available on the UN's website at https://legal.un.org/ilc/texts/instruments/english/draft_articles/1_8_2011.pdf.

[280] Its Operative Paragraph 1 states: "*The General Assembly*, ... 1. *Requests* the Secretary-General to prepare a report on the techniques and procedures used in the elaboration of multilateral treaties, taking also into consideration the debates in the General Assembly at the current session and the observations referred to in paragraph 2 below [(fn 281)], with a view to submission to the Assembly at its thirty-fourth session;" (United Nations (1977), Resolution 32/48 adopted by the General Assembly on 8th December 1977, Operative Paragraph 1; emphasis original).

[281] Its Operative Paragraph 2 specifies: "*The General Assembly*, ... 2. *Invites* Governments and the International Law Commission to submit by 31 July 1979, for inclusion in the report referred to above [(fn 280)], their observations on this subject;" (United Nations (1977), Resolution 32/48 adopted by the General Assembly on 8th December 1977, Operative Paragraph 2; emphasis original).

[282] Elements of the later paragraphs of the ILC's submission to the UN General Assembly on 23rd July 1979 – including almost all of the concluding section – are as follows: "86. Ten conventions have been elaborated and concluded, on the basis of draft articles prepared by the [International Law] Commission, by international conferences convened to that effect by the General Assembly ... . 87. When making a decision that an international conference of plenipotentiaries should be convened to elaborate and conclude a conventional instrument or instruments on the basis of draft articles prepared by the Commission, the General Assembly resolution providing for that decision usually sets forth the task which is before the conference concerned. ... 89. Another decision of importance from the point of view of treaty-making which the General-Assembly normally makes when convening an international conference is that determining what will be the basis for the work of the conference. There have evolved four types of formulae embodying such decisions ... . 90. [For] the first United Nations Conference on the Law of the Sea[, governments were invited to exchange views on the controversial issues relating to the law of the sea in the time remaining before the start of the conference]. On other occasions, the General Assembly made arrangements for the consideration by it of the subject prior to the opening of the conference concerned, including an item to that effect on the agenda of one of its subsequent sessions. ... 91. Another arrangement which the General Assembly used to make when convening an international conference to consider draft articles prepared by the Commission is the request to States to submit to the Secretary-General for circulation written comments and observations on the final draft articles in order that they may be circulated to Governments prior to the opening of the conference. ... 92. On two occasions, States intending to participate in conferences were invited by the General Assembly to submit any amendments to the draft articles prepared by the Commission that they might want to propose in advance of the Conference. Amendments submitted pursuant to that invitation were circulated at the opening of the conferences in question. 93. The resolutions

convening the codification conferences also include provisions which determine the States invited to participate. Such resolutions also provide invitations to the interested specialized agencies and intergovernmental organizations to send observers to the conference. ... 94. For all the codification conferences, the Secretary-General was requested to present recommendations concerning the methods of work and procedures. ... 95. Each United Nations codification conference called to elaborate and conclude an international conventional instrument or instruments on the basis of draft articles prepared by the Commission approves its own rules of procedure as well as the basic methods of work and techniques to be followed in the conference. The articles of the Commission's draft and amendments thereto are considered first at committee level and then by the plenary of the conference. The first United Nations Conference on the Law of the Sea set up five main committees, and the United Nations Conference on Consular Relations two main committees. In other cases, the conferences established a single committee of the whole. All United Nations codification conferences have been assisted by a drafting committee. Working groups are sometimes set up by the conference to consider specific questions and report back to a main committee or to the plenary of the conference. 96. After all articles and amendments thereto have been considered, the preamble of the instrument and the final clauses, the draft convention or conventions are put to the vote as a whole. Once adopted, the conventions, as well as optional protocols, are open for signature and ratification or for accession. Each conference also adopts its final act, to which resolutions adopted by the conference are normally annexed. ... 97. The 1969 Convention on Special Missions and the 1973 Convention on the Prevention and Punishment of Crimes against Internationally Protected Persons, including Diplomatic Agents, were elaborated and adopted, on the basis of the respective draft articles submitted by the Commission, by the General Assembly itself. The draft articles on special missions, prepared by the Commission following the two-reading procedure, had been recommended by the Commission for conclusion of a convention. The draft articles on the prevention and punishment of crimes against diplomatic agents and other internationally protected persons had been provisionally adopted by the Commission and submitted to the General Assembly without any formal recommendations as to the conclusion of a convention on that basis. ... 99. The work of the elaboration of the two conventions was done by the Sixth Committee of the General Assembly, which studied in detail each of the provisions of the draft articles, amended them, prepared the preamble and final clauses of the conventions and, in the case of the articles on special missions, an Optional Protocol concerning the compulsory settlement of disputes arising out of the interpretation or application of the Convention. The Sixth Committee was assisted in both instances by a drafting committee [that] it had established. The General Assembly adopted by resolution the Conventions and the Optional Protocol relevant to the Convention on Special Missions, recommended by the Sixth Committee, and opened the Conventions and the Optional Protocol for signature and ratification or for accession. ... 101. This information shows that the techniques and procedures provided in the Statute of the Commission, as they have evolved during a period of three decades, are well adapted for the object stated in Article 1 of its Statute and further defined in Article 15, i.e., "the progressive development of international law and its codification." 102. Nevertheless, experience has shown that it is not normally feasible in any particular case to separate the elements of progressive development from those of codification, and the Commission, as a permanent body of legal experts, is well qualified to prepare draft conventions or articles in those cases in which elements of progressive development predominate as well as those in which elements of codification predominate. 103. The Commission, while constantly keeping under review its techniques and procedures and adapting them to meet the needs of circumstances as they arise, considers that, on the whole, its rate of progress is satisfactory, in view of the time and resources at its disposal and the assistance which it requires from Governments at all stages. 104. Institutional features which contribute to the efficient performance of its functions by the Commission are: (*a*) Special Rapporteurs, (*b*) the Drafting Committee, and (*c*) Working Groups. (*a*) The institution of Special Rapporteurs was foreseen in the Statute of the Commission. They have served the Commission well, but it will be necessary to provide them with more assistance and more facilities to enable them to perform their duties in the future. (*b*) The Drafting Committee, which has a somewhat wider mandate than a normal drafting committee, is an indispensable and very effective organ of the Commission. (*c*) For preliminary examination of the scope of new topics and for special topics assigned to the Commission by the General Assembly, Working Groups created *ad hoc* have also proved to be valuable. 105. It is essential not only that the Commission should produce drafts of a high technical quality but also that these drafts should reflect the comments and observations of Governments ... . The established procedures do, in fact, provide such opportunities for Governments to make comments and observations and for the Commission to examine them. It may, however, well become necessary for the Commission to make more use of questionnaires addressed to Governments than it has done in the past. 106. ... [T]here is a risk that the rate of progress of the Commission may be impeded by its agenda becoming too congested, and it is for consideration whether topics selected for inclusion in the programme should, where appropriate, be specific rather than general." (International Law Commission (1979), Review of the Multilateral Treaty-Making Process (Paragraph 2 of General Assembly Resolution 32/48), Document A/CN 4/325, Report of the Working Group on review of the multilateral treaty-making process, *Yearbook of the International Law Commission*, 1979, Volume II, Part One, 183-212, 206-210; emphasis original). The Sixth Committee is the principal forum in the General Assembly for discussion of legal issues (final sentence of fn 256). The last sentence of the paragraph that

Effects of Armed Conflicts on Treaties

At its fifty-second session, in 2000, the ILC included the subject 'Effects of armed conflicts on treaties' for inclusion in its future schedule of work [383]. At its fifty-sixth session, in 2004, the ILC placed this topic in its scheme of work [383]. It appointed Sir Ian Brownlie as Special Rapporteur for this topic [383]. At its fifty-seventh and fifty-eighth sessions, in 2005 and 2006 respectively, the ILC considered the Special Rapporteur's first two reports, and a memorandum that the Secretariat of the UN had prepared[283] [383]. At its sixtieth session, in 2008, the ILC adopted, on first reading, a collection of eighteen draft articles regarding the effects of armed conflicts on treaties, along with an annex and commentaries thereon [383]. It transmitted these articles, via the Secretary-General of the UN, to governments for observations and comments – to be submitted to the Secretary-General by 1st January 2010 [383]. After Sir Ian Brownlie resigned from the ILC, it appointed Dr. Lucius Caflisch as Special Rapporteur for the theme 'Effects of armed conflicts on treaties,' at its sixty-first session, in 2009 [383]. At its sixty-second session, in 2010, the ILC had before it the first report of the new Special Rapporteur – which contained his proposals for the reformulation of the draft articles that it had adopted on first reading, taking into account the observations and comments presented by governments [383]. The ILC also had in front of it a compilation of those observations and comments [383]. It referred draft articles 1 to 17 to a drafting committee [383]. At its sixty-third session, in 2011, the ILC completed the second reading of the draft articles, which it adopted together with an annex and commentaries thereon[284] [383].

---

includes the text to fn 228 sets out Article 1 of the Statute of the ILC – which lays down the object of the ILC; the text to fn 485 repeats that statement. The text to fn 486 specifies the definitions of the terms 'progressive development of international law' and 'codification of international law' – which Article 15 of the Statute of the ILC contains.

[283] At its fifty-seventh session, the ILC endorsed the Special Rapporteur's suggestion that the Secretariat circulate a memorandum to governments requesting information concerning their practice regarding this subject, especially their present-day habit (International Law Commission (2023), "Summaries of the Work of the International Law Commission: Effects of armed conflicts on treaties," last updated November 6, 2023, accessed September 6, 2024, <https://legal.un.org/ilc/summaries/1_10.shtml>).

[284] The draft articles are as follows: 1."The present draft articles apply to the effects of armed conflict on the relations of States under a treaty." 2."For the purpose of the present draft articles: (*a*) "treaty" means an international agreement concluded between States in written form and governed by international law, whether embodied in a single instrument or in two or more related instruments and whatever its particular designation, and includes treaties between States to which international organizations are also parties; (*b*) "armed conflict" means a situation in which there is resort to armed force between States or protracted resort to armed force between governmental authorities and organized armed groups." 3."The existence of an armed conflict does not *ipso facto* terminate or suspend the operation of treaties: (*a*) as between States parties to the conflict; (*b*) as between a State party to the conflict and a State that is not." 4."Where a treaty itself contains provisions on its operation in situations of armed conflict, those provisions shall apply." 5."The rules of international law on treaty interpretation shall be applied to establish whether a treaty is susceptible to termination, withdrawal or suspension in the event of an armed conflict." 6."In order to ascertain whether a treaty is susceptible to termination, withdrawal or suspension in the event of an armed conflict, regard shall be had to all relevant factors, including: (*a*) the nature of the treaty, in particular its subject matter, its object and purpose, its content and the number of parties to the treaty; and (*b*) the characteristics of the armed conflict, such as its territorial extent, its scale and intensity, its duration and, in the case of a non-international armed conflict, also the degree of outside involvement." 7."An indicative list of treaties the subject matter of which involves an implication that they continue in operation, in whole or in part, during armed conflict, is to be found in the annex to the present draft articles." 8."1. The existence of an armed conflict does not affect the capacity of a State party to that conflict to conclude treaties in accordance with international law. 2. States may conclude agreements involving termination or suspension of a treaty or part of a treaty that is operative between them during situations of armed conflict, or may agree to amend or modify the treaty." 9."1. A State intending to terminate or withdraw from a treaty to which it is a party, or to suspend the operation of that treaty, as a consequence of an armed conflict[,] shall notify the other State party or States parties to the treaty, of such intention. 2. The notification takes effect upon receipt by the other State party or States parties, unless it provides for a subsequent date. 3. Nothing in the

preceding paragraph shall affect the right of a party to object within a reasonable time, in accordance with the terms of the treaty or other applicable rules of international law, to the termination of or withdrawal from the treaty, or suspension of its operation. 4. If an objection has been raised in accordance with paragraph 3, [then] the States concerned shall seek a solution through the means indicated in Article 33 of the Charter of the United Nations. 5. Nothing in the preceding paragraph shall affect the rights or obligations of States with regard to the settlement of disputes insofar as they have remained applicable." 10."The termination of or the withdrawal from a treaty, or the suspension of its operation, as a consequence of an armed conflict, shall not impair in any way the duty of any State to fulfil any obligation embodied in the treaty to which it would be subject under international law independently of that treaty." 11."Termination, withdrawal from or suspension of the operation of a treaty as a consequence of an armed conflict shall, unless the treaty provides otherwise or the parties otherwise agree, take effect with respect to the whole treaty[,] except where: (*a*) the treaty contains clauses that are separable from the remainder of the treaty with regard to their application; (*b*) it appears from the treaty or is otherwise established that acceptance of those clauses was not an essential basis of the consent of the other Party or Parties to be bound by the treaty as a whole; and (*c*) continued performance of the remainder of the treaty would not be unjust." 12."A State may no longer terminate or withdraw from a treaty or suspend its operation as a consequence of an armed conflict if, after becoming aware of the facts: (*a*) it shall have expressly agreed that the treaty remains in force or continues in operation; or (*b*) it must by reason of its conduct be considered as having acquiesced in the continued operation of the treaty or in its maintenance in force." 13."1. Subsequent to an armed conflict, the States parties may regulate, on the basis of agreement, the revival of treaties terminated or suspended as a consequence of the armed conflict. 2. The resumption of the operation of a treaty suspended as a consequence of an armed conflict shall be determined in accordance with the factors referred to in article 6." 14."A State exercising its inherent right of individual or collective self-defence in accordance with the Charter of the United Nations is entitled to suspend[,] in whole or in part[,] the operation of a treaty to which it is a party insofar as that operation is incompatible with the exercise of that right." 15."A State committing aggression within the meaning of the Charter of the United Nations and resolution 3314 (XXIX) of the General Assembly of the United Nations shall not terminate or withdraw from a treaty or suspend its operation as a consequence of an armed conflict that results from the act of aggression[,] if the effect would be to the benefit of that State." 16."The present draft articles are without prejudice to relevant decisions taken by the Security Council in accordance with the Charter of the United Nations." 17."The present draft articles are without prejudice to the rights and duties of States arising from the laws of neutrality." 18."The present draft articles are without prejudice to the termination, withdrawal or suspension of treaties as a consequence of, *inter alia*: (*a*) a material breach; (*b*) supervening impossibility of performance; or (*c*) a fundamental change of circumstances." (International Law Commission (2011), Report of the International Law Commission on the work of its sixty-third session (26 April – 3 June and 4 July – 12 August 2011), Document A/66/10, Chapter VI. Effects of armed conflicts on treaties, E.1. Text of the draft articles, *Yearbook of the International Law Commission*, 2011, Volume II, Part Two, 107-108; emphasis original). The first and second sentences of the paragraph headed 'VI: Pacific Settlement of Disputes', in the subsection entitled 'The UN Charter' in the section titled 'The United Nations' in Chapter 3, set out paragraph 1 and 2, respectively, of Article 33 of the UN Charter. The UN Charter mentions the word 'aggression' four times – in the title of Chapter VII and in Articles 1(1), 39 and 53(1), but does not define it. In Resolution 3314 (XXIX) of 14th December 1974, the General Assembly approves and adopts the definition of the word 'aggression' that is laid down in its annex, the first three articles of which are as follows: "*Article 1* Aggression is the use of armed force by a State against the sovereignty, territorial sovereignty, territorial integrity or political independence of another State, or in any manner inconsistent with the Charter of the United Nations, as set out in this Definition. ... *Article 2* The first use of armed force by a State in contravention of the [UN] Charter shall constitute *prima facie* evidence of an act of aggression[,] although the Security Council may, in conformity with the Charter, conclude that a determination that an act of aggression has been committed would not be justified in the light of other relevant circumstances, including the fact that the acts concerned or their consequences are not of sufficient gravity. *Article 3* Any of the following acts, regardless of a declaration of war, shall, subject to and in accordance with the provisions of article 2, qualify as an act of aggression: (*a*) The invasion or attack by the armed forces of a State of the territory of another State, or any military occupation, however temporary, resulting from such invasion or attack, or any annexation by the use of force of the territory of another State or part thereof; (*b*) Bombardment by the armed forces of a State against the territory of another State or the use of any weapons by a State against the territory of another State; (*c*) The blockade of the ports or coasts of a State by the armed forces of another State; (*d*) An attack by the armed forces of a State on the land, sea or air forces, or marine and air fleets of another State; (*e*) The use of armed forces of one State which are within the territory of another State with the agreement of the receiving State, in contravention of the conditions provided for in the agreement[,] or any extension of their presence in such territory beyond the termination of the agreement; (*f*) The action of a State in allowing its territory, which it has placed at the disposal of another State, to be used by that other State for perpetrating an act of aggression against a third State; (*g*) The sending by or on behalf of a State of armed bands, groups, irregulars or mercenaries, which carry out acts of armed force against another State of such gravity as to amount to the acts listed above, or its

In Resolution 66/99 of 9th December 2011[285], the UN General Assembly took note of the abovementioned articles, and recommended them to governments for attention [383]. In Resolution 72/121 of 7th December 2017[286], the General Assembly invited states to use these articles as a reference – as appropriate [383].

Subsequent Agreements and Subsequent Practice in Relation to Interpretation of Treaties

At its sixtieth session, in 2008, the ILC identified the subject 'Treaties over time' to be included in both its long-term and its current programmes of work [384]. At its sixty-first session, in 2009, the ILC established a study group to be chaired by Dr. Georg Nolte [384] (now Judge Nolte, Member of the ICJ [385]). The study group agreed that work should commence on subsequent agreements and practice regarding treaties on the basis of consecutive reports which Dr. Nolte provides for his study group's consideration – and that approaching this theme from a wider perspective should be investigated further, that Dr. Nolte should prepare his first report for 2010 on subsequent agreements and practice concerning treaties in the jurisprudence of the ICJ and other international courts and jurisdictions, that contributions on this topic were to be encouraged by other members of the study group, and that such members, if interested, might supply contributions on matters that come within the aforementioned wider view of the subject [384]. At the ILC's sixty-second session, in 2010, the study group started its work on aspects of the theme on the basis of an introductory report prepared by Dr. Nolte on the pertinent jurisprudence of the ICJ and arbitral tribunals [384]. At the ILC's sixty-third session, in 2011, the study group first finished its consideration of Dr. Nolte's introductory report by addressing the issues of possible adjustments to a treaty by subsequent agreements and practice and the relation of these to formal procedures of treaty amendment, as well as considering a working paper on evolutionary interpretation [384]. Then, the study group started its examination of Dr. Nolte's second report, which attended to the jurisprudence under special regimes concerning subsequent agreements and practice regarding treaties [384]. At its sixty-fourth session, in 2012, the ILC decided to alter the format of the work on this subject and to change its title – as recommended by the study group – from 'Treaties over time' to 'Subsequent agreements and subsequent practice in relation to interpretation of treaties,' and to appoint Dr. Nolte as Special Rapporteur for the topic [384]. After examining four consecutive reports from the Special Rapporteur proposing draft conclusions that were referred to a drafting committee, the ILC considered the report of that committee, and adopted, on first reading, a set of thirteen draft

---

substantial involvement therein." (United Nations (1974), Resolution 3314 (XXIX) adopted by the General Assembly on 14th December 1974, Operative Paragraph, and Annex, Articles 1-3; emphasis original). The term '*inter alia*' is from Latin; it means "among other things" (Pearsall, J. (editor) (1998), *The New Oxford Dictionary of English* (Oxford: Oxford University Press), 950).

285 Its Operative Paragraph 3 states: "*The General Assembly*, ... 3. *Takes note* of the articles on the effects of armed conflicts on treaties, presented by the International Law Commission, the text of which is annexed to the present resolution, and commends them to the attention of Governments without prejudice to the question of their future adoption or other appropriate action." (United Nations (2011), Resolution 66/99 adopted by the General Assembly on 9th December 2011, Operative Paragraph 3; emphasis original). Fn 277 lays down Operative Paragraph 4 of General Assembly Resolution 66/98 of 9th December 2011, which commends the ILC for completing its work on the draft articles on the effects of armed conflicts on treaties.

286 Its Operative Paragraph 2 declares: "*The General Assembly*, ... 2. *Emphasizes* the value of the articles on the effects of armed conflicts on treaties in providing guidance to States, and invites States to use the articles as a reference whenever appropriate;" (United Nations (2017), Resolution 72/121 adopted by the General Assembly on 7th December 2017, Operative Paragraph 2; emphasis original).

conclusions with commentaries thereon [384]. The ILC conveyed the draft conclusions, by way of the Secretary-General, to governments for observations and comments – to be submitted to the Secretary-General by 1st January 2018 [384]. At its seventieth session, in 2018, the ILC had the fifth report of the Special Rapporteur before it, in addition to observations and comments received from governments; it began the second reading of the draft conclusions on subsequent agreements and subsequent practice in relation to interpretation of treaties, and subsequently adopted, on second reading, a set of thirteen draft conclusions and commentaries thereon regarding this topic [384]. These conclusions[287] refer to Articles 31 and 32 of the Vienna Convention on the Law of Treaties 1969, which are reproduced here.

---

[287] The draft conclusions are as follows: 1."The present draft conclusions concern the role of subsequent agreements and subsequent practice in the interpretation of treaties." 2."1. Articles 31 and 32 of the Vienna Convention on the Law of Treaties set forth, respectively, the general rule of interpretation and the recourse to supplementary means of interpretation. These rules also apply as customary international law. 2. A treaty shall be interpreted in good faith in accordance with the ordinary meaning to be given to its terms in their context and in the light of its object and purpose, as provided in article 31, paragraph 1 [of the Vienna Convention on the Law of Treaties]. 3. Article 31, paragraph 3 [of the Vienna Convention on the Law of Treaties], provides, *inter alia*, that there shall be taken into account, together with the context, (*a*) any subsequent agreement between the parties regarding the interpretation of the treaty or the application of its provisions; and (*b*) any subsequent practice in the application of the treaty which establishes the agreement of the parties regarding its interpretation. 4. Recourse may be had to other subsequent practice in the application of the treaty as a supplementary means of interpretation under article 32 [of the Vienna Convention on the Law of Treaties]. 5. The interpretation of a treaty consists of a single combined operation, which places appropriate emphasis on the various means of interpretation indicated, respectively, in articles 31 and 32 [of the Vienna Convention on the Law of Treaties]." 3."Subsequent agreements and subsequent practice under article 31, [sub]paragraph[s] 3(*a*) and (*b*) [of the Vienna Convention on the Law of Treaties], being objective evidence of the understanding of the parties as to the meaning of the treaty, are authentic means of interpretation, in the application of the general rule of treaty interpretation reflected in article 31 [of the Vienna Convention on the Law of Treaties]." 4."1. A subsequent agreement as an authentic means of interpretation under article 31, [sub]paragraph 3(*a*) [of the Vienna Convention on the Law of Treaties], is an agreement between the parties, reached after the conclusion of a treaty, regarding the interpretation of the treaty or the application of its provisions. 2. A subsequent practice as an authentic means of interpretation under article 31, [sub]paragraph 3(*b*) [of the Vienna Convention on the Law of Treaties], consists of conduct in the application of a treaty, after its conclusion, which establishes the agreement of the parties regarding the interpretation of the treaty. 3. A subsequent practice as a supplementary means of interpretation under article 32 [of the Vienna Convention on the Law of Treaties] consists of conduct by one or more parties in the application of the treaty, after its conclusion." 5."1. Subsequent practice under articles 31 and 32 [of the Vienna Convention on the Law of Treaties] may consist of any conduct of a party in the application of a treaty, whether in the exercise of its executive, legislative, judicial or other functions. 2. Other conduct, including by non-State actors, does not constitute subsequent practice under articles 31 and 32 [of the Vienna Convention on the Law of Treaties]. Such conduct may, however, be relevant when assessing the subsequent practice of parties to a treaty." 6."1. The identification of subsequent agreements and subsequent practice under article 31, paragraph 3 [of the Vienna Convention on the Law of Treaties], requires, in particular, a determination whether the parties, by an agreement or a practice, have taken a position regarding the interpretation of the treaty. Such a position is not taken if the parties have merely agreed not to apply the treaty temporarily or agreed to establish a practical arrangement (*modus vivendi*). 2. Subsequent agreements and subsequent practice under article 31, paragraph 3 [of the Vienna Convention on the Law of Treaties], may take a variety of forms. 3. The identification of a subsequent practice under article 32 [of the Vienna Convention on the Law of Treaties] requires, in particular, a determination whether conduct by one or more parties is in the application of the treaty." 7."1. Subsequent agreements and subsequent practice under article 31, paragraph 3 [of the Vienna Convention of the Law of Treaties], contribute, in their interaction with other means of interpretation, to the clarification of the meaning of a treaty. This may result in narrowing, widening, or otherwise determining the range of possible interpretations, including any scope for the exercise of discretion which the treaty accords to the parties. 2. Subsequent practice under article 32 [of the Vienna Convention on the Law of Treaties] may also contribute to the clarification of the meaning of a treaty. 3. It is presumed that the parties to a treaty, by an agreement or a practice in the application of the treaty, intend to interpret the treaty, not to amend or to modify it. The possibility of amending or modifying a treaty by subsequent practice of the parties has not been generally recognized. The present draft conclusion is without prejudice to the rules on the amendment or modification of treaties under the Vienna Convention on the Law of Treaties and under customary international law." 8."Subsequent agreements and subsequent practice under articles 31 and 32 [of the Vienna

PART III. OBSERVANCE, APPLICATION AND INTERPRETATION OF TREATIES[288]

SECTION 3. INTERPRETATION OF TREATIES

Convention on the Law of Treaties] may assist in determining whether or not the presumed intention of the parties upon the conclusion of the treaty was to give a term used a meaning which is capable of evolving over time." 9."1. The weight of a subsequent agreement or subsequent practice as a means of interpretation under article 31, paragraph 3 [of the Vienna Convention on the Law of Treaties], depends, *inter alia*, on its clarity and specificity. 2. In addition, the weight of subsequent practice under article 31, [sub]paragraph 3(*b*), depends, *inter alia*, on whether and how it is repeated. 3. The weight of subsequent practice as a supplementary means of interpretation under article 32 [of the Vienna Convention on the Law of Treaties] may depend on the criteria referred to in paragraphs 1 and 2." 10."1. An agreement under article 31, [sub]paragraph[s] 3(*a*) and (*b*) [of the Vienna Convention on the Law of Treaties], requires a common understanding regarding the interpretation of a treaty which the parties are aware of and accept. Such an agreement may, but need not, be legally binding for it to be taken into account. 2. The number of parties that must actively engage in subsequent practice in order to establish an agreement under article 31, [sub]paragraph 3(*b*), may vary. Silence on the part of one or more parties may constitute acceptance of the subsequent practice when the circumstances call for some reaction." 11."1. A Conference of States Parties, under these draft conclusions, is a meeting of parties to a treaty for the purpose of reviewing or implementing the treaty, except where they act as members of an organ of an international organization. 2. The legal effect of a decision adopted within the framework of a Conference of States Parties depends primarily on the treaty and any applicable rules of procedure. Depending on the circumstances, such a decision may embody, explicitly or implicitly, a subsequent agreement under article 31, [sub]paragraph 3(*a*) [of the Vienna Convention on the Law of Treaties], or give rise to subsequent practice under article 31, [sub]paragraph 3(*b*) [of the Vienna Convention on the Law of Treaties], or to subsequent practice under article 32 [of the Vienna Convention on the Law of Treaties]. Decisions adopted within the framework of a Conference of States Parties often provide a non-exclusive range of practical options for implementing the treaty. 3. A decision adopted within the framework of a Conference of States Parties embodies a subsequent agreement or subsequent practice under article 31, paragraph 3 [of the Vienna Convention on the Law of Treaties], insofar as it expresses agreement in substance between the parties regarding the interpretation of a treaty, regardless of the form and the procedure by which the decision was adopted, including adoption by consensus." 12."1. Articles 31 and 32 [of the Vienna Convention on the Law of Treaties] apply to a treaty which is the constituent instrument of an international organization. Accordingly, subsequent agreements and subsequent practice under article 31, paragraph 3 [of the Vienna Convention on the Law of Treaties], are, and subsequent practice under article 32 [of the Vienna Convention on the Law of Treaties] may be, means of interpretation for such treaties. 2. Subsequent agreements and subsequent practice of the parties under article 31, paragraph 3 [of the Vienna Convention on the Law of Treaties], or subsequent practice under article 32 [of the Vienna Convention on the Law of Treaties], may arise from, or be expressed in, the practice of an international organization in the application of its constituent instrument. 3. Practice of an international organization in the application of its constituent instrument may contribute to the interpretation of that instrument when applying articles 31 and 32 [of the Vienna Convention on the Law of Treaties]. 4. Paragraphs 1 to 3 apply to the interpretation of any treaty which is the constituent instrument of an international organization[,] without prejudice to any relevant rules of the organization." 13."1. For the purposes of these draft conclusions, an expert treaty body is a body consisting of experts serving in their personal capacity, which is established under a treaty and is not an organ of an international organization. 2. The relevance of a pronouncement of an expert treaty body for the interpretation of a treaty is subject to the applicable rules of the treaty. 3. A pronouncement of an expert treaty body may give rise to, or refer to, a subsequent agreement or subsequent practice by parties under article 31, paragraph 3 [of the Vienna Convention on the Law of Treaties], or subsequent practice under article 32 [of the Vienna Convention on the Law of Treaties]. Silence by a party shall not be presumed to constitute subsequent practice under article 31, [sub]paragraph 3(*b*) [of the Vienna Convention on the Law of Treaties], accepting an interpretation of a treaty as expressed in a pronouncement of an expert treaty body. 4. This draft conclusion is without prejudice to the contribution that pronouncements of expert treaty bodies make to the interpretation of the treaties under their mandates."(International Law Commission (2018), Report of the International Law Commission on the work of its seventieth session (30 April – 1 June and 2 July – 10 August 2018), Document A/73/10, Chapter IV. Subsequent agreements and subsequent practice in relation to the interpretation of treaties, E.1. Text of the draft conclusions, *Yearbook of the International Law Commission*, 2018, Volume II, Part Two, 24-25; emphasis original). The final sentence of fn 284 defines the term '*inter alia*'.

[288] All capitalized and italicized words, letters and numbers in this quoted passage are in the original document.

Article 31. GENERAL RULE OF INTERPRETATION

1. A treaty shall be interpreted in good faith in accordance with the ordinary meaning to be given to the terms of the treaty in their context and in the light of its object and purpose.
2. The context for the purpose of the interpretation of a treaty shall comprise, in addition to the text, including its preamble and annexes:
   (*a*) Any agreement relating to the treaty which was made between all the parties in connexion with the conclusion of the treaty;
   (*b*) Any instrument which was made by one or more parties in connexion with the conclusion of the treaty and accepted by the other parties as an instrument related to the treaty.
3. There shall be taken into account, together with the context:
   (*a*) Any subsequent agreement between the parties regarding the interpretation of the treaty or the application of its provisions;
   (*b*) Any subsequent practice in the application of the treaty which establishes the agreement of the parties regarding its interpretation;
   (*c*) Any relevant rules of international law applicable in the relations between the parties.
4. A special meaning shall be given to a term if it is established that the parties so intended.

Article 32. SUPPLEMENTARY MEANS OF INTERPRETATION

Recourse may be had to supplementary means of interpretation, including the preparatory work of the treaty and the circumstances of its conclusion, in order to confirm the meaning resulting from the application of article 31, or to determine the meaning when the interpretation according to article 31:

(*a*) Leaves the meaning ambiguous or obscure; or
(*b*) Leads to a result which is manifestly absurd or unreasonable [386].

In Resolution 73/202 of 20th December 2018[289], the UN General Assembly took note of these conclusions on subsequent agreements and subsequent practice in relation to the interpretation of treaties, brought them to the notice of states and of all who might be asked to interpret treaties, and encouraged their broadest possible diffusion [384].

Provisional Application of Treaties

At its sixty-third session, in 2011, the ILC included the subject 'Provisional application of treaties' in its future programme of work [386]. At its sixty-fourth session, in 2013, the ILC placed this topic in its current scheme of work, appointing Mr[290]. Juan Manuel Gómez-Robledo

[289] Its Operative Paragraph 4 declares: "*The General Assembly*, ... 4. *Also takes note* of the conclusions on subsequent agreements and subsequent practice in relation to the interpretation of treaties, the text of which is annexed to the present resolution, with the commentaries thereto, brings them to the attention of States and all who may be called upon to interpret treaties, and encourages their widest possible dissemination." (United Nations (2018), Resolution 73/202 adopted by the General Assembly on 20th December 2018, Operative Paragraph 4; emphasis original)

[290] Judge Gómez-Robledo has held a Doctor of Philosophy degree in International Law from Universidad Nacional Autónoma de México since 2018 (United Nations (2022), United Nations Audiovisual Library of International Law: Mr. Juan Manuel Gómez-Robledo (New York: United Nations), 1-2, 1).

(now Judge Gómez-Robledo, Member of the ICJ [387]) as Special Rapporteur [386]. After considering four of the Special Rapporteur's reports, the ILC, at its seventieth session, in 2018, instructed the Drafting Committee to conclude the first reading of all the draft guidelines on the provisional application of treaties [386]. On the basis of the Drafting Committee's report, the ILC adopted the whole set of draft guidelines on provisional application of treaties – with commentaries – as the draft Guide to Provisional Application of Treaties, on first reading [386]. The ILC transmitted the draft guidelines, via the Secretary-General, to governments and international organizations for observations and comments – requesting that these be communicated to him by 15th December 2019 [386]. At its seventy-first session, in 2019, the Special Rapporteur spoke on informal consultations held on 10th and 18th July 2019 to review his draft model clauses on provisional application of treaties [386]. The ILC noted Dr. Gómez-Robledo's verbal account and decided to annex the proposed draft model clauses to its report to the UN General Assembly – with the aim of seeking comments from governments before the second reading of the draft Guide to Provisional Application of Treaties [386]. At its seventy-second session, in 2021, the ILC examined the sixth report of the Special Rapporteur, together with observations and comments received from governments and international organizations [386]. In his sixth report, Dr. Gómez-Robledo evaluated the observations and comments received from governments and international organizations on the draft Guide to Provisional Application of Treaties and on several of the proposed draft model clauses [386]. He made proposals to be considered on second reading of the draft Guide, taking into account the debate at the ILC [386]. At that session, the ILC adopted, on second reading, the Guide to Provisional Application of Treaties, including the draft guidelines[291] and a draft annex that

[291] The draft guidelines are as follows: 1."The present draft guidelines concern the provisional application of treaties by States or by international organizations." 2."The purpose of the present draft guidelines is to provide guidance regarding the law and practice on the provisional application of treaties, on the basis of article 25 of the Vienna Convention on the Law of Treaties and other relevant rules of international law." 3."A treaty or a part of a treaty is applied provisionally pending its entry into force between the States or international organizations concerned, if the treaty itself so provides, or if in some other manner it has been so agreed." 4."In addition to the case where the treaty so provides, the provisional application of a treaty or a part of a treaty may be agreed between the States or international organizations concerned[,] through: (a) a separate treaty; or (b) any other means or arrangements, including: (i) a resolution, decision or other act adopted by an international organization or at an intergovernmental conference, in accordance with the rules of such organization or conference, reflecting the agreement of the States or international organizations concerned; (ii) a declaration by a State or by an international organization that is accepted by the other States or international organizations concerned." 5."The provisional application of a treaty or a part of a treaty takes effect on such date, and in accordance with such conditions and procedures, as the treaty provides or as is otherwise agreed." 6."The provisional application of a treaty or a part of a treaty produces a legally binding obligation to apply the treaty or a part thereof between the States or international organizations concerned, except to the extent that the treaty otherwise provides or it is otherwise agreed. Such treaty or part of a treaty that is being applied provisionally must be performed in good faith." 7."The present draft guidelines are without prejudice to any question concerning reservations relating to the provisional application of a treaty or part of a treaty." 8."The breach of an obligation arising under a treaty or a part of a treaty that is applied provisionally entails international responsibility in accordance with the applicable rules of international law." 9."1. The provisional application of a treaty or a part of a treaty terminates with the entry into force of that treaty in the relations between the States or international organizations concerned. 2. Unless the treaty otherwise provides or it is otherwise agreed, the provisional application of a treaty or part of a treaty with respect to a State or an international organization shall be terminated if that State or international organization notifies the other States or international organizations concerned of its intention not to become a party to the treaty. 3. Unless the treaty otherwise provides or it is otherwise agreed, a State or an international organization may invoke other grounds for terminating provisional application, in which case it shall notify the other States or international organizations concerned. 4. Unless the treaty otherwise provides or it is otherwise agreed, the termination of the provisional application of a treaty or a part of a treaty does not affect any right, obligation or legal situation created through the execution of such provisional application prior to its termination." 10."1. A State that has agreed to the provisional application of a treaty or a part of a treaty

contained examples of clauses on provisional application [386]. Guideline 2 refers to Article 25 of the Vienna Convention on the Law of Treaties 1969, which is replicated below.

PART II. CONCLUSION AND ENTRY INTO FORCE OF TREATIES[292]

SECTION 3. ENTRY INTO FORCE AND PROVISIONAL APPLICATION OF TREATIES

Article 25. PROVISIONAL APPLICATION

1. A treaty or a part of a treaty is applied provisionally pending its entry into force[,] if:
   (*a*) The treaty itself so provides; or
   (*b*) The negotiating States have in some other manner so agreed.
2. Unless the treaty otherwise provides or the negotiating States have otherwise agreed, the provisional application of a treaty or part of a treaty with respect to a State shall be terminated if that State notifies the other States between which the treaty is being applied provisionally of its intention not to become a party to the treaty.

In Resolution 76/113 of 9th December 2021[293], the UN General Assembly noted the Guide to Provisional Application of Treaties, brought it to the notice of states and international organizations, and encouraged its broadest possible circulation [386].

Succession of States in Respect of Treaties

The ILC considered this theme at its twentieth, twenty-second, twenty-fourth and twenty-sixth sessions, in 1968, 1970, 1972 and 1974, respectively [388]. It appointed Sir Humphrey

may not invoke the provisions of its internal law as justification for its failure to perform an obligation arising under such provisional application. 2. An international organization that has agreed to the provisional application of a treaty or a part of a treaty may not invoke the rules of the organization as justification for its failure to perform an obligation arising under such provisional application." 11."1. A State may not invoke the fact that its consent to the provisional application of a treaty or a part of a treaty has been expressed in violation of a provision of its internal law regarding competence to agree to the provisional application of treaties as invalidating its consent[,] unless that violation was manifest and concerned a rule of its internal law of fundamental importance. 2. An international organization may not invoke the fact that its consent to the provisional application of a treaty or a part of a treaty has been expressed in violation of the rules of the organization regarding competence to agree to the provisional application of treaties as invalidating its consent[,] unless that violation was manifest and concerned a rule of fundamental importance." 12."The present draft guidelines are without prejudice to the right of States or international organizations to agree in the treaty itself or otherwise to the provisional application of the treaty or a part of the treaty with limitations deriving from the internal law of States or from the rules of international organizations." (United Nations (2021), Report of the International Law Commission: Seventy-second session (26 April – 4 June and 5 July – 6 August 2021), Document A/76/10, Chapter V. Provisional application of treaties, E.1. Text of the draft guidelines and the draft annex constituting the Guide to Provisional Application of Treaties, General Assembly Official Records, Seventy-sixth session, Supplement No.10 (A/76/10), 54-55).

292 All capitalized and italicized words, letters and numbers in this quoted passage are in the original document.

293 Its Recital 1, and its Operative Paragraphs 1 and 4, read: "*The General Assembly*, *Having considered* chapter V of the report of the International Law Commission on the work of its seventy-second session, which contains the Guide to Provisional Application of Treaties, ... 1. *Welcomes* the conclusion of the work of the International Law Commission on the provisional application of treaties, and its adoption of the draft guidelines and draft annex constituting the Guide to Provisional Application of Treaties, and the commentaries thereto; ... 4. *Also takes note* of the Guide to Provisional Application of Treaties, including the guidelines, the text of which is annexed to the present resolution, brings the Guide to the attention of States and international organizations for their consideration, and encourages its widest possible dissemination; ... ." (United Nations (2021), Resolution 76/113 adopted by the General Assembly on 9th December 2021, Recital 1, and Operative Paragraphs 1 and 4; emphasis original).

Waldock and Sir Francis Vallat as its successive Special Rapporteurs at its nineteenth and twenty-fifth sessions, in 1967 and 1973, respectively [388]. At its twenty-fourth session, in 1972, the ILC adopted on first reading the provisional draft articles on succession of States and decided to communicate it to governments of Member States of the UN for their observations [388]. In Resolution 2926 (XXVII) of 28th November 1972[294], the UN General Assembly advised the ILC to continue its work on this subject, in view of comments received from Member States [388]. In Resolution 3071 (XXVIII) of 30th November 1973[295], the General Assembly advocated that the ILC complete the second reading of the draft articles on succession of States in respect of treaties at its twenty-sixth session, in 1974, given comments received from Member States [388]. At that session, the ILC adopted the final text of the draft articles on the succession of States in respect of treaties, together with commentaries, and submitted it to the General Assembly, with a recommendation that the latter invite Member States to advance their observations and comments on these articles and convene a conference of plenipotentiaries to examine the draft articles and negotiate a convention on this topic – which it duly did[296] [388]. The United Nations Conference on Succession of States in Respect of Treaties was scheduled for 4th April 1977 to 6th May 1977 in Vienna, and took place as planned [388]. As the work was not complete, the General Assembly approved a resumption of the United Nations Conference on Succession of States in Respect of Treaties in August 1978[297] [388]. The closing date of the event was 23rd August 1978 [388]. On 22nd August 1978, the Conference adopted the Vienna Convention on the Succession of States in respect of Treaties, which comprises a preamble, fifty articles and an annex – which specifies the conciliation procedure to which Article 42 of the Convention relates[298] [388]. The Vienna Convention on the Succession of States in respect of Treaties 1978 was open for signature from 23rd August 1978 until 31st August 1979, and remains open for accession by any state [388]. It entered into force on 6th November 1996 [388]. The Convention applies to effects of one state

[294] Its Recital 3 and Operative Subparagraph 3(b) state: "*The General Assembly*, ... *Welcoming* the draft articles prepared by the International Law Commission on succession of States in respect of treaties, ... 3. *Recommends* that the International Law Commission should: ... (*b*) Proceed with further consideration on succession of States in respect of treaties[,] in the light of comments received from Member States on the present draft; ... ." (United Nations (1972), Resolution 2926 (XXVII) adopted by the General Assembly on 28th November 1972, Recital 3, and Operative Subparagraph 3(b); emphasis original).

[295] Its Operative Subparagraph 3(a) declares: "*The General Assembly*, ... 3. *Recommends* that the International Law Commission should: (*a*) Complete at its twenty-sixth session, in the light of comments received from Member States, the second reading of the draft articles on succession of States in respect of treaties adopted at its twenty-fourth session;" (United Nations (1973), Resolution 3071 (XXVIII) adopted by the General Assembly on 30th November 1973, Operative Subparagraph 3(a); emphasis original).

[296] Operative Paragraph 3 of General Assembly Resolution 3496 (XXX) of 15th December 1975 notes: "*The General Assembly* ... 3. *Decides* to convene a conference of plenipotentiaries in 1977 to consider the draft articles on succession of States in respect of treaties and to embody the results of its work in an international convention and such other instruments as it may deem appropriate;" (United Nations 1975, Resolution 3496 (XXX) adopted by the General Assembly on 15th December 1975, Operative Paragraph 3; emphasis original).

[297] Operative Paragraph 2 of General Assembly Resolution 32/47 of 8th December 1977 reads: "*The General Assembly*, ... 2. *Approves* the convening of a resumed session of the United Nations Conference on Succession of States in Respect of Treaties at Vienna for a period of three weeks, from 31 July to 18 August 1978, with a possible extension of up to one further week should this prove necessary in the view of the Conference;" (United Nations (1977), Resolution 32/47 adopted by the General Assembly on 8th December 1977, Operative Paragraph 2; emphasis original).

[298] The Vienna Convention on the Succession of States in respect of Treaties retains, to a considerable extent, the structure and the text of the draft articles on succession of States in respect of treaties the ILC adopted in 1974 (International Law Commission (2023), "Summaries of the Work of the International Law Commission: Succession of States in respect of treaties," last updated June 30, 2023, accessed September 11, 2024, <https://legal.un.org/ilc/summaries/3_2.shtml>).

succeeding another with regard to treaties between states [389]. It does not apply to the effects of such succession with regard to international agreements made between states and other entities [390]. But it does apply to any treaty that is the constituent instrument of an international organization [391] – such as the Articles of Agreement of the International Bank for Reconstruction and Development, and to any treaty that is concluded within an international organization [392] – such as the Convention on the Abolition of Forced Labour 1957, which was adopted by the International Labour Organization. If a treaty states that, in event of a succession of states, a successor state is to be deemed a party to this treaty, then this clause only takes effect if the successor state accepts in writing to be thus considered [393]. While a succession of states does not affect obligations or rights concerning the use of a territory that are regarded as being attaching to it [394], this is not the case for treaty obligations of the predecessor state that provide for the construction of foreign military bases on the territory to which the succession of states applies [395]. If part of the territory of a state becomes part of another state's territory, then treaties of the predecessor state terminate regarding this territory on the date of the succession of states [396]; treaties of the successor state enter in force over the abovementioned territory from that date, unless it appears from any of these treaties or is otherwise proven that the application of this treaty would conflict with the object and purpose of it or would radically alter the conditions for its functioning [397]. A newly-independent state is not required to maintain in force, or become a party to, any treaty by reason solely of the fact that, at the date of the succession of states, the treaty was effective with regard to the territory to which this succession relates [398]. Subject to two exceptions[299], a newly-independent state may, by a notification of succession, establish its standing as a party to any multilateral treaty that, at the date of the succession of states, was effective in reference to the territory to which this succession relates [399]. Subject to the same two exceptions[300] [400], a newly-independent state may, by a notification of succession, establish its standing as a contracting state to a non-effective multilateral treaty or as a party to a multilateral treaty that comes into force after the date of the succession of states, if, at this date, the predecessor state was a contracting state with regard to the territory to which this succession relates [401]. Subject to those same two exceptions [402], if, prior to the date of succession of states, the predecessor state signed a multilateral treaty subject to ratification, acceptance or approval, and, by this signature, intended that the treaty should include the territory to which the succession of states relates, then the newly-independent state may ratify, accept or approve this treaty as if that state had signed it, and may thereby become a party or a contracting state to it[301] [403]. When making a notification of succession, a newly-independent state may, if the multilateral treaty so allows,

---

[299] This rule does not apply if it appears from a multilateral treaty or is elsewise established that this treaty's application with regard to the newly-independent state would be irreconcilable with the object and purpose of the treaty or would fundamentally change the conditions for its working (United Nations (1978), "Vienna Convention on the Succession of States in respect of Treaties," *United Nations Treaty Series* Registration Number 33356, Article 17(2)). If, under the treaty's terms or because of the object and purpose of the treaty and the limited number of the negotiating states, the participation of another state in the treaty must be deemed to require the consent of all the parties, then the newly-independent state may establish its standing to the treaty solely with this consent (United Nations (1978), "Vienna Convention on the Succession of States in respect of Treaties," Article 17(3)).

[300] Fn 299 comprises these two exceptions.

[301] Unless a different intention emerges from the treaty or is otherwise established, the signature by the predecessor state of a treaty is deemed to express the aim that the treaty should apply to the whole territory for the international relations of which the predecessor state was responsible (United Nations (1978), "Vienna Convention on the Succession of States in respect of Treaties," Article 19(2)).

convey its consent to be bound by part of the treaty, or choose between dissimilar provisions under the conditions set out in the treaty for expressing this consent or making that choice [404]; it may also exercise, under identical conditions to the other parties or contracting states, any right which the treaty provides to withdraw or amend any consent given or choice made by itself or the predecessor state regarding the territory to which the succession of states relates [405]. If the newly-independent state neither so conveys its consent nor withdraws or amends the consent or choice of the predecessor state, then it shall be deemed to be maintaining the consent of the latter state, in compliance with the multilateral treaty, to be bound – with regard to the territory to which the succession of states relates – by part of this treaty, or preserving the choice of that state, in accordance with the treaty, between dissimilar provisions in the application of the treaty with reference to the territory to which the succession of states relates [406]. A notification of succession concerning a multilateral treaty is to be made in writing [407]. There are separate rules for the succession of newly-independent states regarding bilateral treaties[302]. There are clauses on the provisional application of both multilateral[303] and bilateral[304] treaties to territory acquired by succession of newly-independent states, and for the cessation of this provisional application[305]. The rules that concern the succession of a newly-independent state which gains territory from a predecessor state also apply to the succession of a newly-independent state that is formed from two or more territories [408], but with additional specifications[306]. If two or more states unite to form one successor state, then any treaty which is effective at the date of the succession of states with regard to any of them continues in force in connection with the successor state, unless that state and the other state party or states parties to the treaty otherwise agree, or it appears from the treaty or is elsewise established that this treaty's application as regards the successor state would be at variance with its object and purpose or would completely alter the conditions for its functioning [409]; any treaty continuing in force applies solely with regard to the part of the successor state's territory in respect of which the treaty was effective at the date of the succession of states, unless, for a multilateral treaty, the successor state prepares a notification that the treaty will apply in respect of its whole territory[307] [410] – subject to one exception[308] in which case the successor state and the other states parties to the treaty must otherwise agree[309] [411]. If a part or parts of the territory of a

---

[302] Articles 24-26 of the Vienna Convention on the Succession of States in respect of Treaties 1978 sets out these rules.

[303] Article 27 of the Vienna Convention on the Succession of States in respect of Treaties 1978 contains clauses on the provisional application of multilateral treaties.

[304] Article 28 of the Vienna Convention on the Succession of States in respect of Treaties 1978 lays down a rule on the provisional application of bilateral treaties.

[305] Article 29 of the Vienna Convention on the Succession of States in respect of Treaties 1978 comprises clauses on the termination of provisional application for multilateral treaties, a clause on the cessation of provisional application for bilateral treaties, and a definition of 'reasonable notice of termination' made by the newly-independent state.

[306] Paragraphs 2 and 3 of Article 30 of the Vienna Convention on the Succession of States in respect of Treaties 1978 provide for a treaty to apply to the whole territory of the newly-independent state, subject to exceptions detailed therein.

[307] This notification does not apply if it appears from the treaty or is otherwise shown that the application of the treaty as regards the successor state's entire territory would not be compatible with the object and purpose of the treaty, or would radically change the conditions for its working (United Nations (1978), "Vienna Convention on the Succession of States in respect of Treaties," Article 31(3)).

[308] This is the exception that the second sentence of fn 299 sets out.

[309] For a bilateral treaty, the 'unless' clause only applies if the successor state and the other state party to the treaty elsewise agree (United Nations (1978), "Vienna Convention on the Succession of States in respect of Treaties," Article 31(2)(c)).

state separate to form at least one state – whether or not the predecessor state remains in existence, then any treaty that is effective at the date of the succession of states with regard to the entire territory of the predecessor state continues in force with reference to each successor state so created [412], and any treaty which is effective at the date of the succession of states with regard only to that part of the territory of the predecessor state which has become a successor state continues in force in respect of this successor state alone [413]; these rules do not apply if the states otherwise agree [414], or if it appears from the treaty or is elsewise established that the application of the treaty as regards the successor state would be irreconcilable with the object and purpose of the treaty or would fundamentally alter the conditions for its operation [415]. If, after separation of any part of the territory of a state, the predecessor state continues in existence, then any treaty which, at the date of succession of states, was effective in connection with the predecessor state continues in force with regard to its remaining territory, unless: (i) the relevant states otherwise agree [416], (ii) it is proven that the treaty only concerned the treaty which has separated from the predecessor state [417], or (iii) it appears from the treaty or is elsewise established that the application of the treaty as concerns the predecessor state would be contradictory to the object and purpose of the treaty or would radically permute the conditions for its functioning [418]. Any notification concerning the succession of states, in the case of a uniting or separation of states, is to be made in writing [419]. The ordering of settlement of disputes arising between at least two parties to the Vienna Convention on the Succession of States in respect of Treaties 1978, as to the Convention's interpretation or application, is: (i) consultation and negotiation [420], and, if the dispute in question is unresolved within six months of the referral for this, (ii) submission of the dispute by any disputant to the conciliation procedure that the Annex to the Convention provides [421], and, failing resolution of the dispute by this procedure, given prior notification by both disputants to the depositary at the time of signature or ratification of the Convention – or by common consent of the parties, (iii) submission of the dispute to the ICJ or to an arbitral tribunal [422].

Vienna Convention on the Law of Treaties (1969)

The Vienna Convention on the Law of Treaties (1969) applies to treaties which are concluded between states [423]. The Convention applies to any treaty that is the constituent instrument of an international organization – such as the Articles of Agreement of the International Bank for Reconstruction and Development, and to any treaty which is concluded within an international organization – such as the Convention on the Abolition of Forced Labour 1957, adopted by the International Labour Organization [424].

The adoption of the text of a treaty occurs through the consent of all the states partaking in its preparation, bar such adoption at an international conference – which takes place by means of the vote of two-thirds of the states that are represented and voting there, unless by a two-thirds majority vote they decide to apply another rule [425]. The text of a treaty is made authentic and definitive by such procedure as this text may provide or by agreement by the states participating in its formulation [426], or, failing this by the signature, initialling, or signature subject to agreement, by the representatives of these states, of the text of the treaty or the Final Act of a conference that incorporates the text [427].

The consent of a state to be bound by a treaty may be shown by signature, exchange of instruments which constitute a treaty, ratification, acceptance, approval or accession, or by any other method if so agreed [428]. The consent of a state to be bound by a treaty may be indicated by the signature of its representative, if the treaty provides that signature shall demonstrate this consent [429], if it is otherwise proven that the negotiating states were agreed that signature should have this effect [430], or if the aim of the state to give such effect to the signature appears from its representative's full powers or was conveyed during the negotiation [431]. The consent of states to be bound by a treaty which is constituted by instruments exchanged between them, is shown by this interchange, if the instruments specify that their exchange will have such effect [432], or if it is elsewise substantiated that those states were agreed that the exchange of instruments will have this outcome [433]. The consent of a state to be bound by a treaty is manifest by ratification, if the treaty provides for this authorization to be expressed by way of ratification [434], if it is otherwise verified that the negotiating states were agreed that ratification should be obligatory [435], if the state's representative has signed the treaty subject to ratification [436], or if its intention to sign the treaty subject to ratification appears from its representative's full powers or was indicated during the negotiation[310] [437]. The consent of a state to be bound by a treaty is intimated by accession, if the treaty specifies that this permission may be shown by the state by dint of accession [438], if it is elsewise established that the negotiating states were agreed that such consent may be evidenced by this state by means of accession [439], or if all parties have subsequently agreed that this authorization may be revealed by that state by way of accession [440].

Unless the treaty otherwise stipulates, instruments of ratification, acceptance, approval or accession signify the consent of a state to be bound by a treaty, upon their interchange between the contracting states, their placement with the depositary, or their notification to those states or to the depositary – if this is agreed [441]. Without prejudice to the provisions of the Vienna Convention on the Law of Treaties 1969 concerning reservations to treaties[311], the consent of a state to be bound by part of a treaty is effective solely if the treaty permits this or the other contracting states agree to it [442]. The assent of a state to be bound by a treaty that allows a choice between dissimilar provisions is effective only if it is clarified to which of these clauses this consent relates [443]. A state is obligated to refrain from taking actions that would defeat the object and purpose of a treaty, if it has signed the treaty – or exchanged instruments which constitute the treaty – subject to ratification, acceptance or approval, until it has made its intention clear to eschew becoming a party to the treaty [444], or if it has indicated its consent to be bound by the treaty pending the latter's entry into force – and as long as such entry is not inordinately delayed [445].

Every treaty in force is binding upon the parties to it, which must carry out the duties that it lays down in good faith [446]. A party to a treaty may not invoke the rules of its internal law as justification for its failure to perform obligations which this treaty imposes [447].

Unless a different objective appears from the treaty or is otherwise proven, its provisions do not bind a party in connection with any act or fact that took place or any situation which ended before the date of the entry into effect of the treaty regarding that party [448]. Except if

[310] The consent of a state to be bound by a treaty is proven by acceptance or approval, under conditions which are similar to those that apply to ratification (United Nations (1969), "Vienna Convention on the Law of Treaties," *United Nations Treaty Series* Registration Number 18232, Article 14(2)).

[311] These are Articles 19-23 of the Convention, which the text to fns 265-270 sets out.

an intention appears from the treaty or is elsewise demonstrated, a treaty is binding upon each party in respect of its whole territory [449].

Subject to Article 103 of the UN Charter[312], the rights and duties of states parties to successive treaties that concern the identical subject-matter shall be decided as follows [450]. If a treaty stipulates that it is subject to, or that is not to be deemed incompatible with, an earlier or a later treaty, then the provisions of that other treaty prevail [451]. If all the parties to an earlier treaty are also parties to a later treaty, but the earlier treaty is neither suspended or nor terminated under Article 59 of the Vienna Convention on the Law of Treaties 1969[313], then the earlier treaty applies solely to the degree that its provisions are consistent with those of the later treaty [452]. If one or more of the parties to the earlier treaty are not parties to the later treaty, then as between states parties to both treaties the rule in the immediately-preceding sentence applies [453], and as betwixt a state party to both treaties and a state party to merely one of the treaties, the treaty to which both states are parties regulates their mutual rights and obligations [454].

If a treaty has been authenticated in at least two languages, then the text is equally authoritative in each tongue, unless the treaty specifies, or the parties agree, that a particular text is to prevail [455]. In the absence of this priority, if a comparison of the authentic texts reveals a dissimilitude of meaning which the application of Articles 31 and 32 of the Vienna Convention on the Law of Treaties 1969 does not remove[314], then the meaning which best reconciles these texts – having regard to the treaty's object and purpose, is to be adopted [456].

A treaty creates neither rights nor obligations for a third state without its agreement [457]. A right arises for a third state from a clause of a treaty, if the parties to that treaty intend this provision to grant that right either to the third state, to a group of states of which it is one, or to all states, and the third state consents to this[315] [458]; a state which exercises such a right shall observe the conditions for its exercise[316] [459]. An obligation originates for a third state from a provision of a treaty, if the parties to that treaty intend this clause to be the means of instituting that obligation and the third party accepts it in writing[317] [460]. These rules do not preclude a rule which a treaty contains from becoming binding upon a third state as a recognized principle of customary international law [461].

Agreement between the parties is required for a treaty to be amended [462]. Unless a multilateral treaty otherwise provides, its amendment is determined as follows [463]. Any

---

[312] The sentence immediately preceding the text to fn 189 sets out Article 103 of the UN Charter.

[313] This article states: "1. A treaty shall be considered as terminated[,] if all the parties to it conclude a later treaty relating to the same subject-matter[,] and: (*a*) It appears from the later treaty or is otherwise established that the parties intended that the matter should be governed by that treaty; or (*b*) The provisions of the later treaty are so far incompatible with those of the earlier one that the two treaties are not capable of being applied at the same time. 2. The earlier treaty shall be considered as only suspended in operation[,] if it appears from the later treaty or is otherwise established that such was the intention of the parties." (United Nations (1969), "Vienna Convention on the Law of Treaties," Article 59; emphasis original).

[314] The quoted passage to which fn 288 is linked comprises Articles 31 and 32 of the Vienna Convention on the Law of Treaties 1969.

[315] This consent is presumed, as long as the opposite is not shown – unless the treaty otherwise stipulates (United Nations (1969), "Vienna Convention on the Law of Treaties," Article 39).

[316] The parties may neither modify nor revoke this right, if it is proven that the right was intended to be immutable or irrevocable without the third state's concurrence (United Nations (1969), "Vienna Convention on the Law of Treaties," Article 37(2)).

[317] The parties and the third state must assent to modification or revocation of this obligation, unless it is demonstrated that they had elsewise agreed (United Nations (1969), "Vienna Convention on the Law of Treaties," Article 37(1)).

proposal to amend a multilateral treaty as between every party to it must be notified to all its contracting states, each of which shall have the right to participate in the decision as to the action to be taken with respect to this proposal, and in the negotiation and conclusion of any agreement to amend the treaty [464]. Every state that is entitled to become a party to the treaty shall also be eligible to become a party to the amended treaty [465]. The amending agreement does not bind any state that is already a party to the treaty and which does not become a party to this amending agreement [466]; the pre-amended treaty governs its rights and obligations versus parties to both versions of the treaty [467]. Any state that becomes a party to the treaty after the entry into effect of the amending agreement shall – unless it manifests a different intention – be deemed a party to the treaty as amended and to the unamended treaty in connection with any party to the treaty which is not bound by the amending agreement [468]. Two or more parties to a multilateral treaty may make an agreement to modify this treaty as between themselves only, if the treaty provides for the possibility of this type of alteration [469][318], or if the modification is not proscribed by the treaty and neither affects the enjoyment by other parties of their rights or the performance of their obligations under the treaty nor concerns a provision derogation from which is irreconcilable with the effective implementation of the object and purpose of the treaty in general [470].

The validity of a treaty or the consent of a state to be bound by it may only be challenged by means of the application of the Vienna Convention on the Law of Treaties 1969 [471]. The suspension of a treaty's operation, the cessation of the treaty, its denunciation, or the withdrawal of a party, may occur solely as a consequence of the application of its provisions or of the clauses of the Vienna Convention on the Law of Treaties 1969 [472]. These outcomes shall not impair the duty of any state to carry out any obligation that a treaty contains to which that state would be subject under international law separately from the treaty [473].

A party's right, for which a treaty provides or arising in accordance with Article 56 of the Vienna Convention on the Law of Treaties 1969[319], to denounce, withdraw from, or suspend the treaty's functioning, may be exercised only with regard to the entire treaty, unless the treaty otherwise provides or the parties elsewise agree [474]. A ground for withdrawing from, suspending, invalidating or terminating a treaty's operation that is recognized by the Vienna Convention on the Law of Treaties 1969, may be invoked only in respect of the whole treaty, except as provided in Article 60 of the Convention on the Law of Treaties 1969[320] or as follows

---

[318] Unless the treaty otherwise provides, the parties in question must notify the other parties to the treaty of their intention to conclude an agreement to modify it as between themselves only, and of the modification to the treaty for which that agreement provides (United Nations (1969), "Vienna Convention on the Law of Treaties," Article 41(2)).

[319] This article declares: "1. A treaty which contains no provision regarding its termination and which does not provide for denunciation or withdrawal is not subject to denunciation or withdrawal[,] unless: (*a*) It is established that the parties intended to admit the possibility of denunciation or withdrawal; or (*b*) A right of denunciation or withdrawal may be implied by the nature of the treaty. 2. A party shall give not less than twelve months' notice of its intention to denounce or withdraw from a treaty under paragraph 1." (United Nations (1969), "Vienna Convention on the Law of Treaties," Article 56; emphasis original).

[320] This article states: "1. A material breach of a bilateral treaty by one of the parties entitles the other to invoke the breach as a ground for terminating the treaty or suspending its operation[,] in whole or in part. 2. A material breach of a multilateral treaty by one of the parties entitles: (*a*) The other parties by unanimous agreement to suspend the operation of the treaty[,] in whole or in part[,] or to terminate it[,] either: (i) In the relations between themselves and the defaulting State, or (ii) As between all the parties; (*b*) A party specially affected by the breach to invoke it as a ground for suspending the operation of the treaty[,] in whole or in part[,] in the relations between itself and the defaulting State; (*c*) Any party other than the defaulting State to invoke the breach as a ground for suspending the operation of the treaty[,] in whole or in part[,] with respect to itself[,] if the treaty is of such a character that a material breach of its provisions by one party radically changes the position of every party with

[475]. If this ground concerns specific clauses only, then it may be invoked solely with regard to those provisions, where: (a) they are separable from the rest of the treaty in respect of their application, (b) it appears from the treaty or is otherwise evidenced that acceptance of those clauses was not a fundamental basis of the consent of the other party or parties to be bound by the treaty as a complete unit, and (c) continued performance of the remainder of that treaty would not be inequitable [476]. In cases that fall within Articles 49 and 50 of the Vienna Convention on the Law of Treaties 1969[321], the state that is entitled to invoke the fraud of another state (Article 49) or the corruption of its representative by another state (Article 50) may do so with regard either to the entire treaty, or, subject to the immediately-preceding sentence, the particular clauses only [477]. In cases that come under Articles 51, 52 and 53 of the Vienna Convention on the Law of Treaties[322], no separation of the provisions of the relevant treaty is allowed [478]. A state may no longer invoke a ground for withdrawing from, suspending, invalidating or terminating the working of a treaty under Articles 46 to 50 or Articles 60 and 62 of the Vienna Convention on the Law of Treaties 1969[323], if, after realizing

---

respect to the further performance of its obligations under the treaty. 3. A material breach of a treaty, for the purposes of this article, consists in: (*a*) A repudiation of the treaty not sanctioned by the present Convention; or (*b*) The violation of a provision essential to the accomplishment of the object or purpose of the treaty. 4. The foregoing paragraphs are without prejudice to any provision in the treaty applicable in the event of a breach. 5. Paragraphs 1 to 3 do not apply to provisions relating to the protection of the human person contained in treaties of a humanitarian character, in particular to provisions prohibiting any form of reprisals against persons protected by such treaties." (United Nations (1969), "Vienna Convention on the Law of Treaties," Article 60; emphasis original).

321 These articles declare: "[49.] If a State has been induced to conclude a treaty by the fraudulent conduct of another negotiating State, [then] the State may invoke the fraud as invalidating its consent to be bound by the treaty. [50.] If the expression of a State's consent to be bound by a treaty has been procured through the corruption of its representative directly or indirectly by another negotiating State, [then] the State may invoke such corruption as invalidating its consent to be bound by the treaty." (United Nations (1969), "Vienna Convention on the Law of Treaties," Articles 49 and 50).

322 These articles state: "[51.] The expression of a State's consent to be bound by a treaty which has been procured by the coercion of its representative through acts or threats directed against him[,] shall be without any legal effect. [52.] A treaty is void if its conclusion has been procured by the threat or use of force in violation of the principles of international law embodied in the Charter of the United Nations. [53.] A treaty is void if, at the time of its conclusion, it conflicts with a peremptory norm of general international law. For the purposes of the present Convention, a peremptory norm of general international law is a norm accepted and recognized by the international community of States as a whole as a norm from which no derogation is permitted and which can be modified only by a subsequent norm of general international law having the same character." (United Nations (1969), "Vienna Convention on the Law of Treaties," Articles 51-53). If a treaty is void under Article 53 of the Vienna Convention on the Law of Treaties 1969, i.e., for conflicting at the time that it is concluded with a peremptory norm of general international law, then the parties to it must "(*a*) Eliminate[,] as far as possible[,] the consequences of any act performed in reliance on any provision which conflicts with the peremptory norm of general international law; and (*b*) Bring their mutual relations into conformity with the peremptory norm of general international law" (United Nations (1969), "Vienna Convention on the Law of Treaties," Article 71(1); emphasis original).

323 Fn 324 and accompanying text set out Article 46 of the Vienna Convention on the Law of Treaties 1969. The sentence immediately following the text to fn 324 comprises Article 47 of the Vienna Convention on the Law of Treaties 1969. Fn 325, its accompanying text, and the sentence immediately following the text to fn 325, constitute Article 48 of the Vienna Convention on the Law of Treaties 1969. Fn 321 lays down Articles 49 and 50 of the Vienna Convention on the Law of Treaties 1969. Fn 320 contains Article 60 of the Vienna Convention on the Law of Treaties 1969. Article 62 of the Vienna Convention on the Law of Treaties is headed 'Fundamental change of circumstances', and reads as follows: "1. A fundamental change of circumstances which has occurred with regard to those existing at the time of the conclusion of a treaty, and which was not foreseen by the parties, may not be invoked as a ground for terminating or withdrawing from the treaty[,] unless: (*a*) The existence of those circumstances constituted an essential basis of the consent of the parties to be bound by the treaty; and (*b*) The effect of the change is radically to transform the extent of obligations still to be performed under the treaty. 2. A fundamental change of circumstances may not be invoked as a ground for terminating or withdrawing from a treaty: (*a*) If the treaty establishes a boundary; or (*b*) If the fundamental change is the result of a breach by the

the facts: (a) it shall have agreed expressly that the treaty is valid or remains effective or persists in operation – according to the circumstances, or (b) it must, because of its conduct, be deemed as having acquiesced in the treaty's validity or in its continuation in force or in operation – as the case may be [479].

A state may not invoke the fact that its agreement to be bound by a treaty has been expressed in contravention of a provision of its domestic law concerning competence to negotiate treaties as invalidating this assent, unless that infraction was manifest[324] and related to a rule of this law which is of fundamental significance [480]. If the authority of a representative to convey the consent of a state to be bound by a specific treaty has been made subject to a particular restriction, then that representative's omission to abide by this limitation may not be invoked as invalidating the accord communicated by the representative, unless the restriction was disclosed to the other negotiating states before the expressing of this assent [481].

A state may invoke an error in a treaty as invalidating its agreement to be bound by the treaty, if the inaccuracy constituted a central basis of its consent to be so bound and concerns a fact or a situation that was assumed by the state to exist at the moment which the treaty was concluded[325] [482]. But it may not thus invoke a mistake in a treaty, if the state in question contributed to this error by its own conduct or the circumstances were such as to alert that state to a possible inaccuracy [483].

The withdrawal of a party from a treaty, or the termination of a treaty, may take place in accordance with its provisions, or, at any point by consent of all the parties to the treaty – after discussing the matter with the other contracting states [484]. Unless the treaty otherwise specifies, a multilateral treaty does not finish by reason solely of the fact that the number of parties to it falls below the total which is necessary for its entry into effect [485].

The functioning of a treaty in respect of all the parties, or a particular party, may be suspended in line with its provisions, or, at any instant by consent of all the parties to it – after dialogue with the other contracting states [486]. At least two parties to a multilateral treaty may make an agreement to suspend the operation of provisions of this treaty as between themselves only, if: (a) the treaty provides for such a suspension, or (b) the treaty does not preclude this suspension, and the latter affects not the enjoyment by the other parties of their rights under this treaty or the discharge of their obligations and is consistent with the treaty's object and purpose [487].

A party may invoke the impossibility of performing a treaty as a basis for withdrawing from, suspending or terminating it, if the impossibility is caused by the permanent[326] loss or

party invoking it either of an obligation under the treaty or of any other international obligation owed to any other party to the treaty. 3. If, under the foregoing paragraphs, a party may invoke a fundamental change of circumstances as a ground for terminating or withdrawing from a treaty[,] it may also invoke the change as a ground for suspending the operation of the treaty." (United Nations (1969), "Vienna Convention on the Law of Treaties," Article 62; emphasis original).

[324] A transgression is 'manifest', "if it would be objectively evident to any State conducting itself in the matter in accordance with normal practice and in good faith" (United Nations (1969), "Vienna Convention on the Law of Treaties," Article 46(2)).

[325] An error that relates solely to the wording of the text of a treaty affects not its validity; in this instance, Article 79 of the Vienna Convention on the Law of Treaties 1969, which is headed 'Correction of errors in texts or in certified copies of treaties', applies (United Nations (1969), "Vienna Convention on the Law of Treaties," Article 48(3)).

[326] If the impossibility is temporary, then it may be invoked merely as a reason for suspending the treaty's operation (United Nations (1969), "Vienna Convention on the Law of Treaties," Article 61(1)).

ruination of an object that is crucial for the fulfilment of the treaty [488]. A party may not invoke such impossibility of performance, if the impossibility is caused by the non-observance of a duty under the treaty or of any other international obligation which is owed to any other party to this treaty [489].

The severance of diplomatic or consular relations betwixt states parties to a treaty affects not the legal relations that have been formed between them by the treaty, save in so far as the existence of the former relations is necessary for the treaty's application [490]. If a new peremptory norm of general international law is brought to light, then any existing treaty which is at variance with this norm becomes void and aborts [491]. The termination of this treaty releases the parties from any duty further to carry out its obligations under it[327] [492].

A treaty the invalidity of which is proven under the Vienna Convention on the Law of Treaties 1969, is void; the provisions of a void treaty have no legal effect [493]. If acts have been performed in reliance on a void treaty, then: (a) each party to this treaty may require any other party to evidence to the greatest possible degree, in their mutual relations, the situation that would have been if these acts had not been executed, and (b) acts which are performed in good faith before the invalidity was invoked are not made unlawful by reason solely of the treaty's invalidity[328] [494]. Regarding the invalidity of a specific state's consent to be bound by a multilateral treaty, the preceding rules apply to the relations between this state and the parties to that treaty [495].

Unless the treaty states otherwise or parties elsewise agree, the termination of a treaty releases the parties to it from any duty to further perform it, and does not alter any obligation, right or legal situation of the parties which is created by way of carrying out the treaty before its cessation [496]. If a state denounces, or withdraws from, a multilateral treaty, then the immediately-preceding sentence applies to the relations between this state and each of the other parties to the treaty, from the date on which that denunciation or withdrawal becomes effective [497].

Except if the treaty specifies otherwise or the parties elsewise agree, the suspension of a treaty's operation releases the parties to it between which the functioning of the treaty is suspended from the duty to discharge it, in their mutual relations, during the time of the suspension, but does not otherwise change the legal relations between the parties that the treaty has established [498]. Throughout the time of the suspension, the parties shall refrain from acts which tend to hinder the resumption of the working of the treaty [499].

---

[327] This termination "[d]oes not affect any right, obligation or legal situation of the parties created through the execution of the treaty prior to its termination, provided that those rights, obligations or situations may thereafter be maintained only to the extent that their maintenance is not in itself in conflict with the new peremptory norm of general international law" (United Nations (1969), "Vienna Convention on the Law of Treaties," Article 71(2)(b)).

[328] This sentence does not apply in instances that fall under Articles 49, 50, 51 or 52 of the Vienna Convention on the Law of Treaties 1969 with regard to the party to which the fraud, the act of corruption or the coercion is capable of being assigned (United Nations (1969), "Vienna Convention on the Law of Treaties," Article 69(3)). Fn 321 sets out Articles 49 and 50 of the Vienna Convention on the Law of Treaties 1969. The first two sentences of fn 322 comprise Articles 51 and 52, respectively, of the Vienna Convention on the Law of Treaties 1969.

Vienna Convention on the Law of Treaties Between States and International Organizations or Between International Organizations (1986)

The provisions of this convention correspond to those of the Vienna Convention on the Law of Treaties 1969, with necessary adaptations therein for the different application of the former to the latter; the Vienna Convention on the Law of Treaties 1969 applies to treaties between states [423], whereas the Vienna Convention on the Law of Treaties between States and International Organizations or between International Organizations 1986 applies to treaties betwixt a state or states and an international organization or international organizations [500], and to treaties between the last-mentioned [501]. An example of the use of these adaptations is found earlier in this chapter in the comparison of each of Articles 19 to 23 in the 1969 Treaty and the 1986 Treaty[329].

The correspondence between the provisions of these two treaties stretches from Article 1 of each to Article 72 of each. Article 73 of the Vienna Convention on the Law of Treaties between States and International Organizations or between International Organizations 1986 is an additional clause, and reads as follows.

> *Article 73. Relationship to the Vienna Convention on the Law of Treaties*[330]
> As between States parties to the Vienna Convention on the Law of Treaties of 1969, the relations of those States under a treaty between two or more States and one or more international organizations shall be governed by that Convention [502].

The correspondence between the clauses of the two treaties continues 'once removed' until the end of these conventions, i.e., Article 85 of the 1969 Treaty and Article 86 of the 1986 Treaty, which are both headed 'Authentic texts' – and which both specify that the texts of the original version of the present treaty in Chinese, English, French, Russian and Spanish are "equally authentic" [502, 503]. Thus, there is consistency between the two conventions throughout. If one of these treaties needs to be modified, then a corresponding alteration is likely to be required to be made to the other as well.

Comment

The Vienna Convention on the Law of Treaties 1969 is an excellent treaty. It was worked out by first-rate minds patiently and carefully, and is the basis for much of today's international law. However, it is a document that attempts to bring together the positions of states which, in accordance with traditional opinions within this topic, are the primary actors therein. Because the views of the most influential persons within states vary, there are instances in which states would like to follow different routes concerning the subject-matter of a transnational discipline. Regarding conventional international law, a state may wish to accept a treaty as a whole, to accept only a specified part of a treaty, i.e., subject to stipulated reservations or to the exclusion

---

[329] Articles 19, 20, 21, 22 and 23 of the Vienna Convention of the Law of Treaties 1969 are located at the text to fns 265, 266, 267-268, 269 and 270, respectively. Articles 19, 20, 21, 22 and 23 of the Vienna Convention on the Law of Treaties between States or between States and International Organizations 1986 are situated at fns 265, 266, 268, 269 and 270, respectively.

[330] Emphasis original.

of part of it, or to not accept it at all, i.e., not ratify the treaty in the first place or withdraw from it at a later date. Furthermore, there is the possibility that a state may ratify a treaty and then deviate from the implementation of its provisions over this state's territory and/or concerning its relations with some or all other states. The Vienna Convention on the Law of Treaties 1969, and, by extension, the Vienna Convention on the Law of Treaties between States and International Organizations or between International Organizations 1986, cater for such scenarios. Nevertheless, the convoluted way in which its instruments need to accommodate the primacy of states contributes to international law being a complex, messy subject, which displays low levels of legal certainty in comparison to traditional legal disciplines, such as contract and tort[331].

There is also the issue of the extent to which the Vienna Convention on the Law of Treaties 1969 and the Vienna Convention on the Law of Treaties between States and International Organizations or between International Organizations 1986 consider international law to be a superior source of law to national law. Article 27 of the Vienna Convention on the Law of Treaties 1969[332] and its corresponding article in the Vienna Convention on the Law of Treaties between States and International Organizations or between International Organizations 1986[333] make it clear that conventional international law for states parties to treaties is a superior legal source to those parties' respective systems of domestic law. Article 46 of the Vienna Convention on the Law of Treaties[334] and its corresponding article in the Vienna Convention on the Law of Treaties between States and International Organizations or between International Organizations 1986[335] place manifest breaches of a rule of a state's national law of fundamental importance concerning competence to negotiate treaties over that state's consent to be bound

[331] Traditional legal disciplines vary between states, whereas there is only one body of international law. But there tends to be a high degree of uniformity in the former within a single state, and common principles across these disciplines in different states.

[332] The second sentence of the fifth paragraph of the subsection entitled 'Vienna Convention on the Law of Treaties 1969', above in the current section (i.e., that titled 'Primary Sources: International Conventions), sets out Article 27 of the Vienna Convention on the Law of Treaties 1969.

[333] This article is headed 'Internal law of States, rules of international organizations and observance of treaties'; it declares: "1. A State party to a treaty may not invoke the provisions of its internal law as justification for its failure to perform the treaty. 2. An international organization party to a treaty may not invoke the rules of the organization as justification for its failure to perform the treaty. 3. The rules contained in the preceding paragraphs are without prejudice to article 46 [of the Convention on the Law of Treaties between States and International Organizations or between International Organizations 1986]." (United Nations (1986), "Vienna Convention on the Law of Treaties between States and International Organizations or between International Organizations," Article 27). Fn 335 lays down Article 46 of the Convention on the Law of Treaties between States and International Organizations or between International Organizations 1986.

[334] Fn 324 and accompanying text.

[335] This article is headed 'Provisions of internal law of a State and rules of an international organization regarding competence to conclude treaties'; it specifies: "1. A State may not invoke the fact that its consent to be bound by a treaty has been expressed in violation of a provision of its internal law regarding competence to conclude treaties as invalidating its consent[,] unless that violation was manifest and concerned a rule of its internal law of fundamental importance. 2. An international organization may not invoke the fact that its consent to be bound by a treaty has been expressed in violation of the rules of the organization regarding competence to conclude treaties as invalidating its consent[,] unless that violation was manifest and concerned a rule of its internal law of fundamental importance. 3. A violation is manifest[,] if it would be objectively evident to any State or any international organization conducting itself in the matter in accordance with the normal practice of States and, where appropriate, of international organizations and in good faith." (United Nations (1986), "Vienna Convention on the Law of Treaties between States and International Organizations or between International Organizations," Article 46).

by a treaty. This is unnecessary as, according to Article 6 of the Vienna Convention on the Law of Treaties 1969[336], every state has the capacity to conclude treaties [504].

The ILC has been responsible for developing the law for the publication of these two treaties, together with that for the Vienna Convention on the Succession of States in respect of Treaties 1978, as well as for its refinement through standards and accompanying commentaries – including those on reservations to treaties, the effects of armed conflicts on treaties, subsequent agreements and subsequent practice in relation to the interpretation of treaties, and the provisional application of treaties. This work is gradually building a comprehensive system of conventional international law, which is the largest component of the discipline of public international law.

Primary Sources: International Custom

Introduction

It has long been accepted there are two necessary elements for a statement to become a rule of customary international law – the widespread, consistent and repetitive practice of states (*usus longaevus*) and the sincerely-held belief that this practice is legally binding within the global community (*opinio necessitatis sive iuris*)[337] [505]. But it has been difficult to determine a list of statements that have been universally recognized as such. The ILC has attempted to clarify the procedure for identifying elements of customary international law, which resulted in a set of conclusions on this process. The next subsection describes the ILC's work on the topic, which is followed by a subsection on the conclusions on identification of customary international law and, finally, a comment.

Work of the ILC

At its sixty-third session, in 2011, the ILC identified the subject 'Formation and evidence of customary international law' for inclusion in its future programme of work [506]. At its sixty-fourth session, in 2012, the ILC decided to place this theme in its scheme of work, and appointed Sir Michael Wood as Special Rapporteur [506]. At its sixty-fifth session in 2013, the ILC decided to alter the title of the topic to 'Identification of customary international law'[338] [506].

---

[336] The corresponding provision of the Vienna Convention on the Law of Treaties between States and International Organizations or between International Organizations 1986 is headed 'Capacity of international organizations to conclude treaties, and states: "The capacity of an international organization to conclude treaties is governed by the rules of that organization." (United Nations (1986), "Vienna Convention on the Law of Treaties between States and International Organizations or between International Organizations," Article 6).

[337] Article 38(2) of the Statute of the PCIJ, and Article 38(1)(b) of the Statute of the ICJ, refer to "international custom, as evidence of a general practice accepted as law"; the next quoted passage after the text to fn 96 includes Article 38(2) of the Statute of the PCIJ; the quoted passage immediately following the text to fn 207 contains Article 38(1)(b) of the Statute of the ICJ.

[338] The Special Rapporteur showed ambivalence as to the title to be used for this subject: "The scope of the present topic and possible outcomes of the [International Law] Commission's work were discussed during the Commission's debate in 2012, and during the debate in the Sixth Committee at the sixty-seventh session of the General Assembly. The question was raised as to whether the title of the topic, with references both to

At its sixty-sixth session in 2014, the ILC referred to the Drafting Committee the eleven draft conclusions that the Special Rapporteur's second report laid down[339], which provisionally adopted eight of them [506].

At the sixty-seventh session of the ILC, in 2015, the Drafting Committee provisionally adopted all sixteen draft conclusions – the Special Rapporteur's third report included additional

"formation" and "evidence" of customary international law, accurately covered the subject matter envisaged; it was also noted that the various language versions of these references were somewhat inconsistent. It was, moreover, suggested that the central issue was the "identification" of customary international law, and that the reference to "formation" risked making the subject too broad or too theoretical. ... [T]he aim of the topic is to offer some guidance to those called upon to apply rules of customary international law on how to identify such rules in concrete cases. This includes, but is not limited to, judges in domestic courts, and judges and arbitrators in specialized international courts and tribunals. [T]he terms "formation" and "evidence" were intended to indicate that, in order to determine whether a rule of customary international law exists, it is necessary to consider both the requirements for the formation of a rule of customary international law, and the types of evidence that establish the fulfilment of those requirements. It may, nevertheless, be useful to ensure, at an early stage, that the title accurately reflects the intended scope of the topic in the various languages ... and has the same meaning in them all." (International Law Commission (2013), First report on formation and evidence of customary international law, by Sir Michael Wood, Special Rapporteur, Document A/CN.4/663, *Yearbook of the International Law Commission*, 2013, Volume II, Part One, 109-144, 120).

339 These draft conclusions are: 1."1. The present draft conclusions concern the methodology for determining the existence and content of rules of customary international law. 2. The present draft conclusions are without prejudice to the methodology concerning other sources of international law and questions relating to peremptory norms of international law (*jus cogens*)." 2."For the purposes of the present draft conclusions: (*a*) "Customary international law" means those rules of international law that derive from and reflect a general practice accepted as law; (*b*) "International organization" means an intergovernmental organization; (*c*) ..." 3."To determine the existence of a rule of customary international law and its content, it is necessary to ascertain whether there is a general practice accepted as law." 4."In assessing evidence for a general practice accepted as law, regard must be had to the context, including the surrounding circumstances." 5."The requirement, as an element of customary international law, of a general practice means that it is primarily the practice of States that contributes to the creation, or expression, of rules of customary international law." 6."State practice consists of conduct that is attributable to a State, whether in the exercise of executive, legislative, judicial or any other function." 7."1. Practice may take a wide range of forms. It includes both physical and verbal actions. 2. Manifestations of practice include, among others, the conduct of States "on the ground", diplomatic acts and correspondence, legislative acts, judgments of national courts, official publications in the field of international law, statements on behalf of States concerning codification efforts, practice in connection with treaties, and acts in connection with resolutions of organs of international organizations and conferences. 3. Inaction may also serve as practice. 4. The acts (including inaction) of international organizations may also serve as practice." 8."There is no predetermined hierarchy among the various forms of practice. 2. Account is to be taken of all available practice of a particular State. Where the organs of the State do not speak with one voice, less weight is to be given to their practice." 9."1. To establish a rule of customary international law, the relevant practice must be general, meaning that it must be sufficiently widespread and representative. The practice need not be universal. 2. The practice must be generally consistent. 3. Provided that the practice is sufficiently general and consistent, no particular duration is required. 4. In assessing practice, due regard is to be given to the practice of States whose interests are specially affected." 10."1. The requirement, as an element of customary international law, that the general practice be accepted as law means that the practice in question must be accompanied by a sense of legal obligation. 2. Acceptance as law is what distinguishes a rule of customary international law from a mere habit or usage." 11."1. Evidence of acceptance of a general practice as law may take a wide range of forms. These may vary according to the nature of the rule and the circumstances in which the rule falls to be applied. 2. The forms of evidence include, but are not limited to, statements by States which indicate what are or are not rules of customary international law, diplomatic correspondence, the jurisprudence of national courts, the opinions of Government legal advisers, official publications in fields of international law, treaty practice, and action in connection with resolutions of organs of international organizations and of international conferences. 3. Inaction may also service as evidence of acceptance as law. 4. The fact that an act (including inaction) by a State establishes practice for the purpose of identifying a rule of customary international law does not preclude the same act from being evidence that the practice in question is accepted as law." (International Law Commission (2014), Second report on identification of customary international law, by Sir Michael Wood, Special Rapporteur, Document A/CN.4/672, Annex: Proposed draft conclusions on the identification of customary international law, *Yearbook of the International Law Commission*, 2014, Volume II, Part One, 163-203, 202-203; emphasis original).

paragraphs to three of the draft conclusions that were proposed in his second report[340] and five new draft conclusions[341] [506]. Then, the ILC noted the sixteen draft conclusions that the Drafting Committee had provisionally adopted and asked the Secretariat of the UN to prepare a memorandum about the role of judgments of domestic courts in the case law of international courts and tribunals – with a view to determining customary international law [506].

At its sixty-eighth session, in 2016, the ILC had the fourth report of the Special Rapporteur before it – which included suggestions for amendments to the draft conclusions in the light of the comments received[342] [506]. The ILC referred these proposed amendments to the Drafting

---

[340] These additional paragraphs concern draft conclusions 4, 5 and 11, respectively (fn 339), and are highlighted in italics: 4.1. In assessing evidence for a general practice accepted as law, regard must be had to the context, including the surrounding circumstances. "*2. Each element is to be separately ascertained. This generally requires an assessment of specific evidence for each element.*" 5.1. The requirement, as an element of customary international law, of a general practice means that it is primarily the practice of States that contributes to the creation, or expression, of rules of customary international law. 2. See below in the present footnote (i.e., fn 340) "*3. Conduct by other non-State actors is not practice for the purposes of formation or identification of customary international law.*" 11.1. Evidence of acceptance of a general practice as law may take a wide range of forms. These may vary according to the nature of the rule and the circumstances in which the rule falls to be applied. 2. The forms of evidence include, but are not limited to, statements by States which indicate what are or are not rules of customary international law, diplomatic correspondence, the jurisprudence of national courts, the opinions of Government legal advisers, official publications in fields of international law, treaty practice, and action in connection with resolutions of organs of international organizations and of international conferences. 3. Inaction may also service as evidence of acceptance as law", *provided that the circumstances call for some reaction*". 4. The fact that an act (including inaction) by a State establishes practice for the purpose of identifying a rule of customary international law does not preclude the same act from being evidence that the practice in question is accepted as law. (International Law Commission (2015), Third report on identification of customary international law, by Sir Michael Wood, Special Rapporteur, Document A/CN.4/682, Annex: Further proposed draft conclusions, *Yearbook of the International Law Commission*, 2015, Volume II, Part One, 93-134, 134; emphasis added). Paragraph 2 of draft conclusion 5 (above in the current footnote (i.e., fn 340)) was provisionally adopted by the Drafting Committee in 2014; it declares: "In certain cases, the practice of international organizations also contributes to the formation, or expression, of rules of customary international law." (International Law Commission (2015), Third report on identification of customary international law, by Sir Michael Wood, Special Rapporteur, Document A/CN.4/682, *Yearbook of the International Law Commission*, 2015, Volume II, Part One, 93-134, 122). Draft conclusion 2 is deleted; as a result of this, draft conclusion 4 (above in the present footnote) becomes draft conclusion 3, and draft conclusion 5 (above in the current footnote) becomes draft conclusion 4 (International Law Commission (2015), Third report on identification of customary international law, by Sir Michael Wood, Special Rapporteur, Document A/CN.4/682, *Yearbook of the International Law Commission*, 2015, Volume II, Part One, 93-134, 122 and 134).

[341] These five draft conclusions are numbered 12-16, and read as follows: 12."A treaty provision may reflect or come to reflect a rule of customary international law[,] if it is established that the provision in question: (*a*) at the time when the treaty was concluded, codifies an existing rule of customary international law; (*b*) has led to the crystallization of an emerging rule of customary international law; or (*c*) has generated a new rule of customary international law, by giving rise to a general practice accepted as law." 13."Resolutions adopted by international organizations or at international conferences may, in some circumstances, be evidence of customary international law or contribute to its development; they cannot, in and of themselves, constitute it." 14."Judicial decisions and writings may serve as subsidiary means for the identification of rules of customary international law." 15."1. A particular custom is a rule of customary international law that may only be invoked by and against certain States. 2. To determine the existence of a particular custom and its content, it is necessary to ascertain whether there is a general practice among the States concerned that is accepted by each of them as law (*opinion juris*)." 16."A State that has persistently objected to a new rule of customary international law while that rule was in the process of formation is not bound by the rule for so long as it maintains its objection." (International Law Commission (2015), Third report on identification of customary international law, by Sir Michael Wood, Special Rapporteur, Document A/CN.4/682, Annex: Further proposed draft conclusions, *Yearbook of the International Law Commission*, 2015, Volume II, Part One, 93-134, 134; emphasis original).

[342] Amendments – highlighted in italics (other than the phrase '*opinio juris*', which is in italics by virtue of it being Latin) – are suggested to draft conclusions 3, 4, 6, 9 and 12, as follows: 3.(formerly 4.)1."In assessing evidence for a general practice accepted as law, regard must be had to the context, including the surrounding circumstances. 2. Each *of the two* elements is to be separately assessed. This requires an assessment of evidence for each element." 4.(formerly 5.)"1. The requirement, as a constituent element of customary international law,

Committee, and adopted the report of the latter on all sixteen draft conclusions – together with commentaries thereon [506]. The ILC conveyed these draft conclusions, which it had adopted on first reading, via the Secretary-General, to governments for observations and comments – requesting that these be sent to the Secretary-General by 1st January 2018 [506]. It also asked the Secretariat to formulate a memorandum on how to make the evidence of customary international law more-easily available [506].

Following examination of the Special Rapporteur's fifth report at its seventieth session, in 2018, the ILC referred all sixteen draft conclusions to the Drafting Committee, with the instruction that the latter begin the second reading of the draft conclusions on the basis of the Special Rapporteur's proposals, taking into consideration the observations and comments of governments and debate in plenary on Sir Michael Wood's report [506]. The ILC reviewed the Drafting Committee's report, and adopted the whole set of draft conclusions on identification of customary law on second reading, as well as commentaries thereon [506].

By Resolution 73/203 of 20th December 2018, the UN General Assembly noted the conclusions on identification of customary international law and their accompanying commentaries, and brought them to the attention of states and of all who may need to identify these rules – and encouraged their maximum dissemination[343] [506]. It also acknowledged the use of published surveys and digests of practice concerning international law, and encouraged states to strive to support libraries and publications devoted to international law[344] [506].

---

of a general practice *refers* primarily *to* the practice of States *as expressive, or creative*, of rules of customary international law. 2. In certain cases, the practice of international organizations also contributes to the expression, *or creation,* of rules of customary international law. 3. Conduct by other actors is not practice that contributes to the expression, *or creation,* of rules of customary international law, but may be relevant when assessing the practice referred to in paragraphs 1 and 2." 6.(formerly 7.)"1. Practice may take a wide range of forms. It includes both physical and verbal actions. 2. Forms of State practice include, but are not limited to: diplomatic acts and correspondence; conduct in connection with treaties; executive conduct, including operational conduct "on the ground"; legislative and administrative acts; and decisions of national courts. 3. Inaction may also serve as practice. 4. The acts (including inaction) of international organizations may also serve as practice." 9.(formerly 10.)"1. The requirement, as a constituent element of customary international law, that the general practice be accepted as law (*opinio juris*) means that the practice in question must be *accompanied by* a sense of legal obligation. 2. Acceptance as law is what distinguishes a rule of customary international law from a mere habit or usage." 12.(formerly 13.)"1. A resolution adopted by an international organization or at an intergovernmental conference *does not*, of itself, create a rule of customary international law. 2. A resolution adopted by an international organization or at an intergovernmental conference may provide evidence for *determining* the existence and content of a rule of customary international law." (International Law Commission (2016), Fourth report on identification of customary international law, by Sir Michael Wood, Special Rapporteur, Document A/CN.4/695 and Addendum 1, Annex I: Proposed amendments to the draft conclusions, *Yearbook of the International Law Commission*, 2016, Volume II, Part One, 215-249, 227; emphasis original).

343 Operative Paragraph 4 of Resolution 73/203 of 20th December 2018 reads: "*The General Assembly*, ... 4. *Also takes note* of the conclusions on identification of customary international law, the text of which is annexed to the present resolution, with the commentaries thereto, brings them to the attention of States and all who may be called upon to identify rules of customary international law, and encourages their widest possible dissemination;" (United Nations (2018), Resolution 73/203 adopted by the General Assembly on 20th December 2018, Operative Paragraph 4; emphasis original).

344 Operative Paragraph 5 of Resolution 73/203 of 20th December 2018 specifies: "The General Assembly, ... 5. *Acknowledges* the utility of published digests and surveys of practice relating to international law, including those that make legislative, executive and judicial practice widely available, and encourages States to make every effort to support existing publications and libraries specialized in international law" (United Nations (2018), Resolution 73/203 adopted by the General Assembly on 20th December 2018,Operative Paragraph 5; emphasis original).

Conclusions on Identification of Customary International Law

Part One: Introduction
Conclusion 1: Scope

The present conclusions concern the way in which the existence and content of rules of customary international law are to be determined [507].

The terms 'determine' and 'identify' are used interchangeably in the conclusions and the commentaries thereon [508].

Part Two: Basic approach
Conclusion 2: Two constituent elements

To determine the existence and content of a rule of customary international law, it is necessary to ascertain whether there is a general practice that is accepted as law (*opinio juris*[345]) [509].

To prove that a claim which concerns the existence or the content of a rule of customary law is well-founded, one must search for a practice which has secured such acceptance among states that it may be deemed the expression of a legal right or obligation – i.e., that this practice is required, allowed or precluded as a matter of law [510]. This two-element approach applies to all areas of international law [511].

Conclusion 3: Assessment of evidence for the two constituent elements

1. In assessing evidence for the purpose of ascertaining whether there is a general practice and whether that practice is accepted as law (*opinio juris*[346]), regard must be had to the overall context, the nature of the rule, and the particular circumstances in which the evidence in question is to be found [512].
2. Each of the two constituent elements is to be separately ascertained. This requires an assessment of evidence for each element [513].

The requirement that regard be had to the overall context indicates the need to apply the two-element approach, while taking into consideration the subject-matter which the alleged rule of customary international law is assumed to regulate [514]. This implies that, in each instance, any underlying principles of international law which may apply to the matter should be taken into account [514]. Furthermore, certain forms of practice and of evidence of acceptance as law may be especially significant, in keeping with the context [514].

It may sometimes be difficult to find much affirmative state practice in respect of prohibitive rules [514]. Cases that involve these may turn on assessing whether any inaction is accepted as law [514].

When legislation is considered as practice, the interpretation and application of the text may be more important than the text itself [514]. Judgments of national courts will be less consequential if either they are not enforced due to concerns regarding their compatibility with

[345] Emphasis original.
[346] Emphasis original.

international law or they are overturned by the legislature [514]. Casual or spontaneous statements will usually be less significant than those that are prepared carefully [514]. Statements which junior officials make may be less important than those made by senior members of a government [514]. Moreover, practice of a state that runs contrary to its interests or entails large costs for it may be likely to reflect acceptance of this conduct as law [515].

Acceptance as law is to be sought in reference to not only those participating in the practice but also to those in a position to react to that behaviour [515]. In identifying a rule of customary international law, while the existence of a general practice is frequently considered before an inquiry is made into whether such conduct is accepted as law, this order of examination is not obligatory [515].

Part Three: A general practice
Conclusion 4: Requirement of practice

1. The requirement of a general practice, as a constituent element of customary international law, refers primarily to the practice of States that contributes to the formation, or expression, of rules of customary international law [516].
2. In certain cases, the practice of international organizations also contributes to the formation, or expression, or rules of customary international law [517].
3. Conduct of other actors is not practice that contributes to the formation, or expression, or rules of customary international law, but may be relevant when assessing the practice referred to in paragraphs 1 and 2 [518].

In those instances in which the practice of international organizations is relevant, references in the conclusions and commentaries to the practice of states is to be read as including the aforementioned practice [519]. The practice of global organizations in international relations, when accompanied by acceptance as law, may qualify as practice that generates, or attests to, rules of customary international law – but only those whose subject-matter is within the organizations' mandate and/or are addressed specifically to these bodies – such as rules concerning their international responsibility or relating to treaties to which worldwide organizations may be parties [519]. Thus, the practice of these entities, when negotiating treaties, acting as depositaries for treaties, deploying military forces – such as for peacekeeping, administering territories, or taking positions on the extent of the immunities and privileges of the organization and its officials, may be instrumental in the formation, or expression, of rules of customary international law over these spheres [519]. In general, the more directly a practice of a global organization is conducted on behalf of its member states or endorsed by them and the greater the number of member states, the more significant this practice may be in connection with the formation, or expression, of rules of customary international law [519].

The acts of individuals may be relevant to the formation, or expression, of rules of customary international law – but merely to the extent that states have backed or responded to them [520]. Official statements of the International Committee of the Red Cross may contribute to moulding the practice of states which react to these pronouncements [520].

Conclusion 5: Conduct of the state as state practice

State practice consists of conduct of the State, whether in the exercise of its executive, legislative, judicial or other functions [521].

Behaviour within a state, such as its treatment of its nationals, may concern issues of international law [520]. State practice includes that of two or more states acting jointly – such as several states co-operating to launch a satellite into orbit around the earth [520]. In order for a state's practice to play a part in the formation and identification of rules of customary international law, other states must be aware of this conduct [520].

Conclusion 6: Forms of practice

1. Practice may take a wide range of forms. It includes both physical and verbal acts. It may, under certain circumstances, include inaction [522].
2. Forms of State practice include, but are not limited to: diplomatic acts and correspondence; conduct in connection with resolutions adopted by an international organization or at an intergovernmental conference; conduct in connection with treaties; executive conduct, including operational conduct "on the ground"; legislative and administrative acts; and decisions of national courts [523].
3. There is no predetermined hierarchy among the various forms of practice [524].

Inaction can only constitute practice if the state deliberately does not act [525]. Examples of such omissions may include forbearing from instituting criminal proceedings against officials of other states, abstaining from exercising protection to specified naturalized persons, and refraining from using force [525].

Each of the listed forms of state practice is to be interpreted broadly, in order to reflect the many, different ways in which states act and react [525]. 'Executive conduct' refers to any form of executive act, including executive orders and decrees, worldwide or parliamentary statements, and claims before international or national courts [525]. 'Legislative and administrative acts' include the various regulatory arrangements that a public authority effects [525]. 'Operational conduct on the ground' covers seizure of property, law enforcement and military activity [525]. 'Conduct in connection with treaties' embraces acts which are related to negotiating and concluding treaties, and those that are connected with implementing them – such as treaty-host-country agreements and maritime delimitation accords [525]. 'Conduct in connection with resolutions adopted by an international organization or at an intergovernmental conference' includes acts taken by states which concern the negotiation, adoption and implementation of decisions, resolutions and other items that global organizations and intergovernmental conferences adopt – whether or not these are legally-binding [525].

Conclusion 7: Assessing a state's practice

1. Account is to be taken of all available practice of a particular State, which is to be assessed as a whole [526].
2. Where the practice of a particular State varies, the weight to be given to that practice may, depending on the circumstances, be reduced [527].

The practice which is scrutinized regarding the matter of concern must include all available, relevant practice of every organ of the state in question [528]. A difference in the practice between the higher and lower institutions of the same state is unlikely to result in less stress being put on the practice of the former [528]. Practice of departments of a central government will usually be more consequential in the assessment than that of political subdivisions of a state or constituent units of a federal state [528]. The practice of the executive branch of a state is frequently the most pertinent internationally, and, thus, has particular significance in association with the identification of customary international law; however, the constitutional position of the relevant organs of that state may need to be considered [528].

Conclusion 8: The practice must be general

1. The relevant practice must be general, meaning that it must be sufficiently widespread and representative, as well as consistent [529].
2. Provided that the practice is general, no particular duration is required [530].

There is no absolute standard for the pertinent practice being either 'sufficiently widespread and representative' or 'consistent' [528]. While the threshold for each must be appraised taking account of the context, the practice should be of such a character as to enable the discernment an almost-uniform usage [528]. Some contradictions and inconsistencies are not necessarily lethal to the finding of a general practice [531].

While a long duration may give rise to more extensive practice, time immemorial or a sizeable or fixed period of a general practice is not a condition for a rule of customary international law to exist [532]. Nonetheless, some period of time must pass for a general practice to come to light [533].

Part Four: Accepted as law (*opinio juris*)

Conclusion 9: Requirement of acceptance as law (*opinio juris*)

1. The requirement, as a constituent element of customary international law, that the general practice be accepted as law (*opinio juris*) means that the practice in question must be undertaken with a sense of legal right or obligation [534].
2. A general practice that is accepted as law (*opinio juris*) is to be distinguished from mere usage or habit [535].

The practice at issue must be accompanied by a conviction that it is allowed, required or precluded by customary international law [533]. Thus, it is critical to establish, in each case, that states have behaved in a certain manner because they considered themselves to be legally entitled or compelled to do so because of a rule of customary international law [533]. Seeking to observe a treaty commitment is not, in itself, acceptance of law in order to identify customary international law [533]. If a state recognizes that it is bound by a specified obligation by way of both treaty and customary international law, then it would need to prove this [533]. When states act in accordance with a treaty provision by which they are not bound, or apply clauses of a convention in their relations with non-parties to that treaty, then this may evidence the existence of acceptance of law of that provision or those clauses in the absence of any contrary explanation [533].

It is unnecessary to show that all states have accepted as law the rule in question as one of customary international law [536]. It is broad, representative acceptance of that rule as one of law, as well as little or no objection, which is required for it to be recognized as such [536].

Conclusion 10: Forms of evidence of acceptance as law (*opinio juris*)

1. Evidence of acceptance as law (*opinio juris*) may take a wide range of forms [537].
2. Forms of evidence of acceptance as law (*opinio juris*) include, but are not limited to: public statements made on behalf of States; official publications; government legal opinions, diplomatic correspondence, decisions of national courts; treaty provisions; and conduct in connection with resolutions adopted by an international organization or at an intergovernmental conference [538].
3. Failure to react over time to a practice may serve as evidence of acceptance as law (*opinio juris*), provided that States were in a position to react and the circumstances called for some reaction [539].

Statements may manifest the legal conviction of the state, and may frequently be considered as expressions of acceptance of law or otherwise – rather than instances of practice [536]. Among the types of evidence of acceptance as law, an express public statement on a state's behalf that a certain practice is allowed, precluded or mandated under customary international law furnishes the clearest indication that the state has undertaken, or avoided, this practice out of a sense of lawful right or legal obligation [536]. Furthermore, the effect of practice in conformity with the supposed rule may be annulled by contemporaneous statements that there is no such rule [536]. Either way, these statements might be made, for instance, in multilateral debates, on introducing draft legislation in parliament, as assertions made in oral and written pleadings before tribunals and courts, in protests which characterize the behaviour of other states as illegal, and in reply to proposals for codification – either individually or together with others [540].

'Official publications' comprise documents that are published in the name of a state – such as official maps and military manuals – in which acceptance of a rule as law may be found [541]. Published opinions of legal advisers to a government may illuminate the legal position of the relevant state, but not if the state refused to follow the advice contained therein [541]. 'Diplomatic correspondence' may include, for example, notes circulated to diplomatic missions – such as those on privileges and immunities [541]. Domestic legislation may be valuable as evidence of acceptance as law, especially where it has been stated – for instance, in association with the passage of the legislation, that this legislation is mandated under, or gives effect to, customary international law [541]. Judgments of national courts may contain similar statements, when ruling on matters of international law [541]. Diplomatic processes and multilateral drafting may supply valuable, accessible evidence to the legal positions of states regarding the content of customary international law [541]. The guidance in this paragraph and in the immediately-preceding one apply, as appropriate, to the types of evidence of acceptance of law of international organizations [541].

Tolerance of a specified practice may amount to evidence of acceptance as law, if it represents agreement with this conduct [541]. The following two requirements must be fulfilled in each instance, in order to ensure that the inaction does not derive from causes which are unrelated to the legality of the relevant behaviour [541]. First, a reaction to the practice in question would been warranted, as, for example, where the practice is one that affects – usually adversely – the rights or interests of the state refusing or failing to act [541]. Second, the reference in paragraph 3 of Conclusion 10 to states being 'in a position to react' means that the state concerned must have known of the practice, and that it must have had enough capacity and time to act [541].

Part Five: Significance of certain materials for the identification of customary international law

Conclusion 11: Treaties

1. A rule set forth in a treaty may reflect a rule of customary international law[,] if it is established that the treaty rule: (a) codified a rule of customary international law existing at the time when the treaty was concluded; (b) has led to the crystallization of a rule of customary international law that had started to emerge prior to the conclusion of the treaty; or (c) has given rise to a general practice that is accepted as law (*opinio juris*), thus generating a new rule of customary international law [542].
2. The fact that a rule set forth in a number of treaties may, but does not necessarily, indicate that the treaty rule reflects a rule of customary international law [543].

Rules that are present within treaties which have achieved almost-universal acceptance may constitute customary international law [544]. Treaties that are not yet in effect, or which have not yet achieved widespread participation, may be influential in specific circumstances, particularly if they were adopted unopposed or by a huge majority of states [544]. The standpoint of states that are not party to a widely-ratified treaty, both at the point of its conclusion and subsequently, is of relevance to provisions within it reflecting rules of customary international law [544].

Subparagraph 1(a) of Conclusion 11 concerns a situation in which it is shown that a rule within a treaty is declaratory of an existing rule of customary international law [545]. In inquiring whether this is so, the text of the treaty should be examined – as it may include an express statement on this matter [545]. If reservations are expressly allowed to be made with regard to a clause of a treaty, then this provision might not reflect customary international law – although this conclusion is not necessarily beyond doubt [545]. If these indications are missing from the text of the treaty, or if they refer to the treaty in general rather than to any particular rule contained therein, then resort may be made to the treaty's preparatory papers – including any statements made by states during the drafting process that may reveal an intention to codify an existing rule of customary international law [545]. If it is found therein that the negotiating states had considered that the rule at issue was a rule of customary international law, then this would be evidence of the rule's acceptance as law – whose importance would increase the greater the number of negotiating states [545]. Pertinent practice will need to confirm – or co-exist with – the acceptance as customary international law of the treaty rule [545]. This is because the fact that the parties state that the treaty is declaratory of existing law is only one piece of evidence to this effect, and because the rule of customary international law which underlies the text of a treaty may have changed or been supplanted since the negotiation of the convention [545].

Subparagraph 1(b) of Conclusion 11 concerns an instance in which it is proven that a general practice which is accepted as law has solidified around a rule within a treaty that has been developed on the basis of merely a limited quantity of state practice, i.e., the treaty rule has consolidated, and provided further definition to, a rule of customary international law that was only emerging at the time at which the treaty was being drafted [545]. Demonstrating that this is so requires an assessment of whether the rule within the treaty has been accepted as law and is carried out, generally, in practice [545].

Subparagraph 1(c) of Conclusion 11 concerns a case in which it is shown that a rule of law contained in a treaty has given rise to a new rule of customary international law [546]. For this to happen, general practice accepted as law would need to occur rapidly regarding this rule – but this may be insufficient; given that the concordant conduct of the parties to the treaty among themselves probably could be attributed to the obligation which this convention imposes on them – rather than to acceptance of the relevant rule as mandatory under customary international law, the practice of these parties in relation to non-parties to the treaty and of non-parties with reference to parties or among themselves, will have especial value [546].

Conclusion 12: Resolutions of international organizations and intergovernmental conferences

1. A resolution adopted by an international organization or at an intergovernmental conference cannot, of itself, create a rule of customary international law [547].
2. A resolution adopted by an international organization or at an intergovernmental conference may provide evidence for determining the existence and content of a rule of customary international law, or contribute to its development. [548].
3. A provision in a resolution adopted by an international organization or at an intergovernmental conference may reflect a rule of customary international law[,] if it is established that the provision corresponds to a general practice that is accepted as law (*opinio juris*) [549].

Special attention should be given to resolutions of the UN General Assembly, which may offer consequential evidence of the collective opinion of Member States of the UN [546]. Motions adopted by organs of the UN with more-limited membership than that of the General Assembly may be pertinent, too, but their significance in identifying a rule of customary international law is likely to be less than that of the General Assembly's resolutions [546].

Resolutions of organs of worldwide institutions originate from the relevant organization, rather than from its member states [550]. Nevertheless, these instruments may reproduce the collective expression of the views of those countries [550]. Thus, when such resolutions concern legal matters, they may illuminate the attitudes of the member states regarding these issues [550].

If a resolution claims to be declaratory of an existing rule of customary international law, then it may constitute evidence of the acceptance as law of this rule by the states which support the resolution [550]. Conversely, disassociations from a consensus, abstentions or negative votes, as well as explanations of positions and general positions, may form proof that there is no acceptance as law of the rule [550].

As the position of states towards a particular resolution – or rule within a resolution – is frequently motivated by non-legal considerations, ascertaining acceptance as law from these items must be done with care [550]. In each instance, a cautious assessment of various factors in necessary, in order to confirm whether the states concerned meant to accept the existence of a rule of customary international law [550]. The exact wording of a resolution is the starting point in striving to appraise the legal importance of a resolution; reference to 'international law,' the choice or avoidance of certain terms in the text, and the language used, may be noteworthy [550]. The debates and the negotiations before the adoption of the resolution are relevant, especially explanations of vote and similar statements made immediately before and after the vote [550]. The extent of support for the resolution is vital [550].

Conclusion 13: Decisions of courts and tribunals

1. Decisions of international courts and tribunals, in particular of the International Court of Justice, concerning the existence and content of rules of customary international law, are a subsidiary means for the determination of such rules [551].
2. Regard may be had, as appropriate, to decisions of national courts concerning the existence and content of rules of customary international law, as a subsidiary means for the determination of such rules [552].

The value of decisions of international courts and tribunals in offering guidance for ascertaining the existence of rules of customary international law depends upon the quality of the reasoning therein – including, above all, the degree to which this results from a thorough inspection of evidence of an alleged general practice that is accepted as law, and upon the decision's reception – by states and in ensuing case law, particularly [553]. Depending on the circumstances, other considerations might include the rules and procedures which the court or tribunal applies, the nature of that court or tribunal, and the size of the majority by which its decision was adopted [553]. As customary international law may have progressed since the date of a specific decision, judicial pronouncements over this area do not check the law [553].

The term 'international courts and tribunals' covers any transnational entity that exercises judicial powers and which is called upon to examine rules of international customary law [553]. It includes the ICJ, the PCIJ, regional and specialist courts – such as the International Tribunal for the Law of the Sea, the ICC and other global criminal tribunals, the World Trade Organization Dispute Settlement Body, regional human rights courts, interstate arbitral tribunals, and other supranational tribunals that apply international law [553].

The word 'decisions' incorporates judgments, advisory opinions, and orders on interlocutory and procedural matters [553]. The expression 'national courts' embraces those which have an international element operating within at least one domestic legal system, such as 'hybrid' courts and tribunals that have mixed international and national composition and jurisdiction [554].

Conclusion 14: Teachings

Teachings of the most highly qualified publicists of the various nations may serve as subsidiary means for the determination of rules of customary international law [555].

The term 'teachings' – or 'writings' – includes teachings in non-written form, such as audiovisual materials and lectures [554]. While writings are not a source of international law, they may provide guidance to ascertain the existence and content of rules of customary international law [554]. This auxiliary role acknowledges the value that teachings may have in collecting and evaluating state practice, in identifying divergences therein and the possible lack or development of rules, and in appraising the law [554].

Caution should be shown when drawing upon writings, because their worth in determining the existence of a rule of customary international law varies [554]. In advocating development of the law, writers do not always clearly distinguish between this as it is and as they would like it to be [554]. Furthermore, teachings may mirror the individual or national perspectives of their authors [554]. Moreover, writings may differ considerably in quality [554].

The quality of the particular writing matters more than the author's reputation [554]. The factors to be considered regarding the former include the author's approach to the identification of customary international law, and the extent to which his or her text is faithful to this slant [554]. It is important to have regard to writings that are representative of the main legal systems and regions of the world, and in different languages, when identifying customary international law [554].

Part Six: Persistent objector

Conclusion 15: Persistent objector

1. Where a State has objected to a rule of customary international law while that rule was in the process of formation, the rule is not opposable to the State concerned for so long as it maintains its objection [556].
2. The objection must be clearly expressed, made known to other States, and maintained persistently [557].
3. The present conclusion is without prejudice to any question concerning peremptory norms of general international law *(jus cogens)* [558].

A clear verbal objection – in either oral or written form suffices to hold the legal position of the objecting state [559]. It is for the latter to ensure that its protest is announced to other states [559].

The requirement that the objection be 'maintained persistently' applies both before, and after, the rule of customary international law has transpired [559]. Assessing whether this condition has been satisfied must be done pragmatically, taking into consideration the circumstances of the particular case [559]. The protest should be reiterated when the situation is such that a restatement is called for, i.e., where inaction or silence may reasonably lead to the conclusion that the state has abandoned its objection [559]. Repeated protests must be consistent, i.e., without major contradictions [559].

Part Seven: Particular customary international law

Conclusion 16: Particular customary international law

1. A rule of particular customary international law, whether regional, local or other, is a rule of customary international law that applies only among a limited number of States [560].
2. To determine the existence and content of a rule of particular customary international law, it is necessary to ascertain whether there is a general practice among the States concerned that is accepted by them as law (*opinio juris*) among themselves [561].

The preceding conclusions apply to the determination of rules of particular customary international law, except as otherwise provided in the current conclusion [559]. A rule of particular customary international law generates neither rights nor obligations for third states [559], and is distinguished from general customary international law – which, in principle, pertains to all states [559].

Rules of particular customary international law may apply among types of groupings of states [559]. Frequently, reference is made to customary rules of a regional nature, such as those that are distinctive of Latin-American states – for instance, diplomatic asylum [559]. Particular customary international law may extend over a smaller area, for example, a subregion, or even bind just two states [562]. A rule of particular customary international law could develop among states that are connected by a mutual activity, cause or interest other than their location [562].

While the two-element approach requiring a general practice and its acceptance as law applies to the identification of rules of particular customary international law, this practice must be a consistent practice among all the states to which the rule at issue pertains [562]. Each of these countries must have accepted the practice as law between themselves [562]. In this respect, the application of this approach is stricter in the instance of rules of particular customary international law than in the case of those of general customary international law [562].

Comment

The ILC has thoroughly investigated, and provided guidance on, the formation of rules of customary international law. However, it took the Commission until 2011 to identify this fundamental, substantial area of international law for further study. Today, i.e., a few years after the work of the ILC on this topic has been completed, there are clear guidelines on this source of international law, but nothing more. Given the cruciality of having a definite, accessible body of international law readily-available to all, one expects the ILC to proceed to compile a series of detailed volumes as to the precise rules that currently comprise the body of customary international law, and to regularly update these – deleting obsolete rules and including new ones. Ongoing communication with states and other international persons will be indispensable to conserving the quality and reliability of these tomes. Development of them is a vital next step for the ILC, in the interests of legal certainty.

Primary Sources: *Jus Cogens*[347]

Introduction

A peremptory norm of general international law – *jus cogens* – prevails over other sources of international law, and may be modified solely by a subsequent peremptory norm of general international law[348]. A treaty is void, if, at the time that it is concluded, it is incompatible with a peremptory norm of international law[349]. If a new peremptory norm of general international law emerges, then any existing convention which is at variance with this norm becomes void and aborts[350].

In addition to *jus cogens*, international law includes *erga omnes* obligations[351], i.e., those that are to be respected by everyone. These duties prevail over other sources of international

[347] Fn 236 defines the term '*jus cogens*'.

[348] Second sentence of fn 236, and fourth sentence of fn 322.

[349] Third sentence of fn 322.

[350] Sentence immediately preceding the text to fn 327.

[351] '*Erga omnes*' (i.e., 'towards all') obligations are "[o]bligations in whose fulfilment all states have a legal interest[,] because their subject matter is of importance to the international community as a whole. It follows from this that

law, except for *jus cogens*. The purpose of all these high-ranking worldwide norms is to preserve and protect the moral basis for the international legal system.

Work of the ILC

At its sixty-sixth session, in 2014, the ILC included the topic '*Jus cogens*' in its future programme of work [563]. At its sixty-seventh session, in 2015, the Commission selected this subject for its present work scheme, and appointed Dr. Dire Tladi (now Judge Tladi, Member of the ICJ [564]) as Special Rapporteur for the theme [563].

After receiving four reports from the Special Rapporteur in successive sessions, the ILC, at the last of these sessions, i.e., its seventy-first session, in 2019, adopted twenty-three draft conclusions on peremptory norms of general international law (*jus cogens*) on first reading, together with commentaries thereon [563]. It conveyed these draft conclusions, via the Secretary-General, to governments for observations and comments – to be advanced to the Secretary-General by 1st December 2020 [563].

At its seventy-third session, in 2022, the ILC considered the Special Rapporteur's fifth report together with the observations and comments received from governments on the draft conclusions as adopted in first reading [563]. Following its debate on the report, the Committee referred the draft conclusions – as laid down in the Special Rapporteur's fifth report – to the Drafting Committee [563]. The ILC adopted, on second reading, the draft conclusions on identification and legal consequences of peremptory norms of general international law (*jus cogens*), and submitted these to the UN General Assembly [563]. In Resolution 77/103 of 7th December 2022[352], the General Assembly decided that its consideration of this matter would be continued at its next session [381].

Draft Conclusions on Identification and Legal Consequences of Peremptory Norms of General International Law (*Jus Cogens*[353])

Part One: Introduction
Conclusion 1: Scope

---

the breach of such an obligation is of concern not only to the victimized state but also to all the other members of the international community. Thus, in the event of a breach of these obligations, every state must be considered justified in invoking (probably through judicial channels) the responsibility of the guilty state committing the internationally wrongful act. It has been suggested that an example of an *ergo omnes* obligation is that of a people's right to self-determination." (Oxford Reference (2024), "Overview: *erga omnes* obligations," accessed October 6, 2024, <https://www.oxfordreference.com/display/10.1093/oi/authority.20110803095756413>).

352 Its Operative Paragraph 3 states: "*The General Assembly*, ... 3. *Decides* that the consideration of chapter IV of the report of the International Law Commission on the work of its seventy-third session, dealing with the topic "Peremptory Norms of General International Law (*Jus Cogens*)", shall be continued at the seventy-eighth session of the General Assembly, during the consideration of the report of the Commission on the work of its seventy-fourth session;" (United Nations (2022), Resolution 77/103 adopted by the General Assembly on 7th December 2022, Operative Paragraph 3; emphasis original).

353 Fn 236 defines the term '*jus cogens*'.

> The present draft conclusions concern the identification and legal consequences of peremptory norms of general international law (*jus cogens*[354]) [565].

The draft conclusions are mainly concerned with the method for establishing whether a norm of general international law is peremptory, i.e., that it is accepted and recognized by the global community of states as a norm from which no derogation is allowed and which can be modified solely by a subsequent norm of general international law having the same character [566]. *Jus cogens* norms in domestic legal systems, and those of a purely regional or bilateral character, are excluded from the scope of this topic [566]. The word 'norm' is used because it is understood to be broader in meaning than the related words 'rules' and 'principles' and to encompass both; in some instances, these terms can be interchanged [567].

The draft conclusions apply to states, as the principal subjects of international law [567]. If a particular draft conclusion applies to worldwide organizations, then the commentaries make this clear [567].

Conclusion 2: Nature of peremptory norms of general international law (*jus cogens*)

> Peremptory norms of general international law (*jus cogens*[355]) reflect and protect fundamental values of the international community. They are universally applicable and are hierarchically superior to other rules of international law [567].

Support for the connection between peremptory norms of general international law and fundamental values is found in the practice of states, especially in the judgments of national courts [568]. While these values are usually humanitarian in nature, others may also underlie peremptory norms of general international law – provided that they are shared by the worldwide community [569]. This community includes both states and other partakers of international law [569]. Fundamental values are dynamic, and may evolve [569].

The universal application of peremptory norms of general international law (*jus cogens*) means that these are binding on all subjects of international law which they address – including states and global organizations [570]. The notions that peremptory norms of general international law are universally applicable and are hierarchically superior to other rules of international law, come from the non-derogability of these standards [571]. States are not permitted to derogate from a peremptory norm by fashioning their own special laws that are incompatible with it [571].

The universal character of peremptory norms of general international law is reflected in the judgments of national courts and in scholarly writings [571]. Implications of the universal application of these norms include the inapplicability of the persistent objector doctrine or rule to them, and their non-application on a regional or bilateral basis [572].

International courts and tribunals have frequently referred to the hierarchical superiority of peremptory norms of general international law [572]. Acknowledgement of the hierarchical superiority of peremptory norms of general international law can be observed in the practice of states [572].

Proof that a norm 'reflects and protects fundamental values of the international community,' is 'universally applicable' and is 'hierarchically superior to other norms of

[354] Emphasis original.
[355] Emphasis original.

international law' may suffice to back or confirm the peremptory status of a norm [573]. However, this supplementary evidence cannot, in and of itself, form the basis for identifying peremptory norms of general international law [574].

Conclusion 3: Definition of a peremptory norm of general international law (*jus cogens*)

> A peremptory norm of general international law (*jus cogens*[356]) is a norm accepted and recognized by the international community of States as a whole as a norm from which no derogation is permitted and which can be modified only by a subsequent norm of general international law (*jus cogens*[357]) having the same character [575].

Draft conclusion 3 is a reproduction of the second sentence of Article 53 of the Vienna Convention on the Law of Treaties 1969, omitting from therein the phrase 'For the purposes of the present Convention,' and adding the phrase '*jus cogens*' in parentheses after the each of the expressions 'peremptory norm of general international law' and 'subsequent norm of general international law'[358] [575]. While the formulation in Article 53 of the abovementioned treaty is for 'the purposes of the present Convention,' it also applies in other contexts – including in relation to state responsibility [576].

Part Two: Identification of peremptory norms of general international law (*jus cogens*)

Conclusion 4: Criteria for the identification of a peremptory norm of general international law (*jus cogens*)

> To identify a peremptory norm of general international law (*jus cogens*), it is necessary to establish that the norm in question meets the following criteria:
>
> (*a*) it is a norm of general international law; and
> (*b*) it is accepted and recognized by the international community of States as a whole as a norm from which no derogation is permitted and which can be modified only by a subsequent norm of general international law having the same character[359] [577].

The two cumulative criteria in draft conclusion 4 imply a two-step process to the identification of a peremptory norm of general international law (*jus cogens*) [578]. First it is necessary to gather evidence that norm at issue is one of general international law [578]. Second, this norm must be shown to be accepted and recognized by the international community of states in general as having a peremptory character [578].

Conclusion 5: Basis for peremptory norms of general international law (*jus cogens*)

1. Customary international law is the most common basis for peremptory norms of general international law (*jus cogens*[360]) [578].
2. Treaty provisions and general principles of law may also serve as bases for peremptory norms of general international law (*jus cogens*[361]) [578].

[356] Emphasis original.
[357] Emphasis original.
[358] The fourth sentence of fn 322 comprises the second sentence of Article 53 of the Vienna Convention on the Law of Treaties 1969.
[359] The italics for the phrase '*jus cogens*', and for the letters '*a*' and '*b*', are present in the original text.
[360] Emphasis original.
[361] Emphasis original.

The meaning of the term 'general international law' is context-specific [579]. In the context of peremptory norms, the word 'general' in 'norms of general international law' refers to the breadth of applicability of the norm at issue [579]. Norms of general international law are those norms of international law that must have equal effect for all of the international community's members [579].

The words 'basis' in paragraph 1, and 'bases' in paragraph 2, of draft conclusion 5, are to be understood widely and flexibly [579]. They are intended to encapsulate the range of ways which different sources of international law may bring about the emergence of a peremptory norm of general international law [579].

State practice confirms that customary international law is the most prevalent basis for peremptory norms of general international law [579]. The jurisprudence of the ICJ furnishes cogent evidence of the basis of peremptory norms of general international law in customary international law [580]. Moreover, other international courts and tribunals have accepted customary international law as a basis for peremptory norms of general international law [581].

The phrase 'may also' in paragraph 2 of draft conclusion 5 is meant to indicate that, while there is little state practice to underpin the materialization of peremptory norms of general international law from either treaty provisions or general principles of law, the possibility of these sources of international law constituting the basis of peremptory norms of general international law remains [581].

The expression 'treaty provisions' is used in paragraph 2 of draft conclusion 5, rather than the word 'treaties,' to show concern with at least one norm that a treaty contains – rather than with the convention itself [581]. While treaties tend not to be 'general international law' because they do not normally have a general extent of application with equal effect for all members of the international community, there is support in scholarly writings that provisions within treaties can comprise the basis of peremptory norms of general international law [581].

General principles of law are part of general international law, as they have a general scope of application with equal effect for all members of the international community [582]. There is some backing in writings for general principles of law as a basis of peremptory norms of general international law [582].

Conclusion 6: Acceptance and recognition

1. The criterion of acceptance and recognition referred to in draft conclusion 4, subparagraph (*b*[362]), is distinct from acceptance and recognition as a norm of general international law [583].
2. To identify a norm as a peremptory norm of general international law (*jus cogens*[363]), there must be evidence that such a norm is accepted and recognized by the international community of States as a whole as one from which no derogation is permitted and which can only be modified by a subsequent norm of general international law having the same character [583].

Paragraph 1 of draft conclusion 6 attempts to make clear that the acceptance and recognition to which this conclusion refers is distinct from the acceptance and recognition that is necessary for other rules of international law [583]. The former 'acceptance and recognition'

362 Emphasis original.

363 Emphasis original.

differs from, for example, acceptance as law (*opinio juris*), which is a component for the identification of customary international law, or recognition, which is an element for the identification of general principles of law [583].

There is a further criterion, over and above those for the existence of a rule of general international law, that must be fulfilled for peremptory norms of general international law [583]. It is this additional criterion to which draft conclusion 6 refers [583].

Paragraph 2 of draft conclusion 6 describes the acceptance and recognition that is required to raise a norm of general international law to the standing of a peremptory norm of general international law [583]. In order to prove that a norm is a peremptory norm of general international law, it is essential to supply evidence that the norm is accepted and recognized as being one from which no derogation is allowed, and which can be modified solely by a subsequent norm of general international law with the same character [584].

'Acceptance and recognition' as a criterion for the identification of peremptory norms of general international law does not comprise two separate requirements, but denotes the variety of ways that states may demonstrate their view that a norm has a peremptory character [585]. It is adequate to show, as a whole, the acceptance and recognition of the norm of general international law as being peremptory [585].

Conclusion 7: International community of States as a whole

1. It is the acceptance and recognition by the international community of States as a whole that is relevant for the identification of peremptory norms of general international law (*jus cogens*[364]) [585].
2. Acceptance and recognition by a very large and representative majority of States is required for the identification of a norm as a peremptory norm of general international law (*jus cogens*[365]); acceptance and recognition by all States is not required [585].
3. While the positions of other actors may be relevant in providing context and for assessing acceptance and recognition by the international community of States as a whole, these positions cannot, in and of themselves, form part of such acceptance and recognition [585].

Paragraph 1 of draft conclusion 7 specifies that it is acceptance and recognition of the worldwide community of states in general that is pertinent for the identification of peremptory norms of general international law [586]. It is the position of states that is relevant – not that of others [586]. Paragraph 2 of draft conclusion 7 requires acceptance and recognition of a norm as a peremptory norm of general international law by 'a very large and representative majority of states,' which necessitates – as a qualitative assessment – that this acceptance and recognition be across cultures, legal systems and regions [588].

The decisions of international courts and tribunals, and state practice, have continued to associate the elevation of norms of general international law to peremptory standing with acceptance and recognition of states [586]. While peremptory norms of general international law continue to be connected to notions of the conscience of humankind in scholarly writings and in practice, the material presented to exemplify the peremptory character of norms comprises procedures and acts that states have generated – including within global institutions [587].

---

364 Emphasis original.
365 Emphasis original.

Practice and acts of worldwide organizations may furnish evidence of the acceptance and recognition by states, when ascertaining whether a norm has a peremptory character [587]. The positions of non-state entities are insufficient, of themselves, to establish the acceptance and recognition that is requisite to lift a norm of general international law to peremptory status [587]. Paragraph 3 of draft conclusion 7 reflect this [587].

Conclusion 8: Evidence of acceptance and recognition

1. Evidence of acceptance and recognition that a norm of general international law is a peremptory norm (*jus cogens*[366]) may take a wide range of forms [588].
2. Forms of evidence include, but are not limited to: public statements made on behalf of States; official publications; government legal opinions; diplomatic correspondence; constitutional provisions; legislative and administrative acts; decisions of national courts; treaty provisions; resolutions adopted by an international organization or at an intergovernmental conference, and other conduct of States [588].

Any material that is capable of expressing or reflecting states' views, is relevant as evidence of acceptance and recognition that a norm of general international law is a peremptory norm [589]. The question is whether such documents, when taken together, establish the acceptance and recognition of the global community of states as a whole that the norm is one from which no derogation is allowed [590]. The materials must be weighed and assessed jointly, in their context, in order to ascertain whether they evince acceptance and recognition of the worldwide community of states in general of the peremptory character of the norm [590].

Conclusion 9: Subsidiary means for the determination of the peremptory character of norms of general international law

1. Decisions of international courts and tribunals, in particular of the International Court of Justice, are a subsidiary means for determining the peremptory character of norms of general international law. Regard may also be had, as appropriate, to decisions of national courts [590].
2. The works of expert bodies established by States or international organizations and the teachings of the most highly qualified publicists of the various nations may also serve as subsidiary means for determining the peremptory character of norms of general international law [590].

The materials identified in draft conclusion 9 facilitate the identification of acceptance and recognition that a norm of general international law is a peremptory norm, but do not, in themselves, constitute evidence of this acceptance and recognition [590]. There are many examples of decisions of international courts relying on other determinations of transnational courts and tribunals when identifying a peremptory norm of general international law [591]. The ICJ, in its judgment in *Questions relating to the Obligation to Prosecute or to Extradite (Belgium v. Senegal)*[367], opines that the prohibition of torture is part of customary international

[366] Emphasis original.

[367] *Questions relating to the Obligation to Prosecute or to Extradite (Belgium v. Senegal)*, Judgment of 20 July 2012, *I.C.J. Reports 2012*, 422-463.

law, and that this principle has become a peremptory norm of general international law (*jus cogens*)[368] [592].

The ILC uses the phrases 'may also' and 'as appropriate,' in the second sentence of paragraph 1 of draft conclusion 9, to show that, although decisions of national courts may constitute subsidiary ways to determine peremptory norms of general international law, these should be referred to with caution [593]. The emphasis accorded to any one of these judgments depends upon the reasoning applied therein [593].

The use of the expression 'may also' in paragraph 2 of draft conclusion 9, in contradistinction to the word 'are' – which is employed to qualify decisions of international courts and tribunals in paragraph 1 of this draft conclusion, indicates that less weight may be given to works of expert groups and scholarly writings than to judicial determinations [594]. The relevance of these works and writings depends upon several factors, including their reasoning, the extent to which the views given therein are accepted by states, and the degree to which these perspectives are corroborated by either forms of evidence that paragraph 2 of draft conclusion 8[369] lists or determinations of international courts and tribunals [595].

The subsidiary means for the determination of the peremptory character of norms of general international law which draft conclusion 9 identifies are not exhaustive [596]. They are the most prevalent secondary sources that have been counted upon in the identification of peremptory norms of general international law [596].

Part Three: Legal consequences of peremptory norms of general international law (*jus cogens*)

Conclusion 10: Treaties conflicting with a peremptory norm of general international law (*jus cogens*)

1. A treaty is void if, at the time of its conclusion, it conflicts with a peremptory norm of general international law (*jus cogens*[370]). The provisions of such a treaty have no legal force [597].
2. Subject to paragraph 2 of draft conclusion 11[371], if a new peremptory norm of general international law (*jus cogens*[372]) emerges, [then] any existing treaty which is in conflict with that norm becomes void and terminates. The parties to such a treaty are released from any obligation further to perform the treaty [597].

The first sentence of paragraph 1 of draft conclusion 10 replicates the first sentence of Article 53 of the Vienna Convention on the Law of Treaties 1969[373], adding to it the bracketed

[368] At paragraph 99 of its judgment, the ICJ states: "The prohibition [of torture] is grounded in a widespread international practice and on the *opinio juris* of States. It appears in numerous international instruments of universal application (in particular the Universal Declaration of Human Rights of 1948, the 1949 Geneva Conventions for the protection of war victims; the International Covenant on Civil and Political Rights of 1966; General Assembly resolution 3452/30 of 9 December 1975 on the Protection of All Persons from Being Subjected to Torture and Other Cruel, Inhuman or Degrading Treatment or Punishment), and it has been introduced into the domestic law of almost all States; finally, acts of torture are regularly denounced within national and international fora." (*Questions relating to the Obligation to Prosecute or to Extradite (Belgium v. Senegal)*, Judgment of 20 July 2012, *I.C.J. Reports 2012*, 422-463, 457).

[369] The quoted sentence immediately following the text to fn 366, is paragraph 2 of draft conclusion 8.

[370] Emphasis original.

[371] Point 2. in the text to fn 377 sets out paragraph 2 of draft conclusion 11.

[372] Emphasis original.

[373] The third sentence of fn 322 lays down the first sentence of Article 53 of the Vienna Convention on the Law of Treaties 1969.

phrase '*jus cogens*' [598]. The second sentence of that paragraph closely follows the second sentence of paragraph 1 of Article 69 of the Vienna Convention on the Law of Treaties 1969[374] [598].

The first sentence of paragraph 2 of draft conclusion 10 is based upon Article 64 of the Vienna Convention of the Law of Treaties 1969[375] [598]. The second sentence of that paragraph closely adheres to subparagraph 2(a) of Article 71 of the Vienna Convention on the Law of Treaties 1969[376] [598]. The effect of the aforementioned paragraph 2 is to recognize that the provisions of the existing treaty were valid and could give rise to legal consequences before the emergence of the peremptory norm of general international law [598].

Conclusion 11: Separability of treaty provisions conflicting with a peremptory norm of general international law (*jus cogens*)

1. A treaty which, at the time of its conclusion, conflicts with a peremptory norm of general international law (*jus cogens*) is void in whole, and no separation of the provisions of the treaty is permitted [599].
2. A treaty which is in conflict with a new peremptory norm of general international law (*jus cogens*) becomes void and terminates in whole, unless:
   (*a*) the provisions that are in conflict with a peremptory norm of general international law (*jus cogens*) are separable from the remainder of the treaty with regard to their application;
   (*b*) it appears from the treaty or is otherwise established that acceptance of the said provisions was not an essential basis of the consent of the parties to be bound by the treaty as a whole; and
   (*c*) continued performance of the remainder of the treaty would not be unjust[377] [599].

The first part of paragraph 1 of draft conclusion 11 follows the first sentence of Article 53 of the Vienna Convention on the Law of Treaties 1969[378], rephrasing it and adding to it the bracketed phrase '*jus cogens*' and the expression 'in whole' [599]. The second part of that paragraph is based on paragraph 5 of Article 44 of the Vienna Convention on the Law of Treaties 1969[379], which excludes treaties falling within Article 53 of the Vienna Convention on the Law of Treaties 1969[380] from the rules on the separability of treaty provisions in Article 44 of the Vienna Convention on the Law of Treaties 1969[381] [599].

Paragraph 2 of draft conclusion 11 addresses circumstances in which a treaty, or specific provisions of a treaty, clash with a peremptory norm of general international law that emerges after the conclusion of this treaty [599]. The elements which are listed in that paragraph are

[374] The second clause of the sentence immediately following the text to fn 327 sets out the second sentence of Article 69(1) of the Vienna Convention on the Law of Treaties 1969.

[375] The sentence immediately preceding the text to fn 327 lays down Article 64 of the Vienna Convention of the Law of Treaties 1969.

[376] The text to fn 327 sets out Article 71(2)(a) of the Vienna Convention on the Law of Treaties 1969.

[377] The italics for the three occurrences of the phrase '*jus cogens*', and for the letters '*a*', '*b*' and '*c*', are present in the original text.

[378] Fn 373.

[379] The text to fn 322 sets out Article 44(5) of the Vienna Convention on the Law of Treaties 1969.

[380] The third and fourth sentences of fn 322 reproduce Article 53 of the Vienna Convention on the Law of Treaties 1969.

[381] The text to fns 319-322 lays down Article 44 of the Vienna Convention on the Law of Treaties 1969.

taken from paragraph 3 of Article 44 of the Vienna Convention on the Law of Treaties 1969[382] [600]. All three of these elements must be present, in order for provisions that are incompatible with a peremptory norm to be separated from the remainder of the treaty [600]. Whether they are present is to be substantiated by a consideration of all the pertinent circumstances, including the topic of the provision, its relation to other clauses within the treaty and the last-mentioned's working papers [600].

Conclusion 12: Consequences of the invalidity and termination of treaties conflicting with a peremptory norm of general international law (*jus cogens*)

1. Parties to a treaty[,] which is void as a result of being in conflict with a peremptory norm of general international law (*jus cogens*) at the time of the treaty's conclusion[,] have a legal obligation to:
   (*a*) eliminate as far as possible the consequences of any act performed in reliance on any provision of the treaty which conflicts with a peremptory norm of general international law (*jus cogens*); and
   (*b*) bring their mutual relations into conformity with the peremptory norm of general international law (*jus cogens*) [600].
2. The termination of a treaty on account of the emergence of a new peremptory norm of general international law (*jus cogens*) does not affect any right, obligation or legal situation of the parties created through the execution of the treaty prior to the termination of the treaty, provided that those rights, obligations or situations may thereafter be maintained only to the extent that their maintenance is not in itself in conflict with the new peremptory norm of general international law (*jus cogens*)[383] [600].

Paragraph 1 of draft conclusion 12 addresses situations in which a treaty is void, as a result of an incompatibility with a peremptory norm of general international law at the time when the treaty was concluded [601]. That paragraph closely adheres to paragraph 1 of Article 71 of the Vienna Convention on the Law of Treaties 1969[384] – which concerns a treaty that is void under Article 53 of the Vienna Convention on the Law of Treaties 1969[385] [601]. Since, in this case, no treaty comes to be, no reliance can be placed on the treaty's provisions [601].

Under subparagraph 1(a) of draft conclusion 12, the parties to this treaty are legally obliged to remove 'as far as possible' the consequences of any acts which are carried out in reliance on its impugned provisions [601]. Thus, even though the entire treaty is void, there is no obligation to eradicate outcomes of acts that are discharged in reliance on provisions of the treaty which are not incompatible with peremptory norms of international law [601]. Under subparagraph 1(b) of draft conclusion 12, the parties are to align their mutual relations with the peremptory norm of general international law [601].

---

[382] The sentence immediately following the text to fn 320 (or immediately preceding the text to fn 321) sets out Article 44(3) of the Vienna Convention on the Law of Treaties 1969.

[383] The italics for the five instances of the phrase '*jus cogens*', and for the letters '*a*' and '*b*', are present in the original text.

[384] The final sentence of fn 322 lays down Article 71(1) of the Vienna Convention on the Law of Treaties 1969.

[385] The third and fourth sentences of fn 322 replicate Article 53 of the Vienna Convention on the Law of Treaties 1969.

Paragraph 2 of draft conclusion 12 concerns the situation that Article 64 of the Vienna Convention on the Law of Treaties[386] addresses, namely those instances in which a treaty becomes void as a result of a peremptory norm that emerges after the treaty is adopted [601]. The abovementioned paragraph closely follows subparagraph 2(b) of Article 71 of the Vienna Convention on the Law of Treaties 1969[387] [601]. During the period between the treaty's adoption and the coming-to-light of the peremptory norm, the treaty remains valid; as a result, acts which are carried out – and rights and obligations that are generated – pursuant to it, remain valid [601]. Therefore, there can, in general, be no duty to eliminate consequences of acts which are lawfully performed [601]. Thus, while the treaty becomes void, legal situations, rights and obligations that are created by licit conduct under the treaty will not, in principle, be affected [602]. However, these legal situations, rights and responsibilities may be maintained, or relied upon, solely to the extent that their continued existence is not, in itself, an infraction of a peremptory norm of general international law [602].

Conclusion 13: Absent of effect of reservations to treaties on peremptory norms of general international law (*jus cogens*)

1. A reservation to a treaty provision that reflects a peremptory norm of general international law (*jus cogens*[388]) does not affect the binding nature of that norm, which shall continue to apply as such [602].
2. A reservation cannot exclude or modify the legal effect of a treaty in a manner contrary to a peremptory norm of general international law (*jus cogens*[389]) [602].

Paragraph 1 of draft conclusion 13 follows paragraph 1 of Guideline 4.4.3 of the Guide to Practice on Reservations to Treaties[390] [602]. The phrase 'as such,' which is present in both these paragraphs, is intended to show that, even when a peremptory norm of general international law is reflected in a clause in a treaty, this norm continues to exist independently of that provision in the convention [602]. Thus, while the reservation may affect the legal consequences of the clause in the treaty regarding the reserving state, the norm – as a peremptory norm of general international law, will be unaffected and will continue to apply [602]. A state is unable to avoid the binding nature of a peremptory norm of general international law by drafting a reservation to a clause in a treaty which mirrors that norm [603].

Paragraph 2 of draft conclusion 13 replicates paragraph 2 of Guideline 4.4.3 of the Guide to Practice on Reservations to Treaties[391], adding to it the bracketed expression '*jus cogens*'

[386] The sentence immediately preceding the text to fn 327 sets out Article 64 of the Vienna Convention on the Law of Treaties 1969.

[387] Fn 327 lays down Article 71(2)(b) of the Vienna Convention on the Law of Treaties 1969.

[388] Emphasis original.

[389] Emphasis original.

[390] Guideline 4.4.3 of the Guide to Practice on Reservations to Treaties is headed 'Absence of effect on a peremptory norm of general international law (*jus cogens*)'; its paragraph 1 reads: "A reservation to a treaty provision which reflects a peremptory norm of general international law (*jus cogens*) does not affect the binding nature of that norm, which shall continue to apply as such between the reserving State or organization and other States or international organizations." (International Law Commission (2011), Report of the International Law Commission on the work of its sixty-third session (26 April – 3 June and 4 July – 12 August 2011), Document A/66/10, Chapter IV. Reservations to treaties, F.1. Text of the guidelines constituting the Guide to Practice, followed by an annex on the reservations dialogue, *Yearbook of the International Law Commission*, 2011, Volume II, Part Two, 26-38, 35; emphasis original).

[391] Paragraph 2 of Guideline 4.4.3 of the Guide to Practice on Reservation to Treaties states: "A reservation cannot exclude or modify the legal effect of a treaty in a manner contrary to a peremptory norm of general international

[603]. While a reservation to a treaty that sets out a right to education – which is not a peremptory norm of general international law – would neither be incompatible with a peremptory norm of general international law nor constitute a reservation to a clause of a treaty that reflects such a norm, a reservation which restricts the implementation of a right to education to a particular racial group or which excludes such a set from benefiting from the treaty right may be found to contravene the peremptory norm of general international law that prohibits racial discrimination [603].

Conclusion 14: Rules of customary international law conflicting with a peremptory norm of general international law (*jus cogens*)

1. A rule of customary international law does not come into existence[,] if it would conflict with an existing peremptory norm of general international law (*jus cogens*). This is without prejudice to the possible modification of a peremptory norm of general international law (*jus cogens*) by a subsequent norm of general international law having the same character [603].
2. A rule of customary international law not of a peremptory character ceases to exist[,] if and to the extent that it conflicts with a new peremptory norm of general international law (*jus cogens*) [603].
3. The persistent objector rule does not apply to peremptory norms of general international law (*jus cogens*)[392] [603].

Peremptory norms of general international law are hierarchically superior to other rules of international law, and, therefore, override the latter in instances of conflict [604]. Decisions of international courts and tribunals, and determinations of national courts, have recognized that peremptory norms of general international law prevail over conflicting rules of customary international law [604]. The first sentence of paragraph 1 of draft conclusion 14 follows from the superiority of peremptory norms of general international law over customary international law [605].

The second sentence of paragraph 1 of draft conclusion 14 emphasizes that modification of a peremptory norm of general international law is possible – although the threshold for this is very high [605]. The phrase 'having the same character' therein, which is lifted from Article 53 of the Vienna Convention on the Law of Treaties 1969[393], indicates that, to alter a peremptory norm of a general international law, a rule of customary international law must itself be recognized and accepted as one from which no derogation is allowed and which may only be modified by a subsequent peremptory norm of general international law [605]. Thus, there must be, at the moment of emergence of a peremptory norm of general international law, a practice that is accepted as law and which the global community of states as a whole simultaneously accepts and recognizes as having peremptory character [606].

law." (International Law Commission (2011), Report of the International Law Commission on the work of its sixty-third session (26 April – 3 June and 4 July – 12 August 2011), Document A/66/10, Chapter IV. Reservations to treaties, F.1. Text of the guidelines constituting the Guide to Practice, followed by an annex on the reservations dialogue, *Yearbook of the International Law Commission*, 2011, Volume II, Part Two, 26-38, 35).

[392] The italics for the four occurrences of the phrase '*jus cogens*' are present in the original text.

[393] The third and fourth sentences of fn 322 reproduce Article 53 of the Vienna Convention on the Law of Treaties 1969.

In paragraph 2 of draft conclusion 14, the expression 'if and to the extent' is meant to indicate that solely those parts of the rule of customary international law at issue which conflict with the peremptory norm of general international law, will no longer exist [607]. This phrase functions like a separability clause, in order to preserve those parts of the rule of customary international law that are compatible with the peremptory norm of general international law [607].

Regarding paragraph 3 of draft conclusion 14, the rule that, by virtue of their hierarchical superiority and universal application, peremptory norms of general international law are not subject to the persistent objector rule[394], has been supported by statements from states [608]. To the extent that persistent objection from several states implies that a rule of customary international law is not accepted and recognized by the worldwide community of states as a whole as one from which no derogation is allowed, a peremptory norm of general international law might not emerge from this rule [609].

Conclusion 15: Obligations created by unilateral acts of States conflicting with a peremptory norm of general international law (*jus cogens*)

1. A unilateral act of a State manifesting the intention to be bound by an obligation under international law that would be in conflict with a peremptory norm of general international law (*jus cogens*[395]) does not create such an obligation [609].
2. An obligation under international law created by a unilateral act of a State ceases to exist[,] if and to the extent that it conflicts with a new peremptory norm of general international law (*jus cogens*[396]) [609].

Draft conclusion 15 concerns only unilateral acts by a state which it undertakes with the aim of creating obligations just for itself [612]. Paragraph 1 of draft conclusion 15 is incentivized by Article 53 of the Vienna Convention on the Law of Treaties 1969[397] [609]. The ILC, in guiding principle 8 of its guiding principles applicable to unilateral declarations of States capable of creating legal obligations, specifies the rule thus [610].

> A unilateral declaration which is in conflict with a peremptory norm of general international law is void[398] [611].

Even though guiding principle 8 uses the phrase 'is void,' draft conclusion 15 employs broader expressions, i.e., 'does not create such an obligation' and 'ceases to exist,' so as to

---

394 Paragraph 1 of Conclusion 15 of the Conclusions on identification of customary international law, in the subsection entitled 'Conclusions on identification of customary international law', in the section titled 'Primary Sources: International Custom', above in the current chapter (i.e., Chapter 4), contains the persistent objector rule.

395 Emphasis original.

396 Emphasis original.

397 The third and fourth sentences of fn 322 replicate Article 53 of the Vienna Convention on the Law of Treaties 1969.

398 The ILC's commentary states: "The invalidity of a unilateral act which is contrary to a peremptory norm of international law derives from the analogous rule contained in article 53 of the 1969 Vienna Convention [(fn 397)]. Most members of the Commission agreed that there was no obstacle to the application of this rule to the case of unilateral declarations." (International Law Commission (2006), Report of the International Law Commission on the work of its fifty-eighth session (1 May – 9 June and 3 July – 11 August 2006), Document A/61/10, Chapter IX. Unilateral acts of states, D.2. Text of the guiding principles with commentaries thereto adopted by the Commission at its fifty-eighth session, *Yearbook of the International Law Commission*, 2006, Volume II, Part Two, 161-166, 165).

express more fully the wider context (than that of guiding principle 8) of draft conclusion 15 – which is addressing unilateral acts of a state, of which its unilateral declarations are a subset [612]. Therefore, the focus is on the legal obligations that the unilateral act at issue intends to create [612]. These responsibilities are not generated, if they are at variance with a peremptory norm of general international law [612].

Paragraph 1 of draft conclusion 15 describes the unilateral act in question as one 'manifesting the intention to be bound by an obligation under international law' [612]. The words 'manifesting the intention' intend to show that, although it is the state's subjective purpose which is sought, this has to be determined from the complete circumstances and facts of each specific case [613]. Consequently, the subjective intention of the state is to be looked for by relying upon objective facts [614].

The scope of paragraph 2 of draft conclusion 15 differs from that of paragraph 1 of this draft conclusion, because the former refers to obligations of international law that a unilateral act of a state has heretofore created [612]. Paragraph 2 of draft conclusion 15 reflects paragraph 2 of draft conclusion 10[399] and paragraph 2 of draft conclusion 14[400] [612]. It recognizes that, under these circumstances, an obligation comes into being, and only ceases to exist at the instant of the emergence of a new peremptory norm of general international law [612]. The rule in paragraph 2 of draft conclusion 15 is motivated by Article 64 of the Vienna Convention on the Law of Treaties 1969[401] [612].

The obligations that arise from a unilateral act of a state which conflict with a new peremptory norm of general international law emerging after the discharge of this unilateral act, cease to exist merely to the extent that these responsibilities are incompatible with the new peremptory norm of general international law [612]. As in paragraph 2 of draft conclusion 14[402], the phrase 'if and to the extent' is meant to point out that solely those aspects of the obligation at issue which clash with the peremptory norm of general international law, will cease to exist [612].

Conclusion 16: Obligations created by resolutions, decisions or other acts of international organizations conflicting with a peremptory norm of general international law (*jus cogens*)

> A resolution, decision or other act of an international organization that would otherwise have binding effect does not create obligations under international law[,] if and to the extent that they conflict with a peremptory norm of general international law (*jus cogens*[403]) [614].

Draft conclusion 16 is intended to be of broad scope, covering all resolutions, decisions and acts of international organizations that would, but for the peremptory norm of general international law, establish obligations under international law [615]. Examples of a resolution, decision or act of a global institution 'that would otherwise have binding effect' include a

---

[399] The text to fns 371 and 372, together with sentence immediately following that text, consists of paragraph 2 of draft conclusion 10 on identification and legal consequences of peremptory norms of general international law (*jus cogens*).

[400] The sentence immediately preceding the text to fn 392 comprises paragraph 2 of draft conclusion 14 on identification and legal consequences of peremptory norms of general international law (*jus cogens*).

[401] The sentence immediately preceding the text to fn 327 lays down Article 64 of the Vienna Convention of the Law of Treaties 1969.

[402] Fn 400.

[403] Emphasis original.

decision in a resolution of the UNSC which is made under Charter VII of the UN Charter[404], and a decision of the General Assembly that admits a state to membership of the UN [616]. An interpretation of the pertinent decision ascertains whether it would, bar the aforementioned norm, have binding effect [615].[405]

As in paragraph 2 of draft conclusion 14[406] and paragraph 2 of draft conclusion 15[407], the expression 'if and to the extent' are intended to indicate that solely those obligations which are at variance with a peremptory norm of general international law will be affected by the working of draft conclusion 16 [615]. Clauses in a resolution, decision or other act of a transnational organization that are not incompatible with a peremptory norm of general international law will continue to apply, if they are separable from the rest of the act [615].

Article 103 of the UN Charter provides that, if there is a clash between the duties of Member States under the UN Charter and their responsibilities under any other international instrument, then their obligations under the UN Charter will take precedence [271]. If a resolution, decision or other act of the UN does not generate obligations under international law as a result of a conflict with a peremptory norm of general international law, then Article 103 need not be invoked [617]. For this reason, and given the hierarchical superiority of peremptory norms of general international law, draft conclusion 16 applies to binding resolutions, decisions and acts of the UNSC [617].

Draft conclusion 16 should not be read as supplying cover for unilateral repudiation of obligations arising under binding resolutions of the UN – including those of the UNSC that are adopted under Chapter VII of the UN Charter[408] [617]. It is very unlikely that a resolution of the UNSC would, ostensibly, be inconsistent with a peremptory norm of general international law [617].

Conclusion 17: Peremptory norms of general international law (*jus cogens*) as obligations owed to the international community as a whole (obligations *erga omnes*[409])

1. Peremptory norms of general international law (*jus cogens*) give rise to obligations owed to the international community as a whole (obligations *erga omnes*), in relation to which all States have a legal interest [617].

---

[404] Chapter VII of the UN Charter is entitled 'Action with Respect to Threats to the Peace, Breaches of the Peace, and Acts of Aggression', and comprises Articles 39 to 51 inclusive. The paragraph headed 'VII: Action with Respect to Threats to the Peace, Breaches of the Peace, and Acts of Aggression', in the subsection titled 'The UN Charter' in the section entitled 'The UN Charter' in Chapter 3, sets out provisions from Chapter VII of the UN Charter.

[405] The EU publishes acts in the form of regulations, decisions and directives, which are binding on its Member States; other international organizations – such as the African Union, the International Civil Aviation Organization and the World Trade Organization, may also issue resolutions, decisions or other acts that, if it were not for the rule that draft conclusion 16 lays down, would have binding effect (United Nations (2022), Report of the International Law Commission: Seventy-third session (18 April – 3 June and 4 July – 5 August 2022), Document A/77/10, Chapter IV. Peremptory norms of general international law (*jus cogens*), E.2. Text of the draft conclusions and commentaries thereto, General Assembly Official Records, Seventy-seventh Session, Supplement No.10 (A/77/10), 16-89, 63).

[406] The sentence immediately preceding the text to fn 392 consists of paragraph 2 of draft conclusion 14 on identification and legal consequences of peremptory norms of general international law (*jus cogens*).

[407] The text to fn 396 comprises paragraph 2 of draft conclusion 15 on identification and legal consequences of peremptory norms of general international law (*jus cogens*).

[408] Fn 404.

[409] Fn 351 defines the term '*erga omnes* obligations'.

2. Any State is entitled to invoke the responsibility of another State for a breach of a peremptory norm of general international law (*jus cogens*), in accordance with the rules on the responsibility of States for internationally wrongful acts[410] [617].

Statements by the governments of states and by national courts have recognized that peremptory norms of general international law (*jus cogens*), such as the prohibition of genocide and the prohibition of torture, have an *erga omnes* effect, i.e., they give rise to *erga omnes* obligations [618]. While the ICJ has not expressly declared that a link exists between peremptory norms of general international law and *erga omnes* obligations, such a connection could be deduced from some of its judgments and advisory opinions [618]. For instance, every norm that the ICJ has described as one having an *erga omnes* character is also one which has been included in the non-exhaustive list of norms that the ILC has previously referred to as having peremptory status [618]. The relationship between peremptory norms of general international law and *erga omnes* obligations has been acknowledged in scholarly writings [619].

Although all peremptory norms of general international law give rise to *erga omnes* obligations, not all *erga omnes* obligations originate from peremptory norms of general international law [619]. For example, certain rules concerning common spaces, especially common heritage regimes, may generate *erga omnes* obligations independent of whether or not these rules are peremptory norms of general international law [619].

In paragraph 1 of draft conclusion 17, the phrase ‘in relation to which all States have a legal interest’ describes the principal consequence of the *erga omnes* character of peremptory norms of general international law [620]. The expression therein ‘legal interest’ encompasses the protection of the legal norm – including rights and obligations [620]. The phrase ‘in relation to which’ is meant to capture the different ways that states may have an interest in *erga omnes* obligations [620]. The ICJ has referred to the legal interest of states in the protection of rights, and in the prevention of acts, that *erga omnes* obligations cover, and to the legal interest of all states in the observance of, or compliance with, the obligation at issue [620].

Paragraph 2 of draft conclusion 17 precisely describes the implication of the expression ‘in relation to which all states have a legal interest’ in paragraph 1 of the abovementioned draft conclusion [621]. This means that any state is entitled to invoke the responsibility of another state for the latter’s transgression of a peremptory norm of general international law [621]. The words that paragraph 2 of draft conclusion 17 uses follow the text of Article 48 of the ILC’s Articles on Responsibility of States for Internationally Wrongful Acts[411] [621], the first two paragraph of which read as follows.

---

[410] The italics for the two instances of the phrase ‘*jus cogens*’, and the one occurrence of the expression ‘*erga omnes*’, are present in the original text.

[411] It is submitted that paragraph 2 of draft conclusion 17 and the quoted subsections of Article 48 of the Articles on Responsibility of States for Internationally Wrongful Acts do not, on inspection, bear much resemblance to each other. However, the phrase ‘the obligation breached is owed to the international community as a whole’ in subparagraph 48(1)(b) of the Articles on Responsibility of States for Internationally Wrongful Acts is a descriptor for the infraction of an *erga omnes* obligation – a point which is consistent with the wording of paragraph 1 of draft conclusion 17, and the last-mentioned paragraph contains a similar expression, i.e., ‘obligations owed to the international community as a whole’. The commentary identifies the use of the following phrase from paragraph 48(1) of the Articles on Responsibility of States for Internationally Wrongful Acts in paragraph 2 of draft conclusion 17: ‘Any State ... is entitled to invoke the responsibility of another State’ (United Nations (2022), Report of the International Law Commission: Seventy-third session (18 April – 3 June and 4 July – 5 August 2022), Document A/77/10, Chapter IV. Peremptory norms of general international law

1. Any State[,] other than an injured State[,] is entitled to invoke the responsibility of another State in accordance with paragraph 2[,] if:
   (*a*) The obligation breached is owed to a group of States including that State, and is established for the protection of a collective interest of the group; or
   (*b*) The obligation breached is owed to the international community as a whole [622].
2. Any State entitled to invoke responsibility under paragraph 1 may claim from the responsible State:
   (*a*) Cessation of the internationally wrongful act, and assurances and guarantees of non-repetition[,] in accordance with article 30[412]; and
   (*b*) Performance of the obligation of reparation in accordance with the preceding articles, in the interest of the injured State or of the beneficiaries of the obligation breached[413] [623].

The rule that paragraph 2 of draft conclusion 17 contains, is accordant with decisions of international courts and tribunals [621]. The right of an injured State to invoke the responsibility of another State for the violation of a peremptory norm of general international law is to be exercised in accordance with Article 42 of the Articles on Responsibility of States for Internationally Wrongful Acts[414], whereas any state other than an injured state may invoke the responsibility for such a contravention under Article 48 of the Articles on Responsibility of States for Internationally Wrongful Acts[415] [621].

Conclusion 18: Peremptory norms of general international law (*jus cogens*) and circumstances precluding wrongfulness

> No circumstance precluding wrongfulness under the rules on the responsibility of States for internationally wrongful acts may be invoked with regard to any act of a State that is not in conformity with an obligation arising under a peremptory norm of general international law (*jus cogens*[416]) [624].

(*jus cogens*), E.2. Text of the draft conclusions and commentaries thereto, General Assembly Official Records, Seventy-seventh Session, Supplement No.10 (A/77/10), 16-89, 68).

412 This provision declares: "The State responsible for the internationally wrongful act is under an obligation: (*a*) To cease that act, if it is continuing; (*b*) To offer appropriate assurances and guarantees of non-repetition, if circumstances so require." (United Nations (2001), Resolution 56/83 adopted by the General Assembly on 12th December 2001, Annex: Responsibility of States for internationally wrongful acts, Article 30; emphasis original).

413 The italics for the two instances of the letter '*a*', and the two occurrences of the letter '*b*', are present in the original text.

414 This clause reads thus: "A State is entitled as an injured State to invoke the responsibility of another State[,] if the obligation breached is owed to: (*a*) That State individually; or (*b*) A group of States including that State, or the international community as a whole, and the breach of the obligation: (i) Specifically affects that State; or (ii) Is of such a character as radically to change the position of all the other States to which the obligation is owed with respect to the further performance of the obligation." (United Nations (2001), Resolution 56/83 adopted by the General Assembly on 12th December 2001, Annex: Responsibility of States for internationally wrongful acts, Article 42; emphasis original).

415 The text to fns 412 and 413, and the quoted sentence immediately preceding that text, comprise paragraphs 2 and 1 of Article 48 of the Articles on Responsibility of States for Internationally Wrongful Acts, respectively.

416 Emphasis original.

Usually, the presence of certain circumstances may prevent the wrongfulness of an act of a state that would otherwise be unlawful [624]. These include consent[417], self-defence[418], countermeasures[419], an event beyond the control of the state[420], distress[421] and necessity[422]. Draft conclusion 18 specifies an exception to this general rule on the responsibility of states under international law, by providing that, where the infraction in question concerns a peremptory norm of international law (*jus cogens*), the grounds precluding wrongfulness (such

[417] If a state consents to the commission of another state's act, then this "precludes the wrongfulness of that act in relation to the former State to the extent that the act remains within the limits of that consent" (United Nations (2001), Resolution 56/83 adopted by the General Assembly on 12th December 2001, Annex: Responsibility of States for internationally wrongful acts, Article 20).

[418] The wrongfulness of a state's act is ruled out, if this act amounts to a licit measure of self-defence which is taken in compliance with the UN Charter (United Nations (2001), Resolution 56/83 adopted by the General Assembly on 12th December 2001, Annex: Responsibility of States for internationally wrongful acts, Article 21).

[419] The wrongfulness of a state's act that is incompatible "with an international obligation towards another State is precluded[,] if and to the extent that the act constitutes a countermeasure taken against the latter State in accordance with chapter II of part three" (United Nations (2001), Resolution 56/83 adopted by the General Assembly on 12th December 2001, Annex: Responsibility of States for internationally wrongful acts, Article 22). Chapter II of Part III of the Articles on Responsibility of States for Internationally Wrongful Acts is titled 'Countermeasures', and comprises Articles 49-54.

[420] The wrongfulness of a state's act which is inconsistent "with an international obligation of that State is precluded[,] if the act is due to *force majeure*, that is the occurrence of an irresistible force or an unforeseen event beyond the control of the State, making it materially impossible in the circumstances to perform the obligation" (United Nations (2001), Resolution 56/83 adopted by the General Assembly on 12th December 2001, Annex: Responsibility of States for internationally wrongful acts, Article 23(1); emphasis added). Article 23(1) of the Articles on Responsibility of States for Internationally Wrongful Acts is inapplicable, "if: (*a*) The situation of force majeure is due, either alone or in combination with other factors, to the conduct of the State invoking it; or (*b*) The State has assumed the risk of that situation occurring" (United Nations (2001), Resolution 56/83 adopted by the General Assembly on 12th December 2001, Annex: Responsibility of States for internationally wrongful acts, Article 23(2); emphasis original). The term '*force majeure*' is from French; its literal meaning is 'superior force'; "In English, the term is often used in line with its literal French meaning ... . In business circles, "*force majeure*" describes those uncontrollable events (such as war, labor stoppages, or extreme weather) that are not the fault of any party and that make it difficult or impossible to carry out normal business. A company may insert a *force majeure* clause into a contract to absolve itself from liability in the event that it cannot fulfill the terms of a contract (or if attempting to do so will result in loss or damage of goods) for reasons beyond its control." (Merriam-Webster (2024), "*force majeure*," accessed October 27, 2024, <https://www.merriam-webster.com/dictionary/force%20majeure>; emphasis added).

[421] The wrongfulness of a state's act which is at variance "with an international obligation of that State is precluded[,] if the author of the act in question has no other reasonable way, in a situation of distress, of saving the author's life or the lives of other persons entrusted to the author's care" (United Nations (2001), Resolution 56/83 adopted by the General Assembly on 12th December 2001, Annex: Responsibility of States for internationally wrongful acts, Article 24(1)). Article 24(1) of the Articles on Responsibility of States for Internationally Wrongful Acts is inapplicable, "if: (*a*) The situation of the distress is due, either alone or in combination with other factors, to the conduct of the State invoking it; or (*b*) The act in question is likely to create a comparable or greater peril" (United Nations (2001), Resolution 56/83 adopted by the General Assembly on 12th December 2001, Annex: Responsibility of States for internationally wrongful acts, Article 24(2); emphasis original).

[422] It is prohibited to invoke necessity as a basis "for precluding the wrongfulness of an act not in conformity with an international obligation of that State[,] unless the act: (*a*) Is the only way for the State to safeguard an essential interest against a grave and imminent peril; and (*b*) Does not seriously impair an essential interest of the State or States towards which the obligation exists, or of the international community as a whole" (United Nations (2001), Resolution 56/83 adopted by the General Assembly on 12th December 2001, Annex: Responsibility of States for internationally wrongful acts, Article 25(1)). Necessity may not be so invoked, "if: (*a*) The international obligation in question excludes the possibility of invoking necessity; or (*b*) The State has contributed to the situation of necessity" (United Nations (2001), Resolution 56/83 adopted by the General Assembly on 12th December 2001, Annex: Responsibility of States for internationally wrongful acts, Article 25(2); emphasis original).

as consent and self-defence) may not be invoked [624]. This draft conclusion is founded on Article 26 of the Articles on Responsibility of States for Internationally Wrongful Acts[423] [624].

Conclusion 19: Particular consequences of serious breaches of peremptory norms of general international law (*jus cogens*)

1. States shall cooperate to bring to an end through lawful means any serious breach by a State of an obligation arising under a peremptory norm of general international law (*jus cogens*) [625].
2. No State shall recognize as lawful a situation created by a serious breach by a State of an obligation arising under a peremptory norm of general international law (*jus cogens*), nor render aid or assistance in maintaining that situation [625].
3. A breach of an obligation arising under a peremptory norm of general international law (*jus cogens*) is serious[,] if it involves a gross or systematic failure by the responsible State to fulfil that obligation [625].
4. This draft conclusion is without prejudice to the other consequences that any breach by a State of an obligation arising under a peremptory norm of general international law (*jus cogens*) may entail under international law[424] [625].

Draft conclusion 19 is based upon Article 41 of the Articles on Responsibility of States for Internationally Wrongful Acts[425] [625]. It addresses neither consequences that arise from infringements of rules of international law which are not of a peremptory character, nor the outcomes of contraventions of peremptory norms of general international law that are unserious [625].

---

[423] This provision declares: "Nothing in this chapter precludes the wrongfulness of any act of a State which is not in conformity with an obligation arising under a peremptory norm of general international law." (United Nations (2001), Resolution 56/83 adopted by the General Assembly on 12th December 2001, Annex: Responsibility of States for internationally wrongful acts, Article 26). 'This chapter' is Chapter V of Part One of Articles on Responsibility of States for Internationally Wrongful Acts, which is entitled 'Circumstances precluding wrongfulness', and which consists of Articles 20-27. Thus, Article 26 of the Articles on Responsibility of States for Internationally Wrongful Acts does not permit a state to plead consent, self-defence, countermeasures, *force majeure*, distress or necessity, in order to remove its culpability for performing an act which contravenes an obligation that arises under a peremptory norm of international law. Fn 420 defines the term '*force majeure*'.

[424] The italics for the four instances of the phrase '*jus cogens*' are present in the original text.

[425] Article 41 of the Articles on Responsibility of States for Internationally Wrongful Acts is headed 'Particular consequences of a serious breach of an obligation under this chapter'; it reads as follows: "1. States shall cooperate to bring to an end through lawful means any serious breach within the meaning of article 40. 2. No State shall recognize as lawful a situation created by a serious breach within the meaning of article 40, nor render aid or assistance in maintaining that situation. 3. This article is without prejudice to the other consequences referred to in this part and to such further consequences that a breach to which this chapter applies may entail under international law." (United Nations (2001), Resolution 56/83 adopted by the General Assembly on 12th December 2001, Annex: Responsibility of States for internationally wrongful acts, Article 41). 'This part' is Part Two of the Articles on Responsibility of States for Internationally Wrongful Acts, which is titled 'Content of the International Responsibility of a State', and which comprises Articles 28-41. 'This chapter' is Chapter III of Part Two of the Articles on Responsibility of States for Internationally Wrongful Acts, which is entitled 'Serious breaches of obligations under peremptory norms of general international law', and which contains Articles 40 and 41. Article 40 of the Articles on Responsibility of States for Internationally Wrongful Acts is headed 'Application of this chapter'; it specifies: "1. This chapter applies to the international responsibility which is entailed by a serious breach by a State of an obligation arising under a peremptory norm of general international law. 2. A breach of such an obligation is serious[,] if it involves a gross or systematic failure by the responsible State to fulfil the obligation." (United Nations (2001), Resolution 56/83 adopted by the General Assembly on 12th December 2001, Annex: Responsibility of States for internationally wrongful acts, Article 40).

The obligation in paragraph 1 of draft conclusion 19 for states to co-operate to legally terminate any serious transgression by a state of an obligation that arises under a peremptory norm of general international law, has been acknowledged in judicial determinations [626]. This obligation is to be conducted 'through lawful means' [627]. Therefore, the violation of a peremptory norm of general international law may not be used as a justification for the infraction of other rules of international law [627].

While international law does not prohibit unilateral measures by a state to end a serious infringement of a peremptory norm of general international law by another state – provided that these are compatible with international law, the emphasis in paragraph 1 of draft conclusion 19 is upon collective measures (i.e., states 'shall co-operate') [627]. Depending on the kind of breach and the type of the peremptory norm at issue, the UN's collective system is the favoured framework for co-operative action [627].

There are many examples of resolutions of organs of worldwide organizations, especially the UN, which exemplify the duty to co-operate to terminate serious contraventions of obligations that are extensively recognized as arising from peremptory norms of general international law [628]. These include resolutions condemning transgressions of these obligations, resolutions requesting the cessation of violations of such obligations, and resolutions establishing mechanisms of answerability to deal with the infractions [629].

The obligation to co-operate to end serious infringements of peremptory norms of general international law may be implemented by means of non-institutionalized co-operation, including through impromptu arrangements by a collection of states acting jointly to terminate a breach of a peremptory norm [630]. These measures must be consonant with international law [630].

In paragraph 2 of draft conclusion 19, the obligation of non-assistance is a logical consequence of the duty of non-recognition of a situation as lawful [631]. The ILC has already recognized that these responsibilities are part of customary international law [631]. The UNSC has acknowledged the obligation of states not to recognize the situation engendered by a transgression of the prohibition of apartheid, and the duty to respect a people's right to self-determination [632]. The UN General Assembly has made decisions that call for the non-recognition of situations generated by violations of acts that are widely recognized as constituting infractions of peremptory norms of general international law[426] [632]. The

[426] The final sentence of fn 265 of the Text of the draft conclusions on identification and legal consequences of peremptory norms of general international law (*jus cogens*) and commentaries thereto, refers to Operative Paragraph 6 of General Assembly Resolution 68/262 of 27th March 2014 as "the duty not to recognize situations created by the unlawful use of force and threats to territorial integrity in relation to the situation in Crimea" (United Nations (2022), Report of the International Law Commission: Seventy-third session (18 April – 3 June and 4 July – 5 August 2022), Document A/77/10, Chapter IV. Peremptory norms of general international law (*jus cogens*), E.2. Text of the draft conclusions and commentaries thereto, General Assembly Official Records, Seventy-seventh Session, Supplement No.10 (A/77/10), 16-89, 77). That provision declares: "*The General Assembly*, ... 6. *Calls upon* all States, international organizations and specialized agencies not to recognize any alteration of the status of the Autonomous Republic of Crimea and the city of Sevastopol on the basis of the above-mentioned referendum and to refrain from any action of dealing that might be interpreted as recognizing any such altered status." (United Nations (2014), Resolution 68/262 adopted by the General Assembly on 27th March 2014, Operative Paragraph 6; emphasis original). The 'above-mentioned referendum' is "the referendum held in the Autonomous Republic of Crimea and the city of Sevastopol on 16 March 2014", which, "having no validity, cannot form the basis for any alteration of the status of the Autonomous Republic of Crimea or the city of Sevastopol" (United Nations (2014), Resolution 68/262 adopted by the General Assembly on 27th March 2014, Operative Paragraph 5). The applicable peremptory norm of general international law (*jus cogens*) is the prohibition of aggression (United Nations (2022), Report of the International Law Commission: Seventy-third session (18 April – 3 June and 4 July – 5 August 2022), Document A/77/10, Chapter IV. Peremptory norms of

obligation of states not to give assistance or aid to the maintenance of a situation produced by a serious infringement of an obligation arising under a peremptory norm of general international law has been accepted in determinations of the ICJ and resolutions of the UN[427] [633]. The duty in paragraph 2 of draft conclusion 19 concerns 'a situation created by a serious breach,' rather than the transgression itself [634].

Draft conclusions 17, 18 and 19 apply, as appropriate, to international organizations [635]. Regarding the last-mentioned, Articles 41[428] and 42[429] of the Articles on Responsibility of International Organizations are relevant [635].

Part Four: General Provisions

Conclusion 20: Interpretation and application consistent with peremptory norms of general international law (*jus cogens*)

---

general international law (*jus cogens*), E.2. Text of the draft conclusions and commentaries thereto, General Assembly Official Records, Seventy-seventh Session, Supplement No.10 (A/77/10), 16-89, 89). Fn 284 sets out the definition of the word 'aggression', which, in essence, is 'the use of armed force by a state against the sovereignty, territorial sovereignty, territorial integrity or political independence of another state, or in any manner inconsistent with the UN Charter'. As the occupation by Russian troops of Crimea from February 2014 onwards is an act of aggression – in accordance with this definition – against Ukraine, within which Crimea is legally recognized as an autonomous republic, Russia, by invading Crimea, has contravened the prohibition of aggression. This occupation is, in the wording of paragraph 2 of draft conclusion 19, 'a situation created by a serious breach by a state of an obligation arising under a peremptory norm of general international law (*jus cogens*)'. Paragraph 2 of draft conclusion 19 calls upon other states not to recognize this situation as lawful. Therefore, the results of the referendum that took place in Sevastopol on 27th March 2014 should be held by those states to be invalid.

427 Fn 267 of Text of the draft conclusions on identification and legal consequences of peremptory norms of general international law (*jus cogens*) and commentaries thereto, refers to Operative Paragraph 10 of General Assembly Resolution ES-11/1 (LXXVI) of 2nd March 2022, which concerns assistance given by Belarus to Russia in the invasion of Ukraine by Russian forces in February 2022 – in which the pertinent peremptory norm of general international law (*jus cogens*) is the prohibition of aggression (fn 426) (United Nations (2022), Report of the International Law Commission: Seventy-third session (18 April – 3 June and 4 July – 5 August 2022), Document A/77/10, Chapter IV. Peremptory norms of general international law (*jus cogens*), E.2. Text of the draft conclusions and commentaries thereto, General Assembly Official Records, Seventy-seventh Session, Supplement No.10 (A/77/10), 16-89, 78). That clause states: "*The General Assembly*, ... 10. *Deplores* the involvement of Belarus in this unlawful use of force against Ukraine, and calls upon it to abide by its international obligations;" (United Nations (2022), Resolution ES-11/1 (LXXVI) adopted by the General Assembly on 2nd March 2022, Operative Paragraph 10; emphasis original).

428 This provision declares: "1. This Chapter applies to the international responsibility which is entailed by a serious breach by an international organization of an obligation arising under a peremptory norm of general international law. 2. A breach of such an obligation is serious[,] if it involves a gross or systemic failure by the responsible international organization to fulfil the obligation." (United Nations (2011), Resolution 66/100 adopted by the General Assembly on 9th December 2011, Annex: Responsibility of international organizations, Article 41). 'This Chapter' is Chapter III of Part Three of the Articles on Responsibility of International Organizations, which is titled 'Serious breaches of obligations under peremptory norms of general international law', and which contains Articles 41 and 42. Part Three of the Articles on Responsibility of International Organizations is entitled 'Content of the international responsibility of an international organization'.

429 This clause states: "1. States and international organizations shall cooperate to bring to an end through lawful means any serious breach within the meaning of article 41. 2. No State or international organization shall recognize as lawful a situation created by a serious breach within the meaning of article 41, nor render aid or assistance in maintaining that situation. 3. Article 42 is without prejudice to the other consequences referred to in this Part and to such further consequences that a breach to which this Chapter applies may entail under international law." (United Nations (2011), Resolution 66/100 adopted by the General Assembly on 9th December 2011, Annex: Responsibility of international organizations, Article 42). 'Article 41' is Article 41 of the Articles on Responsibility of International Organizations, which fn 428 lays down. 'Article 42' is Article 42 of the Articles on Responsibility of International Organizations, which the current footnote (i.e., fn 429) sets out. 'This Chapter' is Chapter III of Part Three of the Articles on Responsibility of International Organizations (penultimate sentence of fn 428). 'This Part' is Part Three of the Articles on Responsibility of International Organizations (final sentence of fn 428).

> Where it appears that there may be a conflict between a peremptory norm of general international law (*jus cogens*[430]) and another rule of international law, the latter is, as far as possible, to be interpreted and applied so as to be consistent with the former [635].

The word 'conflict' in draft conclusion 20 describes a situation in which two rules of international law infringe on, or impair, each other, if they are applied simultaneously [636]. The phrase 'as far as possible' therein, is meant to emphasize that the limits of interpretation are not to be exceeded, i.e., the non-peremptory canon may not be given a meaning which does not flow from the usual application of the rules and methodology of interpretation in order to attain consistency with peremptory norms of general international law [637]. If it is impossible to reach an interpretation of the non-peremptory regulation that is compatible with the peremptory norm of general international law, then this rule is to be invalidated, in line with draft conclusions 10[431], 14[432], 15[433] and 16[434] [638].

The expression 'another rule of international law' in draft conclusion 20 refers to obligations under this topic, whether arising from a treaty, customary international law, a general principle law, a unilateral act, or an act of an international organization [638]. Consequently, draft conclusion 20 applies in the interpretation of the rules or obligations which are identified in draft conclusions 10, 14, 15 and 16 [638].

Conclusion 21: Recommended procedure

1. A State which invokes a peremptory norm of general international law (*jus cogens*[435]) as a ground for the invalidity or termination of a rule of international law should do so by notifying other States concerned of its claim. The notification should be in writing and should indicate the measure proposed to be taken with respect to the rule of international law in question [638].
2. If none of the other States raises an objection within a period which, except in cases of special urgency, will not be less than three months, [then] the invoking State may carry out the measure which it has proposed [638].
3. If, however, any State concerned raises an objection, [then] the States concerned should seek a solution through the means indicated in Article 33 of the Charter of the United Nations[436]. If no solution is reached within a period of twelve months, and the objecting State offers to submit the matter to the International Court of Justice or to some other procedure entailing binding decisions, [then] the invoking State should not carry out the measure which it has proposed until the dispute is resolved [638].

---

[430] Emphasis original.

[431] The quoted passage that includes the text to fns 370-372 comprises draft conclusion 10 on identification and legal consequences of peremptory norms of general international law (*jus cogens*).

[432] The quoted passage which incorporates the text to fn 392 consists of draft conclusion 14 on identification and legal consequences of peremptory norms of general international law (*jus cogens*).

[433] The text to fns 395 and 396 lays down draft conclusion 15 on identification and legal consequences of peremptory norms of general international law (*jus cogens*).

[434] The text to fn 403 sets out draft conclusion 16 on identification and legal consequences of peremptory norms of general international law (*jus cogens*).

[435] Emphasis original.

[436] The means comprise "negotiation, enquiry, mediation, conciliation, arbitration, judicial settlement, resort to regional agencies or arrangements, or other peaceful means of [the disputants'] choice" (United Nations (1945), "Charter of the United Nations," Article 33(1)).

> 4. This draft conclusion is without prejudice to the procedures set forth in the Vienna Convention on the Law of Treaties, to the relevant rules concerning the jurisdiction of the International Court of Justice, or to other applicable dispute settlement provisions agreed by the States concerned [638].

In drawing up a draft conclusion for dispute resolution regarding the invalidation of rules of international law because of incompatibility with peremptory norms of general international law (*jus cogens*), the ILC had to ensure that it did not appear to be imposing treaty rules on states which were not bound by such provisions, while taking account of concerns about the need to avoid states unilaterally invoking Articles 53[437] and 64[438] on the Vienna Convention on the Law of Treaties 1969 in order to invalidate precepts of international law [639]. The Commission also had to make certain that the procedures for dispute settlement which were established under the Vienna Convention on the Law of Treaties[439], or any other treaty clause, were not undermined by draft conclusion 21 [640]. This draft conclusion sets out a recommended procedure, which is designed to realize this balance [640].

Conclusion 22: Without prejudice to consequences that specific peremptory norms of general international law (*jus cogens*) may otherwise entail

> The present draft conclusions are without prejudice to consequences that specific peremptory norms of general international law (*jus cogens*[440]) may otherwise entail under international law [641].

The issue of legal outcomes of crimes the commission of which peremptory norms of international law (*jus cogens*) – such the prohibitions of genocide, crimes against humanity and war crimes – have banned, has been broached, in particular the possible consequences of those offences for state immunity and the jurisdiction of national courts [642]. As these outcomes are not general consequences of peremptory norms of general international law, but, instead, concern specific peremptory norms of general international law, the current draft conclusions do not address them [642].

Conclusion 23: Non-exhaustive list

> Without prejudice to the existence or subsequent emergence of other peremptory norms of general international law (*jus cogens*[441]), a non-exhaustive list of norms that the International Law Commission has previously referred to as having that status is to be found in the annex to the present draft conclusions [642].

The Annex to the draft conclusions lists the following eight peremptory norms of general international law (*jus cogens*): the prohibition of aggression, the prohibition of genocide, the prohibition of crimes against humanity, the basic rules of international humanitarian law, the

---

[437] The third and fourth sentences of fn 322 reproduce Article 53 of the Vienna Convention on the Law of Treaties 1969.

[438] The sentence immediately preceding the text to fn 327 lays down Article 64 of the Vienna Convention of the Law of Treaties 1969.

[439] Articles 65 and 66 of, and the Annex to, the Vienna Convention on the Law of Treaties 1969, are relevant.

[440] Emphasis original.

[441] Emphasis original.

prohibition of racial discrimination and apartheid, the prohibition of slavery, the prohibition of torture and the right of self-determination [643].

Comment

The commentaries on the draft conclusions on identification and legal consequences of peremptory norms of general international law (*jus cogens*) provide a thorough account of matters concerning *jus cogens*, connecting them both to the Vienna Convention on the Law of Treaties 1969 and to other instruments of international law. This treatment clarifies and objectivizes the rules over this very important area.

Paragraph 1 of draft conclusion 17 states that all *jus cogens* give rise to *erga omnes* obligations[442]. The commentary on that draft conclusion observes that not all *erga omnes* obligations originate from *jus cogens*. Thus, it would be helpful for the ILC to look into what features of any rule of international law cause it to inherit *erga omnes* characteristics. Based on this analysis, the ILC might then publish a comprehensive list of principles of international law that generate *erga omnes* obligations. It could regularly update this list, to reflect the identification of new such rules and to remove any tenets of international law that a big majority of states considered no longer had that effect. The list might identify which rules thereon are *jus cogens* and those which are not.

The ILC could expand its list of *jus cogens* from the eight norms currently listed thereon. The ILC is best-placed to apply the conclusions on identification and legal consequences of peremptory norms of general international law (*jus cogens*) to rules of international law in order to identify further *jus cogens*. It might frequently update its list of *jus cogens*, removing norms from the list that are no longer considered by many states to have peremptory effect, and adding new such norms. It might also apply a moral qualification to this editing process, i.e., concepts such as genocide and torture are so abhorrent to the fundamental welfare of humankind that it should be very, very difficult to be able to remove the peremptory status from the prohibition of them – even in the unlikely event that most states vote in favour of this. States whose leaders propound such views would not be fulfilling their international responsibilities.

Primary Sources: General Principles of Law

Introduction

Subparagraph 1(c) of Article 38 of the Statute of the ICJ refers to "the general principles of law recognized by civilized nations"[443] [344]. The adjective 'civilized' is not used to contrast cultured regimes from rudimentary ones. Rather, it is used to identify principles of law that are used across national legal systems. The phrase has been described as "general principles of fairness and justice which are applied universally in legal systems around the world", and

[442] The sentence immediately preceding the text to fn 410 consists of paragraph 1 of draft conclusion 17.

[443] Article 38(1)(c) of the Statute of the ICJ is point c. in the quoted passage immediately following the text to fn 207.

includes, for instance, the principles of the impartiality of judges, good faith and *res judicata*[444] [644].

Work of the ILC

At its sixty-ninth session, in 2017, the ILC added the subject 'General principles of law' to its future plan of work [645]. At its seventieth session, in 2018, the ILC decided to place this topic in its current scheme of projects, and appointed Dr. Marcelo Vázquez-Bermúdez as Special Rapporteur [645].

The ILC considered three reports of the Special Rapporteur, in 2019, 2021 and 2022, respectively [645]. At its seventy-fourth session, in 2023, the ILC adopted, on first reading, eleven draft conclusions on general principles of law – together with commentaries thereon [645]. The ILC decided to convey these draft conclusions, via the Secretary-General, to governments for observations and comments, requesting that these be presented to the Secretary-General by 1st December 2024 [645].

Draft Conclusions on General Principles of Law Adopted by the ILC on First Reading

Conclusion 1: Scope

> The present draft conclusions concern general principles of law as a source of international law [646].

The phrase 'general principles of law' is employed throughout these draft conclusions to refer to the term 'the general principles of law recognized by civilized nations,' which subparagraph 1(c) of Article 38 of the Statute of the ICJ lists[445] [646]. The draft conclusions aim to clarify the purview of general principles of law, the method for their identification, their functions, and their connection with other sources of international law [646].

Conclusion 2: Recognition

> For a general principle of law to exist, it must be recognized by the community of nations [646].

Recognition features extensively in the practice of states, the jurisprudence of courts and tribunals, and in writings, as the crucial condition for the emergence of a general principle of law [647]. Consequently, to ascertain whether a general principle of law exists at a given moment, all the available evidence must be examined which might show that its recognition has taken place [647].

Conclusion 3: Categories of general principles of law

---

[444] The term '*res judicata*' is from Latin; its literal meaning is 'judged matter'; it is "a matter that has been adjudicated by a competent court and [which] may not be pursued further by the same parties" (Pearsall, J. (editor) (1998), *The New Oxford Dictionary of English*, 1579).

[445] Fn 443.

> General principles of law comprise those:
> (a) that are derived from national legal systems;
> (b) that may be formed within the international legal system [647].

In contradistinction to paragraph (a) of draft conclusion 3 – which utilizes the phrase 'are derived from,' paragraph (b) of this draft conclusion uses the expression 'may be formed' [648]. The term 'may be formed' was deemed appropriate to introduce an element of flexibility to paragraph (b), respecting that there is a debate as to whether the class of general principles of law specified therein exists [649].

Conclusion 4: Identification of general principles of law derived from national legal systems

> To determine the existence and content of a general principle of law derived from national legal systems, it is necessary to ascertain:
> (a) the existence of a principle common to the various legal systems of the world; and
> (b) its transposition to the international legal system [650].

This two-part examination is widely-accepted in state practice and in the literature, and is intended to demonstrate that a general principle law has been 'recognized' as required by subparagraph 1(c) of Article 38 of the Statute of the ICJ[446] [651]. It is an objective method, to be applied by everyone who needs to determine whether a particular general principle of law exists at a specific instant and what the content of this principle is [651].

Use of the word 'transposition' in paragraph (b) of draft conclusion 4 is not aimed at suggesting that an express or a formal act of transposition is requisite [651]. 'Transposition' includes the possibility that the content of the general principle of law which this two-step analysis identifies may not be the same as the principle that is found in the different national legal systems [651].

Conclusion 5: Determination of the existence of a principle common to the various legal systems of the world

> 1. To determine the existence of a principle common to the various legal systems of the world, a comparative analysis of national legal systems is required [651].
> 2. The comparative analysis must be wide and representative, including the different regions of the world [651].
> 3. The comparative analysis includes an assessment of national laws and decisions of national courts, and other relevant materials [651].

Draft conclusion 5 attends to the first step of the two-part methodology for the identification of general principles of law derived from national legal systems, which draft conclusion 4 sets out [651]. This is the determination of the existence of a principle that is common to the various legal systems of the earth [651].

The 'comparative analysis of national legal systems' to which paragraph 1 of draft conclusion 5 refers, does not require that certain methodologies within the sphere of

[446] Fn 443.

comparative law be utilized [652]. While these may, when suitable, furnish guidance, some flexibility is usually maintained in practice [652]. A common denominator across legal systems, as to the nature of the principle, needs to be found [652].

The phrase 'wide and representative, including the different regions of the world' in paragraph 2 of draft conclusion 5 is intended to clarify that, while it is unnecessary to appraise every legal system of the globe to identify a general principle of law, the comparative analysis must be sufficiently exhaustive to take into consideration the legal systems of countries in conformity with the principle of sovereign equality of states [652]. The expression 'different regions of the world' was included, in order to emphasize that it is not enough to show that a principle of law exists in legal systems which represent particular legal families – such as common law, civil law and Islamic law, but that it also necessary to establish that this principle has been recognized extensively in the various regions [652].

The terms 'national laws' and 'decisions of national courts' in paragraph 3 of draft conclusion 5 are to be interpreted broadly, covering the entire range of materials in domestic legal systems which may be pertinent for the identification of a general principle of law – such as constitutions, decrees, legislation and regulations, and determinations of national courts from different levels and districts – including supreme courts, constitutional courts and tribunals, courts of cassation, court of appeal, courts of first instance, and administrative tribunals [653]. The phrase 'other relevant materials' covers other potentially-relevant sources of domestic legal systems – such as doctrine and customary law [654].

Conclusion 6: Determination of transposition to the international legal system

> A principle common to the various legal systems of the world may be transposed to the international legal system insofar as it is compatible with that system [654].

Draft conclusion 6 addresses the second step of the two-part methodology for ascertaining the existence and content of general principles of law derived from national legal systems, which draft conclusion 4 lays down [654]. Draft conclusion 6 employs the words 'may be' to stress that transposition does not happen automatically [655].

A principle which is prevalent in domestic legal orders may be deemed compatible with the international legal system, if it is befitting for application within the framework of this system – when conditions for its application therein exist [655]. An example is the right of access to courts, which is a principle that applies across national legal systems [655]. Transposition of this right to the international legal system would result in a direct breach of the principle of consent to jurisdiction in international law, and would be incapable of functioning at the global level because the conditions for its application are absent, i.e., a court with universal, compulsory jurisdiction to resolve disputes [655].

The use of the expression 'insofar as' in draft conclusion 6 is intended to highlight that there is some flexibility, when determining the possibility of transposing a principle of law to the international legal system [656]. If only part of this principle is consistent with that system, then the principle may be transposed to the extent of its compatible portion [656].

Recognition by the community of nations that a principle common to the different legal systems of the world is transferred to the international legal system, is required, and is implicit when the compatibility test is satisfied [656]. That is to say, if a principle which is common to the various legal systems is appropriate for implementation within the structure of the international legal system, then, when conditions for this exist, it can normally be inferred that the community of nations has recognized that this transposition has occurred [656].

Conclusion 7: Identification of general principles of law formed within the international legal system

1. To determine the existence and content of a general principle of law that may be formed within the international legal system, it is necessary to ascertain that the community of nations has recognized the principle as intrinsic to the international legal system [656].
2. Paragraph 1 is without prejudice to the question of the possible existence of other general principles of law formed within the international legal system [656].

The ILC considers that the presence of this type of general principle of law is justified for the following reasons: (i) there are instances in judicial and state practice which seemed to support the existence of these, (ii) the international legal system must be able to produce general principles of law that are specific to it, and (iii) nothing in the text of subparagraph 1(c) of Article 38 of the Statute of the ICJ[447] or its drafting history restricts general principles of law to those which are derived from domestic legal systems [657]. An examination of operative rules in the international legal system is essential, in order to discover principles that are reflected in those rules or which underlie them, and which are free-standing [658]. This analysis must consider all obtainable evidence of the recognition of the relevant principle by the community of nations, such as statements that states have made, resolutions which have been adopted by worldwide organizations or at intergovernmental conferences, and international instruments that embody the principle [658].

General principles of law which emerge from the international legal system must be proven to be intrinsic to this system [658]. The word 'intrinsic' means that the principle is specific to the aforementioned system, and both mirrors and regulates its fundamental attributes [658]. The ILC's commentary uses the principle of consent to jurisdiction as its first example [658]. This principle is an outcome of the principle that sovereign states are equal and the fact that there is no judiciary at the international level with universal, compulsory jurisdiction to which any dispute may be presented [658]. The principle of consent to jurisdiction inspires, and is reflected in, different international instruments, and has frequently been referred to in determinations of courts and tribunals [658].

Paragraph 2 of draft conclusion 7 was included to display the view of those members of the ILC who backed the existence of general principles of law developed within the international legal system, but considered that paragraph 1 of draft conclusion 7 would be too narrow and would omit other possible principles which, while not intrinsic to the international legal system, may come from within that system – rather than from national legal systems [659]. Several members of the ILC raised the concern that insufficient state practice, jurisprudence and teachings are accessible to totally support the existence of these other possible general principles of law, making it difficult to establish clearly the methodology for their identification [660].

Conclusion 8: Decisions of courts and tribunals

[447] Article 38(1)(c) of the Statute of the ICJ is point c. in the quoted passage immediately following the text to fn 207.

1. Decisions of international courts and tribunals, in particular of the International Court of Justice, concerning the existence and content of general principles of law are a subsidiary means for the determination of such principles [660].
2. Regard may be had, as appropriate, to decisions of national courts concerning the existence and content of general principles of law, as a subsidiary means for the determination of such principles [660].

Decisions of international courts and tribunals are frequently relied upon, in order to ascertain the actuality or non-existence of general principles of law, especially those derived from domestic legal systems, as well as to determine their content [660]. Decisions of national courts have two functions in the identification of general principles of law [661]. First as paragraph 3 of draft conclusion 5[448] indicates, they may be relevant for use in the comparative analysis that is required to ascertain the existence of a principle which is common to the different legal systems of the world [661]. Second, in accordance with paragraph 2 of draft conclusion 8, they may act as a subsidiary means for determining general principles of law – when they investigate the presence and content of a such a principle [661].

The phrase 'subsidiary means' – which is used in subparagraph 1(d) of Article 38 of the ICJ Statute[449] along with both paragraphs of draft conclusion 8 – denotes the ancillary function of judicial decisions in elucidating the law [661]. While a determination of a court or a tribunal may offer helpful guidance for ascertaining the existence or absence of general principles of law, its value may vary considerably, according to its reception – particularly by states and in subsequent cases – and the calibre of the reasoning therein [661].

Paragraph 1 of draft conclusion 8 specifies 'international courts and tribunals,' which comprises any international entity that wields judicial powers and which is called upon to assess general principles of law [661]. It mentions the ICJ [661], which – like the PCIJ – has referred to several general principles of law in its judgments and advisory opinions [662]. The skills and wide range of evidence that are usually available to these courts and tribunals may give significance to their decisions regarding the determination of general principles of law, subject to the abovementioned considerations[450] [662].

For the purposes of draft conclusion 8, the term 'decisions' includes judgements, advisory opinions, awards, and orders on interlocutory and procedural issues [662]. The expression '[r]egard may be had, as appropriate' in paragraph 2 of draft conclusion 8 highlights the need to show caution when attempting to rely on decisions of domestic courts as a subsidiary means to determine the existence and content of a general principle of international law [662]. National courts may embrace international law solely in a particular way and to a limited degree, lack expertise in international law, and have come to their decisions without hearing states' arguments [662].

Conclusion 9: Teachings

---

[448] Point 3. of the fifth quoted passage, above in the current subsection (i.e., that titled 'Draft conclusions on general principles of law adopted by the ILC on first reading'), sets out paragraph 3 of draft conclusion 5 on general principles of law adopted by the ILC on first reading.

[449] Article 38(1)(d) of the Statute of the ICJ refers to "judicial decisions" and writings "as subsidiary means for the determination of rules of law" (United Nations (1945), "Statute of the International Court of Justice," Article 38(1)(d)). Article 38(1)(d) of the Statute of the ICJ is point d. in the quoted passage immediately following the text to fn 207.

[450] These are the reception of the decision and the quality of the reasoning therein (see the last sentence of the paragraph immediately preceding the text to the present footnote (i.e., fn 450)).

Teachings of the most highly qualified publicists of the various nations may serve as a subsidiary means for the determination of general principles of law [662].

The word 'teachings,' also referred to as 'writings,' is to be understood broadly; it includes non-written teachings, such as audiovisual materials and lectures [663]. Teachings may offer guidance in ascertaining the presence and content of general principles of law [663]. This supplementary role recognizes the value that writings may have in: (i) collecting and analyzing domestic laws and other materials, and appraising the compatibility of a principle of law which is common to the different legal systems of the earth with the international legal system, (ii) weighing up pertinent rules in the latter system, relevant resolutions adopted by global organizations or at international conferences, and statements prepared by states, in order to evaluate the recognition of a general principle of law that is formed within the international legal system, (iii) identifying the possible absence or evolution of general principles of law, and (iv) assessing the law [663]. Use of teachings may be especially handy for conquering any linguistic obstacles which are found, when carrying out a comparative analysis of national legal systems [663].

The phrase 'may serve as' in draft conclusion 9 reflects the necessity to manifest caution when drawing upon teachings, because their worthfulness varies for determining the existence and content of a general principle of law [663]. Writings may recommend development of the law, mirror the individual or national standpoints of their authors, and differ substantially in quality [663].

Conclusion 10: Functions of general principles of law

1. General principles of law are mainly resorted to when other rules of international law do not resolve a particular issue[,] in whole or in part [663].
2. General principles of law contribute to the coherence of the international legal system. They may serve, *inter alia*[451]:
   (a) to interpret and complement other rules of international law;
   (b) as a basis for primary rights and obligations, as well as a basis for secondary and procedural rules [664].

Paragraph 1 of conclusion 10 aims to encapsulate the tendency – in doctrine and in state practice, when looking into a specific matter, to first ascertain whether there is a rule within a treaty or of customary international law which may provide a solution, and to turn to general principles of law if these sources of law prove to be insufficient [665]. The words 'are mainly resorted to' within that paragraph clarify that this is not the only way to proceed, and that, in some instances, general principles of law may be used straight away – depending upon the circumstances [665]. The expression 'do not resolve a particular issue, in whole or in part' is intended to make plain that general principles of law may be utilized when a solution for an issue is found neither in treaties nor in custom, or when these sources supply merely a partial solution and general principles of law may be complementary to them [665].

Regarding paragraph 2 of draft conclusion 10, while rules which are derived from the other sources of international law contribute to the international legal system's coherence, some

[451] Emphasis original. The final sentence of fn 284 defines the term '*inter alia*'.

general principles of law seem to be aimed at accomplishing this role more directly [666]. These principles include good faith, *pacta sunt servanda*[452], the principles of *lex specialis*[453] and *lex posterior*[454], basic considerations of humanity, and respect for human dignity [667].

The phrase '*inter alia*'[455] in paragraph 2 of draft conclusion 10 is employed to point out that the functions which subparagraphs 2(a) and 2(b) of draft conclusion 10 lay down for general principles of law in their role of contributing to the coherence of the international legal system, are not exhaustive [667]. The words 'may serve' in paragraph 2 of draft conclusion 10 show that the functions of general principles of law are to be determined case by case, depending upon their content and breadth [667].

Concerning subparagraph 2(a) of draft conclusion 10, it is well-established in practice that general principles of law may be depended upon for interpretative purposes [667]. The term 'complement' in this subparagraph is meant to apply to instances in which a general principle of law is applied at the same time as a treaty provision or a rule of customary international law [668].

In subparagraph 2(b) of draft conclusion 10, the expression 'primary rights and obligations' covers the suggestion that general principles of law may, like any other primary source of international law, generate rights and obligations which are binding upon subjects of international law [668]. Judicial decisions and legal instruments refer – as examples of such general principles of law – to the principle of *uti possidetis*[456], the prohibition of unjust

---

452 The term '*pacta sunt servanda*' is from Latin; it means 'agreements are to be kept'; without this rule, any international agreement would neither be binding on the parties to it nor enforceable (Encyclopaedia Britannica (2024), "*pacta sunt servanda*: law principle," accessed October 25, 2024, <https://www.britannica.com/topic/pacta-sunt-servanda>; Oxford Reference (2024), "Overview: *pacta sunt servanda*," accessed October 25, 2024, <https://www.oxfordreference.com/display/10.1093/oi/authority.20110803100300496>).

453 The full version of this general principle of law is: *lex specialis derogat legi generali*, which is Latin whose translation is 'a special law overrides a general law'; thus, in accordance with the principle, a more specific rule prevails over a more general rule, in the event of a clash between them (International Committee of the Red Cross (2024), "How does law protect in war? *Lex specialis*," accessed October 25, 2024, <https://casebook.icrc.org/a_to_z/glossary/lex-specialis>).

454 The complete formula of this general principle of law is: *lex posterior derogat legi priori*, which is Latin whose translation is 'a later law overrides an earlier law'; hence, in line with the principle, a legal rule that arises after a conflicting legal rule prevails over the latter to the extent of the inconsistency (Oxford Reference (2024), "*Lex posterior derogat (legi) priori*," accessed October 25, 2024, <https://www.oxfordreference.com/display/10.1093/acref/9780195369380.001.0001/acref-9780195369380-e-1282>).

455 The last sentence of fn 284 defines the term '*inter alia*'.

456 The principle of '*uti possidetis*' (Latin: '*as you possess*') or '*uti possidetis iuris*' (Latin: 'as you possess the right') comes from Roman law, as a method for a praetor to determine how the possession of immovable property should be determined between two parties; the formula was: '*Uti eas aedes, quibus de agitur, nec vi nec clam nec precario alter ab altero possidetis, quominus ita possideatis, vim fieri veto.*', which translates literally as: 'As you possess the house in question, the one not having obtained by force, clandestinely, or by permission from the other, I forbid force to be used to the end that you may not continue to possess it.'; when the principle was shifted to international relations, it was applied to states and their territory rather than to private parties and their immovable property, and signified a decisive status instead of a provisional, procedural movement in the burden of proof or a channel for standing; the principle of *uti possidetis* was admitted to international law in the nineteenth century, when its main purpose (in private law) of precluding and nullifying the use of force was no longer present in international law; in contemporary international law, the principle of *uti possidetis* has reverted to its primary object of securing the key worldwide prohibition of forced transfers of territory; the principle of *uti possidetis* was used to upgrade colonial boundaries to international boundaries in Latin America and, later, in Africa and Asia; it does not distinguish between possession-in-law and possession-in-fact; as colonial administrative borders usually cut through the boundaries of the inhabiting populations, their upgrade to international borders pursuant to the application of the principle of *uti possidetis* resulted in nations becoming confined within new states; thus, this non-selective application of the principle of *uti possidetis* in the name of gaining stability and conclusiveness precipitated many claims of the right to self-determination and disputes over boundaries (Peters, A. (2014), '*The Principle of Uti Possidetis Juris: How Relevant is it for Issues of*

enrichment, rudimentary considerations of humanity, the principle that attribution of territory automatically carries with it the waters which appertain to this land, principles underlying the Convention on the Prevention and Punishment of the Crime of Genocide, the prohibition of crimes under international law, the obligation of every state not to knowingly permit its territory to be used for acts that are incompatible with the rights of other countries, freedom of maritime communication, and the right of foundlings to presumed to have been born of nationals of the state in which they are discovered [669].

Regarding the phrase 'secondary rules' in subparagraph 2(b) of draft conclusion 10, international tribunals have deemed that some secondary rules of responsibility stem from general principles of law [670]. These include, the obligation to pay compensatory or moratory interests, the principle of *force majeure*[457] as a ground for preventing wrongfulness, the duty to make reparation for contraventions of international law, principles on succession of individuals in the context of compensation, and *rebus sic stantibus*[458] [670].

The term 'procedural rules' in subparagraph 2(b) of draft conclusion 10, refers to the regulations that govern the process in international courts and tribunals [670]. An example of a general principle of law that acts as a basis for these rules is the principle of *res judicata*[459]. Other such principles of law include *compétence-compétence*[460], *iura novit curia*[461], the principle that no-one may be judge in his or her own cause, review of excess of mandate[462], the

Secession?' in Walter, C., von Ungern-Sternberg, A., and Abushov, K. (eds.) (2014), *Self-Determination and Secession in International Law*, First edition (Oxford: Oxford University Press), 95-137, 97-99; Lone, F. (2012), "*Uti Possidetis Iuris*," last updated March 23, 2012, accessed October 27, 2024, <https://www.oxfordbibliographies.com/display/document/obo-9780199796953/obo-9780199796953-0065.xml>).

457 Fn 420 defines the term '*force majeure*'.

458 The principle of *rebus sic stantibus*, which is from Latin – its literal meaning is 'things standing thus', states that, if there has been a fundamental alteration of circumstances affecting a convention, then a party to that treaty may terminate it or withdraw from it (Encyclopaedia Britannica (2024), "*rebus sic stantibus*: law principle," accessed October 27, 2024, <https://www.britannica.com/topic/rebus-sic-stantibus>).

459 Fn 444 defines the term '*res judicata*'.

460 The *compétence-compétence* (from French) principle holds that an arbitral tribunal – and a court, too, as appropriate – has power to rule on its own jurisdiction; an arbitral tribunal needs to be empowered to make a ruling on its own jurisdiction in order to preclude a party to the relevant arbitration agreement from halting arbitral proceedings, or causing appreciable delay in these, by challenging the jurisdiction of the tribunal (Jones, D. (2009), Competence-Competence, *The International Journal of Arbitration, Mediation and Dispute Management*, 75(1), 56-64, 56).

461 The principle of *iura novit curia* (from Latin) means 'the judge (or court) knows the law'; this principle pertains to the law governing a dispute in civil law jurisdictions, which it requires the judge to apply – as (s)he considers to be appropriate – to the facts that the disputants present before the court (Cica, A. (2014), The Principle of *Iura Novit Curia*. University of Miami School of Law: Young Scholars in International Arbitration – A collection of essays prepared for the ICCA 2014 Congress, 105-124, 105-106).

462 This general principle of law requires a review of an arbitral award by a competent court to be available, on the ground that the arbitral tribunal which made the award exceeded the mandate that the arbitration agreement delineated for it (Houthoff (2024), "Eleven international publishing: Excess of Powers in International Commercial Arbitration – Compliance with the Arbitral Tribunal's Mandate in a Comparative Perspective: Piotr Wiliński," accessed October 28, 2024, <https://www.houthoff.com/-/media/houthoff/publications/pwilinski/flyer----excess-of-powers-in-international-commercial-arbitration.pdf>).

rule of burden of proof[463], the admissibility of indirect evidence[464], and the possibility of trial *in absentia*[465] [670].

Conclusion 11: Relationship between general principles of law and treaties and customary international law

1. General principles of law, as a source of international law, are not in a hierarchical relationship with treaties and customary international law [671].
2. A general principle of law may exist in parallel with a rule of the same or similar content in a treaty or customary international law [671].

---

[463] In an adversarial system of dispute resolution, the burden of proof lies with the party who brings the case; in an inquisitorial system of dispute settlement, the concept of the burden of proof has limited meaning because the court or tribunal retains responsibility for establishing the facts of the case and determining its outcome (Cooper, J. (2008), The burden and standard of proof. Courts and Tribunals Judiciary: Principles in Practice, Spring 2008 (London: Judicial Office), 2-6, 2-3).

[464] In criminal trials in the UK, a court tends to consider evidence – including circumstantial evidence – to be admissible, if it is presented or heard in the court and is probative, non-prejudicial to the defendant, pertinent to the facts of the case, coherent, and provable (Draycott Browne Solicitors (2024), "What is the definition of evidence in UK criminal law?" accessed October 28, 2024, <https://www.draycottbrowne.co.uk/investigations/types-evidence>). In civil proceedings in England and Wales, evidence will – as a general rule – be admissible in the relevant case, unless it falls within the ambit of an exclusionary rule that the law specifies (such as evidence that is subject to legal professional privilege – which is not therein admissible), or the court exercises its discretion to exclude it (Marriott, H. (2020), "Admissibility of evidence in civil proceedings: An overview and case law update," published July 13, 2020, last updated September 1, 2020, accessed October 28, 2024, <https://www.stiveschambers.co.uk/content/uploads/2020/09/HM-Admissibility-of-evidence-in-civil-proceedings.pdf>). The general principle of law on the admissibility of indirect evidence that the ICC accepts, is that circumstantial evidence and inferences of fact are admissible in the pertinent trial, if it can be proven therein that the party who bears the burden of proof is hindered by objective barriers from collecting direct attestation of a relevant element which supports his or her claim (International Criminal Court (2009), *Situation in Uganda in the case of the Prosecutor v. Joseph Kony, Vincent Otti, Okot Odhiambo, Dominic Ongwen*, Judgment of 23 February 2009, The Appeals Chamber of the International Criminal Court, ICC-02/04 OA and ICC-02/04-01/05 OA2, Paragraph 16).

[465] The term '*in absentia*' is from Latin; its literal translation into English is 'in absence'; it means "while not present at the event being referred to" (Pearsall, J. (editor) (1998), *The New Oxford Dictionary of English*, 920). The defendant is required to be present at his or her trial before the ICC (United Nations (1998), "Rome Statute of the International Criminal Court," *United Nations Treaty Series* Registration Number 38544, Article 63(1)). The Rome Statute of the ICC provides for the confirmation of charges to take place in the absence of the accused, but only under the circumstances specified therein: "1. Subject to the provisions of paragraph 2, within a reasonable time after the person's surrender or voluntary appearance before the Court, the Pre-Trial Chamber shall hold a hearing to confirm the charges on which the Prosecutor intends to seek trial. The hearing shall be held in the presence of the Prosecutor and the person charged, as well as his or her counsel. 2. The Pre-Trial Chamber may, upon request of the Prosecutor or on its own motion, hold a hearing in the absence of the person charged to confirm the charges on which the Prosecutor intends to seek trial[,] when the person has: (a) Waived his or her right to be present; or (b) Fled or cannot be found[,] and all reasonable steps have been taken to secure his or her appearance before the Court and to inform the person of the charges and that a hearing to confirm those charges will be held. In that case, the person shall be represented by counsel where the Pre-Trial Chamber determines that it is in the interests of justice." (United Nations (1998), "Rome Statute of the International Criminal Court," Article 61(1)-(2)). As it is difficult to bring offenders before the ICC – as at 21st May 2024, of forty individuals against whom judges of the ICC had authorized arrest warrants, only twenty-one of these had been apprehended and presented at the ICC – proceedings *in absentia* may furnish a potential solution to the inherent drawbacks of international criminal law, such as that of enforcing arrest warrants; considerations of due process – i.e., the denial by proceedings *in absentia* of human and constitutional rights to which the defendant is entitled – have traditionally been a bar to greater use of these proceedings; today, this concern is mitigated by the recommendation of the International Bar Association for all jurisdictions to ensure that judicial guarantees for international criminal justice processes are issued, when proceedings *in absentia* take place (Massimino, I. (2024), The ICC and in-absentia proceedings: Finding a response to the difficulties of executing arrest warrants, *ESIL Reflections*, 13(9), 1-10, 1, 4-6 and 9).

3. Any conflict between a general principle of law and a rule in a treaty or customary international law is to be resolved by applying the generally accepted techniques of interpretation and conflict resolution in international law [671].

Paragraph 1 of draft conclusion 11 follows paragraph 1 of Article 38 of the Statute of the ICJ, which lists international conventions, customary international law and general principles of law as sources of international law without specifying a hierarchy among them[466] [671]. However, nothing prevents states from instituting, for instance, a treaty regime that conceives a different arrangement, such as that in Article 21 of the Rome Statute of the ICC[467] [672].

Regarding paragraph 2 of draft conclusion 11, the ILC intended to emphasize that general principles of law are a separate source of law from conventional international law and customary international law – with their own conditions for identification, and that their presence and applicability as a component of general international law is unaffected if a provision within a treaty or a rule of customary international law attends to the identical, or a similar, subject-matter [672]. This situation may result, for example, when a treaty codifies the whole of a general principle of law, with the effect that a given rule may be located – with the same content – in both the relevant convention and general principles of law [672]. The general principle of law may continue to illuminate the interpretation and application of that treaty, and it would continue to apply as a matter of general international law between the states parties to the convention and non-parties to it, and betwixt states non-parties to the treaty [672].

The phrase 'generally accepted techniques of interpretation and conflict resolution in international law' in paragraph 3 of draft conclusion 11 means certain general principles of law which include *lex specialis derogat legi generali*[468], *lex posterior derogat legi priori*[469], and harmonization[470], together with Articles 31 to 33 of the Vienna Convention on the Law of

---

466 The quoted passage immediately following fn 207 identifies the sources of international law that the ICJ is to apply, which Article 38(1) of the Statute of the ICJ sets out.

467 The first paragraph of the abovementioned article reads as follows: "The Court shall apply: (a) In the first place, this Statute, Elements of Crimes and its Rules of Procedure and Evidence; (b) In the second place, where appropriate, applicable treaties and the principles and rules of international law, including the established principles of the international law of armed conflict; (c) Failing that, general principles of law derived by the Court from national laws of legal systems of the world[,] including, as appropriate, the national laws of States that would normally exercise jurisdiction over the crime, provided that those principles are not inconsistent with this Statute and with international law and internationally recognized norms and standards." (United Nations (1998), "Rome Statute of the International Criminal Court," Article 21(1)).

468 Fn 453 describes the principle *lex specialis derogat legi generali*.

469 Fn 454 relates the principle *lex posterior derogat legi priori*.

470 Harmonization in international law concerns the application of accordant legal standards across territories, thereby raising the level of legal certainty throughout. The following summarizes: "Legal harmonisation in international law is composed of common legislative development, consistent implementation, and uniform interpretation of legal texts across jurisdictions. ... [While] lawmaking and domestic implementation have become more sophisticated[, t]he object of developing legal certainty and predictability is still the main driving force of international harmonisation efforts. ... States, as primary actors of international law, develop and ratify treaties to regulate international relationships, with input from NGOs and industry lobbying groups representing public and private interest[s]. Legal harmonisation can then occur at a domestic, regional, or international level, as states commit to respect and enforce the particular rights and obligations envisaged by the treaties, implementing international law and ensuring that their domestic law is compatible with the international regulation." (Demeter, D., and Nasirova, Z. (2018), International legal harmonisation in theory and practice. Universitatea Spiru Haret: Facultatea de Ştiinţe Juridice, Politice şi Administrative Bucureşti – Centrul de Cercetări Juridice: Legal and Administrative Studies – Proceedings of Conference Legal, Political and Administrative Consequences of Romania's Accession to the European Union, Bucureşti, 17-18 Mai 2018, 66-76, 66). 'NGO' is an abbreviation for 'non-governmental organization'.

Treaties 1969[471] [673]. In settling a conflict to which that paragraph refers, accepted hierarchical relationships, by virtue of the substance of the rule, i.e., *jus cogens*[472] (and *erga omnes* obligations[473]) and particular clauses in treaties (such as Article 103 of the UN Charter[474]), must be taken into account [673].

Comment

The ILC's work on primary sources of international law – bar conventional law, which has a longer history – has been undertaken since 2011. Regarding general principles of law – formally 'the general principles of law recognized by civilized nations,' the draft conclusions and commentaries thereon await their second reading before the ILC, in the light of the observations and comments that have been received from governments on the earlier version – which is described in the immediately-preceding subsection. After publication of these draft conclusions following their second reading and their subsequent approval by the UN General Assembly, it would be useful for the ILC to publish an annotated list of general principles of law and to regularly update this.

Secondary Sources

Introduction

Subparagraph 1(d) of Article 38 of the Statute of the ICJ refers to the subject-matter of the present section, thus.

> 1. The Court, whose function is to decide in accordance with international law such disputes as are submitted to it, shall apply: ... d. subject to the provisions of Article 59 [of the Statute of the ICJ][475], judicial decisions and the teachings of the most highly qualified publicists of the various nations, as subsidiary means for the determination of rules of law [345].

The first sentence of the first paragraph of draft conclusion 6 on subsidiary means for the determination of rules of international law, which, at the time of writing, the ILC has provisionally adopted, reads as follows.

---

[471] Articles 31-33 of the Vienna Convention on the Law of Treaties 1969 are this international instrument's rules on the interpretation of treaties. The quoted passage to which fn 288 is coupled consists of Articles 31 and 32 of the Vienna Convention on the Law of Treaties 1969. The paragraph that includes the text to fn 314 contains paragraphs 1 and 4 of Article 33 of the Vienna Convention on the Law of Treaties 1969.

[472] Fn 236 defines the term '*jus cogens*'. The section titled 'Primary Sources: *Jus Cogens*', above in the current chapter (i.e., Chapter 4), covers peremptory norms of international law (*jus cogens*).

[473] Fn 351 defines the term '*erga omnes* obligations'. Paragraph 1 of draft conclusion 17 on identification and legal consequences of peremptory norms of general international law (*jus cogens*), which the quoted sentence immediately following the text to fn 409 lays down, and the commentary thereon that follows, set out the connection between *jus cogens* and *erga omnes* obligations.

[474] The sentence immediately preceding the text to fn 189 lays down Article 103 of the UN Charter.

[475] The quoted passage immediately following the text to fn 208 comprises Article 59 of the Statute of the ICJ.

Subsidiary means are not a source of international law [674].

In the commentary to paragraph 1 of draft conclusion 1, the ILC explains why it has made this statement.

> (2) Paragraph 1 of draft conclusion 6 is composed of two sentences. The first sentence addresses the nature of subsidiary means [for the determination of the rules of international law,] and provides that subsidiary means are not a source of international law. The Commission found that there is an extensive body of international and national judicial practice and scholarly works, as well as drafting history, to justify this conclusion. (3) ... In formulating the Commission's position, two main alternatives were considered. The first was to provide that the subsidiary means are auxiliary in nature *vis-à-vis*[476] treaties, customary international law and general principles of law[,] and that they are mainly resorted to when determining the rules of international law. (4) The second alternative was to indicate that subsidiary means are not an "autonomous" source of international law or that they are "distinct from" the sources of international law. While it was found that there was merit in each of those approaches, several questions were raised about each of the alternatives, including the possible need to explain them further. The Commission therefore opted for the more direct formulation, stating simply that they are not sources of law. Still, a view was expressed that the proposition contained in the first sentence [of paragraph 1 of draft conclusion 6] was too categorical in [the] light of their use for other purposes[,] and that some nuances of what actually occurs in practice regarding the subsidiary means risk being lost [675].

It is submitted that this slant is non-optimal. The writings of publicists and the *ratio decidendi* of cases and arbitrations with international content have formed a considerable part of public international law in earlier stages of its development. It is only in recent years that the ILC has been ordering sources of non-conventional international law; it would be well-advised to take a gentler line regarding changes to the subject from the past than that of suddenly and categorically de-ranking subsidiary means for determining the rules of international law to non-source status.

It is opined that a better approach than that followed by the ILC is to class teachings and international case law as secondary sources of international law. This wording is used herein, and in the UN Treaty Collection's definition of the word 'convention'[477]. The idea of 'secondary source' implies that it should be resorted to in the absence of, or to augment, findings of relevant rules of international law from the primary sources of international law – from which a lead may emerge as to the identity of further such rules.

---

[476] Emphasis original. The term '*vis-à-vis*' is from French; its literal translation into English is 'face to face'; this hyphenated compound word can be used as a noun, an adverb or a preposition; if it is utilized as the last-mentioned part of speech, then it means "in relation to" or "with regard to" (Pearsall, J. (editor) (1998), *The New Oxford Dictionary of English*, 2065).

[477] This definition uses the following wording: "and – as a secondary source – judicial decisions and the teachings of the most highly qualified publicists" (text to fn 244).

Work of the ILC

At its seventy-second session, in 2021, the ILC introduced the theme 'Subsidiary means for the determination of rules of international law' to its future scheme of work [676]. At its seventy-third session, in 2022, the Commission included this subject in its current programme of assignments, and appointed Dr. Charles Jalloh as Special Rapporteur [676].

At its seventy-fourth session, in 2023, the ILC had in front of it the Special Rapporteur's first report, which included five draft conclusions [676]. The Commission referred these to the Drafting Committee [676]. Subsequently, the ILC provisionally adopted draft conclusions 1, 2 and 3 and the commentaries thereon, and noted draft conclusions 4 and 5 [676].

At its seventy-fifth session, in 2024, the ILC had before it the Special Rapporteur's second report, which contained three further draft conclusions [676]. The Commission referred these to the Drafting Committee [676]. The ILC provisionally adopted draft conclusions 4 and 5 [676]. Later in this session, it provisionally adopted draft conclusions 6, 7 and 8 [676].

Draft Conclusions on Subsidiary Means for the Determination of Rules of International Law Provisionally Adopted Thus Far by the ILC

Conclusion 1: Scope

The present draft conclusions concern the use of subsidiary means for the determination of rules of international law [677].

Conclusion 2: Categories of subsidiary means for the determination of rules of international law

Subsidiary means for the determination of rules of international law include:

(*a*) decisions of courts and tribunals;

(*b*) teachings;

(*c*) any other means generally used to assist in determining rules of international law[478] [677].

Conclusion 3: General criteria for the assessment of subsidiary means for the determination of rules of international law

When assessing the weight of subsidiary means for the determination of rules of international law, regard should be had to, *inter alia*[479]:

(*a*) their degree of representativeness;

(*b*) the quality of the reasoning;

(*c*) the expertise of those involved;

(*d*) the level of agreement among those involved;

(*e*) the reception by States and other entities;

---

478 The italics for the letters '*a*', '*b*' and '*c*' are present in the original text.

479 The final sentence of fn 284 defines the term '*inter alia*'.

(*f*) where applicable, the mandate conferred on the body[480] [678].

Conclusion 4: Decisions of courts and tribunals

1. Decisions of international courts and tribunals, in particular of the International Court of Justice, are a subsidiary means for the determination of the existence and content of rules of international law [674].
2. Decisions of national courts may be used, in certain circumstances, as a subsidiary means for the determination of the existence and content of rules of international law [674].

Conclusion 5: Teachings

Teachings, especially those generally reflecting the coinciding views of persons with competence in international law from the various legal systems and regions of the world, are a subsidiary means for the determination of the existence and content of rules of international law. In assessing the representativeness of teachings, due regard should also be had to, *inter alia*[481], gender and linguistic diversity [674].

Conclusion 6: Nature and function of subsidiary means

1. Subsidiary means are not a source of international law. The function of subsidiary means is to assist with the determination of the existence and content of rules of international law [674].
2. The use of materials as subsidiary means for the determination of the rules of international law is without prejudice to their use for other purposes [674].

Conclusion 7: Absence of legally binding precedent in international law

Decisions of international courts or tribunals may be followed on points of law[,] where those decisions address the same or similar issues as those under consideration. Such decisions do not constitute legally binding precedent[,] unless otherwise provided for in a specific instrument or rule of international law [674].

Conclusion 8: Weight of decisions of courts and tribunals

When assessing the weight of decisions of courts or tribunals, regard should be had to, in addition to the criteria set out in draft conclusion 3[482], *inter alia*[483]:

(*a*) whether the court or tribunal has been conferred with a specific competence with regard to the application of the rule in question;

(*b*) the extent to which the decision is part of a body of concurring decisions; and

---

[480] The italics for the phrase '*inter alia*', and for the letters '*a*', '*b*', '*c*', '*d*', '*e*' and '*f*', are present in the original text.

[481] Emphasis original. The last sentence of fn 284 defines the term '*inter alia*'.

[482] The text to fns 479 and 480 lays down draft conclusion 3 on subsidiary means for the determination of rules of international law.

[483] The final sentence of fn 284 defines the term '*inter alia*'.

(*c*) the extent to which the reasoning remains relevant, taking into account subsequent developments[484] [674].

Comment

The draft conclusions on subsidiary means for the determination of rules of international law are in a developmental stage. More may be added before they undergo their first reading in front of the ILC. It is submitted that these draft conclusions should be through their second reading at the ILC by 2030.

The object of the ILC is "the promotion of the progressive development of international law and its codification"[485] [350]. The Statute of the ILC defines the term 'progressive development of international law' as "the preparation of draft conventions on subjects which have not yet been regulated by international law or in regard to which the law has not yet been sufficiently developed in the practice of States", and the phrase 'codification of international law' as "the more precise formulation and systemization of rules of international law in fields where there has already been extensive State practice, precedent and doctrine"[486] [679]. Over the area of sources of international law – the ILC's work on which is covered above in this chapter, it has fulfilled both of these goals according to their definitions, i.e., the preparation of draft conventions: the Vienna Convention on the Law of Treaties 1969, the Vienna Convention on the Succession of States in respect of Treaties 1978 and the Vienna Convention on the Law of Treaties between States and International Organizations or between International Organizations 1986, and the more-precise formulation and systemization of rules: e.g., the Guide to Practice on Reservations to Treaties, the Conclusions on Subsequent Agreements and Subsequent Practice in relation to Interpretation of Treaties, and the Guidelines on Provisional Application of Treaties. All of these concern conventional international law; it is submitted that the ILC's work on other sources of international law is more preliminary than that on treaties; the production of draft conclusions over the areas of customary international law, *jus cogens*, general principles of law and subsidiary means for the determination of rules of international law does not amount to 'progressive development of international law' within the above definition of this term, as the ILC has not prepared draft conventions on these subjects; nor does this work qualify as 'codification of international law' within the above definition of this phrase; rather, the aforementioned conclusions bring a degree of order to important elements of public international law that have not been structured to date. This is a crucial task that the ILC is accomplishing but, it is opined, insufficient to constitute the eventual form of the law over these areas.

---

[484] The italics for the phrase '*inter alia*', and for the letters '*a*', '*b*' and '*c*', are present in the original text.

[485] This is paragraph 1 of Article 1 of the Statute of the ILC, the wording of which is pursuant to that of subparagraph 1(a) of Article 13 of the UN Charter, which requires the General Assembly to "initiate studies and make recommendations for the purpose of ... encouraging the progressive development of international law and its codification" (third paragraph of the section titled 'Introduction', above in the current chapter (i.e., Chapter 4); text to fn 488).

[486] This is Article 15 of the Statute of the ILC, the wording of which follows the conclusions of the Committee on the Progressive Development of International Law and its Codification as to the meaning of the terms 'progressive development of international law' and 'codification of international law' (fourth paragraph of the subsection entitled 'The third occurrence of 'international law': progressive development and codification', in the section titled 'Introduction', above in the present chapter (i.e., Chapter 4)).

The Preamble of the UN Charter refers to "obligations arising from treaties and other sources of international law" [174], and paragraph 1 of Article 1 of the UN Charter to "the principles of ... international law" [340][487]. It is opined that the drafters of the UN Charter would have wished for legal certainty in the eventual form of international law, as they intended the General Assembly to "initiate studies and make recommendations for the purpose of ... encouraging the progressive development of international law and its codification"[488] [341]. Consequential to this, the responsible entity, i.e., the ILC, must persevere with its work until interested parties are able to reach for a comprehensive manual that clearly states the rules of international law, which, from that point onwards, the ILC should update frequently.

Finally, it is opined that much progress has been made in developing the content of international law during this subject's institutional phase, i.e., from the establishment of the League of Nations on 10th January 1920[489] until today. The research and publications of the ILC – well-ordered on its website – are a major part of this advancement.

Conclusion

This chapter considers the evolution of international law to the current time, within the framework of the UN Charter and paragraph 1 of Article 38 of the Statute of the ICJ, looking at sources of the topic with reference to work of the ILC. The next chapter pronounces on the legality of the invasion of Ukraine.

[487] The first and second paragraphs of the section entitled 'Introduction', above in the current chapter (i.e., Chapter 4) contain, respectively, these two phrases.

[488] The third paragraph of the section titled 'Introduction', above in the present chapter (i.e., Chapter 4), as well as fn 485, embodies this expression.

[489] Text to fn 42.

Chapter 5

The Legality of the Invasion of Ukraine

Abstract

Controversy prior to the dissolution of the USSR over the border between Russia and Ukraine in the expectation of possible independence bore the seeds of the Russian government's future aggression concerning Ukraine. The occupation of Crimea by Russian armed forces in February 2014 was swiftly endorsed by the upper house of the Russian parliament, which promptly and unanimously passed a decree authorizing the use of Russian troops on Ukrainian territory. In February 2022, the Russian parliament requested the President of the Russian Federation to recognize as independent two areas within Donbas, and, as in 2014, sanctioned the use of Russian armed forces on Ukrainian territory. On Thursday 24th February 2022, the President of the Russian Federation gave the order for Russian troops to enter previously-unoccupied areas of Ukraine. Russia's occupation of Crimea in 2014, its support prior to 2022 of forces in Donbas that are non-aligned with the government of Ukraine, and its invasion of Ukraine in 2022, were all part of the same movement and policy from the government and parliament of Russia: namely, to support Russian-speaking populations and areas within the legally-recognized state of Ukraine, to ensure as far as possible the presence of a Russia-friendly government in Ukraine and, in the absence of this, to conquer part – or the whole – of the territory under the legitimate control of the Ukrainian government. Taken together, these actions amount to sundry breaches of paragraphs 3 and 4 of Article 2 of the UN Charter, as well as to contravention of the prohibition of aggression – a peremptory norm of general international law (*jus cogens*). States that have co-operated with Russia in its aggression towards Ukraine have infracted the prohibition of aggression, too. This is by means of violating one or both clauses of paragraph 2 of draft conclusion 19 of the ILC's draft conclusions on identification and legal consequences of peremptory norms of general international law (*jus cogens*). The chapter looks at each of these two clauses separately in relation to Russia's transgression of the prohibition of aggression regarding its activities in Ukraine. The governments of all these countries should cease breaking the rules with immediate effect. Russia should promptly withdraw all its armed forces from the territory of Ukraine. As soon as all Russian – and Russia-aligned – troops have left Ukraine, the terms for a peace settlement can be negotiatied. The ILC has declared the prohibition of racial discrimination to be a peremptory norm of general international law (*jus cogens*). Therefore, the government of Ukraine will be expected to treat its Russian minorities in Crimea, Donbas and elsewhere in the state to the same standard that it acts towards any other Ukrainian national. While such a policy is not in doubt under the current President of Ukraine, it would need to be maintained elsewhere within the regime and into the future.

Keywords: aggression, norm, peremptory, prohibition, resolution, Russia, Ukraine

Introduction

> Every positive law ... is set, directly or circuitously, by a sovereign individual or body, to a member or members of the independent political society wherein its author is supreme.

> ... It is set, directly or circuitously, by a monarch or sovereign number, to a person or persons in a state of subjection to its author. ... The party or parties to whom a law is set, or the party or parties on whom a duty is laid, are necessarily obnoxious to the sanction which enforces the law and the duty. In other words, every law properly so called is set by a superior to an inferior or inferiors: It is set by a party armed with might, to a party or parties whom that might can reach. ... [A] party who is obnoxious to a legal sanction, is a subject of the author to which the sanction is annexed. But as none but members of the community wherein the law obtains are obnoxious to the legal sanction which enforces a positive law, the positive law is imposed exclusively on a member or members of that independent community [680].

Sometime students of the law of England and Wales should be familiar with the work of Mr. John Austin, from whose monograph entitled '*The Province of Jurisprudence Determined*' the above quote is taken. Mr. Austin, an English legal positivist, was writing almost two hundred years ago – before the Judicature Acts of the 1870s, before the Universal Declaration of Human Rights 1948, and before the institutional phase of international law, i.e., in a very different legal environment to that of today. Yet, his description therein of the basic legal order within a hypothetical state is not totally unfamiliar.

In the present book, the concern is not with a regime exercising this perception of law on its people. It is with one whose parliament has wrongfully authorized its government to exert such behaviour over people within a neighbouring state, in breach of precepts and rules of international law, and with states that have supported this. This chapter summarizes.

Applying the Law to the Facts

When the USSR was officially dissolved on 26th December 1991[490], the former Soviet republics became independent states[491]. On that day, the borders between the republics became the international boundaries between them[492].

[490] Fn 3.

[491] Fn 28.

[492] While this development may have been an instance of the exercise of the principle of *uti possidetis* (fn 456), it appears that the matter of international borders between the newly-independent Soviet republics was not comprehensively discussed beforehand by their leaders, and that the continuation of the existing boundaries between these countries from before to after independence was accepted by them – reluctantly in the case of the Russian leadership (see fn 493). A declaration was signed by Dr. Stanislav Shushkevich – Chairman of the Supreme Soviet of the Republic of Belarus, Mr. Boris Yeltsin – President of the Russian Soviet Federative Socialist Republic, and Mr. Leonid Kravchuk – Chairman of the Parliament (Verkovna Rada) of Ukraine, in Minsk on 8th December 1991, in which they proclaimed the foundation of the Commonwealth of Independent States (United Nations (1991), General Assembly: Forty-sixth session – Agenda items 22, 68, 98, 127, 131 and 135, Letter dated 12 December 1991 from the Permanent Representative of Belarus to the United Nations addressed to the Secretary-General, A/46/771, 13 December 1991, Annex I: Declaration by the Heads of State of the Republic of Belarus, the Russian Federation and Ukraine, Operative Paragraph). At that meeting in Minsk, these leaders, together with one other delegate from each Soviet Republic, signed the Agreement establishing the Commonwealth of Independent States, at which they "declare[d] that the Union of Soviet Socialist Republics as a subject of international law and a geopolitical reality no longer exists" (United Nations (1991), General Assembly: Forty-sixth session – Agenda items 22, 68, 98, 127, 131 and 135, Letter dated 12 December 1991 from the Permanent Representative of Belarus to the United Nations addressed to the Secretary-General, A/46/771, 13 December 1991, Annex II: Agreement establishing the Commonwealth of Independent States, Preamble). Paragraph 1 of Article 5 of the Agreement establishing the Commonwealth of Independent States reads: "The High Contracting Parties [(i.e., the Republic of Belarus, the Russian Federation and Ukraine)]

There was contraversy prior to attaining this position[493], which, it is opined, from what it may have harboured in the minds of the leadership of Russia, bore the seeds of the Russian government's future aggression regarding Ukraine.

acknowledge and respect each other's territorial integrity and *the inviolability of existing borders within the Commonwealth.*" (United Nations (1991), General Assembly: Forty-sixth session – Agenda items 22, 68, 98, 127, 131 and 135, Letter dated 12 December 1991 from the Permanent Representative of Belarus to the United Nations addressed to the Secretary-General, A/46/771, 13 December 1991, Annex II: Agreement establishing the Commonwealth of Independent States, Article 5(1); emphasis added). This matter was briefly covered in the Alma Ata Declaration, which was signed in Almaty (formerly Alma-Ata) on 21st December 1991 by a senior governmental representative from each of the following: the Republics of Armenia, Azerbaijan, Belarus, Kazakhstan, Kyrgyzstan, Moldova, Tajikistan and Uzbekistan, the Russian Federation, Turkmenistan and Ukraine; the second recital and the fifth operative paragraph of the Alma Ata Declaration state: "The Independent States ... Recognizing and respecting each other's territorial integrity and *the inviolability of existing borders*, ... With the establishment of the Commonwealth of Independent States, the Union of Soviet Socialist Republics ceases to exist. ..." (United Nations (1991), General Assembly: Forty-seventh session, Security Council: Forty-sixth year, Letter dated 27 December 1991 from the Permanent Representative of Belarus to the United Nations addressed to the Secretary-General, A/47/60 and S/23329, 30 December 1991, Annex II: Alma Ata Declaration, Recital 2 and Operative Paragraph 5; emphasis added).

[493] There is relevant documentation available on-line. Three items are mentioned here. In an obituary of Dr. Shushkevich (fn 492), Mr. George Krol – a retired ambassador from the USA to Belarus, Kazakhstan and Uzbekistan, made the following comments: "Belarusian statesman Stanislav Shushkevich, who died on May 3 [2022], is probably best remembered for hosting the meeting that ended the Soviet Union. On December 8, 1991, in a state guesthouse in the remote Bialowieza Forest, Shushkevich and the leaders of Russia, Boris Yeltsin, and Ukraine, Leonid Kravchuk, signed a series of accords that effectively finished the communist state. ... Shushkevich told me that Yeltsin's people had hijacked the Bialowieza Forest meeting. What had been planned as a bilateral Yeltsin visit became a Russian-managed summit with Ukrainian leader Kravchuk ... aimed at replacing [Mr. Mikhail] Gorbachev's reformed USSR [(of which he was then President)] with a new union essentially run by Russia and Ukraine. Indeed, in the Yeltsin camp's retelling, Belarus was only the handmaiden and host. Belarus itself, Shushkevich admitted to me once, had to agree with whatever Russia wanted, "because in the end we didn't have a choice." Kravchuk, however, while eager for Ukraine to leave the USSR, had no desire, or political power, to commit to joining a new union. Shushkevich said that, failing to get the Ukrainian president's commitment to a new confederation, *at the forest meeting Yeltsin raised with Kravchuk the return of Crimea to Russia*. But *Kravchuk demurred*, asserting that he had no authority from his parliament to discuss the subject. Yeltsin was furious." (Krol, G. (2022), "Memoir | The Shushkevich I knew," published May 12, 2022, accessed November 7, 2024, <https://eurasianet.org/memoir-the-shushkevich-i-knew>; emphasis added). While the history of Crimea is beyond the scope of the current monograph, '*the return of Crimea to Russia*' in the immediately-preceding sentence refers to the transfer of the Crimean oblast from the Russian Soviet Federative Socialist Republic to the Ukrainian Soviet Socialist Republic, further to the decree made by the Presidium of the Supreme Soviet of the USSR on 19th February 1954 (Siegelbaum, L. (2024), "Seventeen Moments in Soviet History: The Gift of Crimea," accessed November 7, 2024, <https://soviethistory.msu.edu/1954-2/the-gift-of-crimea/>). The second and third items are available from the USA's National Security Archive at the George Washington University, from the page headed 'The End of the Soviet Union 1991', at https://nsarchive.gwu.edu/briefing-book/russia-programs/2021-12-21/end-soviet-union-1991. A declassified memorandum sent by Dr. Brent Scowcroft, United States National Security Advisor, to Mr. George H. W. Bush, President of the USA, on 5th September 1991, includes the following statements: "[President Boris] Yel'tsin's popularity and influence ... were obviously boosted by last month's events [(i.e., the August Coup)]. But he made several mistakes in the first days after the coup by moving too quickly and openly to put Russians in control of the Union [of Soviet Socialist Republics]. Before the coup, under Yel'tsin's leadership Russia had for some time moved subtly but unmistakably to infiltrate union institutions, which was already causing some discomfort, particularly in the Asian republics. But Yel'tsin's attempt at what looked almost like a "second coup" during August 22-24 – where he dictated a provisional union government to Gorbachev composed solely of Russians – combined with *his warning on borders to Kazakhstan and Ukraine that they could not depart the Union without leaving behind the Russianized portions of their republics*, frightened other republican leaders. ... Ukraine is the wild card in this. Both Yel'tsin and Gorbachev feel that Ukraine must stay in the Union. It is a huge economy tightly integrated with Russia, and an abrupt separation would be disastrous. Kravchuk may agree, but his political situation is tenuous, and Ukrainian independence is the one cause uniting virtually all political factions in that republic." (Scowcroft, B. (1991), Information: Memorandum for the President – Developments in the USSR, 6506, September 5, 1991, 1-4, 1-2; emphasis added). The third quoted passage is

The occupation of the Crimean peninsula by Russian armed forces in late February 2014[494] was swiftly endorsed by the upper house of the parliament of Russia – which promptly and unanimously passed a decree authorizing the use of Russian troops on Ukrainian territory[495]

---

taken from a transcript of a dinner hosted by King Juan Carlos I of Spain and on 29th October 1991 between the King, President Bush, President Gorbachev and Mr. Felipe González, Prime Minister of Spain, which originated at the Gorbachev Foundation Archive and was translated into English by Dr. Svetlana Savranskaya, a Senior Research Fellow of the National Security Archive; it is noteworthy that I tried to contact Dr. Savranskaya for further information using the e-mail address that she provided on the web page, but received no reply: "Dear Svetlana, I have accessed your page on the National Security Archive, i.e., 'https://nsarchive.gwu.edu/briefing-book/russia-programs/2021-12-21/end-soviet-union-1991'. What I would like to know is how it was decided in 1991 that the post-Soviet Union international borders should follow those of the Soviet Republics. This seems to be a case of *uti possidetis*, but it is crucial to my research on this matter to find out, in essence, what happened in the international political meetings at the time. I would be grateful if you would direct me to any relevant sources. Kind regards, Graeme Baber. (Legal writer)" (Baber, G. (2024), E-mail communication from Dr. Graeme Baber to Dr. Svetlana Savranskaya, National Security Archive, George Washington University, November 6, 2024). Notwithstanding this, it is submitted that the sources that I have been able to access give readers of this footnote (i.e., fn 493) a fair idea as to the positions of the Russian and Ukrainian leaders in 1991 regarding their shared border in the expectation of independence. The translation of the abovementioned transcript includes the following statements: "GORBACHEV. [Y]ou have to keep in mind that[,] whatever Kravchuk is saying (and *he is saying different things – one thing in the Crimea and another in Kiev*), and whatever the Ukrainian Supreme Soviet is adopting, this is not the same as the people's opinion. I am convinced that the people of such a multinational republic as Ukraine will ultimately make a decision in favor of the Union [of Soviet Socialist Republics,] because we cannot simply separate from one another in a country where 75 million people live outside of their ethnic units. There are 15 million Russians in the Ukraine, according to the most conservative estimates. Only 40 per cent of Kazakhstan is Kazakh. JUAN CARLOS. Only? GONZALEZ. Kazakhstan as such is just nonsense. GORBACHEV. Apart from the Union, yes. And that is why [Mr. Nursultan] Nazarbayev [(then President of Kazakhstan)] is firmly pro-Union. We never had any internal borders. How is it possible to divide oneself, how do you cut up everything? Ukraine in its present form emerged only because the Bolsheviks did not have a majority in the Rada [(i.e., the legislature of the Ukrainian Supreme Soviet)], and *they added Kharkov and Donbass to the Ukraine.* And [Mr. Nikita] *Khrushchev* [(First Secretary of the Communist Party of the USSR from 1953 to 1964)] *passed the Crimea from Russia to the Ukraine* as a fraternal gesture. And *when talks started about the secession of Ukraine, then a powerful movement against that began in the Donbass, in the south, and in the Crimea. The Crimea finally made the decision that either Ukraine will be in the Union, or we are returning to Russia.* Kravchuk went to the Crimea, tried to calm them down. The situation is made even more difficult by *the careless statements of Yeltsin and his circle about borders and territorial claims*. This is an explosive topic." (National Security Archive (2021), Record of Dinner Conversation between Gorbachev, Bush, Gonzalez and King Juan Carlos of Spain, Madrid, October 29, 1991, Savranskaya, S. (tr.), 1-19, 10-11; emphasis added).

[494] Eighth and ninth sentences of the penultimate paragraph of the section titled 'The Background', in Chapter 1; fn 29 and accompanying text.

[495] The Observer reports: "*Vladimir Putin gave the green light for an invasion of Ukraine* on Saturday [1st March 2014,] as *the upper house of the Russian parliament unanimously approved his request to send troops into the neighbouring state.* After several days in which Russia appeared to be stealthily laying groundwork for intervention in the Crimean peninsula, the move came suddenly and decisively. The Kremlin said [that] Putin wanted to introduce troops into Ukraine "until the sociopolitical situation is normalised". Less than an hour later, *in a hastily convened extraordinary sitting of Russia's Federation Council ... senators voted unanimously to support Putin's proposal ... . The Russian decree does not limit the use of troops to Crimea, specifying only that Russian military could be deployed "on Ukrainian territory"* ... . Putin's press secretary, Dmitry Peskov, said that no decision to implement the decree had yet been taken. ... The decisive move by Putin come after two days during which the Kremlin's motives were unclear. Armed men seized the Crimean parliament on Thursday [27th February 2014] and the peninsula's airports on Friday [28th February 2014], but claimed to be members of locally organised "self-defence squads" rather than Russian troops. As late as Friday, the foreign ministry [of Russia] was insisting that no irregular troop movements were taking place, despite reports of thousands of Russian military personnel landing in Crimea. Putin has not spoken directly about Ukraine all week. ... Ukraine's new government does include far-right groups, and one of the first laws [that] it passed rescinded provisions for regions with large Russian-speaking populations to use Russian as a second official language. ... Ukraine's new government has disbanded the Berkut riot police involved in clashes with protestors, while *Russia has announced [that] it will give them Russian passports*. The first of them collected passports at a Russian consulate in Crimea on Saturday." (Salem, H., and Walker, S. (2014), Russian parliament approves troop deployment in Ukraine, *The Observer*, Saturday 1 March 2014; emphasis added).

[681]. The parliament of Russia was integrally involved in the period immediately-preceding the large-scale invasion of Ukraine by the Russian military on 24th February 2022[496], requesting the President of the Russian Federation to recognize as independent two areas within Donbas[497] [682, 683], and, as in 2014, sanctioning the use of Russian armed forces on Ukrainian territory[498] [683]. On Thursday 24th February 2022, the President of the Russian Federation gave the order for Russian troops to enter previously unoccupied areas of Ukraine – from Belarus, Crimea, and Russia[499] [684].

It is opined that the Russian occupation of Crimea in 2014, Russia's support prior to 2022 of forces in Donbas that are non-aligned with the government of Ukraine, and its invasion of

---

496 Text to fn 2; fn 499 and accompanying text.

497 Reuters announces: "*Russia's lower house of parliament voted on Tuesday [15th February 2022] to ask President Vladimir Putin to recognise two Russian-backed breakaway regions in eastern Ukraine as independent* … . The move by the State Duma [of Russia], if approved, could further inflame a wider standoff over a Russian military build-up near Ukraine that has fuelled Western fears that Moscow could attack. *Russia denies any invasion plans* … . Recognition of the self-declared Donetsk and Luhansk People's Republics could kill the Minsk peace process in eastern Ukraine, where conflict in the region known as Donbass between [Ukrainian] government forces and Moscow-backed separatists has cost 15,000 lives. "Kyiv is not observing the Minsk agreements. *Our citizens and compatriots who live in Donbass* need our help and support," Vyacheslav Volodin, the State Duma speaker, wrote on social media." (Balmforth, T., and Zverev, A. (2022), Russia's parliament asks Putin to recognise breakaway east Ukrainian regions, *Reuters*, Tuesday 15 February 2022; emphasis added). Human Rights Watch states: "*Russia's parliament adopted a resolution on February 16, 2022[,] requesting President Vladimir Putin to recognize as independent states two areas in eastern Ukraine held by Russia-backed armed groups. On February 21 [2022], President Putin signed two decrees recognizing the two areas' independence* and submitted them to parliament for ratification. Following that, *he issued orders to Russia's armed forces*, which have been amassing at the border with Ukraine for months, *to carry out "peacekeeping" in the self-proclaimed "Donetsk People's Republic ("DNR") and "Luhansk People's Republic ..." ("LNR")*." (Human Rights Watch (2022), Russia, Ukraine & International Law: On Occupation, Armed Conflict and Human Rights: Questions and Answers, *Human Rights Watch*, Wednesday 23 February 2022; emphasis added).

498 Human Rights Watch (fn 497) continues: "*On February 22 [2022], the Federation Council, the upper chamber of Russia's parliament, approved Putin's request to deploy the armed forces.* In public comments on February 22, Putin stated that the boundaries of the territories whose independence Russia has recognized extend to substantial areas of the Donetsk and Luhansk regions that are under Ukrainian government control." (Human Rights Watch (2022), Russia, Ukraine & International Law: On Occupation, Armed Conflict and Human Rights: Questions and Answers, *Human Rights Watch*, Wednesday 23 February 2022; emphasis added).

499 Reuters writes: "President Vladimir Putin authorised "a special military operation" against Ukraine on Thursday morning to eliminate what he called a serious threat, saying his aim was to demilitarise Russia's southern neighbour. In an early morning address on state television, Putin said [that] he had been left with no choice but to launch the operation, the scope of which was not immediately clear[,] but appeared to go well beyond helping Russian-backed separatists in eastern Ukraine. ... The Kremlin chief's announcement followed an appeal from the Russian-backed separatists in eastern Ukraine for military help against what they said was growing Ukrainian aggression. Kyiv has denied any such aggression. Putin told the Ukrainian military to lay down its weapons and go home. ... A Reuters reporter in Kyiv ... heard explosions that sounded like artillery shelling in the distance[,] minutes after Putin finished speaking." (Nikolskaya, P., and Osborn, A. (2022), Russia's Putin authorises 'special military operation' against Ukraine, *Reuters*, Thursday 24 February 2022). Al Jazeera states: "Russia has launched an all-out invasion of Ukraine by land, air and sea … . The attacks began on Thursday [24th February 2022,] after Russian President Vladimir Putin said in a televised address that he had approved a "special military operation". The move came after Moscow earlier recognized rebel-held territories in Luhansk and Donetsk[,] and said [that] they had asked for its "help". Russian missiles rained down on Ukrainian cities. Ukraine reported columns of troops pouring across its borders into the eastern Chernihiv, Kharkiv and Luhansk regions, and landing by sea at the cities of Odesa and Mariupol in the south. Russian troops attacked Ukraine from Belarus as well as Russia with Belarusian support, and an attack was also being launched from annexed Crimea, Ukraine's border guard service said. Explosions could be heard before dawn in the Ukrainian capital, Kyiv. Gunfire rattled out near the main airport and sirens blared across the city. Ukrainian President Volodymyr Zelenskyy said martial law had been declared[,] and he appealed to world leaders to impose all possible sanctions on Russia, including on Putin, who he said wanted to destroy the Ukrainian state." (Al Jazeera (2022), Russian forces launch full-scale invasion of Ukraine: Putin approves 'special military operation' as Russia launches an invasion of Ukraine by land, air and sea, *Al Jazeera*, Thursday 24 February 2022).

Ukraine in 2022, were all part of the same movement and policy from the government and the parliament of Russia: namely, to support Russian-speaking populations and areas within the legally-recognized state of Ukraine, to ensure as far as possible the presence of a Russia-friendly government in Ukraine and, in the absence of this, to conquer part – or the whole – of the territory under the legitmate control of the Ukrainian government. Taken together, these actions amount to sundry breaches of paragraphs 3 and 4 of Article 2 of the UN Charter[500], as well as to contravention of the prohibition of aggression[501] – a peremptory norm of general international law (*jus cogens*)[502].

It is submitted that states which have co-operated with Russia in its aggression towards Ukraine have infracted the prohibition of aggression, too. This allegation requires a more detailed look than that of the transgressions of Russia regarding Ukraine, which are manifest. Paragraph 2 of draft conclusion 19 of the ILC's draft conclusions on identification and legal consequences of peremptory norms of general international law (*jus cogens*) reads thus.

> No State shall recognize as lawful a situation created by a serious breach by a State of an obligation arising under a peremptory norm of general international law (*jus cogens*), nor render aid or assistance in maintaining that situation [625].

The 'obligation arising under a peremptory norm of general international law (*jus cogens*)' is, in this instance, the prohibition of aggression. The 'serious breach' of this obligation is the collection of destructive activities of Russian armed forces in Ukraine – which, as considered above, were committed by the government of Russia and authorized by the parliament of Russia, but were in no way approved by the legitimate government, i.e., the government of Ukraine. Paragraph 2 of draft conclusion 19 refers to 'a situation created by' the aforementioned breach, which all other states are obliged not to recognize as licit, and are prohibited from supplying aid or assistance to maintain it[503]. The two clauses of paragraph 2 of draft conclusion 19 are taken separately.

> *(i) No State shall recognize as lawful a situation created by a serious breach by a State of an obligation arising under a peremptory norm of general international law (jus cogens).*
> *(a) The conquest of Crimea*: The situation created by the unlawful referendum in Crimea after its occupation by Russian troops has already been discussed[504]. 169 of the Member States of the UN voted on the resolution that declared the aforementioned referendum to be invalid[505], of which 100 voted in favour, 58 abstained and 11 voted against [685]. It is

[500] Fn 5 sets out Article 2(3) of the UN Charter. The first sentence of fn 6 lays down Article 2(4) of the UN Charter.

[501] Fn 284 specifies the definition of the word 'aggression', which, in essence, is 'the use of armed force by a state against the sovereignty, territorial sovereignty, territorial integrity or political independence of another state, or in any manner inconsistent with the UN Charter'.

[502] The last paragraph of the subsection entitled 'Draft conclusions on identification and legal consequences of peremptory norms of general international law (*jus cogens*)', in the section titled 'Primary Sources: *Jus Cogens*' in Chapter 4, lists the prohibition of aggression as a peremptory norm of general international law (*jus cogens*), in accordance with the ILC's draft conclusions on identification and legal consequences of peremptory norms of general international law (*jus cogens*).

[503] The ILC draws attention to this in its commentary on draft conclusion 19 (sentence immediately following the text to fn 427).

[504] Fn 426.

[505] This is Resolution 68/262 adopted by the UN General Assembly on 27th March 2014, of which Operative Paragraphs 5 and 6 are the most relevant provisions (fn 426), together with Recital 7 – in which the General

opined that, by acting as such, the states which voted against this resolution were in breach of the peremptory norm of general international law (*jus cogens*) of the prohibition of aggression, by virtue of their non-respect for the first clause of paragraph 2 of draft conclusion 19 on identification and legal consequences of peremptory norms of general international law (*jus cogens*)[506]. As well as being non-derogable, the prohibition of aggression creates *erga omnes* obligations[507]; it is submitted that Russia, and the other states that voted against the abovementioned resolution, failed to take the responsibilities to which this peremptory norm of general international law gives rise. *(b) The subsequent invasion:* The transgressions of the prohibition of aggression pursuant to the first clause paragraph 2 of draft conclusion 19 on identification and legal consequences of peremptory norms of general international law (*jus cogens*) concern resolutions of the UN that declare the invasion and subsequent occupation of Ukrainian territory by Russian troops to be unlawful, which one or more of its Member States voted against. It is opined that these countries have violated the prohibition of aggression. The relevant instruments are UN General Assembly Resolutions ES-11/1 (LXXVI), ES-11/2 (LXXVI), ES-11/4 (LXXVII), ES-11/5 (LXXVII) and ES-11/6 (LXXVII). Table 5.1 and its accompanying footnotes furnish details.

Table 5.1. Voting on UN General Assembly Resolutions concerning the invasion of Ukraine in 2022 and the prohibition of aggression

Resolution	The most relevant provision(s) of the resolution	Number of voting Member States	Votes in favour of the resolution	Abstentions from the vote	Votes against the resolution
ES-11/1 (LXXVI)	Operative Paragraphs 1, 2, 3 and 4[508]	181 [686]	141	35	5[509]

Assembly notes that Ukraine did not authorize the abovementioned referendum (United Nations (2014), Resolution 68/262 adopted by the General Assembly on 27th March 2014, Recital 7).

506 The eleven states that voted against Resolution 68/262 adopted by the General Assembly on 27th March 2014 were Armenia, Belarus, Bolivia, Cuba, the Democratic People's Republic of Korea, Nicaragua, Russia, Sudan, Syria, Venezuela and Zimbabwe (United Nations (2014), "Digital Library: Territorial integrity of Ukraine: resolution / adopted by the General Assembly – 2014," published March 27, 2014, accessed November 9, 2024, <https://digitallibrary.un.org/record/767565?ln=en>).

507 Paragraph 1 of draft conclusion 17 on identification and legal consequences of peremptory norms of general international law (*jus cogens*) specifies this (sentence immediately following the text to fn 409).

508 These clauses read as follows: "*The General Assembly*, ... 1. *Reaffirms its commitment* to the sovereignty, independence, unity and territorial integrity of Ukraine within its internationally recognized borders, extending to its territorial waters; 2. *Deplores in the strongest terms* the aggression by the Russian Federation against Ukraine in violation of Article 2(4) of the [UN] Charter; 3. *Demands* that the Russian Federation immediately cease its use of force against Ukraine and to refrain from any further unlawful threat or use of force against any Member State; 4. *Also demands* that the Russian Federation immediately, completely and unconditionally withdraw all of its military forces from the territory of Ukraine within its internationally recognized borders;" (United Nations (2022), Resolution ES-11/1 (LXXVI) adopted by the General Assembly on 2nd March 2022, Operative Paragraphs 1-4; emphasis original). The first sentence of fn 6 sets out Article 2(4) of the UN Charter.

509 The five states which voted against Resolution ES-11/1 (LXXVI) adopted by the General Assembly on 2nd March 2022 were Belarus, the Democratic People's Republic of Korea, Eritrea, Russia and Syria (United Nations (2022), "Digital Library: Aggression against Ukraine: resolution / adopted by the General Assembly – 2022," published March 2, 2022, accessed November 10, 2024, <https://digitallibrary.un.org/record/3959039>).

Table 5.1. (Continued)

Resolution	The most relevant provision(s) of the resolution	Number of voting Member States	Votes in favour of the resolution	Abstentions from the vote	Votes against the resolution
ES-11/2 (LXXVI)	Recitals 4 and 7; Operative Paragraph 1[510]	183 [687]	140	38	5[511]
ES-11/4 (LXXVII)	Recitals 3, 4 and 6; Operative Paragraphs 1, 2, 3, 4 and 5[512]	183 [688]	143	35	5[513]

[510] These provisions read thus: "*The General Assembly*, ... *Reaffirming its commitment* to the sovereignty, independence, unity and territorial integrity of Ukraine within its internationally recognized borders, extending to its territorial waters, ... *Recalling its demand* that the Russian Federation immediately, completely and unconditionally withdraw all of its military forces from the territory of Ukraine within its internationally recognized borders, ... 1. *Reiterates* the need for the full implementation of resolution ES-11/1 of 2 March 2022, entitled "Aggression against Ukraine"; ... ." (United Nations (2022), Resolution ES-11/2 (LXXVI) adopted by the General Assembly on 24th March 2022, Recitals 4 and 7, and Operative Paragraph 1; emphasis original).

[511] The five states that voted against Resolution ES-11/2 (LXXVI) adopted by the General Assembly on 24th March 2022 were Belarus, the Democratic People's Republic of Korea, Eritrea, Russia and Syria (United Nations (2022), "Digital Library: Humanitarian consequences of the aggression against Ukraine: resolution / adopted by the General Assembly – 2022," published March 24, 2022, accessed November 10, 2024, <https://digitallibrary.un.org/record/3965954?ln=en>).

[512] These clauses read as follows: "*The General Assembly*, ... *Recalling* its resolutions 68/262 of 27 March 2014, entitled "Territorial integrity of Ukraine", ES-11/1 of 2 March 2022, entitled "Aggression against Ukraine", and ES-11/2 of 24 March 2022, entitled "Humanitarian consequences of the aggression against Ukraine", *Noting* that the Donetsk, Kherson, Luhansk and Zaporizhzhia regions of Ukraine are areas that, in part, are or have been under the temporary military control of the Russian Federation, as a result of aggression, in violation of the sovereignty, political independence and territorial integrity of Ukraine, ... *Noting with concern* that the illegal so-called referendums were organized from 23 to 27 September 2022 in these regions as attempts to modify the internationally recognized borders of Ukraine, ... 1. *Reaffirms its commitment* to the sovereignty, independence, unity and territorial integrity of Ukraine within its internationally recognized borders, extending to its territorial waters; 2. *Condemns* the organization by the Russian Federation of illegal so-called referendums in regions within the internationally recognized borders of Ukraine and the attempted illegal annexation of the Donetsk, Kherson, Luhansk and Zaporizhzhia regions of Ukraine, following the organization of the above-mentioned referendums; 3. *Declares* that the unlawful actions of the Russian Federation with regard to the illegal so called referendums held from 23 to 27 September 2022 in parts of the Donetsk, Kherson, Luhansk and Zaporizhzhia regions of Ukraine that, in part, are or have been under the temporary military control of the Russian Federation, and the subsequent illegal annexation of the regions, have no validity under international law and do not form the basis for any alteration of the status of these regions of Ukraine; 4. *Calls upon* all States, international organizations and United Nations specialized agencies not to recognize any alteration by the Russian Federation of the status of any or all of the Donetsk, Kherson, Luhansk or Zaporizhzhia regions of Ukraine, and to refrain from any action or dealing that might be interpreted as recognizing any such altered status; 5. *Demands* that the Russian Federation ... immediately, completely and unconditionally withdraw all of its military forces from the territory of Ukraine within its internationally recognized borders; ... ." (United Nations (2022), Resolution ES-11/4 (LXXVII) adopted by the General Assembly on 12th October 2022, Recitals 3, 4 and 6, and Operative Paragraphs 1-5; emphasis original).

[513] The five states which voted against Resolution ES-11/4 (LXXVII) adopted by the General Assembly on 12th October 2022 were Belarus, the Democratic People's Republic of Korea, Nicaragua, Russia and Syria (United Nations (2022), "Digital Library: Territorial integrity of Ukraine: defending the principles of the Charter of the United Nations: resolution / adopted by the General Assembly – 2022," published October 12, 2022, accessed November 10, 2024, <https://digitallibrary.un.org/record/3990400?ln=en>).

Resolution	The most relevant provision(s) of the resolution	Number of voting Member States	Votes in favour of the resolution	Abstentions from the vote	Votes against the resolution
ES-11/5 (LXXVII)	Recital 6; Operative Paragraph 1[514]	181 [689]	94	73	14[515]
ES-11/6 (LXXVII)	Recital 4; Operative Paragraphs 4 and 5[516]	180 [690]	141	32	7[517]

(ii) No state shall render aid or assistance in maintaining a situation created by a serious breach by a State of an obligation arising under a peremptory norm of general international law (jus cogens). (a) Assistance with Russian attacks on northern Ukraine: At the later admission of Mr. Aleksandr Lukashenko, President of Belarus, this state assisted Russian troops to move from its territory to that of Ukraine in February 2022[518]. In paragraph 10 of UN General Assembly Resolution ES-11/1 (LXXVI) of 2nd March 2022,

[514] These provisions read thus: "*The General Assembly*, ... *Recalling also* its resolutions ES-11/1 of 2 March 2022, entitled "Aggression against Ukraine", ES-11/2 of 24 March 2022, entitled "Humanitarian consequences of the aggression against Ukraine", and ES-11/4 of 12 October 2022, entitled "Territorial integrity of Ukraine: defending the principles of the Charter of the United Nations", in which, among other things, it reaffirmed its commitment to the sovereignty, independence, unity and territorial integrity of Ukraine, ... 1. *Reaffirms* its commitment to the sovereignty, independence, unity and territorial integrity of Ukraine and its demand that the Russian Federation immediately cease its use of force against Ukraine[,] and that the Russian Federation immediately, completely and unconditionally withdraw all of its military forces from the territory of Ukraine within its internationally recognized borders, extending to its territorial waters; ... ." (United Nations (2022), Resolution ES-11/5 (LXXVII) adopted by the General Assembly on 14th November 2022, Recital 6, and Operative Paragraph 1; emphasis original).

[515] The fourteen states that voted against Resolution ES-11/5 (LXXVII) adopted by the General Assembly on 14th November 2022 were the Bahamas, Belarus, Central African Republic, China, Cuba, the Democratic People's Republic of Korea, Eritrea, Ethiopia, Iran, Mali, Nicaragua, Russia, Syria and Zimbabwe (United Nations (2022), "Digital Library: Furtherance of remedy and reparation for aggression against Ukraine: resolution / adopted by the General Assembly – 2022," published November 14, 2022, accessed November 10, 2024, <https://digitallibrary.un.org/record/3994052?ln=en>).

[516] These clauses read as follows: "*The General Assembly*, ... *Recalling* its relevant resolutions adopted at its eleventh emergency special session and its resolution 68/262 of 27 March 2014, ... 4. *Reaffirms its commitment* to the sovereignty, independence, unity and territorial integrity of Ukraine within its internationally recognized borders, extending to its territorial waters; 5. *Reiterates its demand* that the Russian Federation immediately, completely and unconditionally withdraw all of its military forces from the territory of Ukraine within its internationally recognized borders, and calls for a cessation of hostilities; ... ." (United Nations (2023), Resolution ES-11/6 (LXXVII) adopted by the General Assembly on 23rd February 2023, Recital 4, and Operative Paragraphs 4 and 5; emphasis original).

[517] The seven states which voted against Resolution ES-11/6 (LXXVII) adopted by the General Assembly on 23rd February 2023 were Belarus, the Democratic People's Republic of Korea, Eritrea, Mali, Nicaragua, Russia and Syria (United Nations (2023), "Digital Library: Principles of the Charter of the United Nations underlying a comprehensive, just and lasting peace in Ukraine: resolution / adopted by the General Assembly – 2023," published February 23, 2023, accessed November 10, 2024, <https://digitallibrary.un.org/record/4003921?ln=en en>).

[518] The Kyiv Independent reports: "Belarusian dictator Alexander Lukashenko admitted that Russian forces had invaded Ukraine from the territory of Belarus in February 2022[,] in an interview with a pro-Kremlin presenter published on Aug. 17 [2023]. While Lukashenko claimed that "not a single Belarusian was involved," he said that some Russian troops entered Ukraine after the completion of "large-scale" training exercises in Belarus. "The training ended, Russian troops began to withdraw from the territory of Belarus ... They began to leave, and on Feb. 23, 24 [2022], part of these troops began to cross the border of Ukraine and Russia," Lukashenko said to the Ukrainian-born interviewer, Diana Panchenko. ... Though Belarus hasn't officially joined Russia's war, Moscow has used Belarusian territory to launch missiles and drones at Ukraine, as well as trained its troops there." (Court, E. (2023), Lukashenko admits Russian troops invaded Ukraine through Belarus in 2022, *The Kyiv Independent*, Friday 18 August 2023).

the General Assembly expressed its disapproval of Belarus' involvement in the illegal use of force against Ukraine[519]. Permitting Russian armed forces to launch missiles and drones from Belarus after the initial offensive on northern Ukraine[520] amounts to contravention of the second clause of paragraph 2 of draft conclusion 19 on identification and legal consequences of peremptory norms of general international law (*jus cogens*); the relevant peremptory norm is the prohibition of aggression. *(b) The provision of armed forces to aid the Russian war effort:* As of October 2023, no other state had been proven to be sending troops to join those of Russian armed forces in Ukraine [691]. Soldiers from the Democratic People's Republic of Korea are likely to be fighting alongside Russian military personnel in Ukraine in the near future[521], and are already being deployed in the Russian attempt to stop the Ukrainian counteroffensive in neighbouring Russian territory[522]. As the current condition of eastern Ukraine is 'a situation created by a serious breach by a state (i.e., Russia) of an obligation arising under a peremptory norm of general international law (*jus cogens*)' (i.e., the prohibition of aggression), any assistance that the Democratic People's Republic of Korea's (or any other country's) troops provide to Russian armed forces there is an infraction of the prohibition of aggression by virtue of the second clause of paragraph 2 of draft conclusion 19 on identification and legal consequences of peremptory norms of general international law (*jus cogens*) – and combat with Ukrainian soldiers there is a direct infringement of the prohibition of aggression. *(c) The supply of weapons to aid the Russian war effort:* Not only do non-European states furnish arms to Russia – in particular, the Democratic People's Republic of Korea and Iran [692], but until 2020, several European countries did so, too[523]. It is submitted that states who provide weapons to Russia – whether the sales of these are in transactions at their market price or not – are in breach of the second clause of paragraph 2 of draft conclusion 19 on identification and legal consequences of peremptory norms of general international law (*jus cogens*), as the government decision-makers within those countries know, or ought to know, that these weapons are likely to be deployed in further acts of aggression in Ukraine. *(d) Extraordinary or knowingly inappropriate trade with Russia:* It is outside the scope of the present monograph to attempt to determine with precision what trade with Russia would amount to rendering aid or assistance in maintaining the situation created by its serious breach of the prohibition of aggression with regard to its actions in Ukraine. It is opined

[519] Fn 427.

[520] Final sentence of fn 518.

[521] Cable News Network (CNN) states: "North Korean soldiers may be being readied for a move to the front lines of Russia's war against Ukraine[,] after being taught basic Russian commands, South Korean lawmakers told reporters on Tuesday [29th October 2024], citing the country's intelligence officials. About 10,000 North Korean soldiers are receiving military training in eastern Russia, the Pentagon estimated on Monday [28th October 2024]." (Bae, G. and Yeung, J. (2024), North Korean soldiers learning Russian commands and may be sent to Ukraine front lines, South Korean lawmakers say, *CNN*, Tuesday 29 October 2024).

[522] Cable News Network (CNN) writes: "Russia has amassed a large force of tens of thousands – including recently arrived North Korean troops – to carry out an assault on the Ukrainian positions in Russia's Kursk region expected in the coming days, a US official told CNN on Sunday. Ukrainian President Volodymyr Zelensky said [on] Thursday [7th November 2024] that about 11,000 North Korean soldiers are in the region, where Ukraine's three-month military incursion into Russian territory has stalled." (Kostenko, M., Marquardt, A., and McCluskey, M. (2024), Large group of Russian and North Korean forces prepared to retake Russia's Kursk region from Ukraine, *CNN*, Monday 11 November 2024).

[523] These states include – from the largest to the smallest supplier of arms exports to Russia in EUR, from 2015 to 2020, France (152 million EUR), Germany (122 million EUR), Italy (22 million EUR), Austria (19 million EUR), Bulgaria (17 million EUR) and Czech Republic (14 million EUR); these amounts are rounded to the nearest million EUR (Brillaud, L., Curic, A., Maggiore, M., Miñano, L., and Schmidt, N. (2022), "EU member states exported weapons to Russia after the 2014 embargo," published March 17, 2022, accessed November 11, 2024, <https://www.investigate-europe.eu/en/posts/eu-states-exported-weapons-to-russia>).

that trade which would constitute such a contravention of international law would include the supply of dual-use goods to Russia where one of the possible uses of these products is for the construction of armaments (for example, semiconductors and microchips), and the provision of supplies – especially at lower than the market price – of long-life food (such as cans of baked beans), blankets and robust vehicles to Russia – a breach of the law being more persuasive if these items are sold in bulk.

From the above discussion, it can be concluded that Russia and several other states have violated international law regarding the prohibition of aggression, as applied on the legally-recognized territory of Ukraine. This is unacceptable. It is opined that the governments of these countries should cease breaking the rules with immediate effect, and that Russia promptly withdraws all its armed forces from the territory of Ukraine. The international community will not accept – and cannot afford to tolerate – these infractions. As soon as all Russian – and Russia-aligned – troops have left Ukraine, the terms for a peace settlement can be negotiated.

Finally, it is noteworthy that the ILC has declared the prohibition of racial discrimination to be a peremptory norm of general international law (*jus cogens*)[524]. Therefore, the government of Ukraine will be expected to treat its Russian minorities in Crimea, Donbas and elsewhere in the state to the same standard which it acts towards any other Ukrainian national. It is submitted that such a policy is not in doubt under the current President of Ukraine, Mr. Volodymyr Zelensky, but it would need to be maintained elsewhere within the regime and into the future, too.

Conclusion

This chapter considers the legality of the invasion of Ukraine. The next chapter looks at why changes are needed with regard to the UN and to international law.

[524] The Annex to the draft conclusions on identification and legal consequences of peremptory norms of general international law (*jus cogens*) lists the prohibition of racial discrimination as a peremptory norm of general international law (see the sentence immediately following the text to fn 441).

Chapter 6

Why Changes Are Needed to the United Nations and to International Law

Abstract

The fact that the Russian onslaught on Ukrainian territory could be attempted points to areas of the international legal system which might be updated. As opined in Chapter 2, the UN is not entirely based on the principle of sovereign equality of all its Member States. The composition of the UN's Military Staff Committee favours permanent members of the UNSC. If permanent member status is to be continued, then Article 2(1) of the UN Charter should be adapted accordingly. The use of the veto may disable the UNSC, i.e., if a permanent member of the UNSC persistently votes against decisions on measures proposed by the latter on a particular theme, then the UNSC will be unable to take steps concerning that subject. Exercise of the veto may prevent implementation of amendments to the UN Charter. Table 6.1 shows that, from 1946 to 2024, a total of 317 vetoes were cast. Neither France nor the UK has exercised a veto since 1989. If the veto were to be abolished, then a more general curb could be introduced on votes concerning non-procedural decisions before the UNSC. There is no specialized court or tribunal to determine disputes that relate solely to territorial sovereignty. An analagous version of the system for dispute settlement operated within the UNCLOS could be applied to interstate territorial disputes. Applicable paragraphs could be inserted into the UN Charter. This would harness the benefits of compulsory jurisdiction for these disagreements, i.e., the certainty of establishing a method whereby a dispute can be resolved by means of a binding judgment or arbitral award. Adding a further paragraph to Article 36 of the Statute of the ICJ to encourage the completion of declarations under paragraph 2 of this article and to specify which source of binding dispute settlement each state intends to use for the areas of international law that are withheld therein from the compulsory jurisdiction of the ICJ, would encourage states to commit to binding dispute resolution for all their disagreements. Article 38(2) of the Statute of the ICJ should be deleted, because *ex aequo et bono* arbitrations and court cases do not promote legal certainty. A sentence should be added to Article 59 of the Statute of the ICJ which acknowledges the value of *ratio decidendi* of decisions of the Court. Table 6.2 shows there to be 84 reservations concerning the UNCLOS. Drafting a convention in such a way that it permits specified reservations is not necessarily a good idea. While the ILC has made constructive proposals regarding multilateral treaties and reservations, their impact depends upon the governments of states taking note of them. To promote legal certainty, such conventions should be accompanied by no more than a few reservations. A unified system of international law is gently appearing. If, due to excessive treaty reservations, it is deemed necessary to explore the legislative route, then this would need to start with a system which included an organization for drafting and publishing instruments that are not legally-binding upon states.

Keywords: convention, declaration, dispute, *Lotus*, reservation, statute, treaty, veto

Introduction

Chapter 5 makes it clear that the path to independence for Russia and Ukraine involved differing views between the leaders of these former republics of the USSR[525], although it appears that they did not deliberate beforehand over the location of the border between their respective countries[526]. It seems that speed was of the essence in coming to agreement over the dissolution of the USSR and the establishment of the Commonwealth of Independent States, and so, it is submitted, the Russian government yielded to the view of the Ukrainian administration – which did not wish for a change in territorial status to either Crimea or Donbas[527]. Nonetheless, Russia had a case, i.e., both regions contained large ethnic Russian populations – and Ukraine had received both of these areas from Russia at the behest of rulers of the USSR. Therefore, the matter of the boundaries between Russia and Ukraine almost certainly should be been discussed carefully between the leaders of these former Soviet republics before the USSR ceased to exist. As it was not, why did Russia not opt for a method of dispute settlement? Paragraph 1 of Article 33 of the UN Charter specifies that the disputant states must seek a solution thereby, given that continuation of the Russo-Ukrainian boundary dispute "is likely to endanger the maintenance of international peace and security"[528] [7]. Furthermore, Russia – a permanent member of the UNSC – could have raised the matter there, in accordance with Paragraph 2 of Article 33 of the UN Charter[529].

Hence, the issue of the Russo-Ukrainian border was neither satisfactory resolved by dialogue prior to the date of independence of these two states[530], nor by dispute resolution since. Instead, the Russian government – with the approval of the Russian parliament – started a war on legally-recognized Ukrainian territory. In granting permission for Russian armed forces to enter upon this land[531], the parliament of Russia acted beyond its legal authority, as, according to the principle of sovereign equality of states, the Russian parliament and government are only sovereign over legally-recognized Russian territory – and this within the bounds of international law, which is a superior source of law to national law. The eminent jurist and legal philosopher, Dr. Hans Kelsen, describes the matter thus.

> If it is presumed that the States have duties imposed and, consequently, rights conferred upon them by international law, [then] they must be considered as subjected to international law, but the figurative expression "to be subjected" means only the relationship of subjects to a legal order which imposes duties and confers rights upon them. Therefore, the sovereignty of the States, as subjects of international law, is the legal authority of the States under the authority of international law. If sovereignty means "supreme" authority, [then] the sovereignty of States as subjects of international law can mean, not an absolutely but only a relatively supreme authority. A State's legal authority may be said to be "supreme" insofar as it is not subjected to the legal authority of any other State; and the State is then

[525] Fn 493.

[526] First sentence of fn 492.

[527] Both Article 5(1) of the Agreement establishing the Commonwealth of Independent States and the second recital of the Alma Ata Declaration reflect this in their wording, i.e., 'the inviolability of existing borders' (fn 492).

[528] The antepenultimate sentence of fn 149 sets out Article 33(1) of the UN Charter.

[529] The penultimate sentence of fn 149 lays down Article 33(2) of the UN Charter.

[530] This is 26th December 1991, i.e., the date on which the USSR was dissolved (fns 3 and 28).

[531] The Russian parliament authorized Russian troops to enter Ukrainian territory in 2014 (fn 495 and accompanying text) and, again, in 2022 (fn 498 and accompanying text).

> sovereign when it is subjected only to international law, not to the national law of any other State. Consequently, the State's sovereignty under international law is its legal independence from other States [693].

To put the issue a different way in the light of this quote, by authorizing the invasion of Ukraine and by conquering some of its legally-recognized territory, the Russian parliament and government have made Russian-occupied parts of Ukraine places in which the Ukrainian state is not sovereign – which renders it an inferior state to unoccupied countries. It is opined that the Russian leadership has a psychological difficulty with the idea of an independent Ukrainian state, and attributes the choice of the Ukrainian people in selecting its government, and the decisions of its government that are non-aligned with Russian interests as the aforementioned leadership sees these, as a ploy of the West – which, it is also submitted, is wholly untrue.

> [I]n our time, they [(i.e., the West)] began to make "anti-Russia" out of Ukraine. The project is actually not new. People who are at least a little immersed in history know perfectly well: this project goes back to the 19th century, it was cultivated in the Austro-Hungarian Empire, and in Poland, and other countries with one goal – to tear off these historical territories, which today are called Ukraine, from our country. That's what this goal is. There is nothing new, no novelty, everything is repeated [694].

Surely this statement is a denial of Ukrainian statehood, which was made to a Russian audience in order to justify to them the then imminent military attack on Ukraine? The fact that this onslaught could be attempted in the present time does point to some areas of the international legal structure and system which could, perhaps, be updated. The remaining sections in the current chapter, bar the conclusion, address selected areas that may be in need of change.

Permanent Membership of the UNSC

While the UN Charter states that the UN and its Member States, in pursuit of the Purposes of the UN – which are set out therein, shall act in line with seven Principles specified in the Charter, the first of which is that the UN is founded on the principle of the sovereign equality of all its Member States [175], this is a flawed premise, because, as opined in Chapter 2, the UN is not *entirely* based on this principle – since five Member States have permanent seats on the UNSC with the accompanying power to veto non-procedural motions there[532]. All five of these permanent members of the UNSC were on the winning side in the Second World War[533]. The Covenant of the League of Nations furnishes a precedent for permanent status with accompanying veto – it provided for the main victors in the First World War (the Principal Allied and Associated Powers) to be present on the Council of the League of Nations [56], and,

---

[532] The paragraph headed 'I: Purposes and Principles', in the subsection entitled 'The UN Charter', in the section titled 'The United Nations' in Chapter 3, lays down this reasoning.

[533] The permanent members of the UNSC are France, the People's Republic of China (earlier, the Republic of China), Russia (previously, the USSR), the UK and the USA (second paragraph of the subsection entitled 'The Russian veto', in the section titled 'The Problem' in Chapter 1).

subject to two classes of exception stated therein[534], required the agreement of all the Members of the League that were represented at any meeting of the Council to any non-procedural decision taken there[535] [57].

The composition of the UN's Military Staff Committee favours permanent members of the UNSC over all other Member States of the UN[536]. This may have been appropriate in the wake of the Second World War, but, it is submitted, is at variance with the principle of sovereign equality of states, and, furthermore, may not be the most suitable make-up in the world of today.

If permanent member status is to be continued, then paragraph 1 of Article 2 of the UN Charter should be adapted accordingly. The principle of the sovereign equality of all Member States of the UN enshrined therein lies uncomfortably with the current situation of its two-tier membership.

The Veto

Use of the Veto May Disable the UNSC

If a permanent member of the UNSC persistently votes against decisions on measures proposed by the latter on a particular theme – in accordance with the first clause of paragraph 3 of Article 27 of the UN Charter[537], then the UNSC will be unable to take steps concerning that subject. This may arise in a case in which a permanent member vetoes determinations of the UNSC that propose actions to be taken against it for breach, or potential infraction, of one or more provisions of the UN Charter, as well as one in which a permanent member persistently vetoes decisions on measures which the UNSC wishes to take against a Member State of the UN that is allied to this permanent member or which the permanent member wishes to protect.

Exercise of the Veto May Prevent Implementation of Amendments to the UN Charter That Have Been Adopted by the General Assembly

A permanent member of the UNSC may, under Article 108 of the UN Charter[538] or paragraph 2 of Article 109 of the UN Charter[539], refuse to ratify amendments to the UN Charter, in which case these do not enter into force. It is opined that this is a potentially fatal defect in the operation of UN Charter, which may result in no substantial changes being made to it that one

---

[534] Unanimity was required in the Council of the League of Nations to make any non-procedural decision there, "[e]xcept where otherwise expressly provided in this Covenant or by the terms of the present Treaty" (League of Nations – Official Journal (1920), The Covenant of the League of Nations, *League of Nations – Official Journal*, February 2020, 3-11, 4, Article 5).

[535] Text to fn 51.

[536] Fn 174 sets out Article 47 of the UN Charter, which specifies the composition and role of the Military Staff Committee.

[537] The text to fn 14 sets out the first clause of Article 27(3) of the UN Charter.

[538] The penultimate (fourth) sentence of the paragraph headed 'XVIII: Amendments to the UN Charter', in the subsection entitled 'The UN Charter', in the section titled 'The United Nations' in Chapter 3, comprises Article 108 of the UN Charter.

[539] The antepenultimate (third) sentence of the paragraph headed 'XVIII: Amendments to the UN Charter', in the subsection entitled 'The UN Charter', in the section titled 'The United Nations' in Chapter 3, consists of Article 109(2) of the UN Charter.

or more permanent members of the UNSC consider to be against their interests – such as, for instance, abolition of the veto.

An inspection of the five amendments which have been successfully made to the UN Charter reveals that none of these changes significantly reduce the influence of the permanent members of the UNSC. All were introduced in order to cater for the increasing membership of the UN, and the greatest rises both in numbers and percentage terms were in the membership of the ECOSOC rather than in the membership or required voting figures of the UNSC[540].

Practice of the Permanent Members of the UNSC in Their Use of the Veto

All the information in this subsection, and most in the next one, is provided by Security Council Report[541]. Initially, the USSR cast many vetoes – frequently to obstruct admission of a new Member State to the UN, with patterns changing in the use of the veto since the first-mentioned's dissolution [695]. Table 6.1 specifies the numbers of vetoes that each permanent member of the UNSC has cast, together with the matter about which these were exercised, by period, since 1946.

Suggestions That Have Been Made for the Use of the Veto

The final row of Table 6.1 shows that France is the most abstemious user of the veto, followed by China and then the UK. Neither France nor the UK has cast a veto since 23rd December 1989 [697]. It is apt, therefore, that France, along with Mexico, has recommended that the permanent members of the UNSC restrain their use of the veto in cases of genocide, crimes against humanity and war crimes on a big scale, other than in instances in which a permanent member's essential interests are at risk – a proposal that many Member States of the UN have supported, but, fittingly, the UK is the only backer from among the permanent members[542] [695, 698].

There are other submissions for non-utilization of the veto regarding proposals placed before the UNSC for a decision, that advocate restraint of its use in cases of genocide [699]. Such proposals are particularly relevant to the recent Syrian civil war, during which many lives were lost[543] and in relation to which both China and Russia have exercised vetoes[544].

---

540 Table 3.2 details the amendments that have been made to the UN Charter.

541 Security Council Report is a not-for-profit organization that is based in New York City, and whose "mission is to advance the transparency and effectiveness of the UN Security Council"; one of four ways in which it seeks to accomplish this is "by making available timely, balanced, high-quality information about the activities of the Council and its subsidiary bodies" (Security Council Report (2024), "About Security Council Report," accessed November 15, 2024, <https://www.securitycouncilreport.org/about-security-council-report>).

542 Under this French proposal, the Secretary-General of the UN would determine, upon the request of at least fifty members of the UN General Assembly, as to whether a large-scale crime has taken place (Security Council Report (2015), Research Report: The Veto. New York: Security Council Report, 1-9, 5-6).

543 Indeed, the suggestions for veto restraint referred to up until this point were developed against the backdrop of a worsening situation in Syria (Security Council Report (2015), Research Report: The Veto. New York: Security Council Report, 1-9, 4).

544 See the penultimate and antepenultimate rows of Table 6.1.

Table 6.1. Use of the veto by the permanent members of the UNSC [696]

Period	Number of vetoes	Number of vetoes cast by each permanent member					Issue(s) about which the vetoes were exercised
		China	France	UK	USA	USSR/Russia	
1946-1964	113	1	4	3	0	105	Admission of new Member States to the UN: China 1; USSR 51 The Spanish Question (Admission of Spain to the UN): France 1; USSR 7 Congo (Democratic Republic of the Congo): USSR 5 The Greek frontier incidents: USSR 5 Israel and Syria: USSR 4 The Democratic People's Republic of Korea's aggression against the Republic of Korea: USSR 4 The Suez Crisis: France 2; UK 2 Air force planes of USA downed by Soviet military forces over air space of USSR: USSR 3 Regulation and reduction of conventional armaments: USSR 3 Complaint by Lebanon against the United Arab Republic 1958 (Egypt and Syria): USSR 2 India and Pakistan: USSR 2 Letter from Chile on events in Czechoslovakia 1948: USSR 2 Request for an investigation of alleged bacterial warfare: USSR 2 The Indonesian Question (Transfer of sovereignty 1949): USSR 2 Calling on India to withdraw its forces from Goa, Daman and Diu (1961): USSR 1 Complaint by Guatemala concerning bombing of its territory: USSR 1 Complaint of bombing on China's territory: USSR 1 Egypt and Israel: USSR 1 Hungary: USSR 1 Incidents in the Corfu Channel: USSR 1 Lebanon and Syria: USSR 1 Letter from France, the UK and the USA on the Berlin Blockade 1948: USSR 1 Nationalization of the Suez Canal Company by the government of Egypt: USSR 1 Reports from the Atomic Energy Committee: USSR 1 The independence and territorial integrity of Kuwait 1961: USSR 1 The Indonesian Question (Indonesia and the Netherlands 1947): France 1 Thailand: USSR 1 Ukrainian complaint against Greece: USSR 1 Southern Rhodesia (Zimbabwe): UK 1

Period	Number of vetoes	Number of vetoes cast by each permanent member					Issue(s) about which the vetoes were exercised
		China	France	UK	USA	USSR/Russia	
1965-1974	25	2[545]	1	9	6	7	Rhodesia (Zimbabwe): UK 8; USA 2 Expulsion of South Africa from UN Membership: France 1; UK 1; USA 1 India and Pakistan: USSR 3 Indonesia and Malaysia: USSR 1 Israeli breach of Six-Day War ceasefire: China 1; USA 1; USSR 1 Admission of new Member States to the UN: China 1 Cyprus: USSR 1 Czechoslovakian complaint concerning the invasion of Czechoslovakia in 1968: USSR 1 Israel and Palestine: USA 1 Israel and Syria: USSR 1 Panama Canal: USA 1
1975-1984	59	0	10	10	33	6	Namibia and South Africa: France 9; UK 9; USA 9 Israel and Palestine: USA 7 Admission of new Member States to the UN: USA 6 Lebanon: USA 4; USSR 1 Falkland Islands (Malvinas): UK 1; USA 1 American hostages held in Iran: USSR 1 Angolan complaint against South Africa: USA 1 Border dispute between China and Vietnam: USSR 1 Cambodia and Vietnam: USSR 1 Dispute between France and the Comoros over Mayotte: France 1 Downing of the Korean Airliner by the USSR: USSR 1 Egyptian and Lebanese complaint against Israel: USA 1 Grenada: USA 1 Invasion of Afghanistan by the USSR: USSR 1 Israel and Syria: USA 1 Nicaragua: USA 1 Nicaraguan complaint against the USA: USA 1

[545] The vetoes cast by China in the period 1965-1974 were cast by the People's Republic of China, which superseded the Republic of China as a permanent member of the UNSC on 25th October 1971 (Security Council Report (2024), "UN Security Council Working Methods: The Veto," published February 13, 2024, accessed November 16, 2024, <https://www.securitycouncilreport.org/un-security-council-working-methods/the-veto.php>). The sentence immediately preceding the text to fn 12 supplies facts concerning this succession.

Table 6.1. (Continued)

Period	Number of vetoes	Number of vetoes cast by each permanent member					Issue(s) about which the vetoes were exercised
		China	France	UK	USA	USSR/Russia	
1985-1994	45	0	3	10	30	2[546]	Israel and Palestine: USA 8 South Africa: UK 3; USA 3 Nicaraguan complaint against the USA: USA 5 Lebanese complaint against Israel: USA 4 Namibia: UK 2; USA 2 Panama: USA 2; France 1; UK 1 Burkinabe, Libyan, Omani and Syrian complaint against the USA's bombing of Libya: France 1; UK 1; USA 1 Libyan complaint against the USA: France 1; UK 1; USA 1 Angolan complaint against South Africa: UK 1; USA 1 Botswanan, Zambian and Zimbabwean complaint against South Africa: UK 1; USA 1 Bosnia and Herzegovina: Russia 1 Cyprus: Russia 1 Lebanon: USA 1 Syrian complaint against Israel: USA 1
1995-2004	14	2	0	0	11	1	Israel and Palestine: USA 10 Bosnia and Herzegovina: USA 1 Cyprus: Russia 1 Guatemala: China 1 (North) Macedonia: China 1
2005-2014	17	6	0	0	3	8	Syria: China 4; Russia 4 Israel and Palestine: USA 3 Myanmar: China 1; Russia 1 Zimbabwe: China 1; Russia 1 Georgia: Russia 1 Ukraine: Russia 1

546 The vetoes exercised by the USSR/Russia in the period 1985-1994 were exercised by Russia, which followed the USSR as permanent member of the UNSC (fn 12 and accompanying text).

Period	Number of vetoes	Number of vetoes cast by each permanent member					Issue(s) about which the vetoes were exercised
		China	France	UK	USA	USSR/Russia	
2015-2024	44	10	0	0	7	27	Syria: Russia 14; China 6 Israel and Palestine: USA 5; China 2; Russia 2 Non-proliferation of weapons: Russia 3; China 1 Ukraine: Russia 2 Venezuela: China 1; Russia 1 Admission of new Member States to the UN: USA 1 Bosnia and Herzegovina: Russia 1 Climate and security: Russia 1 Counter-terrorism: USA 1 Downing of flight MH17: Russia 1 Mali: Russia 1 Yemen: Russia 1
Total	317	21[547]	18	32	90	156[548]	

[547] The Republic of China cast one veto; the People's Republic of China has exercised twenty vetoes (fn 545).

[548] The USSR cast one hundred and eighteen vetoes; Russia has exercised thirty-eight vetoes (fn 546).

Two older ideas for restraint in employment of the veto by permanent members of the UNSC were put forward by the International Commission on Intervention and State Sovereignty (ICISS) and the five small states (S5) – Costa Rica, Jordan, Liechtenstein, Singapore and Switzerland. The ICISS advised the permanent members of the UNSC not to cast their vetoes to block the adoption of resolutions that sanction military intervention to protect people, for which there is otherwise preponderant support – unless their key interests are involved [700]. The S5 considered that a permanent member exercising a veto, or intending to do this, should circulate an UNSC document to all Member States of the UN in which it furnished an explanation for its decision that is compatible with pertinent international law and the UN Charter's Purposes[549] and Principles[550] [700]. Moreover, the S5 asked the permanent members to refrain from utilizing their vetoes to arrest action of the UNSC which is aimed at precluding or ending genocide, crimes against humanity and war crimes [700].

As mentioned earlier[551], in *Essays on International Law* I suggested two alternative additional paragraphs to Article 27 of the UN Charter, in order to prevent obstruction of proposals by permanent members of the UNSC that were casting vetoes in order to preserve what they considered to be their territorial interests[552]. Nothing which is available from official sources indicates that these possibilities for amendment have been read, let alone considered, by any Member State of the UN or by its Secretariat. Yet, it is submitted, 'the problem' – as expressed in Chapter 1[553] – is unnecessarily causing lives to be lost in wars and civil wars, and, therefore, needs to be addressed urgently.

Comment

The provision of a veto at the UNSC for the five permanent members of the UNSC is not in accordance with the principle of sovereign equality of all its Member States, on which the UN is based[554]. Furthermore, the use of vetoes has proved to be non-optimal. For instance, the USSR prevented many countries from being admitted to the UN by exercising its veto fifty-one times[555]; yet today, the UN has one hundred and ninety-three Member States [701] – comprising most of the world's population and territory.

The UN is likely to act more effectively and efficiently without the use – or existence – of the veto at the UNSC. If this veto were to be abolished, then a more general curb could be introduced on votes concerning non-procedural decisions before the UNSC – such as requiring

549 The text to fns 129-144 lays down the Purposes of the UN.

550 The third, antepenultimate, penultimate and last sentences of the paragraph headed 'I: Purposes and Principles', in the subsection entitled 'The UN Charter, in the section titled 'The United Nations' in Chapter 3, respectively contain the first, fifth, sixth and seventh Principles, i.e., paragraphs 1, 5, 6 and 7 of Article 2 of the UN Charter. The first sentence of fn 4 states the second Principle, i.e., paragraph 2 of Article 2 of the UN Charter. Fn 5 sets out the third Principle, i.e., paragraph 3 of Article 2 of the UN Charter. The first sentence of fn 6 specifies the fourth Principle, i.e., paragraph 4 of Article 2 of the UN Charter.

551 Fn 32 and accompanying text.

552 Fn 32 refers to the relevant pages in *Essays on International Law*.

553 The sentence immediately following the text to fn 32 states the essence of 'the problem'.

554 Paragraph 1 of Article 2 of the UN Charter declares the UN to be founded on this principle. The sentence immediately preceding the text to fn 159 consists of Article 2(1) of the UN Charter.

555 The first entry in the final column of the second row of Table 6.1 shows this.

an affirmative vote from at least nine members of the UNSC *and* less than five or six dissentient votes – as appropriate[556].

Dispute Settlement for Territorial Disagreements

There is no specialized court or tribunal to determine disputes that relate solely to territorial sovereignty. The ICJ may hear these cases where it is asked to do so by one or both of the disputants and when it has jurisdiction to do so. It is also possible for the parties to constitute an *ad hoc* tribunal to arbitrate such disputes. But disputants are required to do neither – in the absence of a treaty to which both are states parties and which specifies a method of dispute resolution for contravention of one or more of its clauses. They are expected to observe paragraph 1 of Article 33 of the UN Charter[557]. However, the procedures specified therein may prove to be inadequate to settle their dispute.

It is submitted that the UNCLOS supplies a good system for resolving disputes regarding the interpretation and application of this convention. Subject to first attempting to settle these matters by peaceful means in accordance with Section 1 of Part XV of the UNCLOS[558], and to the restrictions and exceptions that Section 3 of Part XV of the UNCLOS[559] sets out, any party to the dispute may apply the provisions for compulsory procedures that Section 2 of Part XV of the UNCLOS[560] lays down[561] [702]. The UNCLOS offers to its states parties a selection of dispute resolution processes.

> When signing, ratifying or acceding to this Convention or at any time thereafter, a State shall be free to choose, by means of a written declaration[562], one or more of the following means for the settlement of disputes concerning the interpretation or application of this

---

[556] The threshold for approval should be at least nine affirmative votes and *less than five* dissentient votes regarding decisions of the UNSC taken under Chapter VII of the UN Charter, and at least nine affirmative votes and *less than six* dissentient votes concerning all other non-procedural decisions of the UNSC. This difference recognizes the seriousness of taking decisions that may involve the committal of resources by Member States of the UN. Chapter VII of the UN Charter is entitled 'Action with Respect to Threats to the Peace, Breaches of the Peace, and Acts of Aggression', and comprises Articles 39 to 51 inclusive. The paragraph headed 'VII: Action with Respect to Threats to the Peace, Breaches of the Peace, and Acts of Aggression', in the subsection titled 'The UN Charter' in the section entitled 'The UN Charter' in Chapter 3, lays down provisions from Chapter VII of the UN Charter.

[557] The antepenultimate sentence of fn 149 sets out Article 33(1) of the UN Charter.

[558] Section 1 of Part XV of the UNCLOS is titled 'General Provisions', and comprises Articles 279-285. Part XV of the UNCLOS is entitled 'Settlement of Disputes', and contains Articles 279-299.

[559] Section 3 of Part XV of the UNCLOS is titled 'Limitations and Exceptions to applicability of Section 2', and consists of Articles 297-299.

[560] Section 2 of Part XV of the UNCLOS is entitled 'Compulsory Procedures entailing Binding Decisions', and is composed of Articles 286-296.

[561] The section titled 'Part XV of the UNCLOS: Settlement of Disputes', in Chapter 1 of *The Global Law of the Sea*, i.e., pages 47-66 of Baber, G. (2020), *The Global Law of the Sea* (New York: Nova Science Publishers Inc.), describes the content of Part XV of the UNCLOS.

[562] A written declaration does not affect, and is not influenced by, the duty of a state party to the UNCLOS to accept the jurisdiction of the Seabed Disputes Chamber of the International Tribunal for the Law of the Sea to the extent, and in the way, that Part XI, Section 5 of the UNCLOS provides (United Nations (1982), "United Nations Convention on the Law of the Sea," *United Nations Treaty Series* Registration Number 31363, Article 287(2)). The Seabed Disputes Chamber of the International Tribunal for the Law of the Sea examines disputes which arise under Part XI of the UNCLOS and the Annexes of the UNCLOS that relate to that Part (United Nations (1982), "United Nations Convention on the Law of the Sea," Article 187).

Convention: (a) the International Tribunal for the Law of the Sea ... ; (b) the International Court of Justice; (c) an arbitral tribunal constituted in accordance with Annex VII [of the UNCLOS][563]; (d) a special arbitral tribunal constituted in accordance with Annex VIII [of the UNCLOS] for one or more of the categories of disputes specified therein[564] [703].

A state party to the UNCLOS, which is a party to a dispute to which no declaration-in-force applies, is considered to have accepted arbitration in consonance with Annex VII of the UNCLOS as the method to be used for resolving that dispute [704]. If the disputants have accepted the same procedure for the settlement of their dispute, then it may be submitted only to that process, unless they otherwise agree [705]. If the disputants have not accepted the same method for the resolution of their dispute, then it may submitted solely to arbitration in conformity with Annex VII of the UNCLOS, unless they elsewise agree [706].

It is opined that an analogous version of the system for dispute settlement operated within the UNCLOS could be applied to interstate territorial disputes. Applicable paragraphs could be inserted into the UN Charter. This would harness the benefit of compulsory jurisdiction for these disagreements – i.e., the certainty of establishing a method whereby a dispute can be resolved by means of a binding judgment or arbitral award, while leaving in place – at least for now – the system of declarations operated under paragraph 2 of Article 36 of the Statute of the ICJ[565].

The Statute of the ICJ

Declarations Made under Article 36(2) of the Statute of the ICJ

Neither Russia nor Ukraine has made a declaration recognizing the jurisdiction of the ICJ as compulsory, as invited so to do by paragraph 2 of Article 36 of the Statute of the ICJ [707]. Seventy-four of the UN's one hundred and ninety-three Member States[566] have made these declarations[567] [707, 708].

---

[563] Annex VII of the UNCLOS contains rules which are to govern the arbitration.

[564] These classes of disputes are those regarding the application of the articles of the UNCLOS that relate to fisheries, protection and preservation of the marine environment, marine scientific research and navigation (United Nations (1982), "United Nations Convention on the Law of the Sea," Annex VIII, Article 1).

[565] The text to fns 204 and 205 lays down Article 36(2) of the Statute of the ICJ. The paragraph whose first sentence is the text to fn 206 discusses the use of the phrase 'compulsory jurisdiction' in Article 36(5) of the Statute of the ICJ – which the sentence immediately following the text to fn 206 sets out.

[566] Text to fn 555.

[567] These seventy-four Member States of the UN are Australia, Austria, Barbados, Belgium, Botswana, Bulgaria, Cambodia, Cameroon, Canada, Costa Rica, Côte d'Ivoire, Cyprus, the Democratic Republic of the Congo, Denmark, Djibouti, Dominica, Dominican Republic, Egypt, Equatorial Guinea, Estonia, Eswatini, Finland, Gambia, Georgia, Germany, Greece, Guinea, Guinea-Bissau, Haiti, Honduras, Hungary, India, Iran, Ireland, Italy, Japan, Latvia, Lesotho, Liberia, Liechtenstein, Lithuania, Luxembourg, Madagascar, Malawi, Malta, Marshall Islands, Mauritius, Mexico, the Netherlands, New Zealand, Nicaragua, Nigeria, Norway, Pakistan, Panama, Paraguay, Peru, the Philippines, Poland, Portugal, Romania, Senegal, Slovakia, Somalia, Spain, Sudan, Suriname, Sweden, Switzerland, Timor-Leste, Togo, Uganda, the UK and Uruguay (International Court of Justice (2024), "Declarations recognizing the jurisdiction of the Court as compulsory," accessed November 20, 2024, <https://www.icj-cij.org/declarations/>; United Nations (2024), 4. Declarations recognizing as compulsory the jurisdiction of the International Court of Justice under Article 36, paragraph 2, of the Statute of the Court, I4. Charter of the United Nations and Statute of the International Court of Justice (New York: United Nations), 1-28, 1-3).

Some of these accept the jurisdiction of the ICJ wholeheartedly[568], while others list exceptions[569].

It is opined that the remaining one hundred and nineteen Member States of the UN should complete declarations under Article 36(2) of the Statute of the ICJ, as this raises legal certainty over the area of international dispute settlement and is a move for peace. The more countries that do this, the less one anticipates the possibility of the government of any state initiating cross-border violence in the event of a serious difference of view from that of another national authority.

The insertion of reservations to declarations – as the government of Canada has done[570] – is not, in itself, a difficulty, as long as the areas in which the ICJ is held not to have jurisdiction by a declaring state are covered – as necessary – by another source of binding dispute settlement. Such an exception may be necessary in an instance in which a state has signed an

---

[568] The declaration of Costa Rica furnishes an example, and reads as follows: "The Government of Costa Rica recognizes as compulsory *ipso facto* and without special agreement, in relation to any other State accepting the same obligation, the jurisdiction of the International Court of Justice in all legal disputes of the kinds referred to in Article 36, paragraph 2, of the Statute of the International Court of Justice. This Declaration shall be valid for a period of five years and shall be understood to be tacitly renewed for like periods, unless denounced before the expiration of the said period." (United Nations (2024), 4. Declarations recognizing as compulsory the jurisdiction of the International Court of Justice under Article 36, paragraph 2, of the Statute of the Court, I4. Charter of the United Nations and Statute of the International Court of Justice, 1-28, 5; emphasis original).

[569] The declaration of Canada supersedes earlier declarations by Canada, and was received by the Secretary-General of the UN on 28th August 2023 (United Nations (2024), 4. Declarations recognizing as compulsory the jurisdiction of the International Court of Justice under Article 36, paragraph 2, of the Statute of the Court, I4. Charter of the United Nations and Statute of the International Court of Justice, 1-28, 23, fns 25 and 26). It provides an example of a declaration that lists exceptions to acceptance of the jurisdiction of the ICJ as compulsory, and reads thus: "On behalf of the Government of Canada, (1) I give notice that I hereby terminate the acceptance by Canada of the compulsory jurisdiction of the International Court of Justice hitherto effective by virtue of the declaration made on 10 May 1994 in conformity with paragraph 2 of Article 36 of the Statute of the Court. (2) I declare that the Government of Canada accepts as compulsory *ipso facto* and without special convention, on condition of reciprocity, the jurisdiction of the International Court of Justice, in conformity with paragraph 2 of Article 36 of the Statute of the Court, until such time as notice may be given to terminate the acceptance, over all disputes arising after 10 May 1994, with regard to situations or facts subsequent to the same date, other than: (a) disputes in regard to which the parties have agreed[,] or shall agree[,] to have recourse to some other method of peaceful settlement; (b) disputes with the government of any other country which is a member of the Commonwealth, all of which disputes shall be settled in such manner as the parties have agreed or shall agree; (c) disputes with regard to questions which[,] by international law[,] fall exclusively within the jurisdiction of Canada; (d) disputes in respect of which any other party to the dispute has accepted the compulsory jurisdiction of the International Court of Justice only in relation to[,] or for the purpose of[,] the dispute; or where the acceptance of the Court's compulsory jurisdiction on behalf of any other party to the dispute was deposited or ratified less than twelve months prior to the filing of the application bringing the dispute before the Court; (e) disputes or claims in respect of which the dispute or claim in question has not been notified to Canada by the State or States concerned in writing, including of an intention to submit the dispute or claim to the Court failing an amicable settlement, at least six months in advance of the submission of the dispute or claim to the Court; and (f) disputes arising out of[,] or concerning[,] conservation and management measures taken by Canada with respect to vessels fishing in the NAFO Regulatory Area, as defined in the Convention on Future Multilateral Co-operation in the Northwest Atlantic Fisheries, 1978, and the enforcement of such measures. (3) The Government of Canada also reserves the right at any time, by means of a notification addressed to the Secretary-General of the United Nations, and with effect as from the moment of such notification, either to add to, amend or withdraw any of the foregoing reservations, or any that may hereafter be added. It is respected that this notification be communicated to the governments of all the States that have accepted the Optional Clause and to the Registrar of the International Court of Justice. Ottawa, August 28, 2023. (Signed) The Honorable Mélanie Joly, P.C., M.P. Minister of Foreign Affairs" (United Nations (2024), 4. Declarations recognizing as compulsory the jurisdiction of the International Court of Justice under Article 36, paragraph 2, of the Statute of the Court, I4. Charter of the United Nations and Statute of the International Court of Justice, 1-28, 5; emphasis added).

[570] Fn 569.

bilateral or multilateral treaty that provides for one or more methods of dispute resolution for transgression of provisions of the convention. For instance, if a Member State of the UN has completed a declaration under paragraph 1 of Article 287 of the UNCLOS[571] and deposited this with the Secretary-General of the UN – as paragraph 8 of the same article requires [709], and if it has selected the International Tribunal for the Law of the Sea and/or an arbitral tribunal as the means by which it would prefer disputes regarding the interpretation or application of the UNCLOS to be settled, then it would also need to insert a reservation into its declaration under Article 36(2) of the Statute of the ICJ that excluded these disputes from the jurisdiction of the ICJ – as, for example, Bulgaria has done[572].

It would be helpful if states which make declarations under Article 36(2) of the Statute of the ICJ recognizing the jurisdiction of the Court as compulsory – and that include exceptions to this recognition, would indicate which source of binding dispute resolution the possible disputes arising under each reservation will be subject to. In the abovementioned example of Bulgaria[573], after the phrase ‘boundaries and areas’ and before the comma following the word ‘areas,’ could be added ‘– all of which are subject to the jurisdiction of the International Tribunal for the Law of the Sea’ or words to that effect. It is submitted that adding a further paragraph to Article 36 of the Statute of the ICJ to encourage the completion of declarations under paragraph 2 of this article and to specify which procedure(s) for binding dispute settlement each state intends to use for the areas of international law that are withheld therein from the compulsory jurisdiction of the ICJ, would encourage states to commit to binding dispute resolution for all their disagreements with other states – a result that would improve legal certainty for all countries.

---

[571] Text to fns 562-564.

[572] Bulgaria’s declaration under Article 36(2) of the Statute of the ICJ specifies: “In conformity with Article 36, paragraph 2, of the Statute of the International Court of Justice[,] the Republic of Bulgaria recognizes as compulsory *ipso facto* and without special agreement, in relation to any other State accepting the same obligation, the jurisdiction of the Court in all legal disputes arising out of facts and situations subsequent to[,] or continuing to exist after the entry into force of[,] the present Declaration, concerning: 1. the interpretation of a treaty; 2. any question of international law; 3. the existence of any fact which, if established, would constitute a breach of an international obligation; 4. the nature or extent of the reparation to be made for the breach of an international obligation, except for disputes arising under the United Nations Convention on the Law of the Sea or any other multilateral or bilateral treaty or agreement on the law of the sea, or customary international law on the sea, including, but not limited to[,] disputes concerning navigational rights, exploration and exploitation of living and non-living natural resources, protection and preservation of the marine environment, delimitation of maritime boundaries and areas, ...” (United Nations (2024), 4. Declarations recognizing as compulsory the jurisdiction of the International Court of Justice under Article 36, paragraph 2, of the Statute of the Court, I4. Charter of the United Nations and Statute of the International Court of Justice, 1-28, 4; emphasis added). Bulgaria ratified the UNCLOS on 15th May 1996, and made a declaration under Article 287(1) of the UNCLOS on 2nd December 2015 which states: “In accordance with Article 287, paragraph 1, of the United Nations Convention on the Law of the Sea, the Republic of Bulgaria declares that it accepts the jurisdiction of the International Tribunal for the Law of the Sea for the settlement of disputes concerning the interpretation or application of the Convention.” (United Nations (2024), “United Nations Treaty Collection: Chapter XXI Law of the Sea – 6. United Nations Convention on the Law of the Sea,” last updated November 21, 2024, accessed November 21, 2024, <https://treaties.un.org/pages/ViewDetailsIII.aspx?src=TREATY&mtdsg_no=XXI-6&chapter=21&Temp=mtdsg3&lang=en>).

[573] Fn 572 and accompanying text.

Article 38(2) of the Statute of the ICJ

It is opined that paragraph 2 of Article 38 of the Statute of the ICJ[574] should be deleted. The concept of *ex aequo et bono*[575] is an old-fashioned one, which has been a useful resource for the Court – i.e., the PCIJ, and, subsequently, the ICJ – to settle a dispute when states parties to it very much want this and are prepared to compromise. But *ex aequo et bono* arbitrations and court cases do not promote legal certainty. As international law develops, the pursuit of legal certainty becomes increasingly significant. Therefore, decisions of courts and tribunals should, as far as is reasonably possible, be consistent in their application of the relevant law.

Article 59 of the Statute of the ICJ

Article 59 of the Statute of the ICJ is identical to Article 59 of the Statute of the PCIJ[576]. Neither makes it compulsory – or even advisory – for the Court to follow precedent[577]. Notwithstanding this, the Court tends to do so – which creates a body of international case law. The doctrine of '*stare decisis*'[578] has long been followed in common law systems, and may influence the bench of the ICJ – especially its common law judges. It is submitted that, under these circumstances, a sentence be added to Article 59 of the Statute of the ICJ that acknowledges the value of *ratio decidendi*[579] of decisions of the PCIJ or of previous determinations of the ICJ, while not making it obligatory therein for judges in each case before the Court to follow these rulings.

Comment

The aforementioned provisions of the Statute of the ICJ are those in most need of attention. Given that the Statute of the ICJ has not been amended over its long life, it may soon be time to review it article by article. For instance, as there are presently one hundred and ninety-three

---

[574] The text to fns 209 and 210 contains Article 38(2) of the Statute of the ICJ.

[575] Fn 97 defines the term '*ex aequo et bono*'.

[576] Text to fn 208.

[577] The second quoted passage in the paragraph headed 'Competence of the PCIJ', in the subsection entitled 'The Statute of the PCIJ' in the section titled 'The Permanent Court of International Justice' in Chapter 2, lays down Article 59 of the Statute of the PCIJ. The sentence immediately following the text to fn 208 sets out Article 59 of the Statute of the ICJ.

[578] The term '*stare decisis*' is from Latin; its literal translation into English is 'stand by things decided'; it is "the legal principle of determining points in litigation according to precedent" (Pearsall, J. (editor) (1998), *The New Oxford Dictionary of English*, 1814). LexisNexis supplies more detail: "'*stare decisis at non quieta movere*', 'to stand by things decided and not disturb settled points'. The doctrine of *stare decisis*, or binding precedent, is the principle by which judges are bound by previous judicial decisions[,] especially of superior courts. To 'stand by things decided', the basis for the doctrine of precedent, there is no room for further examination or interpretation of a point or principle of law; the court is bound to the reasoning in the prior decision, unless there is unique exception or the matter is before a higher court.'" (Lexis Nexis (2024), "*Stare decisis* definition," accessed November 21, 2024, <https://www.lexisnexis.co.uk/legal/glossary/stare-decisis>; emphasis added).

[579] The term '*ratio decidendi*' is from Latin; its literal translation into English is 'reason for deciding'; it is "the rule of law on which a decision is based" (Pearsall, J. (editor) (1998), *The New Oxford Dictionary of English*, 1539). LexisNexis furnishes more information: "The *ratio decidendi* is the reason for a court's decision[,] and is part of the judgement delivered at the end of a case. Through analysis of the facts, the judge applies the appropriate rule or principle of law and makes [a] ruling on the verdict of a case." (Lexis Nexis (2024), "*Ratio decidendi* definition," accessed November 21, 2024, <https://www.lexisnexis.co.uk/legal/glossary/ratio-decidendi>; emphasis added).

Member States of the UN[580] – in contrast to fifty-one Founding Member States[581], it may reasonably be argued that the number of current Members of the ICJ should be raised from fifteen to, perhaps, twenty-five – with the full Court remaining at fifteen judges, so that the courtroom in the Peace Palace is spared the need for costly alterations in order to accommodate ten more places at its bench! The procedure for selecting judges might be appraised, with a view to attracting a wider selection of suitable candidates for ICJ Membership – although it should remain the case that each of the current Members of the Court is from a different Member State of the UN.

Reservations to Multilateral Conventions

In Chapter 4, it was submitted[582] that the application of Article 21 of the Vienna Convention on the Law of Treaties 1969[583], and the same article of the Vienna Convention on the Law of Treaties between States and International Organizations or between International Organizations 1986[584] generates a bilateral treaty between a reserving and accepting state or international organization that differs from the main multilateral convention to the extent of the reservation which applies, or the reservations that apply, between them. It was then opined[585] that this is unsatisfactory from the perspective of certainty of international law, especially in instances in which there are many reservations to a multilateral treaty.

There are 170 states parties to the UNCLOS [710]. Table 6.2 lists these, and shows the number of statutory and interpretative declarations that each has made, the number of reservations which each has presented, and the number of objections to reservations that each has lodged – treating substance over form.

Table 6.2 shows there to be 84 reservations, 196 interpretative declarations and 24 objections to reservations concerning the UNCLOS. While this is not an insuperable number of reservations, it nevertheless results in many versions of the treaty – which will augment the difficulty in administering it.

---

580 Text to fn 555.

581 The fifty-one Founding Member States of the UN were Argentina, Australia, Belgium, Bolivia, Brazil, the Byelorussian Soviet Socialist Republic, Canada, Chile, Colombia, Costa Rica, Cuba, Czechoslovakia, Denmark, the Dominican Republic, Ecuador, Egypt, El Salvador, Ethiopia, France, Greece, Guatemala, Haiti, Honduras, India, Iran, Iraq, Lebanon, Liberia, Luxembourg, Mexico, the Netherlands, New Zealand, Nicaragua, Norway, Panama, Paraguay, Peru, the Philippine Commonwealth, Poland, the Republic of China, Saudi Arabia, the Syrian Arab Republic, Turkey, the Ukrainian Soviet Socialist Republic, the UK, the Union of South Africa, Uruguay, the USA, the USSR, Venezuela and Yugoslavia (United Nations (2024), "Dag Hammarskjöld Library: UN Membership – Founding Member States," last updated November 11, 2024, accessed November 22, 2024, <https://research.un.org/en/unmembers/founders>).

582 Sentence immediately following the text to fn 272.

583 The quoted passage that starts 'Article 21' and which includes the text to fns 267 and 268, sets out Article 21 of the Vienna Convention on the Law of Treaties 1969

584 Fn 268 lays down Article 21 of the Vienna Convention on the Law of Treaties between States and International Organizations or between International Organizations 1986.

585 Sentence immediately following that which fn 582 identifies.

Table 6.2. The number of statutory declarations, interpretative declarations, reservations, and objections to reservations that each of the states parties to the UNCLOS has made [710]

State party	Number of declarations made under provisions of the UNCLOS	Number of interpretative declarations	Number of reservations[586]	Number of objections to reservations
Albania	0	0	0	0
Algeria	2	2	2	0
Angola	2	1	1	0
Antigua and Barbuda	0	0	0	0
Argentina	2	5	2	0
Armenia	0	0	0	0
Australia	2	0	1	1
Austria	1	0	0	0
Azerbaijan	0	0	0	0
Bahamas	0	0	0	0
Bahrain	0	0	0	0
Bangladesh	2	6	2	0
Barbados	0	0	0	0
Belarus	2	0	1	1
Belgium	1	3	0	1
Belize	0	0	0	1
Benin	1	0	1	0
Bolivia	0	2	0	0
Bosnia and Herzegovina[587]	0	2	1	0
Botswana	0	0	0	0
Brazil	0	6	0	0
Brunei Darussalam	0	0	0	0
Bulgaria	1	0	0	1
Burkina Faso	0	0	0	0
Cabo Verde	2	8	1	0
Cameroon	0	0	0	0
Canada	2	1	1	0
Chad	0	0	0	0
Chile	2	8	1	0
China	1	3	2	0
Comoros	0	0	0	0
Congo	2	0	1	0
Cook Islands	0	0	0	0
Costa Rica	0	1	0	0
Côte d'Ivoire	0	0	0	0
Croatia[588]	1	2	1[589]	0

[586] This includes any reservations that are presented within a statutory declaration, i.e., the reservation that is enshrined in a declaration which a state makes under paragraph 1 of Article 298 of the UNCLOS.

[587] The data for Bosnia and Herzegovina, Croatia, Montenegro, North Macedonia, Serbia and Slovenia include those for Yugoslavia, with respect to which these countries are successor states, unless one or more of the statements that the government of Yugoslavia had made have been expressly renounced by the government of the relevant successor state (fn 600). Yugoslavia's pronouncement comprised two interpretative declarations and one reservation (United Nations (2024), "United Nations Treaty Collection: Chapter XXI Law of the Sea – 6. United Nations Convention on the Law of the Sea," last updated November 25, 2024, accessed November 25, 2024, <https://treaties.un.org/pages/ViewDetailsIII.aspx?src=TREATY&mtdsg_no=XXI-6&chapter=21&Temp=mtdsg3&lang=en>).

[588] Fn 587.

[589] Croatia's reservation overlaps that of Yugoslavia, but is not identical to it – Table 6.2 records only one reservation for Croatia; Croatia is not an archipelagic state under the UNCLOS (United Nations (2024), "United Nations

Table 6.2. (Continued)

State party	Number of declarations made under provisions of the UNCLOS	Number of interpretative declarations	Number of reservations[586]	Number of objections to reservations
Cuba	2	1	1	0
Cyprus	0	0	0	0
Czech Republic	0	0	0	1[590]
Democratic Republic of the Congo	2	1	1	0
Denmark	2	3	0	0
Djibouti	0	0	0	0
Dominica	0	0	0	0
Dominican Republic	0	0	0	0
Ecuador	2	13	4	0
Egypt	2	6	2	0
Equatorial Guinea	1	0	1	0
Estonia	1	1	0	0
Eswatini	0	0	0	0
EU	1	2	0	0
Fiji	1	0	0	0
Finland	1	3	0	2
France	2	2	2	1
Gabon	1	0	1	0
Gambia	0	0	0	0
Georgia	0	0	0	0
Germany	1	13	0	2
Ghana	0	0	0	0
Greece	1	3	2	0
Grenada	0	0	0	0
Guatemala	0	0	1	0
Guinea	0	1	0	0
Guinea-Bissau	2	0	0	0
Guyana	0	0	0	0
Haiti	0	0	0	0
Honduras	1	0	0	0
Hungary	1	0	0	0
Iceland	1	0	0	0
India	0	1	0	0
Indonesia	1	0	1	0
Iraq	0	1	1	0
Ireland	0	1	0	1
Italy	1	4	1	1

Treaty Collection: Chapter XXI Law of the Sea – 6. United Nations Convention on the Law of the Sea," last updated November 25, 2024, accessed November 25, 2024, <https://treaties.un.org/pages/ViewDetailsIII.aspx?src=TREATY&mtdsg_no=XXI-6&chapter=21&Temp=mtdsg3&lang=en>; Baumert, K, and Melchior, B. (2015), The Practice of Archipelagic States: A Study of Studies, *Ocean Development & International Law*, 46, 60-80, 63).

[590] The Secretary-General of the UN received this objection from the government of Czechoslovakia on 29th May 1985 (United Nations (2024), "United Nations Treaty Collection: Chapter XXI Law of the Sea – 6. United Nations Convention on the Law of the Sea," last updated November 25, 2024, accessed November 25, 2024, <https://treaties.un.org/pages/ViewDetailsIII.aspx?src=TREATY&mtdsg_no=XXI-6&chapter=21&Temp=mtdsg3&lang=en>). Today, it comprises two objections, which are identical in content – one maintained by each of Czechoslovakia's successor states, i.e., the Czech Republic (text to the present footnote – fn 590) and Slovakia (text to fn 597).

State party	Number of declarations made under provisions of the UNCLOS	Number of interpretative declarations	Number of reservations[586]	Number of objections to reservations
Jamaica	0	0	0	0
Japan	0	0	0	0
Jordan	0	0	0	0
Kenya	1	0	1	0
Kiribati	0	1	0	0
Kuwait	0	0	1	0
Laos	0	0	0	0
Latvia	1	0	0	1
Lebanon	0	0	0	0
Lesotho	0	0	0	0
Liberia	0	0	0	0
Lithuania	1	0	1	0
Luxembourg	1	1	0	0
Madagascar	1	0	0	0
Malawi	0	0	0	0
Malaysia	0	6	1	0
Maldives	0	0	0	0
Mali	0	1	0	0
Malta	0	4	3	0
Marshall Islands	0	0	0	0
Mauritania	0	0	0	0
Mauritius	0	0	0	0
Mexico	2	0	1	0
Micronesia	0	0	0	0
Moldova	0	1	0	0
Monaco	0	0	0	0
Mongolia	0	0	0	0
Montenegro[591]	2	2	2	0
Morocco	0	0	2	0
Mozambique	0	0	0	0
Myanmar	0	0	0	0
Namibia	0	0	0	0
Nauru	0	0	0	0
Nepal	0	0	0	0
Netherlands	1	15	0	2
New Zealand	0	0	0	0
Nicaragua	2	2	0	0
Niger	0	0	0	0
Nigeria	1	0	0	0
Niue	0	0	0	0
North Macedonia[592]	0	2	1	0
Norway	2	1	0	0
Oman	1	8	2	0
Pakistan	0	1	1	0
Palau	1	0	1	0
Panama	1	0	1	0
Papua New Guinea	0	0	0	0
Paraguay	0	0	0	0
Philippines	0	5	3	0
Poland	0	0	0	0

[591] Fn 587.
[592] Fn 587.

Table 6.1. (Continued)

State party	Number of declarations made under provisions of the UNCLOS	Number of interpretative declarations	Number of reservations[586]	Number of objections to reservations
Portugal	2	4	1	0
Qatar	0	0	1	0
Republic of Korea	1	1	1	0
Romania	0	3	0	0
Russia, and, prior to 26th December 1991[593], the USSR	3[594]	0	1[595]	1
Rwanda	0	0	0	0
Samoa	0	0	0	0
San Marino	0	0	0	0
São Tomé and Príncipe	0	4	0	0
Saudi Arabia	1	2	4	0
Senegal	0	0	0	0
Serbia[596]	0	2	1	0
Seychelles	0	0	0	0
Sierra Leone	0	0	0	0
Singapore	1	0	1	0
Slovakia	0	0	0	1[597]
Slovenia[598]	2	0[599]	0[600]	0
Solomon Islands	0	0	0	0
Somalia	0	0	0	0
South Africa	0	0	0	0
Spain	2	7	4	0
Sri Lanka	0	0	0	0
St. Kitts and Nevis	0	0	0	0
St. Lucia	0	0	0	0

593 The USSR was officially dissolved on 26th December 1991 (fn 3). The USSR's declarations are recorded under the Russian Federation's section only, and are, therefore, assumed not to apply to any of the former Soviet Republics other than Russia (United Nations (2024), "United Nations Treaty Collection: Chapter XXI Law of the Sea – 6. United Nations Convention on the Law of the Sea," last updated November 25, 2024, accessed November 25, 2024, <https://treaties.un.org/pages/ViewDetailsIII.aspx?src=TREATY&mtdsg_no=XXI-6&chapter=21&Temp=mtdsg3&lang=en>).

594 The USSR made three declarations – under Articles 287(1), 292(1) and 298(1) of the UNCLOS; Russia subsequently made a very similar declaration to that of the USSR under Article 298(1) of the UNCLOS (United Nations (2024), "United Nations Treaty Collection: Chapter XXI Law of the Sea – 6. United Nations Convention on the Law of the Sea," last updated November 25, 2024, accessed November 25, 2024, <https://treaties.un.org/pages/ViewDetailsIII.aspx?src=TREATY&mtdsg_no=XXI-6&chapter=21&Temp=mtdsg3&lang=en>).

595 The two declarations under Article 298(1) of the UNCLOS are recorded as one reservation (fns 586 and 594).

596 Fn 587.

597 Fn 590.

598 Fn 587.

599 Fn 600.

600 The government of Slovenia has expressly disapplied the reservation that Yugoslavia announced (fn 587): "The Republic of Slovenia does not consider itself to be bound by the declaratory statement on the basis of article 310 of the Convention, given by the former SFR of Yugoslavia"; it is submitted that, in the light of its wording, this renouncement by the government of Slovenia also applies to the two interpretative declarations that the government of Yugoslavia had made (United Nations (2024), "United Nations Treaty Collection: Chapter XXI Law of the Sea – 6. United Nations Convention on the Law of the Sea," last updated November 25, 2024, accessed November 25, 2024, <https://treaties.un.org/pages/ViewDetailsIII.aspx?src=TREATY&mtdsg_no=XXI-6&chapter=21&Temp=mtdsg3&lang=en>).

State party	Number of declarations made under provisions of the UNCLOS	Number of interpretative declarations	Number of reservations[586]	Number of objections to reservations
St. Vincent and the Grenadines	1	0	0	0
State of Palestine	0	0	0	0
Sudan	0	2	1	0
Suriname	0	0	0	0
Sweden	1	4	0	2
Switzerland	1	0	0	0
Tanzania	1	0	0	0
Thailand	1	1	1	0
Timor-Leste	2	1	0	0
Togo	2	0	1	0
Tonga	0	0	0	0
Trinidad and Tobago	2	0	1	0
Tunisia	2	1	1	0
Tuvalu	0	0	0	0
Uganda	0	0	0	0
Ukraine	3	0	1	1
UK	2	1	1	3[601]
Uruguay	2	4	3	0
Vanuatu	0	0	0	0
Vietnam	0	2	1	0
Yemen	0	1	2	0
Zambia	0	0	0	0
Zimbabwe	0	0	0	0
Total	103	196	84	24

It is opined that drafting the convention in such a way that it permits specified reservations is not necessarily a good idea. Several countries in Table 6.2 have excluded all of the methods for binding dispute settlement that paragraph 1 of Article 287 of the UNCLOS provides[602], in exercising the declaration that Article 298 of the UNCLOS lays down. It is submitted that the exclusion of these procedures in subparagraph 1(a) of Article 298 of the UNCLOS is particularly damaging, as resolution of disputes regarding the delimitation of maritime boundaries cuts to the heart of the UNCLOS. This subparagraph reads thus.

> When signing, ratifying or acceding to this Convention or at any time thereafter, a State may, without prejudice to the obligations arising under section 1 [of Part XV of the UNCLOS[603]] declare in writing that it does not accept any one or more of the procedures provided for in section 2 [of Part XV of the UNCLOS[604]] with respect to one or more of

[601] In addition to lodging an objection to the pronouncement made the Democratic Republic of the Congo, the government of the UK rejected the statements of Argentina concerning the Falkland Islands (Malvinas) and Spain regarding Gibraltar (United Nations (2024), "United Nations Treaty Collection: Chapter XXI Law of the Sea – 6. United Nations Convention on the Law of the Sea," last updated November 25, 2024, accessed November 25, 2024, <https://treaties.un.org/pages/ViewDetailsIII.aspx?src=TREATY&mtdsg_no=XXI-6&chapter=21&Temp=mtdsg3&lang=en>).

[602] The text to fns 562-564 sets out Article 287(1) of the UNCLOS.

[603] Section 1 of Part XV of the UNCLOS is entitled 'General Provisions', and consists of Articles 279-285.

[604] Section 2 of Part XV of the UNCLOS is titled 'Compulsory Procedures entailing Binding Decisions', and is composed of Articles 286-296. It is opined that the 'procedures provided for in section 2' are the processes for binding dispute settlement that Article 287(1) specifies, i.e., a case submitted to the International Tribunal for the Law of the Sea for judgment, one placed before the ICJ for determination, a case put before an arbitral

the following categories of disputes: (a)(i) disputes concerning the interpretation or application of articles 15[605], 74[606] and 83[607] [of the UNCLOS] relating to sea boundary delimitations, or those involving historic bays or titles, provided that a State having made such a declaration shall, when such a dispute arises subsequent to the entry into force of this Convention and where no agreement within a reasonable time is reached in negotiations between the parties, at the request of any party to the dispute, accept submission of the matter to conciliation under Annex V, section 2 [of the UNCLOS[608]]; and provided further that any dispute that necessarily involves the concurrent consideration of any unsettled dispute concerning sovereignty or other rights over continental or insular

tribunal that is constituted in observance of Annex VII of the UNCLOS, and one presented at a special arbitral tribunal which is constituted in compliance with Article VIII of the UNCLOS.

605 Article 15 of the UNCLOS is headed 'Delimitation of the territorial sea between States with opposite or adjacent coasts', and reads: "Where the coasts of two States are opposite or adjacent to each other, neither of the two States is entitled, failing agreement between them to the contrary, to extend its territorial sea beyond the median line every point of which is equidistant from the nearest points on the baselines from which the breadth of the territorial seas of each of the two States is measured. The above provision does not apply, however, where it is necessary by reason of historic title or other special circumstances to delimit the territorial seas of the two States in a way which is at variance therewith." (United Nations (1982), "United Nations Convention on the Law of the Sea," Article 15).

606 Article 74 of the UNCLOS is headed 'Delimitation of the exclusive economic zone between States with opposite or adjacent coasts', and declares: "1. The delimitation of the exclusive economic zone between States with opposite or adjacent coasts shall be effected by agreement on the basis of international law, as referred to in Article 38 of the Statute of the International Court of Justice, in order to achieve an equitable solution. 2. If no agreement can be reached within a reasonable period of time, [then] the States concerned shall resort to the procedures provided for in Part XV [of the UNCLOS]. 3. Pending agreement as provided for in paragraph 1, the States concerned, in a spirit of understanding and cooperation, shall make every effort to enter into provisional arrangements of a practical nature and, during this transitional period, not to jeopardize or hamper the reaching of the final agreement. Such arrangements shall be without prejudice to the final delimitation. 4. Where there is an agreement in force between the States concerned, questions relating to the delimitation of the exclusive economic zone shall be determined in accordance with the provisions of that agreement." (United Nations (1982), "United Nations Convention on the Law of the Sea," Article 74). The text to fn 207 and the quoted passage which immediately follows that text lay down paragraph 1 of Article 38 of the Statute of the ICJ. The text to fns 209 and 210 sets out paragraph 2 of Article 38 of the Statute of the ICJ. It is opined that 'international law as referred to in Article 38 of the Statute of the ICJ' – mentioned in paragraph 1 of Article 74 of the UNCLOS (first sentence of the present footnote, i.e., fn 606) – comprises the sources of international law to which paragraph 1 of Article 38 of the Statute of the ICJ refers. Part XV of the UNCLOS is titled 'Settlement of Disputes', and contains Articles 279-299.

607 Article 83 of the UNCLOS is headed 'Delimitation of the continental shelf between States with opposite or adjacent coasts', and specifies: "1. The delimitation of the continental shelf between States with opposite or adjacent coasts shall be effected by agreement on the basis of international law, as referred to in Article 38 of the Statute of the International Court of Justice, in order to achieve an equitable solution. 2. If no agreement can be reached within a reasonable period of time, [then] the States concerned shall resort to the procedures provided for in Part XV [of the UNCLOS]. 3. Pending agreement as provided for in paragraph 1, the States concerned, in a spirit of understanding and cooperation, shall make every effort to enter into provisional arrangements of a practical nature and, during this transitional period, not to jeopardize or hamper the reaching of the final agreement. Such arrangements shall be without prejudice to the final delimitation. 4. Where there is an agreement in force between the States concerned, questions relating to the delimitation of the continental shelf shall be determined in accordance with the provisions of that agreement." (United Nations (1982), "United Nations Convention on the Law of the Sea," Article 83). Article 83 of the UNCLOS is identical to Article 74 of the UNCLOS (fn 606), other than replacing the phrase 'exclusive economic zone' in paragraphs 1 and 4 of the latter with the expression 'continental shelf' in paragraphs 1 and 4 of the former. Therefore, the last four sentences of fn 606 apply to the equivalent terms in Article 83 of the UNCLOS to those in Article 74 of the UNCLOS.

608 Annex V of the UNCLOS is entitled 'Conciliation'; its Section 2 is titled 'Compulsory submission to Conciliation Procedure pursuant to Section 3 of Part XV', and consists of Articles 11-14 – the last of which applies the conciliation procedure laid down in Articles 2-10 of Section 1 of Annex V of the UNCLOS (United Nations (1982), "United Nations Convention on the Law of the Sea," Annex V, Article 14). Section 3 of Part XV of the UNCLOS is entitled 'Limitations and Exceptions to applicability of Section 2', and is composed of Articles 297-299.

> land territory shall be excluded from such submission; (ii) after the conciliation comission has presented its report, which shall state the reasons on which it is based, the parties shall negotiate an agreement on the basis of that report; if these negotiations do not result in an agreement, [then] the parties shall, by mutual consent, submit the question to one of the procedures provided for in section 2 [of Part XV of the UNCLOS[609]], unless the parties otherwise agree; (iii) this subparagraph does not apply to any sea boundary dispute finally settled by an arrangement between the parties, or to any such dispute which is to be settled in accordance with a bilateral or multilateral agreement binding upon those parties; ... [711].

If the parties opt for conciliation, then they are free to reject the conclusions of the conciliation commission. Under these circumstances, both or all the disputants need to agree to submit their delimitation dispute to a procedure for binding dispute resolution. What happens if they do not so agree? The possibilities for conflict between them remain.

It is opined that the ILC is aware of at least some of the difficulties concerning reservations to multilateral conventions. For instance, paragraph 1 of Guideline 2.5.3 of its Guide to Practice on Reservations to Treaties suggests that states or worldwide organizations which have introduced reservations to a treaty "should undertake a periodic review of such reservations and consider withdrawing those which no longer serve their purpose" [712]. In this review, paragraph 2 of Guideline 2.5.3 advises, these entities "should devote special attention to the aim of preserving the integrity of multilateral treaties" [712]. And the reservations dialogue in the Annex to the Guide to Practice on Reservations to Treaties expresses similar sentiments.

> *The International Law Commission*, ... *Bearing in mind* the need to achieve a satisfactory balance between the objectives of safeguarding the integrity of multilateral treaties and securing the widest possible participation therein, *Recognizing* the role that reservations to treaties may play in achieving this balance, ... *I. Considers that:* I. States and international organizations intending to formulate reservations should do so as precisely and narrowly as possible, consider limiting their scope[,] and ensure that they are not incompatible with the object and purpose of the treaty to which they relate; ... 4. States and international organizations should periodically review their reservations with a view to limiting their scope or withdrawing them[,] where appropriate; ... 7. States and international organizations, as well as monitoring bodies, if they deem it useful, should encourage the withdrawal of reservations, the reconsideration of the need for a reservation or the gradual reduction of the scope of a reservation through partial withdrawals; 8. States and international organizations should address the concerns and reactions of other States, international organizations and monitoring bodies and take them into account, to the extent possible, with a view to reconsidering, modifying or withdrawing a reservation[610]; ... [713].

It is submitted that these are constructive proposals concerning multilateral treaties and reservations. But will the governments of states take note of them? The more that substantial multilateral conventions, such as the UNCLOS, are free from – or close to being unimpeded by – the ballast of reservations, the greater the progress which is being made towards a uniform, comprehensive model of international law.

---

[609] Fn 604.

[610] The italics for the phrases '*The International Law Commission*', '*Bearing in mind*' and '*I: Considers that:*', and for the word '*Recognizing*', are present in the original text.

The Direction of International Law

From the 1920s to the 2020s: Revisiting the Case of the S.S. "Lotus"

The institutional phase of international law commences with the establishment of the League of Nations on 10th January 1920[611]. The Covenant of the League of Nations was included, as Part I, in the Peace Treaties that officially ended the First World War[612]. One of these was the Treaty of Sèvres, which went unratified and was replaced by the Treaty of Lausanne recognizing the boundaries of Turkey[613] (as it then was[614]).

In its Article 15, the Treaty of Lausanne – subject to one exception not relevant to the case[615], stated that all matters of jurisdiction, as between Turkey and the other states parties, were to be determined in line with the principles of international law [714]. The PCIJ considered that the phrase 'principles of international law' meant "international law as it is applied between all nations belonging to the community of States" [714]. The Court considered whether there was any such principle which prevented Turkey from prosecuting under Turkish law a French national (Monsieur Demons) on board a French ship (the *S.S. "Lotus"*) for permitting it to collide – with serious consequences – into a Turkish vessel (the *S.S. "Boz-Court"*) on the high seas [715], and decided that there was not [716]. It held that, in the absence of a prohibitory principle of international law, France and Turkey held concurrent jurisdiction over the collision – which rendered it legal for the latter to try Monsieur Demons in the Turkish courts.

> The offence for which Lieutenant Demons appears to have been prosecuted was an act – of negligence or imprudence – having its origin on board the *Lotus*[616], whilst its effects made themselves felt on board the *Boz-Kourt*[617]. These two elements are, legally, entirely inseparable, so much so that their separation renders the offence non-existent. Neither the exclusive jurisdiction of either State, nor the limitations of the jurisdiction of each to the occurrences which took place on the respective ships would appear calculated to satisfy the requirements of justice and effectively to protect the interests of the two States. It is only natural that each should be able to exercise jurisdiction and to do so in respect of the incident as a whole. It is therefore a case of concurrent jurisdiction [717].

The phrases 'satisfy the requirements of justice' and 'protect the interests of the two States' are noteworthy – they demonstrate an equitable approach to settling the dispute. The opportunity for the PCIJ to apply equity and assert concurrent jurisdiction was given by the fact that the separation of the act (strictly French jurisdiction) from its effects (strictly Turkish

---

[611] Text to fns 33 and 42.
[612] Sentence immediately preceding the text to fn 37; final sentence of the paragraph that includes the text to fn 38.
[613] Text to fn 38.
[614] Fn 38 and accompanying text.
[615] This is Article 16 of the Treaty of Lausanne, which specifies how jurisdiction is allocated between Turkey and other states parties to this convention over issues of the personal status of their nationals within Turkey (Hertogen, A. (2015), Letting *Lotus* Bloom, *The European Journal of International Law*, 26(4), 901-926, 906, fn 28).
[616] Emphasis original.
[617] Emphasis original.

jurisdiction) – which, it is opined, is in accordance with the theoretical application of the law of state sovereignty[618] – 'renders the offence obsolete.'

The Case of the S.S. Lotus[619] was decided in September 1927, i.e., before the Statute of the PCIJ was amended in September 1929[620]. The original version of the Statute of the PCIJ is therefore consulted. The last sentence of Article 38 therein reads as follows.

> This provision[621] shall not prejudice the power of the Court to decide a case *ex aequo et bono*[622], if the parties agree thereto [94].

It is submitted that the PCIJ determined *The Case of the S.S. Lotus ex aequo et bono*, which required the agreement of the parties under Article 38 of the Statute of the PCIJ. The Court did not seek their concurrence, and, therefore, was acting at variance with this provision – and, consequently, beyond its jurisdiction, in adjudicating this dispute in the way that it did. Could the Turkish government have compensated the families of the victims of the collision without attempting to prosecute Monsieur Demons? This is only of academic interest today, and, in any case, the lack of a specific rule of international law over this area has, since 1927, been addressed. Paragraph 1 of Article 11 of the Convention on the High Seas 1958 reads thus.

> In the event of a collision or of any other incident of navigation concerning a ship on the high seas, involving the penal or disciplinary responsibility of the master or of any other person in the service of the ship, *no penal or disciplinary proceedings may be instituted against such persons except before the judicial or administrative authorities either of the flag State or of the State of which such person is a national*[623] [718].

As between states parties to the UNCLOS, that treaty prevails over the Geneva Conventions on the Law of the Sea of 29th April 1958 [719], which includes the Convention on the High Seas 1958[624]. Paragraph 1 of Article 97 of the UNCLOS contains an identical provision – save two minor changes[625] – to paragraph 1 of Article 11 of the Convention on the High Seas 1958.

> In the event of a collision or any other incident of navigation concerning a ship on the high seas, involving the penal or disciplinary responsibility of the master or of any other person in the service of the ship, no penal or disciplinary proceedings may be instituted against

---

[618] The *S.S. "Lotus"* is a vessel flying the French flag, and Monsieur Demons is a French national on board the *S.S. "Lotus"* – giving France sovereignty. The *S.S. "Boz-Court"* is a vessel flying the Turkish flag, granting Turkey sovereignty.

[619] Judgment of 7 September 1927, *P.C.I.J. Series A No. 10 (1927)*, 4-33.

[620] Fn 83 and accompanying text.

[621] It is submitted that 'This provision' refers to the first paragraph of Article 38 of the Statute of the PCIJ, which the first quoted passage in the paragraph headed 'Competence of the PCIJ', in the subsection titled 'The Statute of the PCIJ' in the section entitled 'The Permanent Court of International Justice' in Chapter 2, lays down.

[622] Emphasis original. Fn 97 defines the term '*ex aequo et bono*'.

[623] Emphasis added.

[624] The other such treaties over which the UNCLOS prevails as between its states parties are the Convention on Fishing and Conservation of the Living Resources of the High Seas 1958, the Convention on the Continental Shelf 1958, and the Convention on the Territorial Sea and the Contiguous Zone 1958.

[625] The drafters of the UNCLOS deleted the word 'of' from the phrase 'or of any other incident' in Article 11(1) of the Convention on the High Seas 1958 to read 'or any other incident' in Article 97(1) of the UNCLOS, and changed 'such persons' in Article 11(1) of the Convention on the High Seas 1958 to 'such person' in Article 97(1) of the UNCLOS.

such person except before the judicial or administrative authorities either of the flag State or of the State of which such person is a national [720].

Under either of these paragraphs, Monsieur Demons would not have been liable to prosecution under Turkish law regarding his part in the collision between the *S.S. "Lotus"* and the *S.S. "Boz-Court,"* as he was a French national on board a ship whose flag state was France at the moment that the incident took place.

Does Such Development in International Law Indicate a Wider Trend?

The judgment in *The Case of the S.S. Lotus*[626] as interpreted in the immediately-preceding subsection as an application of equity, and the filling of the relevant lacuna of international law with a pertinent treaty provision, may represent a direction from few rules to more regulations – and may proceed to a thorough system for directing the cross-border decisions and actions of the governments of states. This would be a constructive result, from the perspective of legal certainty.

It is opined that, in the history of the law of England and Wales, the law administered in the local courts was customary law[627] – which was subsumed by common law, as, from the time of King Henry II[628], the monarch's jurisdiction gradually spread across the territory. If the common law system was not considered to be adequate, then a disputant could petition the King – then, the King's Council, and, later, the Lord Chancellor, who presided over the Court of Chancery – which administered equity (in contrast to common law) [721]. The Court of Chancery was dissolved and its jurisdiction transferred to the Chancery Division of the High Courts, as a result of the restructuring of the courts of England and Wales set out in the Judicature Acts of 1873 and 1875 [722]. As a result of the merging of the common law courts with the equity-administering Court of Chancery, the senior judiciary in the late 19th century and the 20th century were challenged with the need to apply common law to cases on the basis of precedent but with the possibility of applying equitable remedies, where these were available and relevant[629]. But this was not all. The various governments have, during that time and up until today, introduced increasing volumes of legislative and regulatory instruments which have – it is submitted – replaced, subsumed or subordinated the common law in most fields. Consequently, the law of the twenty-first century in England and Wales is primarily one of the statute book, in which the main roles of the system's judges are those of interpretation and application of the various parliamentary end-products.

---

626 Judgment of 7 September 1927, *P.C.I.J. Series A No. 10 (1927)*, 4-33.

627 In pre-Norman Britain, each hundred had a court in which criminal matters and private disputes were resolved by customary law; these institutions persisted into medieval times (Encyclopaedia Britannica (1998), "hundred," published July 20, 1998, last updated February 24, 2012, accessed November 28, 2024, <https://www.britannica.com/topic/hundred-English-government>).

628 Milners (Solicitors) writes: "Henry ... oversaw the creation of common law and legal "circuits". Laws created in Westminster replaced local customs. This new common law was implemented by travelling judges who went around the country's circuits settling cases." (Milners (2023), "A (very) brief history of the legal system in England and Wales," published March 24, 2023, accessed November 28, 2024, <https://www.milnerslaw.co.uk/a-very-brief-history-of-the-legal-system-in-england-and-wales/>).

629 It is submitted that the leading proponent of this thinking was the long-standing Master of the Rolls, Lord Denning, whose most-illustrative book – *The Due Process of Law* – was published in 1980 by Butterworths and re-published in 2005 by Oxford University Press, USA.

Can a forerunning analogy be identified from the description in the immediately-preceding paragraph regarding international law? As seen from the above revisitation[630] to *The Case of the S.S. Lotus*[631], provisions from multilateral treaties are tending to fill lacunae in international law over time. Further to Chapter 4, the ILC is gradually covering the ground for it to be able to compile a dynamic catalogue of rules over each of the non-conventional sources of international law. Today, this subject comprises many regulations – a great number of which have emerged from interpretations of state practice by the ILC, the ICJ and other courts and tribunals, and drafters of multilateral conventions. The relevant background is the general practice of states, rather than that of one or a few states. To promote legal certainty, multilateral treaties should be accompanied by no more than a few reservations – and are better still with none. Nearly all states are Member States of the UN. Thus, a unified system of international law is gently appearing – if yet still some distance away.

Other necessary components of a uniform system of international law are access of all states to mechanisms for binding dispute settlement, and an awareness and acceptance by their governments that this law is a superior source of law to national law. It is opined that the administrations of a majority of states are law-abiding in their international obligations, and would welcome a stable system of governing law. It is submitted that this could be the natural – and, at best, the optimal – outcome of the evolution of the subject, just as it may be in the case of the law of England and Wales – even though the statutory input in the latter instance has been considerable. If, in practice, it proves to be very difficult or impossible to accomplish the establishment of meaningful multilateral treaties – with few or no reservations – over most subject areas of international law, then it may be necessary to explore the legislative route. This would need to start with a system which included an organization for drafting and publishing instruments that are not legally-binding upon states – standards, principles, guidelines and recommendations – in order to evaluate, in practice, whether global law-making could conceivably work.

Comment

Having ascertained that the international legal system is in need of being updated, this chapter describes some areas of the UN and of international law that may be in need of change, and indicates, in principle, what might be done to correct these deficiencies or advance the current situation. Some of the topics in the above sections, such as the vetoes of the permanent members of the UNSC, have needed to be modified or abolished for a long time – but little or nothing has been done, and the lack of adjustment has contributed to ensuing conflicts and the suffering that these have caused. Notwithstanding this, there are concrete measures that can be taken; the ground for some of these is covered in this section and in those preceding it.

---

[630] See the subsection titled 'From the 1920s to the 2020s: revisiting the Case of the S.S. "Lotus"', above in the current section, i.e., that entitled 'The direction of international law'.

[631] Judgment of 7 September 1927, *P.C.I.J. Series A No. 10 (1927)*, 4-33.

Conclusion

This chapter considers why changes are needed to the UN and to international law, and describes some areas of the international legal system where appropriate alterations may be introduced. The next chapter sets out specific amendments, deletions and additions that might be made thereto.

Chapter 7

Suggested Changes to the United Nations and to International Law

Abstract

The main instruments of the international order have not undergone any significant amendment since the time at which they were set up, but are now being challenged. Consequently, changes to them are necessary. This chapter presents those modifications that this author proposes, based on his perception of the international legislative framework and of the current circumstances in relation to that structure, and on the work undertaken in earlier chapters of this monograph. Recommendations for amendment to the UN Charter are put forward first, followed by the suggestion of the establishment of a Parliament of the United Nations, and thence by proposals for adjustment to the Statute of the ICJ and one for the editing of a draft conclusion of the ILC. Article 2(1) of the UN Charter is altered in the light of the continuation of permanent member status at the UNSC for five Member States of the UN. The veto of the permanent members of the UNSC is removed; an alternative check on voting at the UNSC is inserted in its stead. The composition of the Military Staff Committee is rebalanced to include representatives of the non-permanent members of the UNSC. A procedure is introduced to Chapter VIII of the UN Charter to extend a choice of methods for binding dispute resolution to Member States in respect of territorial disagreements relating to the location of their international borders on land, which includes the establishment of a Tribunal for Determining International Borders on Land. A summary procedure is added to Article 94 of the UN Charter to address alleged contraventions of one or more articles of the Charter. Chapter XVIII of the UN Charter is modified to remove the veto power of permanent members of the UNSC over the entry into force of amendments to the UN Charter. A Parliament of the United Nations becomes a principal organ of the UN; an initial version of its statute is drafted. A paragraph is placed in Article 36 of the Statute of the ICJ to encourage Member States to make a declaration recognizing as compulsory the jurisdiction of the ICJ and to specify therein the procedure(s) for binding dispute resolution to which disputes arising within those areas of international law that they exclude from the compulsory jurisdiction of the ICJ, are to be submitted. Paragraph 2 of Article 38 of the Statute of the ICJ – which provides for judgments *ex aequo et bono*, is deleted. Provision is made in Article 59 of the UN Charter for judges to consult *ratio decidendi* of cases of the ICJ and the PCIJ with similar facts. Finally, one of the draft conclusions on subsidiary means for the determination of rules of international law is adjusted in order to alter the accepted status of these means.

Keywords: amendment, binding, Charter, dispute, parliament, seat, Statute, states

Introduction

There is a tide in affairs of men
Which, taken at the flood, leads on to fortune;
Omitted, all the voyage of their life

> Is bound in shallows and in miseries.
> On such a full sea are we now afloat,
> And we must take the current when it serves,
> Or lose our ventures [723].

William Shakespeare's Marcus Brutus was only too aware of the necessity of grasping the main opportunity that his life presented. As history records, the foremost beneficiary of the events of this time was the then-young Octavius Caesar, who became a long-standing ruler of ancient Rome and its Empire under the name of Caesar Augustus – from which the present nomenclature for the month of August is derived.

It is submitted that the current period offers an analogous moment in the sense that the primary instruments of the international order have not undergone any significant amendment since the time at which they were set up, but are being challenged by acts of significant national defiance. That changes to them are necessary, is undeniable. But what alterations thereto should be made? The sections which follow present those modifications that this author proposes, based on his perception of the international legislative framework and of the current circumstances in relation to that structure, and on the work undertaken in earlier chapters of this monograph. Recommendations for amendment to the UN Charter are put forward first, followed by the suggestion of the establishment of a Parliament of the United Nations, and thence by proposals for adjustment to the Statute of the ICJ and one for the editing of a draft conclusion of the ILC. The chapter then concludes.

Amendments to the UN Charter

Paragraph 1 of Article 2 of the UN Charter

In concord with the comments in Chapters 3[632] and 6[633], and the suggestion made in Chapter 6[634], change paragraph 1 of Article 2 of the UN Charter from "The Organization is based upon the principle of sovereign equality of all its Members" [175] to the following.

> 1. Within the framework that international law provides, each Member is sovereign over its territory.

Article 27 of the UN Charter

Pursuant to 'the problem' that is identified in Chapter 1[635] – the technical basis for which is synopsized in Chapter 3[636], and the remarks made in Chapter 6[637], and in consonance with the

[632] Text to fns 159-162.
[633] Text to fn 554.
[634] Sentence immediately following the paragraph containing fn 536.
[635] The section entitled 'The Problem' in Chapter 1 identifies and explores 'the problem', which is summarized in the penultimate paragraph of that section, i.e., in the paragraph immediately following the text to fn 32.
[636] Text to fns 159-161.
[637] Text to fns 554 and 555.

recommendation made in Chapter 6[638], the upcoming alterations should be made to Article 27 of the UN Charter. Replace the phrase "including the concurring votes of the permanent members" in the first clause of paragraph 3 of Article 27 of the UN Charter[639] with the following: ", subject to fulfilment of the condition in paragraph 4". Article 27(3) will then read thus.

> 3. Decisions of the Security Council on all other matters shall be made by an affirmative vote of nine members, subject to fulfilment of the condition in paragraph 4.

Add new paragraph 4 to Article 27 of the UN Charter, which is to be worded so.

> 4. Decisions of the Security Council under Chapter VII shall require less than five dissentient votes. All other non-procedural decisions of the Security Council shall require less than six dissentient votes.

The First Sentence of Paragraph 2 of Article 47 of the UN Charter

Further to the comment made in Chapter 6[640], the first sentence of paragraph 2 of Article 47 of the UN Charter should be changed to reflect a fairer balance in representation of UN Member States on the Military Staff Committee to that which it currently requires[641]. The following alternative attempts to do this.

> 2. The Military Staff Committee shall consist of the Chiefs of Staff of each of the members of the Security Council or their representatives. …

Chapter VIII of the UN Charter: Regional Arrangements

In keeping with the advice furnished in Chapter 3[642], erase the second sentence of paragraph 1 of Article 53 of the UN Charter and the current content of paragraph 2 of Article 53 of the UN Charter. Reclassify Article 54 of the UN Charter[643] as paragraph 2 of Article 53 of the UN Charter. In conformity with the proposal put forward in Chapter 6[644], insert the following new content into Article 54 of the UN Charter.

> 1. The Members of the United Nations are required to select, by means of a written declaration to be deposited with the Secretary-General, at least one of the following methods of binding dispute resolution for territorial disputes relating to the location of their international borders on land, which are unable to be settled by means of either diplomacy or a method of non-binding dispute resolution: (a) the Tribunal for

---

638 Fn 556 and accompanying text.
639 Text to fn 14.
640 Text to fn 536 and the immediately-following sentence.
641 Point 2. in fn 174 sets out paragraph 2 of Article 47 of the UN Charter.
642 Fn 178.
643 Sentence immediately-following the text to fn 178.
644 Paragraph containing the text to fn 565.

Determining International Borders on Land; (b) the International Court of Justice; (c) an arbitral tribunal comprising five arbitrators, one of whom is appointed by each of the two main parties to the dispute and three of whom are independent arbitrators each from a different non-disputing Member who are appointed by the Secretary-General and of whom one shall be the chairperson of the tribunal.

2. The Tribunal for Determining International Borders on Land is hereby established, and is constituted in accordance with its Statute. It shall operate as specified by its Rules of Procedure.
3. If the disputants have accepted the same procedure for the settlement of the dispute, then it may be submitted only to that procedure, unless they otherwise agree.
4. If the disputants have not accepted the same procedure for the settlement of the dispute, then it may be submitted only to arbitration in accordance with subparagraph 1(c), unless they otherwise agree.
5. A Member that is a party to a dispute not covered by a declaration in force, shall be deemed to have accepted arbitration in accordance with subparagraph 1(c).
6. A declaration under paragraph 1 may be withdrawn only in the event that a state's membership of the United Nations has come to an end. Such withdrawal does not affect the status of any ongoing disputes to which that state is a party.
7. A declaration under paragraph 1 may be modified at any time, subject to prior notice of three months of the intended alteration being given to the Secretary-General, with whom the amended declaration is to be deposited. This change does not in any way affect proceedings pending before a court or tribunal having jurisdiction under this article, unless the parties otherwise agree.

Article 94 of the UN Charter

In order to counter infractions of the UN Charter – two of which are posited in Chapter 1[645], the introduction a summary procedure for binding judgment is recommended. Accordingly, add the following new paragraph 3 to Article 94 of the UN Charter.

> If a Member of the United Nations considers, on reasonable grounds, that another Member of the United Nations has contravened one or more articles of this Charter, then it may make an application in writing addressed to the President of the International Court of Justice and copied to the Secretary-General, stating the article(s) or paragraph(s) of the article(s) thereof which the latter Member has allegedly breached – providing as well the name of that Member, a description of the nature of the infraction, and the period of time for which it considers the other Member to have been flouting the relevant provision(s). If the President of the International Court of Justice considers that there is a reasonable probability that there has been a violation of the UN Charter, and that the offence continues to be perpetrated, then (s)he shall promptly arrange a trial before a chamber of the International Court of Justice between the relevant Members and inform them and the Secretary-General of the details. The judgment of the International Court of Justice is binding upon the parties to the case.

[645] Fns 5 and 6 and accompanying text, and the sentence immediately following that text.

Chapter XVIII of the UN Charter: Amendments

Due to the difficulty concerning amendments to the UN Charter that is identified in Chapter 6[646], Article 108 of the UN Charter[647] and paragraph 2 of Article 109 of the UN Charter[648] should be modified to remove the veto power of each of the permanent members of the UNSC over the entry into force of such amendments. From both of these provisions, delete the phrase "including all the permanent members of the Security Council". Then, Article 108 of the UN Charter reads thus.

> Amendments to the present Charter shall come into force for all Members of the United Nations when they have been adopted by a vote of two thirds of the members of the General Assembly and ratified in accordance with their respective constitutional processes by two thirds of the Members of the United Nations.

Paragraph 2 of Article 109 of the UN Charter, after amendment, is as follows.

> 2. Any alteration of the present Charter recommended by a two-thirds vote of the conference shall take effect when ratified in accordance with their respective constitutional processes by two thirds of the Members of the United Nations.

Paragraph 1 of Article 7 of the UN Charter

Further to the reference in Chapter 6[649] to the possible need for an organization to draft and publish international instruments – initially without legally-binding effect, establish a Parliament of the United Nations and draft its statute. To found this institution, add the phrase "a Parliament of the United Nations" to paragraph 1 of the Article 7 of the UN Charter[650], which then reads so.

> There are established as principal organs of the United Nations: a General Assembly, a Security Council, a Parliament of the United Nations, an Economic and Social Council, a Trusteeship Council, an International Court of Justice and a Secretariat.

The next section, i.e., that entitled 'Statute of the Parliament of the United Nations,' drafts the Statute of the Parliament of the United Nations – including the initial allotment of seats therein to Member States of the UN.

---

646 Text to fn 539.

647 The penultimate (fourth) sentence of the paragraph headed 'XVIII: Amendments to the UN Charter', in the subsection entitled 'XVIII: Amendments to the UN Charter', in the section titled 'The United Nations' in Chapter 3, lays down Article 108 of the UN Charter.

648 The antepenultimate (third) sentence of the paragraph headed 'XVIII: Amendments to the UN Charter', in the subsection entitled 'XVIII: Amendments to the UN Charter', in the section titled 'The United Nations' in Chapter 3, specifies Article 109(2) of the UN Charter.

649 The relevant text in Chapter 6 comprises the last two sentences of the final paragraph of the subsection entitled 'Does such development in international law indicate a wider trend?', in the section titled 'The Direction of International Law' therein.

650 Sentence immediately-following the text to fn 165.

Statute of the Parliament of the United Nations

Statute of the Parliament of the United Nations

Article 1

The Parliament of the United Nations established by the Charter of the United Nations as the representative governmental organ of the United Nations shall be constituted and shall function in accordance with the provisions of the present Statute.

Chapter I: Organization of the Parliament

Article 2

The Parliament shall be composed of a body of parliamentarians, elected from among persons of high moral character, who possess the qualifications and experience required in their respective Member States of the United Nations, for appointment to the highest legislative offices.

Article 3

The selection of parliamentarians shall be performed by the national authorities of each Member State, in consultation with the Secretariat of the United Nations – who shall be kept up-to-date as to the procedures in place and notified of any proposed changes to them.

Article 4

1. A parliamentary term shall be four years.
2. Parliamentarians may stand for up to three terms in office.

Article 5

1. The Parliament shall have a Speaker and no more than five Deputy Speakers, all of whom shall be appointees from among the senior members of the Secretariat.
2. The total length of office of a Speaker or Deputy Speaker shall not exceed twelve years, including that of a person who has held both levels of office.

Article 6

1. Every Member State shall be represented in the Parliament.
2. No Member State shall have fewer than two seats therein.

Article 7

1. The Parliament shall initially have a total of six hundred and fifty-seven seats.
2. The total number of seats within the Parliament may be amended by a resolution of the General Assembly of the United Nations.

Article 8

The more-populous Member States shall have more representatives in the Parliament than the less-populous Member States. In this matter, a balance is to be struck between the principle of equality of states and the principle of equality of persons.

Article 9

1. In the light of Article 8, and heeding paragraph 2 of Article 6, the recommended method for allocation of seats in the Parliament to representatives of Member States is by logarithmic scale of population therein. Accordingly, Member States shall receive the following allocations of seats to the Parliament.

Population of less than one million people	Two seats
One million people ≤ population < ten million people	Three seats
Ten million people ≤ population < one hundred million people	Four seats
One hundred million people ≤ population < one billion people	Five seats
Population of greater than one billion people	Six seats

2. Based on the method in paragraph 1, Annex I shows the initial allocation of seats in the Parliament to Member States. Annex II lists the Member States that have a specified number of seats therein. These allotments of seats may be adjusted by a resolution of the General Assembly.

Chapter II: Competence of the Parliament

Article 10

1. The Parliament shall be empowered to issue non-binding international instruments, which shall include standards, principles, guidelines and recommendations.

2. The United Nations reserves the right, in accordance with the wishes of the majority of its Member States, to authorize the Parliament to issue binding legislative instruments over agreed areas of international law. Member States shall be required to implement all such measures over their territories. The specific subject areas over which binding legislative instruments may be issued shall be subject to a regular process of review.

Article 11

The subject areas over which the Parliament is empowered to publish international instruments shall include, but not be limited to, the following: [To be decided].

Chapter III: Procedure

[To be decided]

Table 7.1. Annex I to the Statute of the Parliament of the United Nations

Name of the UN Member State	Population [724, 725]	Number of seats
Afghanistan	42,647,492	4
Albania	2,791,765	3
Algeria	46,814,308	4
Andorra	81,938	2
Angola	37,885,849	4
Antigua and Barbuda	93,772	2
Argentina	45,696,159	4
Armenia	2,973,840	3
Australia	26,713,205	4
Austria	9,120,813	3
Azerbaijan	10,336,577	4
the Bahamas	401,283	2
Bahrain	1,607,049	3
Bangladesh	174,458,352	5
Barbados	282,467	2
Belarus	9,056,696	3
Belgium	11,738,763	4
Belize	417,072	2
Benin	14,462,724	4
Bhutan	791,524	2
Bolivia	12,413,315	4
Bosnia and Herzegovina	3,164,253	3
Botswana	2,521,139	3
Brazil	212,342,620	5
Brunei Darussalam	462,721	2
Bulgaria	6,757,689	3
Burkina Faso	23,548,781	4
Burundi	14,047,786	4
Cabo Verde	524,877	2
Cambodia	17,638,801	4
Cameroon	29,123,744	4
Canada	39,742,430	4
Central African Republic	5,330,690	3
Chad	20,299,123	4
Chile	19,764,771	4
China	1,417,955,444	6
Colombia	52,886,363	4
Comoros	866,268	2
Congo	6,332,961	3
Costa Rica	5,129,910	3
Côte d'Ivoire	31,934,230	4
Croatia	3,875,325	3
Cuba	10,979,783	4
Cyprus	1,358,282	3
the Czech Republic (Czechia)	10,735,859	4
the Democratic People's Republic of Korea	26,498,823	4
the Democratic Republic of the Congo	110,767,444	5
Denmark	5,977,412	3
Djibouti	1,168,722	3
Dominica	66,205	2
the Dominican Republic	11,427,557	4
Ecuador	18,135,478	4

Name of the UN Member State	Population [724, 725]	Number of seats
Egypt	117,308,325	5
El Salvador	6,338,193	3
Equatorial Guinea	1,892,516	3
Eritrea	3,535,603	3
Estonia	1,360,546	3
Eswatini	1,242,822	3
Ethiopia	133,493,294	5
Fiji	928,784	2
Finland	5,617,310	3
France	66,548,530	4
Gabon	2,538,952	3
the Gambia	2,759,988	3
Georgia	3,807,670	3
Germany	84,349,963	4
Ghana	34,427,414	4
Greece	10,047,817	4
Grenada	117,207	2
Guatemala	18,406,359	4
Guinea	14,754,785	4
Guinea-Bissau	2,201,352	3
Guyana	831,087	2
Haiti	11,772,557	4
Honduras	10,825,703	4
Hungary	9,676,135	3
Iceland	393,396	2
India	1,456,393,814	6
Indonesia	284,430,961	5
Iran	91,926,496	4
Iraq	46,042,015	4
Ireland	5,255,017	3
Israel	9,387,021	3
Italy	59,342,867	4
Jamaica	2,839,175	3
Japan	123,477,716	5
Jordan	11,552,876	4
Kazakhstan	20,592,571	4
Kenya	56,432,944	4
Kiribati	134,518	2
Kuwait	4,934,507	3
Kyrgyzstan	7,186,009	3
Laos	7,769,819	3
Latvia	1,871,871	3
Lebanon	5,805,962	3
Lesotho	2,337,423	3
Liberia	5,612,817	3
Libya	7,381,023	3
Liechtenstein	39,870	2
Lithuania	2,859,110	3
Luxembourg	673,036	2
Madagascar	31,964,956	4
Malawi	21,655,286	4
Malaysia	35,557,673	4
the Maldives	527,799	2
Mali	24,478,595	4
Malta	539,607	2

Table 7.1. (Continued)

Name of the UN Member State	Population [724, 725]	Number of seats
The Marshall Islands	37,548	2
Mauritania	5,169,395	3
Mauritius	1,271,169	3
Mexico	131,319,483	5
Micronesia	526,923	2
Moldova	3,034,961	3
Monaco	38,631	2
Mongolia	3,475,540	3
Montenegro	638,479	2
Morocco	38,081,173	4
Mozambique	34,631,766	4
Myanmar	54,500,091	4
Namibia	3,030,131	3
Nauru	11,947	2
Nepal	29,651,054	4
the Netherlands	18,228,742	4
New Zealand	5,213,944	3
Nicaragua	6,916,140	3
Niger	27,032,412	4
Nigeria	234,719,163	5
North Macedonia	1,823,009	3
Norway	5,576,660	3
Oman	5,281,538	3
Pakistan	252,933,513	5
Palau	17,695	2
Palestine[651]	5,495,443	3
Panama	4,515,577	3
Papua New Guinea	10,576,502	4
Paraguay	6,929,153	3
Peru	34,217,848	4
the Philippines	116,241,958	5
Poland	38,539,201	4
Portugal	10,425,292	4
Qatar	3,048,423	3
the Republic of Korea	51,717,590	4
Romania	19,015,088	4
Russia	144,471,529	5
Rwanda	14,256,567	4
Saint Kitts and Nevis	46,843	2
Saint Lucia	179,744	2
Saint Vincent and the Grenadines	100,616	2
Samoa	218,019	2
San Marino	33,581	2
São Tomé and Príncipe	235,536	2
Saudia Arabia	33,962,757	4
Senegal	18,501,984	4

[651] The website of the UN notes: "Palestine is a "Permanent Observer State" at the UN, enjoying the status that allows it to participate in all of the Organization's proceedings, except for voting on draft resolutions and decisions in its main organs and bodies …" (United Nations (2024), "UN News: Global perspective Human stories – Palestine's status at the UN explained," published April 18, 2024, accessed December 1, 2024, <https://news.un.org/en/story/2024/04/1148351>). It is submitted that Palestine – officially the State of Palestine – should be included in states entitled to contribute to, and hold seats at, the Parliament of the United Nations.

Name of the UN Member State	Population [724, 725]	Number of seats
Serbia	6,736,216	3
the Seychelles	130,418	2
Sierra Leone	8,642,022	3
Singapore	5,832,387	3
Slovakia	5,506,760	3
Slovenia	2,118,697	3
the Solomon Islands	819,198	2
Somalia	19,009,151	4
South Africa	64,007,187	4
South Sudan	11,943,408	4
Spain	47,910,526	4
Sri Lanka	23,103,565	4
Sudan	50,448,963	4
Suriname	634,431	2
Sweden	10,606,999	4
Switzerland	8,921,981	3
Syria	24,672,760	4
Tajikistan	10,590,927	4
Tanzania	68,560,157	4
Thailand	71,647,630	4
Timor-Leste	1,400,638	3
Togo	9,515,236	3
Tonga	104,175	2
Trinidad and Tobago	1,507,782	3
Tunisia	12,277,109	4
Türkiye	87,563,306	4
Turkmenistan	7,494,498	3
Tuvalu	9,646	2
Uganda	50,015,092	4
the UK	69,138,192	4
Ukraine	37,860,221	4
the United Arab Emirates	11,027,129	4
Uruguay	3,386,588	3
the USA	346,207,988	5
Uzbekistan	36,361,859	4
Vanuatu	327,777	2
Venezuela	28,405,543	4
Vietnam	101,245,759	5
Yemen	40,583,164	4
Zambia	21,314,956	4
Zimbabwe	16,634,373	4
Total		657

Table 7.2. Annex II to the Statute of the Parliament of the United Nations

Number of seats	2	3	4	5	6
Member State	Andorra	Albania	Afghanistan	Bangladesh	China
	Antigua and Barbuda	Armenia	Algeria	Brazil	India
	the Bahamas	Austria	Angola	the Democratic Republic of the Congo	
	Barbados	Bahrain	Argentina	Egypt	
	Belize	Belarus	Australia	Ethiopia	

Table 7.2. (Continued)

Number of seats	2	3	4	5	6
	Bhutan	Bosnia and Herzegovina	Azerbaijan	Indonesia	
	Brunei Darussalam	Botswana	Belgium	Japan	
	Cabo Verde	Bulgaria	Benin	Mexico	
	Comoros	Central African Republic	Bolivia	Nigeria	
	Dominica	Congo	Burkina Faso	Pakistan	
	Fiji	Costa Rica	Burundi	the Philippines	
	Grenada	Croatia	Cambodia	Russia	
	Guyana	Cyprus	Cameroon	the USA	
	Iceland	Denmark	Canada	Vietnam	
	Kiribati	Djibouti	Chad		
	Liechtenstein	El Salvador	Chile		
	Luxembourg	Equatorial Guinea	Colombia		
	the Maldives	Eritrea	Côte d'Ivoire		
	Malta	Estonia	Cuba		
	the Marshall Islands	Eswatini	the Czech Republic (Czechia)		
	Micronesia	Finland	the Democratic People's Republic of Korea		
	Monaco	Gabon	the Dominican Republic		
	Montenegro	the Gambia	Ecuador		
	Nauru	Georgia	France		
	Palau	Guinea-Bissau	Germany		
	Saint Kitts and Nevis	Hungary	Ghana		
	Saint Lucia	Ireland	Greece		
	Saint Vincent and the Grenadines	Israel	Guatemala		
	Samoa	Jamaica	Guinea		
	San Marino	Kuwait	Haiti		
	São Tomé and Príncipe	Kyrgyzstan	Honduras		
	the Seychelles	Laos	Iran		
	the Solomon Islands	Latvia	Iraq		
	Suriname	Lebanon	Italy		
	Tonga	Lesotho	Jordan		
	Tuvalu	Liberia	Kazakhstan		
	Vanuatu	Libya	Kenya		
		Lithuania	Madagascar		
		Mauritania	Malawi		
		Mauritius	Malaysia		
		Moldova	Mali		
		Mongolia	Morocco		
		Namibia	Mozambique		
		New Zealand	Myanmar		
		Nicaragua	Nepal		
		North Macedonia	the Netherlands		
		Norway	Niger		

Number of seats	2	3	4	5	6
		Oman	Papua New Guinea		
		Palestine[652]	Peru		
		Panama	Poland		
		Paraguay	Portugal		
		Qatar	the Republic of Korea		
		Serbia	Romania		
		Sierre Leone	Rwanda		
		Singapore	Saudi Arabia		
		Slovakia	Senegal		
		Slovenia	Somalia		
		Switzerland	South Africa		
		Timor-Leste	South Sudan		
		Togo	Spain		
		Trinidad and Tobago	Sri Lanka		
		Turkmenistan	Sudan		
		Uruguay	Sweden		
			Syria		
			Tajikistan		
			Tanzania		
			Thailand		
			Tunisia		
			Türkiye		
			Uganda		
			the UK		
			Ukraine		
			the United Arab Emirates		
			Uzbekistan		
			Venezuela		
			Yemen		
			Zambia		
			Zimbabwe		

Amendments to the Statute of the ICJ

Article 36 of the Statute of the ICJ

Add the following paragraph is to Article 36 of the Statute of the ICJ, in accordance with the recommendation made in Chapter 6[653].

> 7. All states parties to the present Statute are encouraged to make a declaration under paragraph 2 of the current article. In this declaration, it is recommended that states parties specify the procedure or procedures for binding dispute settlement to which disputes arising within those areas of international law that they exclude – if any – from the compulsory jurisdiction of the Court[654], are to be submitted.

---

[652] Fn 651.
[653] Sentence immediately following the text to fn 573.
[654] In this sentence, 'the Court' is the ICJ – this terminology for it being that used throughout the Statute of the ICJ.

Article 38 of the Statute of the ICJ

Delete paragraph 2 of Article 38 of the Statute of the ICJ, in line with the suggestion proposed in Chapter 6[655]. Reclassify paragraph 1 of Article 38 of the Statute of the ICJ as Article 38 of the Statute of the ICJ.

Article 59 of the Statute of the ICJ

Reclassify Article 59 of the Statute of the ICJ as paragraph 1 of Article 59 of the Statute of the ICJ. Add the following new paragraph 2 to Article 59 of the Statute of the ICJ, in fulfilment of the advice given in Chapter 6[656].

> 2. Notwithstanding paragraph 1 of the current article, the reasons for the decisions that the Court[657], and the Permanent Court of International Justice, have taken, may be considered to be persuasive – and should be consulted – by judges, in instances in which these relate to cases with similar facts.

Amendment to the Draft Conclusions of the ILC

In the light of the argument put forth in the subsection entitled 'Introduction,' in the section titled 'Secondary Sources' in Chapter 4, delete the first sentence of the first paragraph of draft conclusion 6 on subsidiary means for the determination of rules of international law, i.e., "1. Subsidiary means are not a source of international law" [674], and replace it with the following statement.

> 1. Subsidiary means are a secondary source of international law. …

Conclusion

This chapter sets out the author's suggested changes to the UN and to international law. The next chapter lays down concluding thoughts.

---

655 Text to fn 574.
656 Text to fn 579.
657 Fn 654.

Chapter 8

Conclusion

Abstract

Sienese painter Ambrogio Lorenzetti captures well the contrast in his murals named *Effects of Good Government in the City* and *Effects of Bad Government in the City*. Good government seems to be a rare experience. St. Augustine, Bishop of Hippo – now Annaba, Algeria – from 395 to 430, was a strong, effective leader. He demonstrated the following qualities in attending to his episcopal obligations: faith, competence, diligence, commitment, objectivity, awareness, a sense of responsibility, humility and courtesy. There would be plenty of demand for St. Augustine in the senior ranks of the international legal system, if he were here today. Thus, it is possible for this structure to work well, having incorporated into it changes such as those suggested in the present book, if it were populated with individuals who displayed leadership qualities and management capabilities that resemble those of St. Augustine. There are various matters of territorial status which have not yet been satisfactorily addressed. It is important that everyone in the world is represented at the UN. It is arguable that, for a minority of populations, this is not currently so. The ILC has ten topics on its long-term programme of work. Two of these – compensation for the damage caused by internationally wrongful acts and due diligence in international law – were added recently. Table 8.1 lists the cases pending before the ICJ. These include an application by Armenia against Azerbaijan, and one by Azerbaijan against Armenia, which allege that the defendant state is in breach of the International Convention on the Elimination of All Forms of Racial Discrimination – both of which the Court has found it has jurisdiction to determine. The two pending cases before the ITLOS are *The M/T "Heroic Idun" (No. 2) Case (Marshall Islands/Equatorial Guinea)* and *The "Zheng He" Case (Luxembourg v. Mexico)*. It is good to see that states are continuing to entrust settlement of their disputes to official methods of binding dispute resolution. This book is true to its title. The problem of the wrongful exercise of the veto at the UNSC is identified, and, rather than addressing this matter in the narrow sense, the monograph looks to discover the need for broader changes to the legal framework. It proceeds by following the institutional development of international law, from the First World War through the Second World War and the establishment of the UN, to the work of the ILC on sources of this law up until the present time. Comments are made throughout as to provisions and approaches that are non-optimal, and recommendations are proposed as to how these might be improved. The monograph's climax is its Chapter 7, in which changes to the main instruments of the international order are proposed.

Keywords: Augustine, government, international, law, responsibility, state, UN

Introduction

If you have bought from a bookstore, or loaned from a library, a copy of my monograph entitled '*Achieving the Sustainable Development Goals Punctually: An Impossible Remit?*'[658], then you would have observed on its front cover a beautiful, ordered scene – a photograph taken from Cortona in central Italy over rooftops of this town and across adjacent fields. That holiday included a visit to the *Palazzo Pubblico* in Siena, which presented in the *Museo Civico* – located in the *Palazzo* – a series of frescoes of the Sienese painter Ambrogio Lorenzetti titled *Allegory and Effects of Good and Bad Government*[659] [726]. The most memorable of these was the mural called *Effects of Good Government in the City*, which shows neat, smart buildings, with people quietly going about their business in an ordered way in the foreground [727] – in contrast to the nearby painting known as *Effects of Bad Government in the City*.

What one would give to be treated to an experience of good government! It seems to be a rare blessing at all levels of authority, in different places, and during various times.

Good Government: St. Augustine of Hippo

St. Augustine of Hippo (354-430) had the reputation of being an exemplary bishop of the early Latin Church (395-430) [728]. Pope Benedict XVI summarizes St. Augustine's work as Bishop of Hippo, thus.

> [H]e preached several times a week to his faithful, supported the poor and orphans, supervised the formation of the clergy and the organization of mens' and womens' monasteries. ... He was very active in the government of his Diocese – with remarkable, even civil, implications -in the more than 35 years of his Episcopate, and the Bishop of Hippo actually exercised a vast influence in his guidance of the Catholic Church in Roman Africa and, more generally, in the Christianity of his time, coping with religious tendencies and tenacious, disruptive heresies such as Manichaeism, Donatism and Pelagianism, which endangered the Christian faith in the one God, rich in mercy [728].

What made St. Augustine such a strong, effective leader? It was his faith, as the following excerpts from Book VII of his most-famous work *The Confessions of St. Augustine*[660] make clear.

> O Truth Who are Eternity! And Love Who art Truth! And Eternity who art Love! Thou art my God, to Thee do I sigh night and day. Thee when I first knew, Thou liftedst me up, that

---

[658] Baber, G. (2020), *Achieving the Sustainable Development Goals Punctually: An Impossible Remit?* (Newcastle-upon-Tyne: Cambridge Scholars Publishing).

[659] Ambrogio Lorenzetti (*c.*1285-*c.*1348) painted these wall decorations between 1337 and 1339 in the *Sala della Pace* in the *Palazzo Pubblico* in Siena (Encyclopaedia Britannica (1998), "Ambrogio Lorenzetti," published July 20, 1998, last updated March 22, 2024, accessed December 7, 2024, <https://www.britannica.com/biography/Ambrogio-Lorenzetti>). These frescoes portray the allegory of the government of the 'Nine' lords of Siena (1287-1355) and the possible effect of their rule on the city of Siena and on the nearby countryside (Municipality of Siena Culture and Tourism Directorate (2024), "visitsiena: Civic Museum of Siena," accessed December 7, 2024, <https://visitsienaofficial.it/en/civic-museum-of-siena/>).

[660] Fn 665.

> I might see there was what I might see, and that I was not yet such as to see. And Thou didst beat back the weakness of my sight, streaming forth Thy beams of light upon me most strongly, and I trembled with love and awe: and I perceived myself to be far off from Thee, in the region of unlikeness, as if I heard this voice from on high: "I am the food of grown men, grow, and thou shalt feed upon Me; nor shalt thou convert Me, like the food of thy flesh into thee, but thou shalt be converted into Me." [729].
> Then I sought a way of obtaining strength sufficient to enjoy Thee; and found it not, until I embraced that Mediator betwixt God and men, the Man Christ Jesus, who is over all, God blessed for evermore, calling unto me, and saying, I am the way, the truth, and the life, and mingling that food which I was unable to receive, with our flesh. For, the Word was made flesh, that Thy wisdom, whereby Thou createdst all things, might provide milk for our infant state [730].

How did St. Augustine go about his duties? Pope Benedict mentions his commitment to preaching and episcopal practical work[661]. He also makes the following observations.

> Augustine is also the Father of the Church who left the greatest number of works. Possidius, his biographer, said it seemed impossible that one man could have written so many things in his lifetime [728].

This is the type of remark that one might make about Johann Sebastian Bach[662], and his contemporary, Georg Philipp Telemann[663]. These composers were competent, diligent and committed[664]. The same could be said of St. Augustine – albeit in a different field, in a different place, and at a different time.

St. Augustine's renowned Sermon 340 gives further clues as to the qualities that he brought to the role of Bishop of Hippo. First, there is the separation of his faith from his duty, which enabled him to distinguish personal objectives from professional ones, In other words, helped by his belief, St. Augustine strove for objectivity in undertaking his episcopate.

---

[661] First quoted passage in the current section, i.e., that entitled 'Good government: St. Augustine of Hippo'.

[662] The Bach museum in Leipzig comments: "No sooner had Bach arrived in Leipzig than he threw himself wholeheartedly into composing church music. In a mere few years, he managed to create up to five annual cycles of church cantatas, about 60 compositions per year. In addition, he wrote such works as the Magnificat, the Ascension Oratorio, the St. John Passion and the St. Matthew Passion" (Rucker, H., and Wiese, K. (2024), Clear the Stage for J.S. Bach – Act 1: Church Music in Praise of God (Leipzig: Bach-Museum Leipzig), 1).

[663] Encyclopaedia Britannica writes: "Telemann's printed compositions number more than 50 opuses, among them (counting each as one item) the famous collection *Musique de table* (published in 1733; containing three orchestral suites, three concerti, three quartets, three trios, and three sonatas); the first music periodical, *Der getreue Music-Meister* 1728-29; containing 70 compositions); *Der harmonische Gottesdienst* (1725-26; 72 church cantatas); and 36 fantasias for harpsichord. ... Apart from being a prolific composer, he was also a keen writer; his two autobiographies of 1718 and 1739 are comparatively well documented. He published a long poem after his first wife's death, and many words in his vocal compositions came from his own pen. Especially noteworthy are Telemann's many prefaces to collections of his music, which contain a great amount of practical advice on how his compositions (as well as those of his contemporaries) should be performed." (Bergmann, W. (1998), "Georg Philipp Telemann," published July 20, 1998, last updated June 22, 2024, accessed December 8, 2024, <https://www.britannica.com/biography/Georg-Philipp-Telemann>; emphasis original).

[664] For instance, the Bach museum in Leipzig notes: "The Leipzig chorale cantata cycle was unparalleled in its consistency, as Bach meticulously executed an objective he had outlined back in 1708 in a letter to the town council of Mülhausen – to carry out the "ultimate goal, namely a well-regulated church music to the Glory of God and in conformance with your [the parishioners'] wishes."" (Rucker, H., and Wiese, K. (2024), Clear the Stage for J.S. Bach – Act 1: Church Music in Praise of God (Leipzig: Bach-Museum Leipzig), 4).

> For you I am a bishop, with you, after all, I am a Christian. The first is the name of an office undertaken, the second a name of grace; that one means danger, this one salvation [731].

He was aware of what the role of a bishop entailed in his day, and had a sense of responsibility towards performing it.

> The turbulent have to be corrected, the faint-hearted cheered up, the weak supported; the gospel's opponents need to be refuted, its insidious enemies guarded against; the unlearned need to be taught, the indolent stirred up, the argumentative checked; the proud must be put in their place, the desperate set on their feet, those engaged in quarrels reconciled; the needy have to be helped, the oppressed to be liberated, the good to be given your backing, the bad to be tolerated; all must be loved [732].

He was humble and courteous in asking for the help of lay members of his diocese to carry out the abovementioned tasks.

> In all the vast and varied activity involved in fulfilling such manifold responsibilities, please give me your help by both your prayers and your obedience. In this way[,] I will find pleasure not so much in being in charge of you as in being of use to you [732].

Good Government: Applying the Augustinian Method

In essence, then, St. Augustine demonstrated the following qualities in addressing his episcopal obligations: faith, competence, diligence, commitment, objectivity, awareness, a sense of responsibility, humility and courtesy. If the model for the international legal framework that the previous chapters of this monograph, taken together, develop, is accepted, then how could these attributes be applied to its establishment, implementation, maintenance and progression? The ensuing subsections contain a few statements thereon, according to the contributor's role.

Heads and Senior Members of the National Governments of States

Step forward President, Prime Minister or Foreign Minister Augustinus Aurelius[665], in office in 2025. Mr. Aurelius would be proud of his territory and its heritage, and would want to do his best to effectively and fairly serve his people in a constructive, peaceable way. With this in mind, and realizing the huge responsibility of the job – to which he was dedicated, he would politely co-opt their participation in helping his state to work effectively.

---

[665] Augustinus Aurelius (style: 'Graeme Baber'), or Aurelius Augustinus (style: 'Baber Graeme'), is a secular, non-canonized alternative designation to St. Augustine of Hippo – not to be confused with the name of Roman emperor Marcus Aurelius – which is appropriate for referring to St. Augustine in the present subsection (i.e., that titled 'Heads and senior members of the governments of states') and the next two (i.e., those entitled 'Officials of the UN' and 'International judges, advocates and scholars', below in the current section, i.e., that titled 'Good government: applying the Augustinian method'), as well as for referencing St. Augustine's book entitled '*The Confessions of St. Augustine*'.

Mr. Aurelius would wish to avoid – although not evade – situations in which his state was engaged in territorial disputes with neighbouring countries, and, with this in mind, would support an integrated international framework. He would not wish to omit to sign or ratify a multilateral convention, unless he understood its content – or part of this – to be substantially at variance with the interests of his state. He would also wish to refrain from appending reservations to it, other than in an exceptional case in which one or more provisions of the treaty compromised the position of his country. He would prefer his state to abide by all the provisions of the multilateral conventions to which it was a party.

Mr. Aurelius would not want his country to be trading with those states who were contravening international law – especially any peremptory norm of general international law (*jus cogens*), until and unless these infractions ceased. Under no circumstances would he advocate support of such nations. He would tend to be in favour of voting for measures at the UN that required or requested these countries to terminate their violations.

Officials of the UN

Step forward Secretary-General, Deputy Secretary-General, Under Secretary-General or Assistant Secretary-General Augustus Aurelius, in office in 2025. Mr. Aurelius would wish to see the UN work as well as possible. Therefore, he would back any proposed measures which freed up the operation of the UNSC[666] or discouraged breaches of the UN Charter[667]. He would also want to support the creation and functioning of any appropriate new structures, such as the Parliament of the United Nations proposed in Chapter 7[668], and to try to ensure that these were launched effectively and smoothly.

International Judges, Advocates and Scholars

Step forward Judge Aurelius, Augustinus Aurelius KC, or Dr. Aurelius. He would wish to see the international legal framework, and the operation of the ICJ in particular, be optimal and efficient, and would apply himself to his duties as consciencious1y as possible with a view to contributing to such a result.

---

[666] The subsection titled 'Article 27 of the UN Charter', in the section entitled 'Amendments to the UN Charter' in Chapter 7, sets out modifications to Article 27 of the UN Charter that would have this effect.

[667] The subsection titled 'Article 94 of the UN Charter', in the section entitled 'Amendments to the UN Charter' in Chapter 7, introduces a new paragraph 3 to Article 94 of the UN Charter that lays down a summary procedure for binding dispute resolution, which may be initiated in the face of evidence of continuing transgression by a UN Member State of one or more provisions of the Charter.

[668] The subsection titled 'Paragraph 1 of Article 7 of the UN Charter', in the section entitled 'Amendments to the UN Charter' in Chapter 7, amends Article 7(1) of the UN Charter to establish a Parliament of the United Nations as a principal organ of the UN. The section titled 'Statute of the Parliament of the United Nations', in Chapter 7, drafts the Statute of the Parliament of the United Nations.

Comment

There would be plenty of demand for St. Augustine in the senior ranks of the international legal system, if he were here today. The Church would not need him nearly so much. It is possible for this structure to work well, having incorporating into it changes such as those suggested in the present book, if it were populated with individuals who displayed leadership qualities and management capabilities that resemble those of St. Augustine.

The Future: What Issues Are Still to Be Addressed?

Introduction

There are various matters of territorial status that have not yet been satisfactorily addressed, which include – but are not limited to – those of Hong Kong, Taiwan, Western Sahara, and the Paracel and Spratly Islands in the South China Sea. There is scope for the UN's list of 193 Member States to rise further, which would affect, among other things, the number and allocation of seats in the proposed Parliament of the United Nations[669].

It is important that everyone in the world is represented at the UN and in its funds and programmes[670], specialized agencies[671] and regional commissions[672]. It is arguable that, for a minority of populations, this is not currently so. It may be helpful to set out the future work lists of the ILC, the ICJ and the ITLOS. A subsection is devoted to each of these.

The ILC

The following topics are on the ILC's long-term programme of work, from the earliest-added to the most recent: (i) ownership and protection of wrecks beyond the limits of national maritime jurisdiction, (ii) jurisdictional immunity of international organizations, (iii) protection of personal data in transborder flow of information, (iv) extraterritorial jurisdiction, (v) the fair and equitable treatment standard in international investment law, (vi) evidence before international courts and tribunals, (vii) universal criminal jurisdiction, (viii) reparation to individuals for gross violations of international human rights law and serious violations of international humanitarian law, (ix) compensation for the damage caused by international wrongful acts, and (x) due diligence in international law [733]. Subjects (ix) and (x) were added recently – in 2024 [733]. Therefore, each of these merits a description.

It is argued that topic (ix) fits the ILC's programme of work, because it would enable the Commission to address compensation in general and sufficiently-detailed terms to mirror its significance in the law of state responsibility [734]. This theme mainly focuses on Article 36 of the Articles on Responsibility of States for Internationally Wrongful Acts [735]. That article is headed 'Compensation,' and reads thus.

---

[669] Fn 668.
[670] See *The United Nations System* (fn 122) at pages 21-25.
[671] See *The United Nations System* at pages 25-33.
[672] See *The United Nations System* at pages 33-36.

1. The State responsible for an internationally wrongful act is under an obligation to compensate for the damage caused thereby, insofar as such damage is not made good by restitution.
2. The compensation shall cover any financially assessable damage[,] including loss of profits insofar as it is established [736].

Topic (x) comprises an obligation or standard of care to be applied to a state's actions on its territory or to activities that are subject to its control or jurisdiction, which harm the rights and interests of other countries [737]. The duty of due diligence is situated at the link between the sovereign right of states to act within their territory and their responsibility as members of the global community [738]. While previous work of the ILC has attended to the obligation of due diligence, it has not comprehensively dealt with this duty as a stand-alone responsibility with broader application than interstate environmental damage [739]. Theme (x) will examine matters that are connected with the duty of due diligence, including whether there are conditions under which due diligence emerges that are specific to the due diligence standard of care, the extent of the relevant state's control over the sources of impairment, the degree and nature of the variability of the standard of behaviour – and the extent of vigilance or care – that the obligation of due diligence requires, whether there is a minimum level of risk of, and seriousness of, injury, which is necessary for the duty of due diligence to be activated – and questions concerning the pertinent knowledge that is required and foreseeability of the possibility of harm, and the reasonableness of the standard of conduct regarding the activities of a state or of non-state participants who are subject to that country's control or jurisdiction [740].

The ICJ

It is notable that Armenia and Azerbaijan have both filed applications against each other for alleged contravention of the International Convention on the Elimination of All Forms of Racial Discrimination. The ICJ rejected both of the preliminary objections raised by Azerbaijan and one of the three preliminary objections introduced by Armenia, and found that, subject to the two preliminary objections of Armenia which it upheld, it had jurisdiction to entertain these applications on the basis of Article 22 of the Convention[673] [742, 743].

[673] This provision reads as follows: "Any dispute between two or more States Parties with respect to the interpretation or application of this Convention, which is not settled by negotiation or by the procedures expressly provided for in this Convention, shall, at the request of any of the parties to the dispute, be referred to the International Court of Justice, for decision, unless the disputants agree to another mode of settlement." (United Nations (1966), "International Convention on the Elimination of All Forms of Racial Discrimination," *United Nations Treaty Series* Registration Number 9464, Article 22).

Table 8.1. Cases pending before the ICJ on 10th December 2024 [741]

Cases currently being heard or under deliberation	
1	Land and Maritime Delimitation and Sovereignty over Islands (Gabon/Equitorial Guinea)
2	Obligation of States in respect of Climate Change
Pending cases	
1	Gabčíkovo-Nagymaros Project (Hungary/Slovakia)
2	Certain Iranian Assets (Iran v. USA)
3	Arbitral Award of 3 October 1899 (Guyana v. Venezuela)
4	Alleged Violations of the 1955 Treaty of Amity, Economic Relations, and Consular Rights (Iran v. USA)
5	Relocation of the United States Embassy to Jerusalem (Palestine v. USA)
6	Guatemala's Territorial, Insular and Maritime Claim (Guatemala/Belize)
7	Application of the Convention on the Prevention and Punishment of the Crime of Genocide (The Gambia v. Myanmar: 7 States intervening)
8	Application of the International Convention on the Elimination of All Forms of Racial Discrimination (Armenia v. Azerbaijan)
9	Application of the International Convention on the Elimination of All Forms of Racial Discrimination (Azerbaijan v. Armenia)
10	Application of the Convention on the Prevention and Punishment of the Crime of Genocide (Ukraine v. Russia)
11	Questions of jurisdictional immunities of the State and measures of constraint against State-owned property (Germany v. Italy)
12	Request relating to the Return of Property Confiscated in Criminal Proceedings (Equatorial Guinea v. France)
13	Sovereignty over the Sapodilla Cayes/Cayos Zapotillos (Belize v. Honduras)
14	Application of the Convention against Torture and Other Cruel, Inhuman or Degrading Treatment or Punishment (Canada and the Netherlands v. Syria)
15	Alleged Violations of State Immunities (Iran v. Canada)
16	Aerial Incident of 8 January 2020 (Canada, Sweden, Ukraine and UK v. Iran)
17	Right to Strike under ILO Convention No. 87
18	Application of the Convention on the Prevention and Punishment of the Crime of Genocide in the Gaza Strip (South Africa v. Israel)
19	Alleged Breaches of Certain International Obligations in respect of the Occupied Palestinian Territory (Nicaragua v. Germany)
20	Embassy of Mexico in Quito (Mexico v. Ecuador)
21	Glas Espinel (Ecuador v. Mexico)

The ITLOS

The two pending cases before the ITLOS are *The M/T "Heroic Idun" (No. 2) Case (Marshall Islands/Equatorial Guinea)* and *The "Zheng He" Case (Luxembourg v. Mexico)* [744]. A paragraph is dedicated to each.

The Marshall Islands instituted arbitral proceedings under Article VII of the UNCLOS against Equatorial Guinea regarding their dispute concerning the *M/T "Heroic Idun"* and her crew, and, subsequently, the parties agreed to transfer the case to a special chamber of the ITLOS [745]. Four Orders have been made to date [746], the last of which authorizes the Marshall Islands to submit a Reply to the Counter-Memorial that Equatorial Guinea presented, by 25th November 2024, and Equatorial Guinea to file a Rejoinder by 24th March 2025, and reserves the subsequent procedure for a future decision [747].

The ITLOS presents the facts of *The "Zheng He" Case (Luxembourg v. Mexico)* in its Press Release dated 4th June 2024.

> [O]n 5 October 2023, the "*Zheng He*"[674] left the port of Freeport, Bahamas, bound for the port of Tampico, Mexico ... . On 23 October 2023, the "*Zheng He*"[675] was given permission to dock at the port of Tampico[,] where it was to remain for refuelling and maintenance and to await further instructions. On 24 October 2023, the Mexican authorities imposed a first customs sanction against the "*Zheng He*"[676]. On 1 November 2023, the vessel was visited by Mexican tax officials and detained on the basis that the vessel was to be considered as a good, whose entry into Mexican territory was to be treated as an import, subjecting the owner of the vessel to the payment of customs duty proportionate to the value of the vessel [748].

On 7th June 2024, Luxembourg submitted a request under paragraph 1 of Article 290 of the UNCLOS[677] to the ITLOS for the latter to prescribe specified provisional measures [749]. After the hearing on 11th and 12th July 2024[678] [750], the ITLOS issued an Order which found that the circumstances did not require it to exercise its authority to set down provisional measures under that paragraph [751]. On 8th August 2024, the President of the ITLOS furnished an Order, which fixed time limits of 10th February 2025 for Luxembourg to file its Memorial and 11th August 2025 for Mexico to submit its Counter-Memorial, and which reserved the subsequent procedure for a succeeding decision [752].

Comment

From the above paragraphs, it appears that normal business is proceeding at the ILC, the ICJ and the ITLOS. It is good to see that states are continuing to entrust determination of their disputes to official methods of binding dispute resolution.

Conclusion

This chapter sets out concluding issues, taking the theme of good government using the excellent forerunner St. Augustine of Hippo, and applying his qualities, as Augustinus Aurelius, to the international legal framework – with an emphasis on its development as proposed in the

---

674 Emphasis added. The "*Zheng He*" is a vessel that flies the flag of Luxembourg (International Tribunal for the Law of the Sea (2024), Press Release 351, 4 June 2024 (Hamburg: International Tribunal for the Law of the Sea).

675 Emphasis added.

676 Emphasis added.

677 This paragraph states: "If a dispute has been duly submitted to a court or tribunal which considers that *prima facie* it has jurisdiction under this Part or Part XI, section 5, [then] the court or tribunal may prescribe any provisional measures which it considers appropriate under the circumstances to preserve the respective rights of the parties to the dispute or to prevent serious harm to the marine environment, pending the final decision." (United Nations (1982), "United Nations Convention on the Law of the Sea," Article 290(1); emphasis original). 'This Part' is Part XV of the UNCLOS, which is entitled 'Settlement of Disputes, and which consists of Articles 279-299. 'Part XI, section 5' is Section 5 of Part XI (titled 'The Area') of the UNCLOS, which is entitled 'Settlement of Disputes and Advisory Opinions', and which contain Articles 186-191.

678 The President of the ITLOS issued an Order on 13th June 2024, which specified these dates for the hearing concerning Luxembourg's request for the prescription of provisional measures, and which reserved the subsequent procedure for a later determination (International Tribunal for the Law of the Sea (2024), *The "Zheng He" Case (Luxembourg v. Mexico)*, Order of 13 June 2024, *List of Cases No. 33 Order 2024/1*).

present monograph. Then, the chapter presents the future work lists of the ILC, the ICJ and the ITLOS.

This book is true to its title *International Law Changes in the Light of the Invasion of Ukraine*. The problem of the wrongful exercise of the veto at the UNSC is identified, and, rather than addressing this matter in the narrow sense, the monograph looks to discover the need for broader changes to the legal framework. The book proceeds by following the institutional development of international law, from the First World War through the Second World War and the establishment of the UN, to the work of the ILC on sources of this law up until the present time. Comments are made throughout as to provisions and approaches that are non-optimal, and recommendations are proposed as to how these might be improved. The monograph's climax is its Chapter 7, in which changes to the main instruments of the international order are put forward. Good day.

About the Author

Graeme Baber, PhD, is a jurist and a legal researcher, specializing in financial law and international law. His previous monographs are *The Impact of Legislation and Regulation on the Freedom of Movement of Capital in Estonia, Poland and Latvia* (2010), *The Free Movement of Capital and Financial Services: An Exposition?* (2014), *The European Union and the Global Financial Crisis: A View from 2016* (2016), *Essays on International Law* (2017), *International Financial Law: Quo Vadis?* (2017), *Preferential Trade Agreements and International Law* (2018), *The United Nations System: A Synopsis* (2019), *The Global Law of the Sea: Baselines and Boundary Delimitation* (2020), *Achieving the Sustainable Development Goals Punctually: An Impossible Remit?* (2020), *The British Judges of the International Court of Justice: An Explication? Overview, McNair and Lauterpacht* (2021), *The British Judges of the International Court of Justice: An Explication? The Later Jurists* (2022), *An Overview of Banking Law in Four English-Language Jurisdictions* (2023), and *An Overview of Corporate Securities Law in Four English-Language Jurisdictions* (2023). Graeme has published many papers. He is also an experienced teacher of university students.

Since 2014, Graeme has written seven monographs, four papers, and a book chapter, which Nova has published. The first of the books is *The European Union and the Global Financial Crisis: A View from 2016*, which compares – in places in which this is possible – the securities and banking legislation after the financial crisis with that preceding it. The second is *International Financial Law: Quo Vadis?*, which describes worldwide instruments set by the Financial Stability Board, the Bank for International Settlements, the Basel Committee for Banking Supervision, the International Organization of Securities Commissions, and the International Monetary Fund – giving views as to the structure and workings of the global financial architecture and as to the progression of this topic in the near and medium-term. The third is *The Global Law of the Sea: Baselines and Boundary Delimitation*. The fourth and fifth, which are Graeme's tenth and eleven monographs, respectively, are *The British Judges of the International Court of Justice: An Explication? Overview, McNair and Lauterpacht* and *The British Judges of the International Court of Justice: An Explication? The Later Jurists*. Pursuant to his earlier research contributing to *The Global Law of the Sea: Baselines and Boundary Delimitation* and a subsequent summary article concerning the life, scholarship and judgments of the eminent Swiss jurist Max Huber, in these two books, he investigates the academic and judicial output of the seven people who served as British members of the International Court of Justice between 1946 and 2018. The sixth and seventh are *An Overview of Banking Law in Four English-Language Jurisdictions*, and *An Overview of Corporate Securities Law in Four English-Language Jurisdictions*, which review legislation over the area of banking law and corporate securities law, respectively, in Australia, Canada, New Zealand and the USA and which offer a common introduction to the law in each of these territories.

References

[1] United Nations (2024). "Member States." Accessed June 8, 2024. https://www.un.org/en/about-us/member-states.

[2] United Nations (1945). "Charter of the United Nations," *United Nations Treaty Series* Registration Number N/A, Article 23, Paragraphs (1) and (3).

[3] Baber, G. (2019). *The United Nations System* (Newcastle-upon-Tyne: Cambridge Scholars Publishing), 8.

[4] United Nations (2024). "Dag Hammarskjöld Library: Ask DAG – Where can I find the letters of 24 December 1991 regarding the continuation of the membership of the USSR by the Russian Federation?" Last updated April 25, 2024. Accessed June 10, 2024. https://ask.un.org/faq/378083.

[5] United Nations (1945). "Charter of the United Nations," Article 27(3).

[6] United Nations (1945). "Charter of the United Nations," Article 33.

[7] United Nations (1945). "Charter of the United Nations," Article 33(1).

[8] United Nations (1945). "Charter of the United Nations," Article 36(1).

[9] United Nations (1945). "Charter of the United Nations," Article 37(2).

[10] United Nations (1945). "Charter of the United Nations," Article 38.

[11] United Nations (1945). "Charter of the United Nations," Article 52(3).

[12] United Nations (1945). "Charter of the United Nations," Article 52(1).

[13] United Nations (1945). "Charter of the United Nations," Article 51.

[14] International Court of Justice (1986). *Case concerning Military and Paramilitary Activities in and against Nicaragua (Nicaragua v. United States of America), The Merits*, Judgment of 27 June 1986, *I.C.J. Reports 1986*, 14-150, 103.

[15] International Court of Justice (1986). *Case concerning Military and Paramilitary Activities in and against Nicaragua (Nicaragua v. United States of America), The Merits*, Judgment of 27 June 1986, *I.C.J. Reports 1986*, 14-150, 104-105.

[16] International Court of Justice (1986). *Case concerning Military and Paramilitary Activities in and against Nicaragua (Nicaragua v. United States of America), The Merits*, Judgment of 27 June 1986, *I.C.J. Reports 1986*, 14-150, 105.

[17] International Court of Justice (1986). *Case concerning Military and Paramilitary Activities in and against Nicaragua (Nicaragua v. United States of America), The Merits*, Judgment of 27 June 1986, *I.C.J. Reports 1986*, 14-150, 94.

[18] United Nations (2022). Resolution ES-11/1 (LXXVI) adopted by the General Assembly on 2nd March 2022, Operative Paragraph 3.

[19] United Nations (2022). Resolution ES-11/2 (LXXVI) adopted by the General Assembly on 24th March 2022, Operative Paragraph 1.

[20] United Nations (2022). Resolution ES-11/2 (LXXVI) adopted by the General Assembly on 24th March 2022, Operative Paragraph 2.

[21] International Court of Justice (2022). *Allegations of Genocide under the Convention on the Prevention and Punishment of the Crime of Genocide (Ukraine v. Russian Federation), Provisional Measures*, Order of 16 March 2002, *I.C.J. Reports 2022*, 211-231, 231.

[22] United Nations (1945). "Charter of the United Nations," Article 94(1).

[23] United Nations (1945). "Statute of the International Court of Justice," *United Nations Treaty Series* Registration Number N/A, Article 59.

[24] United Nations (1948). "Convention on the Prevention and Punishment of the Crime of Genocide," *United Nations Treaty Series* Registration Number 1021, Article 1.

[25] United Nations (1998). "Rome Statute of the International Criminal Court," *United Nations Treaty Series* Registration Number 38544, Article 6.

[26] United Nations (1998). "Rome Statute of the International Criminal Court," Article 7.

[27] United Nations (1998). "Rome Statute of the International Criminal Court," Article 8.

[28] United Nations (1998). "Rome Statute of the International Criminal Court," Article 8 *bis*.

[29] United Nations (2024). "United Nations Treaty Collection: Chapter XVIII Penal Matters – 10. Rome Statute of the International Criminal Court," Last updated June 13, 2024. Accessed June 13, 2024. https://treaties.un.org/Pages/ViewDetails.aspx?src=TREATY&mtdsg_no=XVIII-10&chapter=18 &clang=_en.

[30] Tams, C. (2019). 'Chapter 10 – Peace Through International Adjudication: The Permanent Court of International Justice and the Post-War Order' *in* Erpelding, M., Hess, B., and Ruiz Fabri, H. (eds.) (2019), *Peace Through Law: The Versailles Peace Treaty and Dispute Settlement After World War I*, First edition (Baden-Baden: Nomos Verlagsgesellschaft), 222.

[31] Tams, C. (2019). 'Chapter 10 – Peace Through International Adjudication: The Permanent Court of International Justice and the Post-War Order' *in* Erpelding, M., Hess, B., and Ruiz Fabri, H. (eds.) (2019), *Peace Through Law: The Versailles Peace Treaty and Dispute Settlement After World War I*, First edition, 224.

[32] Tams, C. (2019). 'Chapter 10 – Peace Through International Adjudication: The Permanent Court of International Justice and the Post-War Order' *in* Erpelding, M., Hess, B., and Ruiz Fabri, H. (eds.) (2019), *Peace Through Law: The Versailles Peace Treaty and Dispute Settlement After World War I*, First edition, 224-225.

[33] History.com Staff. (2020). "Outbreak of World War I." Published August 24, 2018. Updated November 10, 2020. Accessed June 24, 2024. https://www.history.com/topics/world-war-i/outbreak-of-world-war-i.

[34] RTÉ (2018). "WWI: Scale and horror of the conflict." Published November 7, 2018. Accessed June 24, 2024. https://www.rte.ie/news/2018/1107/1008936-world-war-one-numbers/.

[35] Mémorial de l'Armistice (2018). "The Armistice of 1918." Accessed June 25, 2024. https://armistice-museum.com/understanding-the-history/the-armistice-of-1918/.

[36] Bell, J., Danforth, L., and Dimitrov, P. (2023). "history of Bulgaria." Published August 30, 2023. Updated April 19, 2024. Accessed June 25, 2024. https://www.britannica.com/topic/history-of-Bulgaria/The-principality.

[37] Encyclopaedia Britannica (1998). "Armistice of Mudros: Turkish history [1918]." Published July 20, 1998. Last updated October 23, 2023. Accessed June 25, 2024. https://www.britannica.com/event/Armistice-of-Mudros.

[38] Imperial War Museums (2024). "The Peace Treaties that Ended The First World War." Accessed June 25, 2024. https://www.iwm.org.uk/history/the-peace-treaties-that-ended-the-first-world-war.

[39] Encyclopaedia Britannica (1998). "Paris Peace Conference 1919-1920." Published July 20, 1998. Last updated April 19, 2024. Accessed June 25, 2024. https://www.britannica.com/event/Paris-Peace-Conference.

[40] Demirci, S. (1997). *The Lausanne Conference: The Evolution of Turkish and British Diplomatic Strategies 1922-1923*. Dissertation for the Degree of Doctor of Philosophy in International History at the London School of Economics and Political Science, March 1997 (Ann Arbor: ProQuest LLC), 2.

[41] Encyclopaedia Britannica (1998). "Treaty of Lausanne: Allies-Turkey [1923]." Published July 20, 1998. Last updated June 7, 2024. Accessed June 25, 2024. https://www.britannica.com/event/Treaty-of-Lausanne-1923.

[42] British Broadcasting Corporation (2024). "Bitesize: Paris Peace Treaties and the League of Nations, to 1933: Terms of the Paris Peace Treaties." Accessed June 25, 2024. https://www.bbc.co.uk/bitesize/guides/zbg4t39/revision/4.

[43] Erpelding, M. (2019). 'Introduction: Versailles and the Broadening of 'Peace Through Law' *in* Erpelding, M., Hess, B., and Ruiz Fabri, H. (eds.) (2019), *Peace Through Law: The Versailles Peace*

Treaty and Dispute Settlement After World War I, First edition (Baden-Baden: Nomos Verlagsgesellschaft), 13.

[44] League of Nations – Official Journal (1920). The Covenant of the League of Nations. *League of Nations – Official Journal*, February 2020, 3-11, 3, Preamble.

[45] Erpelding, M. (2019). 'Introduction: Versailles and the Broadening of 'Peace Through Law' *in* Erpelding, M., Hess, B., and Ruiz Fabri, H. (eds.) (2019), *Peace Through Law: The Versailles Peace Treaty and Dispute Settlement After World War I*, First edition, 12.

[46] Tennessee Virtual Archive (2024). "League to Enforce Peace convention invitation to Governor Rye." Accessed June 26, 2024. https:// teva.contentdm.oclc.org/digital/collection/p15138coll18/id/2590/.

[47] The Nobel Prize (2024). "Woodrow Wilson: Facts." Accessed June 26, 2024. https://www.nobelprize.org/prizes/peace/1919/wilson/facts/.

[48] The Nobel Prize (2024). "Woodrow Wilson: Biographical." Accessed June 27, 2024. https://www.nobelprize.org/prizes/peace/1919/wilson/biographical/.

[49] Wilson, W. (1917). "Peace Without Victory" speech, January 22, 1917. 64th Cong., 23 Sess., Senate Document No. 685: "A League for Peace".

[50] National Archives (2022). "Milestone Documents: President Woodrow Wilson's 14 Points (1918)." Last reviewed February 8, 2022. Accessed June 27, 2024. https://www.archives.gov/milestone-documents/ president-woodrow-wilsons-14-points.

[51] International Criminal Court (ICC) Legal Tools Database (2008). "Covenant of the League of Nations." Published November 10, 2008. Accessed June 28, 2024. https://legal-tools.org/doc/106a5f.

[52] United Nations (2024). "The League of Nations." Accessed June 29, 2024. https://www.ungeneva.org/en/about/league-of-nations/overview.

[53] League of Nations – Official Journal (1920). The Covenant of the League of Nations. *League of Nations – Official Journal*, February 2020, 3-11, 3, Article 1.

[54] League of Nations – Official Journal (1920). The Covenant of the League of Nations. *League of Nations – Official Journal*, February 2020, 3-11, 3, Article 2.

[55] League of Nations – Official Journal (1920). The Covenant of the League of Nations. *League of Nations – Official Journal*, February 2020, 3-11, 3, Article 3.

[56] League of Nations – Official Journal (1920). The Covenant of the League of Nations. *League of Nations – Official Journal*, February 2020, 3-11, 4, Article 4.

[57] League of Nations – Official Journal (1920). The Covenant of the League of Nations. *League of Nations – Official Journal*, February 2020, 3-11, 4, Article 5.

[58] League of Nations – Official Journal (1920). The Covenant of the League of Nations. *League of Nations – Official Journal*, February 2020, 3-11, 4, Article 6.

[59] League of Nations – Official Journal (1920). The Covenant of the League of Nations. *League of Nations – Official Journal*, February 2020, 3-11, 5, Article 7.

[60] League of Nations – Official Journal (1920). The Covenant of the League of Nations. *League of Nations – Official Journal*, February 2020, 3-11, 5, Article 8.

[61] League of Nations – Official Journal (1920). The Covenant of the League of Nations. *League of Nations – Official Journal*, February 2020, 3-11, 5, Article 10.

[62] League of Nations – Official Journal (1920). The Covenant of the League of Nations. *League of Nations – Official Journal*, February 2020, 3-11, 5-6, Article 11.

[63] League of Nations – Official Journal (1920). The Covenant of the League of Nations. *League of Nations – Official Journal*, February 2020, 3-11, 8, Article 18.

[64] League of Nations – Official Journal (1920). The Covenant of the League of Nations. *League of Nations – Official Journal*, February 2020, 3-11, 9-10, Article 22.

[65] League of Nations – Official Journal (1920). The Covenant of the League of Nations. *League of Nations – Official Journal*, February 2020, 3-11, 10, Article 23.

[66] United Nations (2024). "Transition to the United Nations." Accessed July 2, 2024. https://www.ungeneva.org/en/about/league-of-nations/transition.

[67] United Nations (2024). "Predecessor: The League of Nations." Accessed July 2, 2024. https://www.un.org/en/about-us/history-of-the-un/predecessor.

[68] United Nations (2012). United Nations Audiovisual Library of International Law: Statute of the International Court of Justice (New York: United Nations), 1.

[69] Permanent Court of International Justice (1926). Resolution concerning the establishment of a Permanent Court of International Justice passed by the Assembly of the League of Nations, Geneva, December 13th, 1920. Statute of the Court. *P.C.I.J. Series D No.1*, 4.

[70] Permanent Court of International Justice (1926). Protocol of Signature for the Permanent Court of International Justice provided for by Article 14 of the Covenant of the League of Nations. *P.C.I.J. Series D No.1*, 5-6, 5.

[71] International Court of Justice (2024). "History." Accessed July 4, 11 and 12, 2024, and August 9 and 10, 2024. https://www.icj-cij.org/history.

[72] League of Nations – Official Journal (1920). The Covenant of the League of Nations. *League of Nations – Official Journal*, February 2020, 3-11, 5-6, Article 12.

[73] International Criminal Court (ICC) Legal Tools Database (2024). Covenant of the League of Nations, 1919, as amended (The Hague: International Criminal Court), Article 12.

[74] International Criminal Court (ICC) Legal Tools Database (2024). Covenant of the League of Nations, 1919, as amended, Article 13.

[75] International Criminal Court (ICC) Legal Tools Database (2024). Covenant of the League of Nations, 1919, as amended, Article 15.

[76] League of Nations – Official Journal (1920). The Covenant of the League of Nations. *League of Nations – Official Journal*, February 2020, 3-11, 7, Article 15.

[77] League of Nations – Official Journal (1920). The Covenant of the League of Nations. *League of Nations – Official Journal*, February 2020, 3-11, 7, Article 16.

[78] United Nations (2012). United Nations Audiovisual Library of International Law: Statute of the International Court of Justice, 2.

[79] Permanent Court of International Justice (1926). Statute of the Court. *P.C.I.J. Series D No.1*, 7-27, 7-8, Articles 2 and 3.

[80] Permanent Court of International Justice (1926). Statute of the Court. *P.C.I.J. Series D No.1*, 7-27, 8, Article 4.

[81] Permanent Court of International Justice (1926). Statute of the Court. *P.C.I.J. Series D No.1*, 7-27, 11, Article 13.

[82] Permanent Court of International Justice (1926). Statute of the Court. *P.C.I.J. Series D No.1*, 7-27, 11, Article 14.

[83] Permanent Court of International Justice (1926). Statute of the Court. *P.C.I.J. Series D No.1*, 7-27, 11-12, Article 16.

[84] Permanent Court of International Justice (1926). Statute of the Court. *P.C.I.J. Series D No.1*, 7-27, 12, Article 17.

[85] Permanent Court of International Justice (1926). Statute of the Court. *P.C.I.J. Series D No.1*, 7-27, 13, Article 21.

[86] Permanent Court of International Justice (1926). Statute of the Court. *P.C.I.J. Series D No.1*, 7-27, 13, Article 22.

[87] Permanent Court of International Justice (1926). Statute of the Court. *P.C.I.J. Series D No.1*, 7-27, 13-14, Article 24.

[88] Permanent Court of International Justice (1926). Statute of the Court. *P.C.I.J. Series D No.1*, 7-27, 14, Article 25.

[89] Permanent Court of International Justice (1926). Statute of the Court. *P.C.I.J. Series D No.1*, 7-27, 16, Article 29.

[90] Permanent Court of International Justice (1926). Statute of the Court. *P.C.I.J. Series D No.1*, 7-27, 16, Article 30.

[91] Permanent Court of International Justice (1926). Statute of the Court. *P.C.I.J. Series D No.1*, 7-27, 16, Article 31.

[92] Permanent Court of International Justice (1926). Statute of the Court. *P.C.I.J. Series D No.1*, 7-27, 19, Article 36.

[93] Permanent Court of International Justice (1926). Statute of the Court. *P.C.I.J. Series D No.1*, 7-27, 20, Article 36.

[94] Permanent Court of International Justice (1926). Statute of the Court. *P.C.I.J. Series D No.1*, 7-27, 20, Article 38.

[95] Permanent Court of International Justice (1926). Statute of the Court. *P.C.I.J. Series D No.1*, 7-27, 25, Article 59.

[96] Permanent Court of International Justice (1926). Statute of the Court. *P.C.I.J. Series D No.1*, 7-27, 21, Article 39.

[97] Permanent Court of International Justice (1926). Statute of the Court. *P.C.I.J. Series D No.1*, 7-27, 21, Article 40.

[98] Permanent Court of International Justice (1926). Statute of the Court. *P.C.I.J. Series D No.1*, 7-27, 22, Article 41.

[99] Permanent Court of International Justice (1926). Statute of the Court. *P.C.I.J. Series D No.1*, 7-27, 22, Article 43.

[100] Permanent Court of International Justice (1926). Statute of the Court. *P.C.I.J. Series D No.1*, 7-27, 22, Article 45.

[101] Permanent Court of International Justice (1926). Statute of the Court. *P.C.I.J. Series D No.1*, 7-27, 24, Article 50.

[102] Permanent Court of International Justice (1926). Statute of the Court. *P.C.I.J. Series D No.1*, 7-27, 24, Article 51.

[103] Permanent Court of International Justice (1926). Statute of the Court. *P.C.I.J. Series D No.1*, 7-27, 24, Article 53.

[104] Permanent Court of International Justice (1926). Statute of the Court. *P.C.I.J. Series D No.1*, 7-27, 25, Article 55.

[105] Permanent Court of International Justice (1926). Statute of the Court. *P.C.I.J. Series D No.1*, 7-27, 25, Article 56.

[106] Permanent Court of International Justice (1926). Statute of the Court. *P.C.I.J. Series D No.1*, 7-27, 25, Article 57.

[107] Permanent Court of International Justice (1926). Statute of the Court. *P.C.I.J. Series D No.1*, 7-27, 26, Article 60.

[108] Permanent Court of International Justice (1926). Statute of the Court. *P.C.I.J. Series D No.1*, 7-27, 26, Article 61.

[109] Permanent Court of International Justice (1926). Statute of the Court. *P.C.I.J. Series D No.1*, 7-27, 26, Article 62.

[110] Permanent Court of International Justice (1926). Statute of the Court. *P.C.I.J. Series D No.1*, 7-27, 27, Article 63.

[111] CFR Education (2023). "Why Did World War II Happen?" Last updated July 25, 2023. Accessed July 16, 2024. https://education.cfr.org/learn/reading/why-did-world-war-ii-happen.

[112] Government of the United States of America (1944). *Events leading up to World War II: Chronological history of certain major international events leading up to and during World War II with the ostensible reasons advanced for their occurrence, 1931-1944*, 78th Congress, 2nd Session, House Document No. 541 (Washington: United States Government Printing Office), 85, 146-148, 166-167 and 180-181.

[113] Hughes, T., and Royde-Smith, J. (1998). "World War II: 1939-1945." Published August 23, 1998. Last updated July 13, 2024. Accessed July 18, 2024. https://www.britannica.com/event/World-War-II.

[114] Government of the United States of America (1944). *Events leading up to World War II: Chronological history of certain major international events leading up to and during World War II with the ostensible reasons advanced for their occurrence, 1931-1944*, 78th Congress, 2nd Session, House Document No. 541, 210.

[115] Government of the United States of America (1944). *Events leading up to World War II: Chronological history of certain major international events leading up to and during World War II with the ostensible reasons advanced for their occurrence, 1931-1944*, 78th Congress, 2nd Session, House Document No. 541, 204.

[116] Government of the United States of America (1944). *Events leading up to World War II: Chronological history of certain major international events leading up to and during World War II with the ostensible reasons advanced for their occurrence, 1931-1944*, 78th Congress, 2nd Session, House Document No. 541, 211.

[117] Government of the United States of America (1944). *Events leading up to World War II: Chronological history of certain major international events leading up to and during World War II with the ostensible reasons advanced for their occurrence, 1931-1944*, 78th Congress, 2nd Session, House Document No. 541, 212.

[118] Government of the United States of America (1944). *Events leading up to World War II: Chronological history of certain major international events leading up to and during World War II with the ostensible reasons advanced for their occurrence, 1931-1944*, 78th Congress, 2nd Session, House Document No. 541, 213.

[119] Government of the United States of America (1944). *Events leading up to World War II: Chronological history of certain major international events leading up to and during World War II with the ostensible reasons advanced for their occurrence, 1931-1944*, 78th Congress, 2nd Session, House Document No. 541, 214.

[120] Government of the United States of America (1944). *Events leading up to World War II: Chronological history of certain major international events leading up to and during World War II with the ostensible reasons advanced for their occurrence, 1931-1944*, 78th Congress, 2nd Session, House Document No. 541, 215.

[121] Government of the United States of America (1944). *Events leading up to World War II: Chronological history of certain major international events leading up to and during World War II with the ostensible reasons advanced for their occurrence, 1931-1944*, 78th Congress, 2nd Session, House Document No. 541, 216.

[122] Government of the United States of America (1944). *Events leading up to World War II: Chronological history of certain major international events leading up to and during World War II with the ostensible reasons advanced for their occurrence, 1931-1944*, 78th Congress, 2nd Session, House Document No. 541, 256.

[123] Encyclopaedia Britannica (2018). "Tripartite Pact." Published February 27, 2018. Last updated September 20, 2023. Accessed July 18, 2024. https://www.britannica.com/topic/Tripartite-Pact.

[124] Government of the United States of America (1944). *Events leading up to World War II: Chronological history of certain major international events leading up to and during World War II with the ostensible reasons advanced for their occurrence, 1931-1944*, 78th Congress, 2nd Session, House Document No. 541, 307.

[125] Harry S. Truman Presidential Library and Museum (2024). "Invasion of Manchuria." Accessed July 18, 2024. https://www.trumanlibrary.gov/education/presidential-inquiries/invasion-manchuria.

[126] Government of the United States of America (1944). *Events leading up to World War II: Chronological history of certain major international events leading up to and during World War II with the ostensible reasons advanced for their occurrence, 1931-1944*, 78th Congress, 2nd Session, House Document No. 541, 308-309.

[127] Government of the United States of America (1944). *Events leading up to World War II: Chronological history of certain major international events leading up to and during World War II with the ostensible reasons advanced for their occurrence, 1931-1944*, 78th Congress, 2nd Session, House Document No. 541, 309-310.

[128] Government of the United States of America (1944). *Events leading up to World War II: Chronological history of certain major international events leading up to and during World War II with the ostensible reasons advanced for their occurrence, 1931-1944*, 78th Congress, 2nd Session, House Document No. 541, 310-312.

[129] Government of the United States of America (1944). *Events leading up to World War II: Chronological history of certain major international events leading up to and during World War II with the ostensible reasons advanced for their occurrence, 1931-1944*, 78th Congress, 2nd Session, House Document No. 541, 312.

[130] Mullen, M., Onion, A., Sullivan, M., and Zapata, C. (2009). "World War II." Published October 29, 2009. Updated March 13, 2024. Accessed July 18 and 20, 2024. https://www.history.com/topics/world-war-ii/world-war-ii-history.

[131] Chmielewski, K. (2023). "Casualties of World War II." Published August 31, 2023. Updated May 15, 2024. Accessed July 18, 2024. https://www.britannica.com/event/casualties-of-World-War-II-2231003.

[132] The National WWII Museum New Orleans (2024). "Research Starters: Worldwide Deaths in World War II." Accessed July 18, 2024. https://www.nationalww2museum.org/students-teachers/student-resources/research-starters/research-starters-worldwide-deaths-world-war.

[133] Encyclopaedia Britannica (2024). "How many people died during World War II?" Accessed July 18, 2024. https://www.britannica.com/question/How-many-people-died-during-World-War-II.

[134] Keegan, J. (1998). "Normandy Invasion." Published July 20, 1998. Last updated June 8, 2024. Accessed July 19, 2024. https://www.britannica.com/event/Normandy-Invasion.

[135] Encyclopaedia Britannica (2024). "How did World War II end?" Accessed July 19, 2024. https://www.britannica.com/question/How-did-World-War-II-end.

[136] Gouvernement de France (2024). "Chemins de Mémoire: An ordinary red-brick school." Accessed July 19, 2024. https://www.cheminsdememoire.gouv.fr/en/ordinary-red-brick-school-0.

[137] National Archives (2023). "Milestone Documents: Surrender of Germany (1945)." Last reviewed January 10, 2023. Accessed July 19 and 20, 2024. https://www.archives.gov/milestone-documents/surrender-of-germany.

[138] Encyclopaedia Britannica (2021). "Atomic bombings of Hiroshima and Nagasaki." Published May 3, 2021. Last updated June 21, 2024. Accessed July 19, 2024. https://www.britannica.com/event/atomic-bombings-of-Hiroshima-and-Nagasaki.

[139] Lowe, K. (2020). "How and when did WW2 end?" Published September 1, 2020. Accessed July 19, 2024. https://www.historyextra.com/period/second-world-war/how-when-ww2-end-ve-day-vj-day-fighting-atomic-bombs-japan-world-europe/.

[140] The National WWII Museum New Orleans (2024). "The End of World War II 1945." Accessed July 19, 2024. https://www.nationalww2museum.org/war/topics/end-world-war-ii-1945.

[141] Government of the United States of America (2009). "U.S. Department of State Archive: The Potsdam Conference, 1945." Published January 20, 2009. Accessed July 20, 2024. https://2001-2009.state.gov/r/pa/ho/time/wwii/93275.htm.

[142] Government of the United States of America (2024). "Department of State – Office of the Historian: Foreign Relations of the United States, 1946, Paris Peace Conference: Proceedings, Volume III." Accessed July 20, 2024. https://history.state.gov/historicaldocuments/frus1946v03/introduction.

[143] Munez, E. (2023). "Paris Peace Treaties 1947." Published May 1, 2023. Accessed July 20, 2024. https://www.britannica.com/topic/Paris-Peace-Treaties-1947.

[144] Oxford Reference (2024). "Overview: Paris Peace Treaties." Accessed July 20, 2024. https://www.oxfordreference.com/display/10.1093/oi/authority.20110803100306594.

[145] Baber, G. (2019). *The United Nations System*, 4.

[146] Yale University (2008). Yale Law School Lillian Goldman Law Library The Avalon Project – Inter-Allied Meeting Held in London at St. James's Palace on June 12, 1941: Resolution, Article 3.

[147] Encyclopaedia Britannica (1998). "Atlantic Charter." Published July 20, 1998. Last updated March 11, 2024. Accessed July 22, 2024. https://www.britannica.com/event/Atlantic-Charter.

[148] Yale University (2008). Yale Law School Lillian Goldman Law Library The Avalon Project – Atlantic Charter: August 14, 1941, Principle 1.

[149] Yale University (2008). Yale Law School Lillian Goldman Law Library The Avalon Project – Atlantic Charter: August 14, 1941, Principle 2.

[150] Yale University (2008). Yale Law School Lillian Goldman Law Library The Avalon Project – Atlantic Charter: August 14, 1941, Principle 3.

[151] Yale University (2008). Yale Law School Lillian Goldman Law Library The Avalon Project – Atlantic Charter: August 14, 1941, Principle 4.

[152] Yale University (2008). Yale Law School Lillian Goldman Law Library The Avalon Project – Atlantic Charter: August 14, 1941, Principle 5.

[153] Yale University (2008). Yale Law School Lillian Goldman Law Library The Avalon Project – Atlantic Charter: August 14, 1941, Principle 6.
[154] Yale University (2008). Yale Law School Lillian Goldman Law Library The Avalon Project – Atlantic Charter: August 14, 1941, Principle 7.
[155] Yale University (2008). Yale Law School Lillian Goldman Law Library The Avalon Project – Atlantic Charter: August 14, 1941, Principle 8.
[156] United Nations (2024). "Model United Nations: The History of the UN." Accessed July 23 and 26, 2024. https://www.un.org/en/model-united-nations/history-united-nations.
[157] Yale University (2008). Yale Law School Lillian Goldman Law Library The Avalon Project – Declaration by the United Nations: January 1, 1942, Recital 1.
[158] Yale University (2008). Yale Law School Lillian Goldman Law Library The Avalon Project – Declaration by the United Nations: January 1, 1942, Article 1.
[159] Yale University (2008). Yale Law School Lillian Goldman Law Library The Avalon Project – Declaration by the United Nations: January 1, 1942, Article 2.
[160] Government of the United States of America (2024). "Department of State – Office of the Historian: The Tehran Conference, 1943." Accessed July 23, 2024. https://history.state.gov/milestones/1937-1945/tehran-conf.
[161] Encyclopaedia Britannica (1998). "Dumbarton Oaks Conference." Published July 20, 1998. Last updated August 14, 2023. Accessed July 23, 2024. https://www.britannica.com/event/Dumbarton-Oaks-Conference.
[162] Derecho Internacional Público (2024). Dumbarton Oaks – Washington Conversations on International Peace and Security Organization, October 7, 1944: Proposals for the Establishment of a General International Organization, Chapter 1.
[163] United Nations (1945). "Charter of the United Nations," Article 1.
[164] Derecho Internacional Público (2024). Dumbarton Oaks – Washington Conversations on International Peace and Security Organization, October 7, 1944: Proposals for the Establishment of a General International Organization, Chapter VI, Section A.
[165] Derecho Internacional Público (2024). Dumbarton Oaks – Washington Conversations on International Peace and Security Organization, October 7, 1944: Proposals for the Establishment of a General International Organization, Chapter VI, Section B, Paragraph 1.
[166] Derecho Internacional Público (2024). Dumbarton Oaks – Washington Conversations on International Peace and Security Organization, October 7, 1944: Proposals for the Establishment of a General International Organization, Chapter VI, Section B, Paragraph 3.
[167] Derecho Internacional Público (2024). Dumbarton Oaks – Washington Conversations on International Peace and Security Organization, October 7, 1944: Proposals for the Establishment of a General International Organization, Chapter VI, Section B, Paragraph 4.
[168] Derecho Internacional Público (2024). Dumbarton Oaks – Washington Conversations on International Peace and Security Organization, October 7, 1944: Proposals for the Establishment of a General International Organization, Chapter VI, Section C, Paragraph 1.
[169] Derecho Internacional Público (2024). Dumbarton Oaks – Washington Conversations on International Peace and Security Organization, October 7, 1944: Proposals for the Establishment of a General International Organization, Chapter VI, Section C, Paragraph 2.
[170] Derecho Internacional Público (2024). Dumbarton Oaks – Washington Conversations on International Peace and Security Organization, October 7, 1944: Proposals for the Establishment of a General International Organization, Chapter VI, Section C, Paragraph 3.
[171] Mullen, M., Onion, A., Sullivan, M., and Zapata, C. (2009). "Yalta Conference." Published October 29, 2009. Updated November 1, 2022. Accessed July 26, 2024. https://www.history.com/topics/world-war-ii/yalta-conference.
[172] United Nations (2024). "The San Francisco Conference." Accessed July 26, 2024. https://www.un.org/en/about-us/history-of-the-un/san-francisco-conference.
[173] Government of the United States of America (2024). "Department of State – Office of the Historian: The Formation of the United Nations, 1945." Accessed July 26, 2024. https://history.state.gov/milestones/1937-1945/un.

[174] United Nations (1945). "Charter of the United Nations," Preamble.
[175] United Nations (1945). "Charter of the United Nations," Article 2(1).
[176] United Nations (1945). "Charter of the United Nations," Article 2(5).
[177] United Nations (1945). "Charter of the United Nations," Article 2(6).
[178] United Nations (1945). "Charter of the United Nations," Article 2(7).
[179] United Nations (1945). "Charter of the United Nations," Article 4(2).
[180] United Nations (1945). "Charter of the United Nations," Article 5.
[181] United Nations (1945). "Charter of the United Nations," Article 7(1).
[182] United Nations (1945). "Charter of the United Nations," Article 8.
[183] United Nations (1945). "Charter of the United Nations," Article 10.
[184] United Nations (1945). "Charter of the United Nations," Article 12(1).
[185] United Nations (1945). "Charter of the United Nations," Article 11(1).
[186] United Nations (1945). "Charter of the United Nations," Article 11(2).
[187] United Nations (1945). "Charter of the United Nations," Article 11(3).
[188] United Nations (1945). "Charter of the United Nations," Article 13.
[189] United Nations (1945). "Charter of the United Nations," Article 14.
[190] United Nations (1945). "Charter of the United Nations," Article 15(1).
[191] United Nations (1945). "Charter of the United Nations," Article 15(2).
[192] United Nations (1945). "Charter of the United Nations," Article 17(1).
[193] United Nations (1945). "Charter of the United Nations," Article 18(2).
[194] United Nations (1945). "Charter of the United Nations," Article 18(3).
[195] United Nations (1945). "Charter of the United Nations," Article 18(1).
[196] United Nations (1945). "Charter of the United Nations," Article 20.
[197] United Nations (1945). "Charter of the United Nations," Articles 21 and 22.
[198] United Nations (1945). "Charter of the United Nations," Article 23(1).
[199] United Nations (1945). "Charter of the United Nations," Article 23(2).
[200] United Nations (1945). "Charter of the United Nations," Article 27(1).
[201] United Nations (1945). "Charter of the United Nations," Article 30.
[202] United Nations (1945). "Charter of the United Nations," Article 29.
[203] United Nations (1945). "Charter of the United Nations," Article 33(2).
[204] United Nations (1945). "Charter of the United Nations," Article 34.
[205] United Nations (1945). "Charter of the United Nations," Article 35(1).
[206] United Nations (1945). "Charter of the United Nations," Article 35(2).
[207] United Nations (1945). "Charter of the United Nations," Article 37(1).
[208] United Nations (1945). "Charter of the United Nations," Article 39.
[209] United Nations (1945). "Charter of the United Nations," Article 40.
[210] United Nations (1945). "Charter of the United Nations," Article 41.
[211] United Nations (1945). "Charter of the United Nations," Article 42.
[212] United Nations (1945). "Charter of the United Nations," Article 43(1).
[213] United Nations (1945). "Charter of the United Nations," Article 43(2).
[214] United Nations (1945). "Charter of the United Nations," Article 44.
[215] United Nations (1945). "Charter of the United Nations," Article 45.
[216] United Nations (1945). "Charter of the United Nations," Article 46.
[217] United Nations (1945). "Charter of the United Nations," Article 48(2).
[218] United Nations (1945). "Charter of the United Nations," Article 49.
[219] United Nations (1945). "Charter of the United Nations," Article 50.
[220] United Nations (1945). "Charter of the United Nations," Article 52(2).
[221] United Nations (1945). "Charter of the United Nations," Article 53(1).
[222] United Nations (1945). "Charter of the United Nations," Article 54.
[223] United Nations (1945). "Charter of the United Nations," Article 55(a).
[224] United Nations (1945). "Charter of the United Nations," Article 55(b).
[225] United Nations (1945). "Charter of the United Nations," Article 55(c).
[226] United Nations (1945). "Charter of the United Nations," Article 56.

[227] United Nations (1945). "Charter of the United Nations," Article 57(1).
[228] United Nations (1945). "Charter of the United Nations," Article 63(1).
[229] United Nations (1945). "Charter of the United Nations," Article 58.
[230] United Nations (1945). "Charter of the United Nations," Article 59.
[231] United Nations (1945). "Charter of the United Nations," Article 60.
[232] United Nations (1945). "Charter of the United Nations," Article 61(1).
[233] United Nations (1945). "Charter of the United Nations," Article 61(2).
[234] United Nations (1945). "Charter of the United Nations," Article 61(4).
[235] United Nations (1945). "Charter of the United Nations," Article 62(1).
[236] United Nations (1945). "Charter of the United Nations," Article 62(2).
[237] United Nations (1945). "Charter of the United Nations," Article 62(4).
[238] United Nations (1945). "Charter of the United Nations," Article 62(3).
[239] United Nations (1945). "Charter of the United Nations," Article 63(2).
[240] United Nations (1945). "Charter of the United Nations," Article 65.
[241] United Nations (1945). "Charter of the United Nations," Article 66(1).
[242] United Nations (1945). "Charter of the United Nations," Article 66(2).
[243] United Nations (1945). "Charter of the United Nations," Article 66(3).
[244] United Nations (1945). "Charter of the United Nations," Article 67(2).
[245] United Nations (1945). "Charter of the United Nations," Article 67(1).
[246] United Nations (1945). "Charter of the United Nations," Article 68.
[247] United Nations (1945). "Charter of the United Nations," Article 69.
[248] United Nations (1945). "Charter of the United Nations," Article 70.
[249] United Nations (1945). "Charter of the United Nations," Article 71.
[250] United Nations (1945). "Charter of the United Nations," Article 72(1).
[251] United Nations (1945). "Charter of the United Nations," Article 72(2).
[252] United Nations (1945). "Charter of the United Nations," Article 73.
[253] United Nations (1945). "Charter of the United Nations," Article 74.
[254] United Nations (2024). "The United Nations and Decolonization: Non-Self-Governing Territories." Accessed August 6, 2024. https://www.un.org/dppa/decolonization/en/nsgt.
[255] United Nations (1945). "Charter of the United Nations," Article 75.
[256] United Nations (2024). "The United Nations and Decolonization: International Trusteeship System." Accessed August 7, 2024. https://www.un.org/dppa/decolonization/en/history/international-trusteeship-system-and-trust-territories.
[257] United Nations (1945). "Charter of the United Nations," Article 88.
[258] United Nations (1945). "Charter of the United Nations," Article 92.
[259] United Nations (1945). "Charter of the United Nations," Article 93(1).
[260] United Nations (1945). "Charter of the United Nations," Article 93(2).
[261] United Nations (1945). "Charter of the United Nations," Article 94(1).
[262] United Nations (1945). "Charter of the United Nations," Article 97.
[263] United Nations (1945). "Charter of the United Nations," Article 99.
[264] United Nations (1945). "Charter of the United Nations," Article 98.
[265] United Nations (1945). "Charter of the United Nations," Article 100(1).
[266] United Nations (1945). "Charter of the United Nations," Article 100(2).
[267] United Nations (1945). "Charter of the United Nations," Article 101(1).
[268] United Nations (1945). "Charter of the United Nations," Article 101(2).
[269] United Nations (1945). "Charter of the United Nations," Article 102(1).
[270] United Nations (1945). "Charter of the United Nations," Article 102(2).
[271] United Nations (1945). "Charter of the United Nations," Article 103.
[272] United Nations (1945). "Charter of the United Nations," Article 104.
[273] United Nations (1945). "Charter of the United Nations," Article 105(1).
[274] United Nations (1945). "Charter of the United Nations," Article 109(1).
[275] United Nations (1945). "Charter of the United Nations," Article 109(2).
[276] United Nations (1945). "Charter of the United Nations," Article 108.

[277] United Nations (2024). "Amendments to Articles 23, 27, 61, 109." Accessed August 9, 2025. https://www.un.org/en/about-us/un-charter/amendments.
[278] United Nations (1945). "Charter of the United Nations," Article 110(1).
[279] United Nations (1945). "Charter of the United Nations," Article 110(2).
[280] United Nations (1945). "Charter of the United Nations," Article 110(3).
[281] United Nations (1945). "Charter of the United Nations," Article 111.
[282] International Court of Justice (2024). "Basic Documents." Accessed August 12, 2024. https://www.icj-cij.org/basic-documents.
[283] United Nations (1945). "Statute of the International Court of Justice," Articles 2 and 3(1).
[284] United Nations (1945). "Statute of the International Court of Justice," Article 4(1).
[285] United Nations (1945). "Statute of the International Court of Justice," Article 13(1).
[286] United Nations (1945). "Statute of the International Court of Justice," Article 15.
[287] United Nations (1945). "Statute of the International Court of Justice," Article 16(1).
[288] United Nations (1945). "Statute of the International Court of Justice," Article 17(1).
[289] United Nations (1945). "Statute of the International Court of Justice," Article 17(2).
[290] United Nations (1945). "Statute of the International Court of Justice," Article 21(1).
[291] United Nations (1945). "Statute of the International Court of Justice," Article 21(2).
[292] United Nations (1945). "Statute of the International Court of Justice," Article 22(1).
[293] United Nations (1945). "Statute of the International Court of Justice," Article 24(1)-(2).
[294] United Nations (1945). "Statute of the International Court of Justice," Article 25(1).
[295] United Nations (1945). "Statute of the International Court of Justice," Article 26(1).
[296] United Nations (1945). "Statute of the International Court of Justice," Article 26(2).
[297] United Nations (1945). "Statute of the International Court of Justice," Article 26(3).
[298] United Nations (1945). "Statute of the International Court of Justice," Article 29.
[299] United Nations (1945). "Statute of the International Court of Justice," Article 27.
[300] United Nations (1945). "Statute of the International Court of Justice," Article 30(1).
[301] United Nations (1945). "Statute of the International Court of Justice," Article 31(1).
[302] United Nations (1945). "Statute of the International Court of Justice," Article 31(2)-(3).
[303] United Nations (1945). "Statute of the International Court of Justice," Article 31(5).
[304] United Nations (1945). "Statute of the International Court of Justice," Article 34(1).
[305] United Nations (1945). "Statute of the International Court of Justice," Article 35(1).
[306] United Nations (1945). "Statute of the International Court of Justice," Article 36(1).
[307] United Nations (1945). "Statute of the International Court of Justice," Article 36(2).
[308] United Nations (1945). "Statute of the International Court of Justice," Article 36(3).
[309] United Nations (1945). "Statute of the International Court of Justice," Article 36(5).
[310] United Nations (1945). "Statute of the International Court of Justice," Article 37.
[311] United Nations (1945). "Statute of the International Court of Justice," Article 38(1).
[312] United Nations (1945). "Statute of the International Court of Justice," Article 38(2).
[313] United Nations (1945). "Statute of the International Court of Justice," Article 39(1).
[314] United Nations (1945). "Statute of the International Court of Justice," Article 39(3).
[315] United Nations (1945). "Statute of the International Court of Justice," Article 40(1).
[316] United Nations (1945). "Statute of the International Court of Justice," Article 41(1).
[317] United Nations (1945). "Statute of the International Court of Justice," Article 43(1).
[318] United Nations (1945). "Statute of the International Court of Justice," Article 43(2)-(3).
[319] United Nations (1945). "Statute of the International Court of Justice," Article 43(5).
[320] United Nations (1945). "Statute of the International Court of Justice," Article 45.
[321] United Nations (1945). "Statute of the International Court of Justice," Article 50.
[322] United Nations (1945). "Statute of the International Court of Justice," Article 51.
[323] United Nations (1945). "Statute of the International Court of Justice," Article 53(1).
[324] United Nations (1945). "Statute of the International Court of Justice," Article 53(2).
[325] United Nations (1945). "Statute of the International Court of Justice," Article 55(1).
[326] United Nations (1945). "Statute of the International Court of Justice," Article 55(2).
[327] United Nations (1945). "Statute of the International Court of Justice," Article 56(1).

[328] United Nations (1945). "Statute of the International Court of Justice," Article 56(2).
[329] United Nations (1945). "Statute of the International Court of Justice," Article 57.
[330] United Nations (1945). "Statute of the International Court of Justice," Article 60.
[331] United Nations (1945). "Statute of the International Court of Justice," Article 62(1).
[332] United Nations (1945). "Statute of the International Court of Justice," Article 62(2).
[333] United Nations (1945). "Statute of the International Court of Justice," Article 65(1).
[334] United Nations (1945). "Statute of the International Court of Justice," Article 65(2).
[335] United Nations (1945). "Statute of the International Court of Justice," Article 66(1).
[336] United Nations (1945). "Statute of the International Court of Justice," Article 66(2).
[337] United Nations (1945). "Statute of the International Court of Justice," Article 66(4).
[338] United Nations (1945). "Statute of the International Court of Justice," Article 69.
[339] United Nations (1945). "Statute of the International Court of Justice," Article 70.
[340] United Nations (1945). "Charter of the United Nations," Article 1(1).
[341] United Nations (1945). "Charter of the United Nations," Article 13(1)(a).
[342] United Nations (1945). "Statute of the International Court of Justice," Article 38(1)(a).
[343] United Nations (1945). "Statute of the International Court of Justice," Article 38(1)(b).
[344] United Nations (1945). "Statute of the International Court of Justice," Article 38(1)(c).
[345] United Nations (1945). "Statute of the International Court of Justice," Article 38(1)(d).
[346] International Law Commission (2024). "About the Commission: Origin and background – Drafting and implementation of Article 13, paragraph 1, of the Charter of the United Nations." Accessed August 21 and 22, 2024. https://legal.un.org/ilc/drafting.shtml.
[347] United Nations (1946). Resolution 94 (I) adopted by the General Assembly on 11th December 1946, Recital 1.
[348] United Nations (1946). Resolution 94 (I) adopted by the General Assembly on 11th December 1946.
[349] International Law Commission (2024). "About the Commission: Organization, programme and methods of work." Accessed August 22, 2024. https://legal.un.org/ilc/methods.shtml.
[350] United Nations (1947). "Statute of the International Law Commission," Adopted by the General Assembly in Resolution 174 (II) of 21st November 1947, as amended by Resolutions 485 (V) of 12th December 1950, 984 (X) of 3rd December 1955, 985 (X) of 3rd December 1955 and 36/39 of 18th November 1981, Article 1(1).
[351] United Nations (1947). "Statute of the International Law Commission," Article 2(1)-(2).
[352] United Nations (1947). "Statute of the International Law Commission," Articles 3 and 4.
[353] United Nations (1947). "Statute of the International Law Commission," Articles 2(1) and 8.
[354] United Nations (1947). "Statute of the International Law Commission," Article 10.
[355] United Nations (1947). "Statute of the International Law Commission," Article 16.
[356] United Nations (1947). "Statute of the International Law Commission," Article 17(1).
[357] United Nations (1947). "Statute of the International Law Commission," Article 18(1).
[358] United Nations (1947). "Statute of the International Law Commission," Article 18(2).
[359] United Nations (1947). "Statute of the International Law Commission," Article 19(1).
[360] United Nations (1947). "Statute of the International Law Commission," Article 19(2).
[361] United Nations (1947). "Statute of the International Law Commission," Article 20.
[362] United Nations (1947). "Statute of the International Law Commission," Article 21(1).
[363] United Nations (1947). "Statute of the International Law Commission," Article 21(2).
[364] United Nations (1947). "Statute of the International Law Commission," Article 22.
[365] United Nations (1947). "Statute of the International Law Commission," Article 23(1).
[366] United Nations (1947). "Statute of the International Law Commission," Article 23(2).
[367] International Law Commission (2023). "Summaries of the Work of the International Law Commission." Last updated August 9, 2023. Accessed August 26, 2024. https://legal.un.org/ilc/summaries/summaries.shtml.
[368] United Nations (1969). "Vienna Convention on the Law of Treaties," *United Nations Treaty Series* Registration Number 18232, Article 2(1)(a).
[369] United Nations (1986). "Vienna Convention on the Law of Treaties between States and International Organizations or between International Organizations," A/CONF.129/15, Official Records of the

United Nations Conference on the Law of Treaties between States and International Organizations or between International Organizations, Volume II, 93-109, 95, Article 2(1)(a).

[370] United Nations (2024). "United Nations Treaty Collection: Definitions – Definition of key terms used in the UN Treaty Collection." Accessed August 28, 2024. https://treaties.un.org/Pages/overview.aspx?path=overview/definition/page1_en.xml.

[371] International Law Commission (2023). "Summaries of the Work of the International Law Commission: Law of treaties." Last updated June 23, 2023. Accessed August 29, 2024. https://legal.un.org/ilc/summaries/1_1.shtml.

[372] International Law Commission (2017). "Summaries of the Work of the International Law Commission: Question of treaties concluded between States and international organizations or between two or more international organizations." Last updated December 4, 2017. Accessed August 29, 2024. https://legal.un.org/ilc/summaries/1_2.shtml.

[373] United Nations (1986). "Vienna Convention on the Law of Treaties between States and International Organizations or between International Organizations," Articles 84(3) and 85(1).

[374] United Nations (2024). "United Nations Treaty Collection: Chapter XXIII Law of Treaties – 3. Vienna Convention on the Law of Treaties between States and International Organizations or between International Organizations." Last updated August 29, 2024. Accessed August 29, 2024. https://treaties.un.org/Pages/ViewDetails.aspx?src=TREATY&mtdsg_no=XXIII-3&chapter=23&clang=_en.

[375] International Law Commission (2015). "Summaries of the Work of the International Law Commission: Extended participation in general multilateral treaties concluded under the auspices of the League of Nations." Last updated July 15, 2015. Accessed August 31, 2024. https://legal.un.org/ilc/summaries/1_5.shtml.

[376] International Law Commission (2023). "Summaries of the Work of the International Law Commission: Reservations to multilateral conventions." Last updated June 22, 2023. Accessed August 31, 2024, and September 1, 2024. https://legal.un.org/ilc/summaries/1_6.shtml.

[377] United Nations (1969). "Vienna Convention on the Law of Treaties," Articles 19-23.

[378] United Nations (1978). "Vienna Convention on the Succession of States in respect of Treaties," *United Nations Treaty Series* Registration Number 33356, Article 20(1).

[379] United Nations (1978). "Vienna Convention on the Succession of States in respect of Treaties," Article 20(2).

[380] United Nations (1978). "Vienna Convention on the Succession of States in respect of Treaties," Article 20(3).

[381] International Law Commission (2023). "Summaries of the Work of the International Law Commission: Reservations to treaties." Last updated June 29, 2023. Accessed September 4, 2024. https://legal.un.org/ilc/summaries/1_8.shtml.

[382] International Law Commission (2015). "Summaries of the Work of the International Law Commission: Review of the multilateral treaty-making process." Last updated July 15, 2015. Accessed September 5, 2024. https://legal.un.org/ilc/summaries/1_7.shtml.

[383] International Law Commission (2023). "Summaries of the Work of the International Law Commission: Effects of armed conflicts on treaties." Last updated November 6, 2023. Accessed September 6 and 7, 2024. https://legal.un.org/ilc/summaries/1_10.shtml.

[384] International Law Commission (2024). "Summaries of the Work of the International Law Commission: Subsequent agreements and subsequent practice in relation to interpretation of treaties." Last updated July 18, 2024. Accessed September 8 and 9, 2024. https://legal.un.org/ilc/summaries/1_11.shtml.

[385] International Court of Justice (2024). "Judge Georg Nolte." Accessed September 8, 2024. https://www.icj-cij.org/index.php/node/4058.

[386] International Law Commission (2024). "Summaries of the Work of the International Law Commission: Provisional application of treaties." Last updated July 18, 2024. Accessed September 10 and 11, 2024. https://legal.un.org/ilc/summaries/1_12.shtml.

[387] International Court of Justice (2024). "Current Members." Accessed September 10, 2024. https://www.icj-cij.org/index.php/current-members.

[388] International Law Commission (2023). "Summaries of the Work of the International Law Commission: Succession of States in respect of treaties." Last updated June 30, 2023. Accessed September 11, 2024. https://legal.un.org/ilc/summaries/3_2.shtml.
[389] United Nations (1978). "Vienna Convention on the Succession of States in respect of Treaties," Article 1.
[390] United Nations (1978). "Vienna Convention on the Succession of States in respect of Treaties," Article 3.
[391] United Nations (1978). "Vienna Convention on the Succession of States in respect of Treaties," Article 4(a).
[392] United Nations (1978). "Vienna Convention on the Succession of States in respect of Treaties," Article 4(b).
[393] United Nations (1978). "Vienna Convention on the Succession of States in respect of Treaties," Article 10(2).
[394] United Nations (1978). "Vienna Convention on the Succession of States in respect of Treaties," Article 12(1)-(2).
[395] United Nations (1978). "Vienna Convention on the Succession of States in respect of Treaties," Article 12(3).
[396] United Nations (1978). "Vienna Convention on the Succession of States in respect of Treaties," Article 15(a).
[397] United Nations (1978). "Vienna Convention on the Succession of States in respect of Treaties," Article 15(b).
[398] United Nations (1978). "Vienna Convention on the Succession of States in respect of Treaties," Article 16.
[399] United Nations (1978). "Vienna Convention on the Succession of States in respect of Treaties," Article 17(1).
[400] United Nations (1978). "Vienna Convention on the Succession of States in respect of Treaties," Article 18(3)-(4).
[401] United Nations (1978). "Vienna Convention on the Succession of States in respect of Treaties," Article 18(1)-(2).
[402] United Nations (1978). "Vienna Convention on the Succession of States in respect of Treaties," Article 19(3)-(4).
[403] United Nations (1978). "Vienna Convention on the Succession of States in respect of Treaties," Article 19(1).
[404] United Nations (1978). "Vienna Convention on the Succession of States in respect of Treaties," Article 21(1).
[405] United Nations (1978). "Vienna Convention on the Succession of States in respect of Treaties," Article 21(2).
[406] United Nations (1978). "Vienna Convention on the Succession of States in respect of Treaties," Article 21(3).
[407] United Nations (1978). "Vienna Convention on the Succession of States in respect of Treaties," Article 22(1).
[408] United Nations (1978). "Vienna Convention on the Succession of States in respect of Treaties," Article 30(1).
[409] United Nations (1978). "Vienna Convention on the Succession of States in respect of Treaties," Article 31(1).
[410] United Nations (1978). "Vienna Convention on the Succession of States in respect of Treaties," Article 31(2)(a).
[411] United Nations (1978). "Vienna Convention on the Succession of States in respect of Treaties," Article 31(2)(b).
[412] United Nations (1978). "Vienna Convention on the Succession of States in respect of Treaties," Article 34(1)(a).
[413] United Nations (1978). "Vienna Convention on the Succession of States in respect of Treaties," Article 34(1)(b).

[414] United Nations (1978). "Vienna Convention on the Succession of States in respect of Treaties," Article 34(2)(a).
[415] United Nations (1978). "Vienna Convention on the Succession of States in respect of Treaties," Article 34(2)(b).
[416] United Nations (1978). "Vienna Convention on the Succession of States in respect of Treaties," Article 35(a).
[417] United Nations (1978). "Vienna Convention on the Succession of States in respect of Treaties," Article 35(b).
[418] United Nations (1978). "Vienna Convention on the Succession of States in respect of Treaties," Article 35(c).
[419] United Nations (1978). "Vienna Convention on the Succession of States in respect of Treaties," Article 38(1).
[420] United Nations (1978). "Vienna Convention on the Succession of States in respect of Treaties," Article 41.
[421] United Nations (1978). "Vienna Convention on the Succession of States in respect of Treaties," Article 42.
[422] United Nations (1978). "Vienna Convention on the Succession of States in respect of Treaties," Articles 43-44.
[423] United Nations (1969). "Vienna Convention on the Law of Treaties," Article 1.
[424] United Nations (1969). "Vienna Convention on the Law of Treaties," Article 5.
[425] United Nations (1969). "Vienna Convention on the Law of Treaties," Article 9.
[426] United Nations (1969). "Vienna Convention on the Law of Treaties," Article 10(a).
[427] United Nations (1969). "Vienna Convention on the Law of Treaties," Article 10(b).
[428] United Nations (1969). "Vienna Convention on the Law of Treaties," Article 11.
[429] United Nations (1969). "Vienna Convention on the Law of Treaties," Article 12(1)(a).
[430] United Nations (1969). "Vienna Convention on the Law of Treaties," Article 12(1)(b).
[431] United Nations (1969). "Vienna Convention on the Law of Treaties," Article 12(1)(c).
[432] United Nations (1969). "Vienna Convention on the Law of Treaties," Article 13(a).
[433] United Nations (1969). "Vienna Convention on the Law of Treaties," Article 13(b).
[434] United Nations (1969). "Vienna Convention on the Law of Treaties," Article 14(1)(a).
[435] United Nations (1969). "Vienna Convention on the Law of Treaties," Article 14(1)(b).
[436] United Nations (1969). "Vienna Convention on the Law of Treaties," Article 14(1)(c).
[437] United Nations (1969). "Vienna Convention on the Law of Treaties," Article 14(1)(d).
[438] United Nations (1969). "Vienna Convention on the Law of Treaties," Article 15(a).
[439] United Nations (1969). "Vienna Convention on the Law of Treaties," Article 15(b).
[440] United Nations (1969). "Vienna Convention on the Law of Treaties," Article 15(c).
[441] United Nations (1969). "Vienna Convention on the Law of Treaties," Article 16.
[442] United Nations (1969). "Vienna Convention on the Law of Treaties," Article 17(1).
[443] United Nations (1969). "Vienna Convention on the Law of Treaties," Article 17(2).
[444] United Nations (1969). "Vienna Convention on the Law of Treaties," Article 18(a).
[445] United Nations (1969). "Vienna Convention on the Law of Treaties," Article 18(b).
[446] United Nations (1969). "Vienna Convention on the Law of Treaties," Article 26.
[447] United Nations (1969). "Vienna Convention on the Law of Treaties," Article 27.
[448] United Nations (1969). "Vienna Convention on the Law of Treaties," Article 28.
[449] United Nations (1969). "Vienna Convention on the Law of Treaties," Article 29.
[450] United Nations (1969). "Vienna Convention on the Law of Treaties," Article 30(1).
[451] United Nations (1969). "Vienna Convention on the Law of Treaties," Article 30(2).
[452] United Nations (1969). "Vienna Convention on the Law of Treaties," Article 30(3).
[453] United Nations (1969). "Vienna Convention on the Law of Treaties," Article 30(4)(a).
[454] United Nations (1969). "Vienna Convention on the Law of Treaties," Article 30(4)(b).
[455] United Nations (1969). "Vienna Convention on the Law of Treaties," Article 33(1).
[456] United Nations (1969). "Vienna Convention on the Law of Treaties," Article 33(4).
[457] United Nations (1969). "Vienna Convention on the Law of Treaties," Article 34.

[458] United Nations (1969). "Vienna Convention on the Law of Treaties," Article 36(1).
[459] United Nations (1969). "Vienna Convention on the Law of Treaties," Article 36(2).
[460] United Nations (1969). "Vienna Convention on the Law of Treaties," Article 35.
[461] United Nations (1969). "Vienna Convention on the Law of Treaties," Article 38.
[462] United Nations (1969). "Vienna Convention on the Law of Treaties," Article 39.
[463] United Nations (1969). "Vienna Convention on the Law of Treaties," Article 40(1).
[464] United Nations (1969). "Vienna Convention on the Law of Treaties," Article 40(2).
[465] United Nations (1969). "Vienna Convention on the Law of Treaties," Article 40(3).
[466] United Nations (1969). "Vienna Convention on the Law of Treaties," Article 40(4).
[467] United Nations (1969). "Vienna Convention on the Law of Treaties," Articles 30(4)(b) and 40(4).
[468] United Nations (1969). "Vienna Convention on the Law of Treaties," Article 40(5).
[469] United Nations (1969). "Vienna Convention on the Law of Treaties," Article 41(1)(a).
[470] United Nations (1969). "Vienna Convention on the Law of Treaties," Article 41(1)(b).
[471] United Nations (1969). "Vienna Convention on the Law of Treaties," Article 42(1).
[472] United Nations (1969). "Vienna Convention on the Law of Treaties," Article 42(2).
[473] United Nations (1969). "Vienna Convention on the Law of Treaties," Article 43.
[474] United Nations (1969). "Vienna Convention on the Law of Treaties," Article 44(1).
[475] United Nations (1969). "Vienna Convention on the Law of Treaties," Article 44(2).
[476] United Nations (1969). "Vienna Convention on the Law of Treaties," Article 44(3).
[477] United Nations (1969). "Vienna Convention on the Law of Treaties," Article 44(4).
[478] United Nations (1969). "Vienna Convention on the Law of Treaties," Article 44(5).
[479] United Nations (1969). "Vienna Convention on the Law of Treaties," Article 45.
[480] United Nations (1969). "Vienna Convention on the Law of Treaties," Article 46(1).
[481] United Nations (1969). "Vienna Convention on the Law of Treaties," Article 47.
[482] United Nations (1969). "Vienna Convention on the Law of Treaties," Article 48(1).
[483] United Nations (1969). "Vienna Convention on the Law of Treaties," Article 48(2).
[484] United Nations (1969). "Vienna Convention on the Law of Treaties," Article 54.
[485] United Nations (1969). "Vienna Convention on the Law of Treaties," Article 55.
[486] United Nations (1969). "Vienna Convention on the Law of Treaties," Article 57.
[487] United Nations (1969). "Vienna Convention on the Law of Treaties," Article 58.
[488] United Nations (1969). "Vienna Convention on the Law of Treaties," Article 61(1).
[489] United Nations (1969). "Vienna Convention on the Law of Treaties," Article 61(2).
[490] United Nations (1969). "Vienna Convention on the Law of Treaties," Article 63.
[491] United Nations (1969). "Vienna Convention on the Law of Treaties," Article 64.
[492] United Nations (1969). "Vienna Convention on the Law of Treaties," Article 71(2)(a).
[493] United Nations (1969). "Vienna Convention on the Law of Treaties," Article 69(1).
[494] United Nations (1969). "Vienna Convention on the Law of Treaties," Article 69(2).
[495] United Nations (1969). "Vienna Convention on the Law of Treaties," Article 69(4).
[496] United Nations (1969). "Vienna Convention on the Law of Treaties," Article 70(1).
[497] United Nations (1969). "Vienna Convention on the Law of Treaties," Article 70(2).
[498] United Nations (1969). "Vienna Convention on the Law of Treaties," Article 72(1).
[499] United Nations (1969). "Vienna Convention on the Law of Treaties," Article 72(2).
[500] United Nations (1978). "Vienna Convention on the Succession of States in respect of Treaties," Article 1(a).
[501] United Nations (1978). "Vienna Convention on the Succession of States in respect of Treaties," Article 1(b).
[502] United Nations (1969). "Vienna Convention on the Law of Treaties," Article 85.
[503] United Nations (1978). "Vienna Convention on the Succession of States in respect of Treaties," Article 86.
[504] United Nations (1969). "Vienna Convention on the Law of Treaties," Article 6.
[505] International Law Commission (2024). "B. Formation and evidence of customary law." Accessed September 23, 2024. https://legal.un.org/ilc/sessions/66/pdfs/english/icil_czech_republic.pdf.

[506] International Law Commission (2024). "Summaries of the Work of the International Law Commission: Identification of customary international law." Last updated July 18, 2024. Accessed September 23 and 24, 2024. https://legal.un.org/ilc/summaries/1_13.shtml.
[507] United Nations (2018). Resolution 73/203 adopted by the General Assembly on 20th December 2018, Annex: Identification of customary international law, Conclusion 1.
[508] International Law Commission (2018). Report of the International Law Commission on the work of its seventieth session (30 April – 1 June and 2 July – 10 August 2018), Document A/73/10, Chapter V. Identification of customary international law, E.2. Text of the draft conclusions and commentaries thereto, *Yearbook of the International Law Commission*, 2018, Volume II, Part Two, 91-113, 93.
[509] United Nations (2018). Resolution 73/203 adopted by the General Assembly on 20th December 2018, Annex: Identification of customary international law, Conclusion 2.
[510] International Law Commission (2018). Report of the International Law Commission on the work of its seventieth session (30 April – 1 June and 2 July – 10 August 2018), Document A/73/10, Chapter V. Identification of customary international law, E.2. Text of the draft conclusions and commentaries thereto, *Yearbook of the International Law Commission*, 2018, Volume II, Part Two, 91-113, 93-94.
[511] International Law Commission (2018). Report of the International Law Commission on the work of its seventieth session (30 April – 1 June and 2 July – 10 August 2018), Document A/73/10, Chapter V. Identification of customary international law, E.2. Text of the draft conclusions and commentaries thereto, *Yearbook of the International Law Commission*, 2018, Volume II, Part Two, 91-113, 94.
[512] United Nations (2018). Resolution 73/203 adopted by the General Assembly on 20th December 2018, Annex: Identification of customary international law, Conclusion 3(1).
[513] United Nations (2018). Resolution 73/203 adopted by the General Assembly on 20th December 2018, Annex: Identification of customary international law, Conclusion 3(2).
[514] International Law Commission (2018). Report of the International Law Commission on the work of its seventieth session (30 April – 1 June and 2 July – 10 August 2018), Document A/73/10, Chapter V. Identification of customary international law, E.2. Text of the draft conclusions and commentaries thereto, *Yearbook of the International Law Commission*, 2018, Volume II, Part Two, 91-113, 95.
[515] International Law Commission (2018). Report of the International Law Commission on the work of its seventieth session (30 April – 1 June and 2 July – 10 August 2018), Document A/73/10, Chapter V. Identification of customary international law, E.2. Text of the draft conclusions and commentaries thereto, *Yearbook of the International Law Commission*, 2018, Volume II, Part Two, 91-113, 96.
[516] United Nations (2018). Resolution 73/203 adopted by the General Assembly on 20th December 2018, Annex: Identification of customary international law, Conclusion 4(1).
[517] United Nations (2018). Resolution 73/203 adopted by the General Assembly on 20th December 2018, Annex: Identification of customary international law, Conclusion 4(2).
[518] United Nations (2018). Resolution 73/203 adopted by the General Assembly on 20th December 2018, Annex: Identification of customary international law, Conclusion 4(3).
[519] International Law Commission (2018). Report of the International Law Commission on the work of its seventieth session (30 April – 1 June and 2 July – 10 August 2018), Document A/73/10, Chapter V. Identification of customary international law, E.2. Text of the draft conclusions and commentaries thereto, *Yearbook of the International Law Commission*, 2018, Volume II, Part Two, 91-113, 97.
[520] International Law Commission (2018). Report of the International Law Commission on the work of its seventieth session (30 April – 1 June and 2 July – 10 August 2018), Document A/73/10, Chapter V. Identification of customary international law, E.2. Text of the draft conclusions and commentaries thereto, *Yearbook of the International Law Commission*, 2018, Volume II, Part Two, 91-113, 98.
[521] United Nations (2018). Resolution 73/203 adopted by the General Assembly on 20th December 2018, Annex: Identification of customary international law, Conclusion 5.
[522] United Nations (2018). Resolution 73/203 adopted by the General Assembly on 20th December 2018, Annex: Identification of customary international law, Conclusion 6(1).
[523] United Nations (2018). Resolution 73/203 adopted by the General Assembly on 20th December 2018, Annex: Identification of customary international law, Conclusion 6(2).
[524] United Nations (2018). Resolution 73/203 adopted by the General Assembly on 20th December 2018, Annex: Identification of customary international law, Conclusion 6(3).

[525] International Law Commission (2018). Report of the International Law Commission on the work of its seventieth session (30 April – 1 June and 2 July – 10 August 2018), Document A/73/10, Chapter V. Identification of customary international law, E.2. Text of the draft conclusions and commentaries thereto, *Yearbook of the International Law Commission*, 2018, Volume II, Part Two, 91-113, 99.

[526] United Nations (2018). Resolution 73/203 adopted by the General Assembly on 20th December 2018, Annex: Identification of customary international law, Conclusion 7(1).

[527] United Nations (2018). Resolution 73/203 adopted by the General Assembly on 20th December 2018, Annex: Identification of customary international law, Conclusion 7(2).

[528] International Law Commission (2018). Report of the International Law Commission on the work of its seventieth session (30 April – 1 June and 2 July – 10 August 2018), Document A/73/10, Chapter V. Identification of customary international law, E.2. Text of the draft conclusions and commentaries thereto, *Yearbook of the International Law Commission*, 2018, Volume II, Part Two, 91-113, 100.

[529] United Nations (2018). Resolution 73/203 adopted by the General Assembly on 20th December 2018, Annex: Identification of customary international law, Conclusion 8(1).

[530] United Nations (2018). Resolution 73/203 adopted by the General Assembly on 20th December 2018, Annex: Identification of customary international law, Conclusion 8(2).

[531] International Law Commission (2018). Report of the International Law Commission on the work of its seventieth session (30 April – 1 June and 2 July – 10 August 2018), Document A/73/10, Chapter V. Identification of customary international law, E.2. Text of the draft conclusions and commentaries thereto, *Yearbook of the International Law Commission*, 2018, Volume II, Part Two, 91-113, 101.

[532] International Law Commission (2018). Report of the International Law Commission on the work of its seventieth session (30 April – 1 June and 2 July – 10 August 2018), Document A/73/10, Chapter V. Identification of customary international law, E.2. Text of the draft conclusions and commentaries thereto, *Yearbook of the International Law Commission*, 2018, Volume II, Part Two, 91-113, 101-102.

[533] International Law Commission (2018). Report of the International Law Commission on the work of its seventieth session (30 April – 1 June and 2 July – 10 August 2018), Document A/73/10, Chapter V. Identification of customary international law, E.2. Text of the draft conclusions and commentaries thereto, *Yearbook of the International Law Commission*, 2018, Volume II, Part Two, 91-113, 102.

[534] United Nations (2018). Resolution 73/203 adopted by the General Assembly on 20th December 2018, Annex: Identification of customary international law, Conclusion 9(1).

[535] United Nations (2018). Resolution 73/203 adopted by the General Assembly on 20th December 2018, Annex: Identification of customary international law, Conclusion 9(2).

[536] International Law Commission (2018). Report of the International Law Commission on the work of its seventieth session (30 April – 1 June and 2 July – 10 August 2018), Document A/73/10, Chapter V. Identification of customary international law, E.2. Text of the draft conclusions and commentaries thereto, *Yearbook of the International Law Commission*, 2018, Volume II, Part Two, 91-113, 103.

[537] United Nations (2018). Resolution 73/203 adopted by the General Assembly on 20th December 2018, Annex: Identification of customary international law, Conclusion 10(1).

[538] United Nations (2018). Resolution 73/203 adopted by the General Assembly on 20th December 2018, Annex: Identification of customary international law, Conclusion 10(2).

[539] United Nations (2018). Resolution 73/203 adopted by the General Assembly on 20th December 2018, Annex: Identification of customary international law, Conclusion 10(3).

[540] International Law Commission (2018). Report of the International Law Commission on the work of its seventieth session (30 April – 1 June and 2 July – 10 August 2018), Document A/73/10, Chapter V. Identification of customary international law, E.2. Text of the draft conclusions and commentaries thereto, *Yearbook of the International Law Commission*, 2018, Volume II, Part Two, 91-113, 103-104.

[541] International Law Commission (2018). Report of the International Law Commission on the work of its seventieth session (30 April – 1 June and 2 July – 10 August 2018), Document A/73/10, Chapter V. Identification of customary international law, E.2. Text of the draft conclusions and commentaries thereto, *Yearbook of the International Law Commission*, 2018, Volume II, Part Two, 91-113, 104.

[542] United Nations (2018). Resolution 73/203 adopted by the General Assembly on 20th December 2018, Annex: Identification of customary international law, Conclusion 11(1).

[543] United Nations (2018). Resolution 73/203 adopted by the General Assembly on 20th December 2018, Annex: Identification of customary international law, Conclusion 11(2).

[544] International Law Commission (2018). Report of the International Law Commission on the work of its seventieth session (30 April – 1 June and 2 July – 10 August 2018), Document A/73/10, Chapter V. Identification of customary international law, E.2. Text of the draft conclusions and commentaries thereto, *Yearbook of the International Law Commission*, 2018, Volume II, Part Two, 91-113, 105.

[545] International Law Commission (2018). Report of the International Law Commission on the work of its seventieth session (30 April – 1 June and 2 July – 10 August 2018), Document A/73/10, Chapter V. Identification of customary international law, E.2. Text of the draft conclusions and commentaries thereto, *Yearbook of the International Law Commission*, 2018, Volume II, Part Two, 91-113, 106.

[546] International Law Commission (2018). Report of the International Law Commission on the work of its seventieth session (30 April – 1 June and 2 July – 10 August 2018), Document A/73/10, Chapter V. Identification of customary international law, E.2. Text of the draft conclusions and commentaries thereto, *Yearbook of the International Law Commission*, 2018, Volume II, Part Two, 91-113, 107.

[547] United Nations (2018). Resolution 73/203 adopted by the General Assembly on 20th December 2018, Annex: Identification of customary international law, Conclusion 12(1).

[548] United Nations (2018). Resolution 73/203 adopted by the General Assembly on 20th December 2018, Annex: Identification of customary international law, Conclusion 12(2).

[549] United Nations (2018). Resolution 73/203 adopted by the General Assembly on 20th December 2018, Annex: Identification of customary international law, Conclusion 12(3).

[550] International Law Commission (2018). Report of the International Law Commission on the work of its seventieth session (30 April – 1 June and 2 July – 10 August 2018), Document A/73/10, Chapter V. Identification of customary international law, E.2. Text of the draft conclusions and commentaries thereto, *Yearbook of the International Law Commission*, 2018, Volume II, Part Two, 91-113, 108.

[551] United Nations (2018). Resolution 73/203 adopted by the General Assembly on 20th December 2018, Annex: Identification of customary international law, Conclusion 13(1).

[552] United Nations (2018). Resolution 73/203 adopted by the General Assembly on 20th December 2018, Annex: Identification of customary international law, Conclusion 13(2).

[553] International Law Commission (2018). Report of the International Law Commission on the work of its seventieth session (30 April – 1 June and 2 July – 10 August 2018), Document A/73/10, Chapter V. Identification of customary international law, E.2. Text of the draft conclusions and commentaries thereto, *Yearbook of the International Law Commission*, 2018, Volume II, Part Two, 91-113, 109.

[554] International Law Commission (2018). Report of the International Law Commission on the work of its seventieth session (30 April – 1 June and 2 July – 10 August 2018), Document A/73/10, Chapter V. Identification of customary international law, E.2. Text of the draft conclusions and commentaries thereto, *Yearbook of the International Law Commission*, 2018, Volume II, Part Two, 91-113, 110.

[555] United Nations (2018). Resolution 73/203 adopted by the General Assembly on 20th December 2018, Annex: Identification of customary international law, Conclusion 14.

[556] United Nations (2018). Resolution 73/203 adopted by the General Assembly on 20th December 2018, Annex: Identification of customary international law, Conclusion 15(1).

[557] United Nations (2018). Resolution 73/203 adopted by the General Assembly on 20th December 2018, Annex: Identification of customary international law, Conclusion 15(2).

[558] United Nations (2018). Resolution 73/203 adopted by the General Assembly on 20th December 2018, Annex: Identification of customary international law, Conclusion 15(3).

[559] International Law Commission (2018). Report of the International Law Commission on the work of its seventieth session (30 April – 1 June and 2 July – 10 August 2018), Document A/73/10, Chapter V. Identification of customary international law, E.2. Text of the draft conclusions and commentaries thereto, *Yearbook of the International Law Commission*, 2018, Volume II, Part Two, 91-113, 112.

[560] United Nations (2018). Resolution 73/203 adopted by the General Assembly on 20th December 2018, Annex: Identification of customary international law, Conclusion 16(1).

[561] United Nations (2018). Resolution 73/203 adopted by the General Assembly on 20th December 2018, Annex: Identification of customary international law, Conclusion 16(2).

[562] International Law Commission (2018). Report of the International Law Commission on the work of its seventieth session (30 April – 1 June and 2 July – 10 August 2018), Document A/73/10, Chapter V. Identification of customary international law, E.2. Text of the draft conclusions and commentaries thereto, *Yearbook of the International Law Commission*, 2018, Volume II, Part Two, 91-113, 113.

[563] International Law Commission (2024). "Summaries of the Work of the International Law Commission: Peremptory norms of general international law (*jus cogens*)." Last updated July 16, 2024. Accessed October 6 and 7, 2024. https://legal.un.org/ilc/summaries/1_14.shtml.

[564] International Court of Justice (2024). "Judge Dire Tladi." Accessed October 6, 2024. https://www.icj-cij.org/node/203535.

[565] United Nations (2022). Report of the International Law Commission: Seventy-third session (18 April – 3 June and 4 July – 5 August 2022), Document A/77/10, Chapter IV. Peremptory norms of general international law (*jus cogens*), E.2. Text of the draft conclusions and commentaries thereto, General Assembly Official Records, Seventy-seventh Session, Supplement No.10 (A/77/10), 16-89, 16.

[566] United Nations (2022). Report of the International Law Commission: Seventy-third session (18 April – 3 June and 4 July – 5 August 2022), Document A/77/10, Chapter IV. Peremptory norms of general international law (*jus cogens*), E.2. Text of the draft conclusions and commentaries thereto, General Assembly Official Records, Seventy-seventh Session, Supplement No.10 (A/77/10), 16-89, 17.

[567] United Nations (2022). Report of the International Law Commission: Seventy-third session (18 April – 3 June and 4 July – 5 August 2022), Document A/77/10, Chapter IV. Peremptory norms of general international law (*jus cogens*), E.2. Text of the draft conclusions and commentaries thereto, General Assembly Official Records, Seventy-seventh Session, Supplement No.10 (A/77/10), 16-89, 18.

[568] United Nations (2022). Report of the International Law Commission: Seventy-third session (18 April – 3 June and 4 July – 5 August 2022), Document A/77/10, Chapter IV. Peremptory norms of general international law (*jus cogens*), E.2. Text of the draft conclusions and commentaries thereto, General Assembly Official Records, Seventy-seventh Session, Supplement No.10 (A/77/10), 16-89, 19-20.

[569] United Nations (2022). Report of the International Law Commission: Seventy-third session (18 April – 3 June and 4 July – 5 August 2022), Document A/77/10, Chapter IV. Peremptory norms of general international law (*jus cogens*), E.2. Text of the draft conclusions and commentaries thereto, General Assembly Official Records, Seventy-seventh Session, Supplement No.10 (A/77/10), 16-89, 22.

[570] United Nations (2022). Report of the International Law Commission: Seventy-third session (18 April – 3 June and 4 July – 5 August 2022), Document A/77/10, Chapter IV. Peremptory norms of general international law (*jus cogens*), E.2. Text of the draft conclusions and commentaries thereto, General Assembly Official Records, Seventy-seventh Session, Supplement No.10 (A/77/10), 16-89, 22-23.

[571] United Nations (2022). Report of the International Law Commission: Seventy-third session (18 April – 3 June and 4 July – 5 August 2022), Document A/77/10, Chapter IV. Peremptory norms of general international law (*jus cogens*), E.2. Text of the draft conclusions and commentaries thereto, General Assembly Official Records, Seventy-seventh Session, Supplement No.10 (A/77/10), 16-89, 23.

[572] United Nations (2022). Report of the International Law Commission: Seventy-third session (18 April – 3 June and 4 July – 5 August 2022), Document A/77/10, Chapter IV. Peremptory norms of general international law (*jus cogens*), E.2. Text of the draft conclusions and commentaries thereto, General Assembly Official Records, Seventy-seventh Session, Supplement No.10 (A/77/10), 16-89, 24.

[573] United Nations (2022). Report of the International Law Commission: Seventy-third session (18 April – 3 June and 4 July – 5 August 2022), Document A/77/10, Chapter IV. Peremptory norms of general international law (*jus cogens*), E.2. Text of the draft conclusions and commentaries thereto, General Assembly Official Records, Seventy-seventh Session, Supplement No.10 (A/77/10), 16-89, 26.

[574] United Nations (2022). Report of the International Law Commission: Seventy-third session (18 April – 3 June and 4 July – 5 August 2022), Document A/77/10, Chapter IV. Peremptory norms of general international law (*jus cogens*), E.2. Text of the draft conclusions and commentaries thereto, General Assembly Official Records, Seventy-seventh Session, Supplement No.10 (A/77/10), 16-89, 26-27.

[575] United Nations (2022). Report of the International Law Commission: Seventy-third session (18 April – 3 June and 4 July – 5 August 2022), Document A/77/10, Chapter IV. Peremptory norms of general international law (*jus cogens*), E.2. Text of the draft conclusions and commentaries thereto, General Assembly Official Records, Seventy-seventh Session, Supplement No.10 (A/77/10), 16-89, 27.

[576] United Nations (2022). Report of the International Law Commission: Seventy-third session (18 April – 3 June and 4 July – 5 August 2022), Document A/77/10, Chapter IV. Peremptory norms of general international law (*jus cogens*), E.2. Text of the draft conclusions and commentaries thereto, General Assembly Official Records, Seventy-seventh Session, Supplement No.10 (A/77/10), 16-89, 28.

[577] United Nations (2022). Report of the International Law Commission: Seventy-third session (18 April – 3 June and 4 July – 5 August 2022), Document A/77/10, Chapter IV. Peremptory norms of general international law (*jus cogens*), E.2. Text of the draft conclusions and commentaries thereto, General Assembly Official Records, Seventy-seventh Session, Supplement No.10 (A/77/10), 16-89, 29.

[578] United Nations (2022). Report of the International Law Commission: Seventy-third session (18 April – 3 June and 4 July – 5 August 2022), Document A/77/10, Chapter IV. Peremptory norms of general international law (*jus cogens*), E.2. Text of the draft conclusions and commentaries thereto, General Assembly Official Records, Seventy-seventh Session, Supplement No.10 (A/77/10), 16-89, 30.

[579] United Nations (2022). Report of the International Law Commission: Seventy-third session (18 April – 3 June and 4 July – 5 August 2022), Document A/77/10, Chapter IV. Peremptory norms of general international law (*jus cogens*), E.2. Text of the draft conclusions and commentaries thereto, General Assembly Official Records, Seventy-seventh Session, Supplement No.10 (A/77/10), 16-89, 31.

[580] United Nations (2022). Report of the International Law Commission: Seventy-third session (18 April – 3 June and 4 July – 5 August 2022), Document A/77/10, Chapter IV. Peremptory norms of general international law (*jus cogens*), E.2. Text of the draft conclusions and commentaries thereto, General Assembly Official Records, Seventy-seventh Session, Supplement No.10 (A/77/10), 16-89, 32.

[581] United Nations (2022). Report of the International Law Commission: Seventy-third session (18 April – 3 June and 4 July – 5 August 2022), Document A/77/10, Chapter IV. Peremptory norms of general international law (*jus cogens*), E.2. Text of the draft conclusions and commentaries thereto, General Assembly Official Records, Seventy-seventh Session, Supplement No.10 (A/77/10), 16-89, 33.

[582] United Nations (2022). Report of the International Law Commission: Seventy-third session (18 April – 3 June and 4 July – 5 August 2022), Document A/77/10, Chapter IV. Peremptory norms of general international law (*jus cogens*), E.2. Text of the draft conclusions and commentaries thereto, General Assembly Official Records, Seventy-seventh Session, Supplement No.10 (A/77/10), 16-89, 35.

[583] United Nations (2022). Report of the International Law Commission: Seventy-third session (18 April – 3 June and 4 July – 5 August 2022), Document A/77/10, Chapter IV. Peremptory norms of general international law (*jus cogens*), E.2. Text of the draft conclusions and commentaries thereto, General Assembly Official Records, Seventy-seventh Session, Supplement No.10 (A/77/10), 16-89, 36.

[584] United Nations (2022). Report of the International Law Commission: Seventy-third session (18 April – 3 June and 4 July – 5 August 2022), Document A/77/10, Chapter IV. Peremptory norms of general international law (*jus cogens*), E.2. Text of the draft conclusions and commentaries thereto, General Assembly Official Records, Seventy-seventh Session, Supplement No.10 (A/77/10), 16-89, 36-37.

[585] United Nations (2022). Report of the International Law Commission: Seventy-third session (18 April – 3 June and 4 July – 5 August 2022), Document A/77/10, Chapter IV. Peremptory norms of general international law (*jus cogens*), E.2. Text of the draft conclusions and commentaries thereto, General Assembly Official Records, Seventy-seventh Session, Supplement No.10 (A/77/10), 16-89, 37.

[586] United Nations (2022). Report of the International Law Commission: Seventy-third session (18 April – 3 June and 4 July – 5 August 2022), Document A/77/10, Chapter IV. Peremptory norms of general international law (*jus cogens*), E.2. Text of the draft conclusions and commentaries thereto, General Assembly Official Records, Seventy-seventh Session, Supplement No.10 (A/77/10), 16-89, 38.

[587] United Nations (2022). Report of the International Law Commission: Seventy-third session (18 April – 3 June and 4 July – 5 August 2022), Document A/77/10, Chapter IV. Peremptory norms of general international law (*jus cogens*), E.2. Text of the draft conclusions and commentaries thereto, General Assembly Official Records, Seventy-seventh Session, Supplement No.10 (A/77/10), 16-89, 39.

[588] United Nations (2022). Report of the International Law Commission: Seventy-third session (18 April – 3 June and 4 July – 5 August 2022), Document A/77/10, Chapter IV. Peremptory norms of general international law (*jus cogens*), E.2. Text of the draft conclusions and commentaries thereto, General Assembly Official Records, Seventy-seventh Session, Supplement No.10 (A/77/10), 16-89, 40.

[589] United Nations (2022). Report of the International Law Commission: Seventy-third session (18 April – 3 June and 4 July – 5 August 2022), Document A/77/10, Chapter IV. Peremptory norms of general international law (*jus cogens*), E.2. Text of the draft conclusions and commentaries thereto, General Assembly Official Records, Seventy-seventh Session, Supplement No.10 (A/77/10), 16-89, 41.
[590] United Nations (2022). Report of the International Law Commission: Seventy-third session (18 April – 3 June and 4 July – 5 August 2022), Document A/77/10, Chapter IV. Peremptory norms of general international law (*jus cogens*), E.2. Text of the draft conclusions and commentaries thereto, General Assembly Official Records, Seventy-seventh Session, Supplement No.10 (A/77/10), 16-89, 43.
[591] United Nations (2022). Report of the International Law Commission: Seventy-third session (18 April – 3 June and 4 July – 5 August 2022), Document A/77/10, Chapter IV. Peremptory norms of general international law (*jus cogens*), E.2. Text of the draft conclusions and commentaries thereto, General Assembly Official Records, Seventy-seventh Session, Supplement No.10 (A/77/10), 16-89, 44.
[592] International Court of Justice (2012). *Questions relating to the Obligation to Prosecute or to Extradite*, Judgment of 20 July 2012, *I.C.J. Reports 2012*, 422-463, 457.
[593] United Nations (2022). Report of the International Law Commission: Seventy-third session (18 April – 3 June and 4 July – 5 August 2022), Document A/77/10, Chapter IV. Peremptory norms of general international law (*jus cogens*), E.2. Text of the draft conclusions and commentaries thereto, General Assembly Official Records, Seventy-seventh Session, Supplement No.10 (A/77/10), 16-89, 45.
[594] United Nations (2022). Report of the International Law Commission: Seventy-third session (18 April – 3 June and 4 July – 5 August 2022), Document A/77/10, Chapter IV. Peremptory norms of general international law (*jus cogens*), E.2. Text of the draft conclusions and commentaries thereto, General Assembly Official Records, Seventy-seventh Session, Supplement No.10 (A/77/10), 16-89, 45-46.
[595] United Nations (2022). Report of the International Law Commission: Seventy-third session (18 April – 3 June and 4 July – 5 August 2022), Document A/77/10, Chapter IV. Peremptory norms of general international law (*jus cogens*), E.2. Text of the draft conclusions and commentaries thereto, General Assembly Official Records, Seventy-seventh Session, Supplement No.10 (A/77/10), 16-89, 46.
[596] United Nations (2022). Report of the International Law Commission: Seventy-third session (18 April – 3 June and 4 July – 5 August 2022), Document A/77/10, Chapter IV. Peremptory norms of general international law (*jus cogens*), E.2. Text of the draft conclusions and commentaries thereto, General Assembly Official Records, Seventy-seventh Session, Supplement No.10 (A/77/10), 16-89, 47.
[597] United Nations (2022). Report of the International Law Commission: Seventy-third session (18 April – 3 June and 4 July – 5 August 2022), Document A/77/10, Chapter IV. Peremptory norms of general international law (*jus cogens*), E.2. Text of the draft conclusions and commentaries thereto, General Assembly Official Records, Seventy-seventh Session, Supplement No.10 (A/77/10), 16-89, 48.
[598] United Nations (2022). Report of the International Law Commission: Seventy-third session (18 April – 3 June and 4 July – 5 August 2022), Document A/77/10, Chapter IV. Peremptory norms of general international law (*jus cogens*), E.2. Text of the draft conclusions and commentaries thereto, General Assembly Official Records, Seventy-seventh Session, Supplement No.10 (A/77/10), 16-89, 50.
[599] United Nations (2022). Report of the International Law Commission: Seventy-third session (18 April – 3 June and 4 July – 5 August 2022), Document A/77/10, Chapter IV. Peremptory norms of general international law (*jus cogens*), E.2. Text of the draft conclusions and commentaries thereto, General Assembly Official Records, Seventy-seventh Session, Supplement No.10 (A/77/10), 16-89, 51.
[600] United Nations (2022). Report of the International Law Commission: Seventy-third session (18 April – 3 June and 4 July – 5 August 2022), Document A/77/10, Chapter IV. Peremptory norms of general international law (*jus cogens*), E.2. Text of the draft conclusions and commentaries thereto, General Assembly Official Records, Seventy-seventh Session, Supplement No.10 (A/77/10), 16-89, 52.
[601] United Nations (2022). Report of the International Law Commission: Seventy-third session (18 April – 3 June and 4 July – 5 August 2022), Document A/77/10, Chapter IV. Peremptory norms of general international law (*jus cogens*), E.2. Text of the draft conclusions and commentaries thereto, General Assembly Official Records, Seventy-seventh Session, Supplement No.10 (A/77/10), 16-89, 53.
[602] United Nations (2022). Report of the International Law Commission: Seventy-third session (18 April – 3 June and 4 July – 5 August 2022), Document A/77/10, Chapter IV. Peremptory norms of general

international law (*jus cogens*), E.2. Text of the draft conclusions and commentaries thereto, General Assembly Official Records, Seventy-seventh Session, Supplement No.10 (A/77/10), 16-89, 54.
[603] United Nations (2022). Report of the International Law Commission: Seventy-third session (18 April – 3 June and 4 July – 5 August 2022), Document A/77/10, Chapter IV. Peremptory norms of general international law (*jus cogens*), E.2. Text of the draft conclusions and commentaries thereto, General Assembly Official Records, Seventy-seventh Session, Supplement No.10 (A/77/10), 16-89, 55.
[604] United Nations (2022). Report of the International Law Commission: Seventy-third session (18 April – 3 June and 4 July – 5 August 2022), Document A/77/10, Chapter IV. Peremptory norms of general international law (*jus cogens*), E.2. Text of the draft conclusions and commentaries thereto, General Assembly Official Records, Seventy-seventh Session, Supplement No.10 (A/77/10), 16-89, 56.
[605] United Nations (2022). Report of the International Law Commission: Seventy-third session (18 April – 3 June and 4 July – 5 August 2022), Document A/77/10, Chapter IV. Peremptory norms of general international law (*jus cogens*), E.2. Text of the draft conclusions and commentaries thereto, General Assembly Official Records, Seventy-seventh Session, Supplement No.10 (A/77/10), 16-89, 57.
[606] United Nations (2022). Report of the International Law Commission: Seventy-third session (18 April – 3 June and 4 July – 5 August 2022), Document A/77/10, Chapter IV. Peremptory norms of general international law (*jus cogens*), E.2. Text of the draft conclusions and commentaries thereto, General Assembly Official Records, Seventy-seventh Session, Supplement No.10 (A/77/10), 16-89, 57-58.
[607] United Nations (2022). Report of the International Law Commission: Seventy-third session (18 April – 3 June and 4 July – 5 August 2022), Document A/77/10, Chapter IV. Peremptory norms of general international law (*jus cogens*), E.2. Text of the draft conclusions and commentaries thereto, General Assembly Official Records, Seventy-seventh Session, Supplement No.10 (A/77/10), 16-89, 58.
[608] United Nations (2022). Report of the International Law Commission: Seventy-third session (18 April – 3 June and 4 July – 5 August 2022), Document A/77/10, Chapter IV. Peremptory norms of general international law (*jus cogens*), E.2. Text of the draft conclusions and commentaries thereto, General Assembly Official Records, Seventy-seventh Session, Supplement No.10 (A/77/10), 16-89, 59.
[609] United Nations (2022). Report of the International Law Commission: Seventy-third session (18 April – 3 June and 4 July – 5 August 2022), Document A/77/10, Chapter IV. Peremptory norms of general international law (*jus cogens*), E.2. Text of the draft conclusions and commentaries thereto, General Assembly Official Records, Seventy-seventh Session, Supplement No.10 (A/77/10), 16-89, 60.
[610] United Nations (2022). Report of the International Law Commission: Seventy-third session (18 April – 3 June and 4 July – 5 August 2022), Document A/77/10, Chapter IV. Peremptory norms of general international law (*jus cogens*), E.2. Text of the draft conclusions and commentaries thereto, General Assembly Official Records, Seventy-seventh Session, Supplement No.10 (A/77/10), 16-89, 60-61.
[611] International Law Commission (2006). Report of the International Law Commission on the work of its fifty-eighth session (1 May – 9 June and 3 July – 11 August 2006), Document A/61/10, Chapter IX. Unilateral acts of states, D.2. Text of the guiding principles with commentaries thereto adopted by the Commission at its fifty-eighth session, *Yearbook of the International Law Commission*, 2006, Volume II, Part Two, 161-166, 165.
[612] United Nations (2022). Report of the International Law Commission: Seventy-third session (18 April – 3 June and 4 July – 5 August 2022), Document A/77/10, Chapter IV. Peremptory norms of general international law (*jus cogens*), E.2. Text of the draft conclusions and commentaries thereto, General Assembly Official Records, Seventy-seventh Session, Supplement No.10 (A/77/10), 16-89, 61.
[613] United Nations (2022). Report of the International Law Commission: Seventy-third session (18 April – 3 June and 4 July – 5 August 2022), Document A/77/10, Chapter IV. Peremptory norms of general international law (*jus cogens*), E.2. Text of the draft conclusions and commentaries thereto, General Assembly Official Records, Seventy-seventh Session, Supplement No.10 (A/77/10), 16-89, 61-62.
[614] United Nations (2022). Report of the International Law Commission: Seventy-third session (18 April – 3 June and 4 July – 5 August 2022), Document A/77/10, Chapter IV. Peremptory norms of general international law (*jus cogens*), E.2. Text of the draft conclusions and commentaries thereto, General Assembly Official Records, Seventy-seventh Session, Supplement No.10 (A/77/10), 16-89, 62.
[615] United Nations (2022). Report of the International Law Commission: Seventy-third session (18 April – 3 June and 4 July – 5 August 2022), Document A/77/10, Chapter IV. Peremptory norms of general

international law (*jus cogens*), E.2. Text of the draft conclusions and commentaries thereto, General Assembly Official Records, Seventy-seventh Session, Supplement No.10 (A/77/10), 16-89, 63.

[616] United Nations (2022). Report of the International Law Commission: Seventy-third session (18 April – 3 June and 4 July – 5 August 2022), Document A/77/10, Chapter IV. Peremptory norms of general international law (*jus cogens*), E.2. Text of the draft conclusions and commentaries thereto, General Assembly Official Records, Seventy-seventh Session, Supplement No.10 (A/77/10), 16-89, 62-63.

[617] United Nations (2022). Report of the International Law Commission: Seventy-third session (18 April – 3 June and 4 July – 5 August 2022), Document A/77/10, Chapter IV. Peremptory norms of general international law (*jus cogens*), E.2. Text of the draft conclusions and commentaries thereto, General Assembly Official Records, Seventy-seventh Session, Supplement No.10 (A/77/10), 16-89, 64.

[618] United Nations (2022). Report of the International Law Commission: Seventy-third session (18 April – 3 June and 4 July – 5 August 2022), Document A/77/10, Chapter IV. Peremptory norms of general international law (*jus cogens*), E.2. Text of the draft conclusions and commentaries thereto, General Assembly Official Records, Seventy-seventh Session, Supplement No.10 (A/77/10), 16-89, 65.

[619] United Nations (2022). Report of the International Law Commission: Seventy-third session (18 April – 3 June and 4 July – 5 August 2022), Document A/77/10, Chapter IV. Peremptory norms of general international law (*jus cogens*), E.2. Text of the draft conclusions and commentaries thereto, General Assembly Official Records, Seventy-seventh Session, Supplement No.10 (A/77/10), 16-89, 66.

[620] United Nations (2022). Report of the International Law Commission: Seventy-third session (18 April – 3 June and 4 July – 5 August 2022), Document A/77/10, Chapter IV. Peremptory norms of general international law (*jus cogens*), E.2. Text of the draft conclusions and commentaries thereto, General Assembly Official Records, Seventy-seventh Session, Supplement No.10 (A/77/10), 16-89, 67.

[621] United Nations (2022). Report of the International Law Commission: Seventy-third session (18 April – 3 June and 4 July – 5 August 2022), Document A/77/10, Chapter IV. Peremptory norms of general international law (*jus cogens*), E.2. Text of the draft conclusions and commentaries thereto, General Assembly Official Records, Seventy-seventh Session, Supplement No.10 (A/77/10), 16-89, 68.

[622] United Nations (2001). Resolution 56/83 adopted by the General Assembly on 12th December 2001, Annex: Responsibility of States for internationally wrongful acts, Article 48(1).

[623] United Nations (2001). Resolution 56/83 adopted by the General Assembly on 12th December 2001, Annex: Responsibility of States for internationally wrongful acts, Article 48(2).

[624] United Nations (2022). Report of the International Law Commission: Seventy-third session (18 April – 3 June and 4 July – 5 August 2022), Document A/77/10, Chapter IV. Peremptory norms of general international law (*jus cogens*), E.2. Text of the draft conclusions and commentaries thereto, General Assembly Official Records, Seventy-seventh Session, Supplement No.10 (A/77/10), 16-89, 69.

[625] United Nations (2022). Report of the International Law Commission: Seventy-third session (18 April – 3 June and 4 July – 5 August 2022), Document A/77/10, Chapter IV. Peremptory norms of general international law (*jus cogens*), E.2. Text of the draft conclusions and commentaries thereto, General Assembly Official Records, Seventy-seventh Session, Supplement No.10 (A/77/10), 16-89, 70.

[626] United Nations (2022). Report of the International Law Commission: Seventy-third session (18 April – 3 June and 4 July – 5 August 2022), Document A/77/10, Chapter IV. Peremptory norms of general international law (*jus cogens*), E.2. Text of the draft conclusions and commentaries thereto, General Assembly Official Records, Seventy-seventh Session, Supplement No.10 (A/77/10), 16-89, 71.

[627] United Nations (2022). Report of the International Law Commission: Seventy-third session (18 April – 3 June and 4 July – 5 August 2022), Document A/77/10, Chapter IV. Peremptory norms of general international law (*jus cogens*), E.2. Text of the draft conclusions and commentaries thereto, General Assembly Official Records, Seventy-seventh Session, Supplement No.10 (A/77/10), 16-89, 72.

[628] United Nations (2022). Report of the International Law Commission: Seventy-third session (18 April – 3 June and 4 July – 5 August 2022), Document A/77/10, Chapter IV. Peremptory norms of general international law (*jus cogens*), E.2. Text of the draft conclusions and commentaries thereto, General Assembly Official Records, Seventy-seventh Session, Supplement No.10 (A/77/10), 16-89, 73.

[629] United Nations (2022). Report of the International Law Commission: Seventy-third session (18 April – 3 June and 4 July – 5 August 2022), Document A/77/10, Chapter IV. Peremptory norms of general

international law (*jus cogens*), E.2. Text of the draft conclusions and commentaries thereto, General Assembly Official Records, Seventy-seventh Session, Supplement No.10 (A/77/10), 16-89, 73-74.

[630] United Nations (2022). Report of the International Law Commission: Seventy-third session (18 April – 3 June and 4 July – 5 August 2022), Document A/77/10, Chapter IV. Peremptory norms of general international law (*jus cogens*), E.2. Text of the draft conclusions and commentaries thereto, General Assembly Official Records, Seventy-seventh Session, Supplement No.10 (A/77/10), 16-89, 75.

[631] United Nations (2022). Report of the International Law Commission: Seventy-third session (18 April – 3 June and 4 July – 5 August 2022), Document A/77/10, Chapter IV. Peremptory norms of general international law (*jus cogens*), E.2. Text of the draft conclusions and commentaries thereto, General Assembly Official Records, Seventy-seventh Session, Supplement No.10 (A/77/10), 16-89, 76.

[632] United Nations (2022). Report of the International Law Commission: Seventy-third session (18 April – 3 June and 4 July – 5 August 2022), Document A/77/10, Chapter IV. Peremptory norms of general international law (*jus cogens*), E.2. Text of the draft conclusions and commentaries thereto, General Assembly Official Records, Seventy-seventh Session, Supplement No.10 (A/77/10), 16-89, 77.

[633] United Nations (2022). Report of the International Law Commission: Seventy-third session (18 April – 3 June and 4 July – 5 August 2022), Document A/77/10, Chapter IV. Peremptory norms of general international law (*jus cogens*), E.2. Text of the draft conclusions and commentaries thereto, General Assembly Official Records, Seventy-seventh Session, Supplement No.10 (A/77/10), 16-89, 77-78.

[634] United Nations (2022). Report of the International Law Commission: Seventy-third session (18 April – 3 June and 4 July – 5 August 2022), Document A/77/10, Chapter IV. Peremptory norms of general international law (*jus cogens*), E.2. Text of the draft conclusions and commentaries thereto, General Assembly Official Records, Seventy-seventh Session, Supplement No.10 (A/77/10), 16-89, 78.

[635] United Nations (2022). Report of the International Law Commission: Seventy-third session (18 April – 3 June and 4 July – 5 August 2022), Document A/77/10, Chapter IV. Peremptory norms of general international law (*jus cogens*), E.2. Text of the draft conclusions and commentaries thereto, General Assembly Official Records, Seventy-seventh Session, Supplement No.10 (A/77/10), 16-89, 79.

[636] United Nations (2022). Report of the International Law Commission: Seventy-third session (18 April – 3 June and 4 July – 5 August 2022), Document A/77/10, Chapter IV. Peremptory norms of general international law (*jus cogens*), E.2. Text of the draft conclusions and commentaries thereto, General Assembly Official Records, Seventy-seventh Session, Supplement No.10 (A/77/10), 16-89, 79-80.

[637] United Nations (2022). Report of the International Law Commission: Seventy-third session (18 April – 3 June and 4 July – 5 August 2022), Document A/77/10, Chapter IV. Peremptory norms of general international law (*jus cogens*), E.2. Text of the draft conclusions and commentaries thereto, General Assembly Official Records, Seventy-seventh Session, Supplement No.10 (A/77/10), 16-89, 80.

[638] United Nations (2022). Report of the International Law Commission: Seventy-third session (18 April – 3 June and 4 July – 5 August 2022), Document A/77/10, Chapter IV. Peremptory norms of general international law (*jus cogens*), E.2. Text of the draft conclusions and commentaries thereto, General Assembly Official Records, Seventy-seventh Session, Supplement No.10 (A/77/10), 16-89, 81.

[639] United Nations (2022). Report of the International Law Commission: Seventy-third session (18 April – 3 June and 4 July – 5 August 2022), Document A/77/10, Chapter IV. Peremptory norms of general international law (*jus cogens*), E.2. Text of the draft conclusions and commentaries thereto, General Assembly Official Records, Seventy-seventh Session, Supplement No.10 (A/77/10), 16-89, 81-83.

[640] United Nations (2022). Report of the International Law Commission: Seventy-third session (18 April – 3 June and 4 July – 5 August 2022), Document A/77/10, Chapter IV. Peremptory norms of general international law (*jus cogens*), E.2. Text of the draft conclusions and commentaries thereto, General Assembly Official Records, Seventy-seventh Session, Supplement No.10 (A/77/10), 16-89, 83.

[641] United Nations (2022). Report of the International Law Commission: Seventy-third session (18 April – 3 June and 4 July – 5 August 2022), Document A/77/10, Chapter IV. Peremptory norms of general international law (*jus cogens*), E.2. Text of the draft conclusions and commentaries thereto, General Assembly Official Records, Seventy-seventh Session, Supplement No.10 (A/77/10), 16-89, 84.

[642] United Nations (2022). Report of the International Law Commission: Seventy-third session (18 April – 3 June and 4 July – 5 August 2022), Document A/77/10, Chapter IV. Peremptory norms of general

international law (*jus cogens*), E.2. Text of the draft conclusions and commentaries thereto, General Assembly Official Records, Seventy-seventh Session, Supplement No.10 (A/77/10), 16-89, 85.

[643] United Nations (2022). Report of the International Law Commission: Seventy-third session (18 April – 3 June and 4 July – 5 August 2022), Document A/77/10, Chapter IV. Peremptory norms of general international law (*jus cogens*), E.2. Text of the draft conclusions and commentaries thereto, General Assembly Official Records, Seventy-seventh Session, Supplement No.10 (A/77/10), 16-89, 89.

[644] Duke University (2024). "Duke Law School: International Legal Research Tutorial – General Principles of Law." Accessed October 20, 2024. https://law.duke.edu/ilrt/cust_law_10.htm.

[645] International Law Commission (2024). "Summaries of the Work of the International Law Commission: General principles of law." Last updated October 8, 2024. Accessed October 20, 2024. https://legal.un.org/ilc/summaries/1_15.shtml.

[646] United Nations (2023). Report of the International Law Commission: Seventy-fourth session (24 April – 2 June and 3 July – 4 August 2023), Document A/78/10, Chapter IV. General principles of law, C.2. Text of the draft conclusions and commentaries thereto, General Assembly Official Records, Seventy-eighth Session, Supplement No.10 (A/78/10), 13-35, 13.

[647] United Nations (2023). Report of the International Law Commission: Seventy-fourth session (24 April – 2 June and 3 July – 4 August 2023), Document A/78/10, Chapter IV. General principles of law, C.2. Text of the draft conclusions and commentaries thereto, General Assembly Official Records, Seventy-eighth Session, Supplement No.10 (A/78/10), 13-35, 14.

[648] United Nations (2023). Report of the International Law Commission: Seventy-fourth session (24 April – 2 June and 3 July – 4 August 2023), Document A/78/10, Chapter IV. General principles of law, C.2. Text of the draft conclusions and commentaries thereto, General Assembly Official Records, Seventy-eighth Session, Supplement No.10 (A/78/10), 13-35, 14-15.

[649] United Nations (2023). Report of the International Law Commission: Seventy-fourth session (24 April – 2 June and 3 July – 4 August 2023), Document A/78/10, Chapter IV. General principles of law, C.2. Text of the draft conclusions and commentaries thereto, General Assembly Official Records, Seventy-eighth Session, Supplement No.10 (A/78/10), 13-35, 15.

[650] United Nations (2023). Report of the International Law Commission: Seventy-fourth session (24 April – 2 June and 3 July – 4 August 2023), Document A/78/10, Chapter IV. General principles of law, C.2. Text of the draft conclusions and commentaries thereto, General Assembly Official Records, Seventy-eighth Session, Supplement No.10 (A/78/10), 13-35, 16.

[651] United Nations (2023). Report of the International Law Commission: Seventy-fourth session (24 April – 2 June and 3 July – 4 August 2023), Document A/78/10, Chapter IV. General principles of law, C.2. Text of the draft conclusions and commentaries thereto, General Assembly Official Records, Seventy-eighth Session, Supplement No.10 (A/78/10), 13-35, 17.

[652] United Nations (2023). Report of the International Law Commission: Seventy-fourth session (24 April – 2 June and 3 July – 4 August 2023), Document A/78/10, Chapter IV. General principles of law, C.2. Text of the draft conclusions and commentaries thereto, General Assembly Official Records, Seventy-eighth Session, Supplement No.10 (A/78/10), 13-35, 18.

[653] United Nations (2023). Report of the International Law Commission: Seventy-fourth session (24 April – 2 June and 3 July – 4 August 2023), Document A/78/10, Chapter IV. General principles of law, C.2. Text of the draft conclusions and commentaries thereto, General Assembly Official Records, Seventy-eighth Session, Supplement No.10 (A/78/10), 13-35, 19-20.

[654] United Nations (2023). Report of the International Law Commission: Seventy-fourth session (24 April – 2 June and 3 July – 4 August 2023), Document A/78/10, Chapter IV. General principles of law, C.2. Text of the draft conclusions and commentaries thereto, General Assembly Official Records, Seventy-eighth Session, Supplement No.10 (A/78/10), 13-35, 20.

[655] United Nations (2023). Report of the International Law Commission: Seventy-fourth session (24 April – 2 June and 3 July – 4 August 2023), Document A/78/10, Chapter IV. General principles of law, C.2. Text of the draft conclusions and commentaries thereto, General Assembly Official Records, Seventy-eighth Session, Supplement No.10 (A/78/10), 13-35, 21.

[656] United Nations (2023). Report of the International Law Commission: Seventy-fourth session (24 April – 2 June and 3 July – 4 August 2023), Document A/78/10, Chapter IV. General principles of law, C.2.

Text of the draft conclusions and commentaries thereto, General Assembly Official Records, Seventy-eighth Session, Supplement No.10 (A/78/10), 13-35, 22.
[657] United Nations (2023). Report of the International Law Commission: Seventy-fourth session (24 April – 2 June and 3 July – 4 August 2023), Document A/78/10, Chapter IV. General principles of law, C.2. Text of the draft conclusions and commentaries thereto, General Assembly Official Records, Seventy-eighth Session, Supplement No.10 (A/78/10), 13-35, 22-23.
[658] United Nations (2023). Report of the International Law Commission: Seventy-fourth session (24 April – 2 June and 3 July – 4 August 2023), Document A/78/10, Chapter IV. General principles of law, C.2. Text of the draft conclusions and commentaries thereto, General Assembly Official Records, Seventy-eighth Session, Supplement No.10 (A/78/10), 13-35, 23.
[659] United Nations (2023). Report of the International Law Commission: Seventy-fourth session (24 April – 2 June and 3 July – 4 August 2023), Document A/78/10, Chapter IV. General principles of law, C.2. Text of the draft conclusions and commentaries thereto, General Assembly Official Records, Seventy-eighth Session, Supplement No.10 (A/78/10), 13-35, 24-25.
[660] United Nations (2023). Report of the International Law Commission: Seventy-fourth session (24 April – 2 June and 3 July – 4 August 2023), Document A/78/10, Chapter IV. General principles of law, C.2. Text of the draft conclusions and commentaries thereto, General Assembly Official Records, Seventy-eighth Session, Supplement No.10 (A/78/10), 13-35, 25.
[661] United Nations (2023). Report of the International Law Commission: Seventy-fourth session (24 April – 2 June and 3 July – 4 August 2023), Document A/78/10, Chapter IV. General principles of law, C.2. Text of the draft conclusions and commentaries thereto, General Assembly Official Records, Seventy-eighth Session, Supplement No.10 (A/78/10), 13-35, 26.
[662] United Nations (2023). Report of the International Law Commission: Seventy-fourth session (24 April – 2 June and 3 July – 4 August 2023), Document A/78/10, Chapter IV. General principles of law, C.2. Text of the draft conclusions and commentaries thereto, General Assembly Official Records, Seventy-eighth Session, Supplement No.10 (A/78/10), 13-35, 27.
[663] United Nations (2023). Report of the International Law Commission: Seventy-fourth session (24 April – 2 June and 3 July – 4 August 2023), Document A/78/10, Chapter IV. General principles of law, C.2. Text of the draft conclusions and commentaries thereto, General Assembly Official Records, Seventy-eighth Session, Supplement No.10 (A/78/10), 13-35, 28.
[664] United Nations (2023). Report of the International Law Commission: Seventy-fourth session (24 April – 2 June and 3 July – 4 August 2023), Document A/78/10, Chapter IV. General principles of law, C.2. Text of the draft conclusions and commentaries thereto, General Assembly Official Records, Seventy-eighth Session, Supplement No.10 (A/78/10), 13-35, 28-29.
[665] United Nations (2023). Report of the International Law Commission: Seventy-fourth session (24 April – 2 June and 3 July – 4 August 2023), Document A/78/10, Chapter IV. General principles of law, C.2. Text of the draft conclusions and commentaries thereto, General Assembly Official Records, Seventy-eighth Session, Supplement No.10 (A/78/10), 13-35, 29.
[666] United Nations (2023). Report of the International Law Commission: Seventy-fourth session (24 April – 2 June and 3 July – 4 August 2023), Document A/78/10, Chapter IV. General principles of law, C.2. Text of the draft conclusions and commentaries thereto, General Assembly Official Records, Seventy-eighth Session, Supplement No.10 (A/78/10), 13-35, 29-30.
[667] United Nations (2023). Report of the International Law Commission: Seventy-fourth session (24 April – 2 June and 3 July – 4 August 2023), Document A/78/10, Chapter IV. General principles of law, C.2. Text of the draft conclusions and commentaries thereto, General Assembly Official Records, Seventy-eighth Session, Supplement No.10 (A/78/10), 13-35, 30.
[668] United Nations (2023). Report of the International Law Commission: Seventy-fourth session (24 April – 2 June and 3 July – 4 August 2023), Document A/78/10, Chapter IV. General principles of law, C.2. Text of the draft conclusions and commentaries thereto, General Assembly Official Records, Seventy-eighth Session, Supplement No.10 (A/78/10), 13-35, 31.
[669] United Nations (2023). Report of the International Law Commission: Seventy-fourth session (24 April – 2 June and 3 July – 4 August 2023), Document A/78/10, Chapter IV. General principles of law, C.2.

Text of the draft conclusions and commentaries thereto, General Assembly Official Records, Seventy-eighth Session, Supplement No.10 (A/78/10), 13-35, 31-32.
[670] United Nations (2023). Report of the International Law Commission: Seventy-fourth session (24 April – 2 June and 3 July – 4 August 2023), Document A/78/10, Chapter IV. General principles of law, C.2. Text of the draft conclusions and commentaries thereto, General Assembly Official Records, Seventy-eighth Session, Supplement No.10 (A/78/10), 13-35, 32.
[671] United Nations (2023). Report of the International Law Commission: Seventy-fourth session (24 April – 2 June and 3 July – 4 August 2023), Document A/78/10, Chapter IV. General principles of law, C.2. Text of the draft conclusions and commentaries thereto, General Assembly Official Records, Seventy-eighth Session, Supplement No.10 (A/78/10), 13-35, 33.
[672] United Nations (2023). Report of the International Law Commission: Seventy-fourth session (24 April – 2 June and 3 July – 4 August 2023), Document A/78/10, Chapter IV. General principles of law, C.2. Text of the draft conclusions and commentaries thereto, General Assembly Official Records, Seventy-eighth Session, Supplement No.10 (A/78/10), 13-35, 34.
[673] United Nations (2023). Report of the International Law Commission: Seventy-fourth session (24 April – 2 June and 3 July – 4 August 2023), Document A/78/10, Chapter IV. General principles of law, C.2. Text of the draft conclusions and commentaries thereto, General Assembly Official Records, Seventy-eighth Session, Supplement No.10 (A/78/10), 13-35, 35.
[674] United Nations (2024). Report of the International Law Commission: Seventy-fifth session (29 April – 31 May and 1 July – 2 August 2024), Document A/79/10, Chapter V. Subsidiary means for the determination of rules of international law, C. Text of the draft conclusions on subsidiary means for the determination of rules of international law provisionally adopted thus far by the Commission, General Assembly Official Records, Seventy-ninth Session, Supplement No.10 (A/79/10), 30-53, 31.
[675] United Nations (2024). Report of the International Law Commission: Seventy-fifth session (29 April – 31 May and 1 July – 2 August 2024), Document A/79/10, Chapter V. Subsidiary means for the determination of rules of international law, C. Text of the draft conclusions on subsidiary means for the determination of rules of international law provisionally adopted thus far by the Commission, General Assembly Official Records, Seventy-ninth Session, Supplement No.10 (A/79/10), 30-53, 41-42.
[676] International Law Commission (2024). "Summaries of the Work of the International Law Commission: Subsidiary means for the determination of rules of international law." Last updated September 27, 2024. Accessed October 31, 2024. https://legal.un.org/ilc/summaries/1_16.shtml.
[677] United Nations (2024). Report of the International Law Commission: Seventy-fifth session (29 April – 31 May and 1 July – 2 August 2024), Document A/79/10, Chapter V. Subsidiary means for the determination of rules of international law, C. Text of the draft conclusions on subsidiary means for the determination of rules of international law provisionally adopted thus far by the Commission, General Assembly Official Records, Seventy-ninth Session, Supplement No.10 (A/79/10), 30-53, 30.
[678] United Nations (2024). Report of the International Law Commission: Seventy-fifth session (29 April – 31 May and 1 July – 2 August 2024), Document A/79/10, Chapter V. Subsidiary means for the determination of rules of international law, C. Text of the draft conclusions on subsidiary means for the determination of rules of international law provisionally adopted thus far by the Commission, General Assembly Official Records, Seventy-ninth Session, Supplement No.10 (A/79/10), 30-53, 30-31.
[679] United Nations (1947). "Statute of the International Law Commission," Article 15.
[680] Austin, J. (1832). *The Province of Jurisprudence Determined.* London: Richard Taylor (University of London), 378-379.
[681] Salem, H., and Walker, S. (2014). Russian parliament approves troop deployment in Ukraine, *The Observer*, Saturday 1 March 2014.
[682] Balmforth, T., and Zverev, A. (2022). Russia's parliament asks Putin to recognise breakaway east Ukrainian regions, *Reuters*, Tuesday 15 February 2022.
[683] Human Rights Watch (2022). Russia, Ukraine & International Law: On Occupation, Armed Conflict and Human Rights: Questions and Answers, *Human Rights Watch*, Wednesday 23 February 2022.

[684] Walker, N. (2024). "Research Briefing: Conflict in Ukraine: A timeline (current conflict, 2022 – present)." Published September 16, 2024. Accessed November 8, 2024. https://commonslibrary.parliament.uk/research-briefings/cbp-9847/.

[685] United Nations (2014). Digital Library: Territorial integrity of Ukraine: resolution / adopted by the General Assembly – 2014. Published March 27, 2014. Accessed November 9, 2024. https://digitallibrary.un.org/record/767565?ln=en.

[686] United Nations (2022). "Digital Library: Aggression against Ukraine: resolution / adopted by the General Assembly – 2022." Published March 2, 2022. Accessed November 10, 2024. https://digitallibrary.un.org/record/3959039.

[687] United Nations (2022). "Digital Library: Humanitarian consequences of the aggression against Ukraine: resolution / adopted by the General Assembly – 2022." Published March 24, 2022. Accessed November 10, 2024. https://digitallibrary.un.org/record/3965954?ln=en.

[688] United Nations (2022). "Digital Library: Territorial integrity of Ukraine: defending the principles of the Charter of the United Nations: resolution / adopted by the General Assembly – 2022." Published October 12, 2022. Accessed November 10, 2024. https://digitallibrary.un.org/record/3990400?ln=en.

[689] United Nations (2022). "Digital Library: Furtherance of remedy and reparation for aggression against Ukraine: resolution / adopted by the General Assembly – 2022." Published November 14, 2022. Accessed November 10, 2024. https://digitallibrary.un.org/record/3994052?ln=en.

[690] United Nations (2023). "Digital Library: Principles of the Charter of the United Nations underlying a comprehensive, just and lasting peace in Ukraine: resolution / adopted by the General Assembly – 2023." Published February 23, 2023. Accessed November 10, 2024. https://digitallibrary.un.org/record/4003921?ln=en.

[691] World Population Review (2024). "Countries Sending Troops to Ukraine 2024." Accessed November 11, 2024. https://worldpopulationreview.com/country-rankings/countries-sending-troops-to-ukraine.

[692] Howell, J. (2024). "Which kontris dey supply weapons give Russia?" Published October 16, 2024. Accessed November 11, 2024. https://www.bbc.com/pidgin/articles/cevywyxlxvjo.

[693] Kelsen, H. (1944). The Principle of Sovereign Equality of States as a Basis for International Organization, *The Yale Law Journal*, 53(2), 207-220, 208.

[694] Mirage News (2022). "Full Text of Putin State of Nation Speech 21 Feb 2022." Published February 22, 2022. Accessed November 13, 2024. https://www.miragenews.com/full-text-of-putin-state-of-nation-speech-21-951701/.

[695] Security Council Report (2024). "UN Security Council Working Methods: The Veto." Published February 13, 2024. Accessed November 16 and 18, 2024. https://www.securitycouncilreport.org/un-security-council-working-methods/the-veto.php.

[696] Security Council Report (2024). The Security Council Veto. New York: Security Council Report, 1-17, 1-17.

[697] Security Council Report (2024). The Security Council Veto. New York: Security Council Report, 1-17, 5.

[698] Security Council Report (2015). Research Report: The Veto. New York: Security Council Report, 1-9, 5-6.

[699] Security Council Report (2015). Research Report: The Veto. New York: Security Council Report, 1-9, 6.

[700] Security Council Report (2015). Research Report: The Veto. New York: Security Council Report, 1-9, 4.

[701] United Nations (2024). "About Us." Accessed November 19, 2024. https://www.un.org/en/about-us.

[702] United Nations (1982). "United Nations Convention on the Law of the Sea," *United Nations Treaty Series* Registration Number 31363, Article 286.

[703] United Nations (1982). "United Nations Convention on the Law of the Sea," Article 287(1).

[704] United Nations (1982). "United Nations Convention on the Law of the Sea," Article 287(3).

[705] United Nations (1982). "United Nations Convention on the Law of the Sea," Article 287(4).

[706] United Nations (1982). "United Nations Convention on the Law of the Sea," Article 287(5).

[707] International Court of Justice (2024). "Declarations recognizing the jurisdiction of the Court as compulsory." Accessed November 20, 2024. https://www.icj-cij.org/declarations/.

[708] United Nations (2024). 4. Declarations recognizing as compulsory the jurisdiction of the International Court of Justice under Article 36, paragraph 2, of the Statute of the Court, I4. Charter of the United Nations and Statute of the International Court of Justice (New York: United Nations), 1-28, 1-3.

[709] United Nations (1982). "United Nations Convention on the Law of the Sea," Article 287(8).

[710] United Nations (2024). "United Nations Treaty Collection: Chapter XXI Law of the Sea – 6. United Nations Convention on the Law of the Sea." Last updated November 25, 2024. Accessed November 22, 23, 24 and 25, 2024. https://treaties.un.org/pages/ViewDetailsIII.aspx?src=TREATY&mtdsg_no=XXI-6&chapter=21&Temp=mtdsg3&lang=en.

[711] United Nations (1982). "United Nations Convention on the Law of the Sea," Article 298(1).

[712] International Law Commission (2011). Report of the International Law Commission on the work of its sixty-third session (26 April – 3 June and 4 July – 12 August 2011), Document A/66/10, Chapter IV. Reservations to treaties, F.1. Text of the guidelines constituting the Guide to Practice, followed by an annex on the reservations dialogue, *Yearbook of the International Law Commission*, 2011, Volume II, Part Two, 26-38, 29.

[713] International Law Commission (2011). Report of the International Law Commission on the work of its sixty-third session (26 April – 3 June and 4 July – 12 August 2011), Document A/66/10, Chapter IV. Reservations to treaties, F.1. Text of the guidelines constituting the Guide to Practice, followed by an annex on the reservations dialogue, *Yearbook of the International Law Commission*, 2011, Volume II, Part Two, 26-38, 37-38.

[714] Permanent Court of International Justice (1927). *The Case of the S.S. "Lotus"*, Judgment of 7 September 1927, *P.C.I.J. Series A No. 10 (1927)*, 4-33, 16.

[715] Permanent Court of International Justice (1927). *The Case of the S.S. "Lotus"*, Judgment of 7 September 1927, *P.C.I.J. Series A No. 10 (1927)*, 4-33, 10 and 21-22.

[716] Permanent Court of International Justice (1927). *The Case of the S.S. "Lotus"*, Judgment of 7 September 1927, *P.C.I.J. Series A No. 10 (1927)*, 4-33, 23, 25-27 and 30.

[717] Permanent Court of International Justice (1927). *The Case of the S.S. "Lotus"*, Judgment of 7 September 1927, *P.C.I.J. Series A No. 10 (1927)*, 4-33, 30-31.

[718] United Nations (1958). "Convention on the High Seas," *United Nations Treaty Series* Registration Number 6465, Article 11(1).

[719] United Nations (1982). "United Nations Convention on the Law of the Sea," Article 311(1).

[720] United Nations (1982). "United Nations Convention on the Law of the Sea," Article 97(1).

[721] Milners (2023). "A (very) brief history of the legal system in England and Wales." Published March 24, 2023. Accessed November 28, 2024. https://www.milnerslaw.co.uk/a-very-brief-history-of-the-legal-system-in-england-and-wales/.

[722] Courts and Tribunals Judiciary (2024). "An Introduction to the Chancery Division." Accessed November 28, 2024. https://www.judiciary.uk/courts-and-tribunals/business-and-property-courts/chancery-division/the-work-of-the-chancery-division/introduction-to-the-chancery-division/.

[723] Shakespeare, W. (1599). 'The Tragedy of Julius Caesar' *in* Jowett, J., Montgomery, W., Taylor, G., and Wells, S. (eds.) (1986), *William Shakespeare: The Complete Works* (Oxford: Oxford University Press), 675-703, 697-698.

[724] Worldometer (2024). "World Population: Top 20 Largest Countries by Population (Live)". Accessed December 1, 2024. https://www.worldometers.info/world-population/#top20.

[725] Worldometer (2024). "Countries in the world by population (2024)." Accessed December 1, 2024. https://www.worldometers.info/world-population/population-by-country/.

[726] Municipality of Siena Culture and Tourism Directorate (2024). "visitsiena: Allegory and Effects of Good and Bad Government." Accessed December 7, 2024. https://visitsienaofficial.it/en/allegory-and-effects-of-good-and-bad-government/.

[727] Encyclopaedia Britannica (2024). "The Effects of Good Government in the City." Accessed December 7, 2024. https://www.britannica.com/art/The-Effects-of-Good-Government-in-the-City#/media/1/2235274/291140Access%20Date.

[728] Libreria Editrice Vaticana (2008). "Benedict XVI General Audience: Paul VI Audience Hall – Wednesday, 9 January 2008." Accessed December 7 and 8, 2024. https://www.vatican.va/content/benedict-xvi/en/audiences/2008/documents/hf_ben-xvi_aud_20080109.html.

[729] Aurelius, A. (400). *The Confessions of St. Augustine.* Pusey, E. (tr.) (Grand Rapids: Christian Classics Ethereal Library), 154.

[730] Aurelius, A. (400). *The Confessions of St. Augustine.* Pusey, E. (tr.) (Grand Rapids: Christian Classics Ethereal Library), 162.

[731] Rotelle, J. (ed.) (1994). *The Works of Saint Augustine: A Translation for the 21st Century, Part III – Sermons, Volume 9: Sermons 306-340A.* Hill, E. (tr.) (New York: New City Press), 292.

[732] Rotelle, J. (ed.) (1994). *The Works of Saint Augustine: A Translation for the 21st Century, Part III – Sermons, Volume 9: Sermons 306-340A.* Hill, E. (tr.) (New York: New City Press), 293.

[733] International Law Commission (2024). "Current status of the work of the Commission and forthcoming deadlines." Last updated September 18, 2024. Accessed December 10, 2024. https://legal.un.org/ilc/status.shtml.

[734] United Nations (2024). Report of the International Law Commission: Seventy-fifth session (29 April – 31 May and 1 July – 2 August 2024), Document A/79/10, Annex I. Compensation for the damage caused by internationally wrongful acts, General Assembly Official Records, Seventy-ninth Session, Supplement No.10 (A/79/10), 125-145, 128.

[735] United Nations (2024). Report of the International Law Commission: Seventy-fifth session (29 April – 31 May and 1 July – 2 August 2024), Document A/79/10, Annex I. Compensation for the damage caused by internationally wrongful acts, General Assembly Official Records, Seventy-ninth Session, Supplement No.10 (A/79/10), 125-145, 130.

[736] United Nations (2001). Resolution 56/83 adopted by the General Assembly on 12th December 2001, Annex: Responsibility of States for internationally wrongful acts, Article 36.

[737] United Nations (2024). Report of the International Law Commission: Seventy-fifth session (29 April – 31 May and 1 July – 2 August 2024), Document A/79/10, Annex II. Due Diligence in International Law, General Assembly Official Records, Seventy-ninth Session, Supplement No.10 (A/79/10), 146-162, 147.

[738] United Nations (2024). Report of the International Law Commission: Seventy-fifth session (29 April – 31 May and 1 July – 2 August 2024), Document A/79/10, Annex II. Due Diligence in International Law, General Assembly Official Records, Seventy-ninth Session, Supplement No.10 (A/79/10), 146-162, 148.

[739] United Nations (2024). Report of the International Law Commission: Seventy-fifth session (29 April – 31 May and 1 July – 2 August 2024), Document A/79/10, Annex II. Due Diligence in International Law, General Assembly Official Records, Seventy-ninth Session, Supplement No.10 (A/79/10), 146-162, 151.

[740] United Nations (2024). Report of the International Law Commission: Seventy-fifth session (29 April – 31 May and 1 July – 2 August 2024), Document A/79/10, Annex II. Due Diligence in International Law, General Assembly Official Records, Seventy-ninth Session, Supplement No.10 (A/79/10), 146-162, 153.

[741] International Court of Justice (2024). "Pending cases." Accessed December 10, 2024. https://www.icj-cij.org/pending-cases.

[742] International Court of Justice (2024). *Application of the International Convention on the Elimination of All Forms of Racial Discrimination (Armenia v. Azerbaijan), Preliminary Objections*, Judgment of 12 November 2024, *2024 12 November General List No. 180*, 1-32, 31.

[743] International Court of Justice (2024). *Application of the International Convention on the Elimination of All Forms of Racial Discrimination (Azerbaijan v. Armenia), Preliminary Objections*, Judgment of 12 November 2024, *2024 12 November General List No. 181*, 1-32, 30-31.

[744] International Tribunal for the Law of the Sea (2024). "Cases: Docket – List of pending cases and current status." Accessed December 11, 2024. https://www.itlos.org/en/main/cases/docket/.

[745] International Tribunal for the Law of the Sea (2023). Press Release 335, 2 May 2023 (Hamburg: International Tribunal for the Law of the Sea).

[746] International Tribunal for the Law of the Sea (2024). "The M/T "Heroic Idun" (No. 2) Case (Marshall Islands/Equatorial Guinea)." Accessed December 11, 2024. https://www.itlos.org/en/main/cases/list-of-cases/the-m/t-heroic-idun-no-2-case-marshall-islands/equatorial-guinea/.

[747] International Tribunal for the Law of the Sea (2024). *The M/T "Heroic Idun" (No. 2) Case (Marshall Islands/Equatorial Guinea)*, Order of 25 July 2024, *List of Cases No. 32 Order 2024/2*, 1-3, 2-3.

[748] International Tribunal for the Law of the Sea (2024). Press Release 351, 4 June 2024 (Hamburg: International Tribunal for the Law of the Sea).

[749] International Tribunal for the Law of the Sea (2024). Press Release 352, 10 June 2024 (Hamburg: International Tribunal for the Law of the Sea), 1-2, 1.

[750] International Tribunal for the Law of the Sea (2024). Press Release 354, 13 June 2024 (Hamburg: International Tribunal for the Law of the Sea), 1-2, 1.

[751] International Tribunal for the Law of the Sea (2024). *The "Zheng He" Case (Luxembourg v. Mexico)*, Order of 27 July 2024, *List of Cases No. 33 Order 2024/2*, 1-41, 40.

[752] International Tribunal for the Law of the Sea (2024). *The "Zheng He" Case (Luxembourg v. Mexico)*, Order of 8 August 2024, *List of Cases No. 33 Order 2024/3*, 1-3, 2.

Bibliography

Al Jazeera (2022). Russian forces launch full-scale invasion of Ukraine: Putin approves 'special military operation' as Russia launches an invasion of Ukraine by land, air and sea, *Al Jazeera*, Thursday 24 February 2022.

Aurelius, A. (400). *The Confessions of St. Augustine.* Pusey, E. (tr.). Grand Rapids: Christian Classics Ethereal Library.

Austin, J. (1832). *The Province of Jurisprudence Determined.* London: Richard Taylor (University of London).

Baber, G. (2017). *Essays on International Law.* Newcastle-upon-Tyne: Cambridge Scholars Publishing.

Baber, G. (2019). *The United Nations System.* Newcastle-upon-Tyne: Cambridge Scholars Publishing.

Baber, G. (2020). *The Global Law of the Sea.* New York: Nova Science Publishers Inc.

Baber, G. (2024). E-mail communication from Dr. Graeme Baber to Dr. Svetlana Savranskaya, National Security Archive, George Washington University, November 6, 2024.

Bae, G., and Yeung, J. (2024). North Korean soldiers learning Russian commands and may be sent to Ukraine front lines, South Korean lawmakers say, *CNN*, Tuesday 29 October 2024.

Balmforth, T., and Zverev, A. (2022). Russia's parliament asks Putin to recognise breakaway east Ukrainian regions, *Reuters*, Tuesday 15 February 2022.

Baumert, K, and Melchior, B. (2015). The Practice of Archipelagic States: A Study of Studies, *Ocean Development & International Law*, 46, 60-80.

Bell, J., Danforth, L., and Dimitrov, P. (2023). "History of Bulgaria." Published August 30, 2023. Updated April 19, 2024. Accessed June 25, 2024. https://www.britannica.com/topic/history-of-Bulgaria/The-principality.

Bergmann, W. (1998). "*Georg Philipp Telemann.*" Published July 20, 1998, Last updated June 22, 2024. Accessed December 8, 2024. https://www.britannica.com/biography/Georg-Philipp-Telemann.

Bielieskov, M. (2021). "*The Russian and Ukrainian Spring 2021 War Scare.*" Published September 21, 2021. Accessed June 8, 2024. https://www.csis.org/analysis/russian-and-ukrainian-spring-2021-war-scare.

Brillaud, L., Curic, A., Maggiore, M., Miñano, L., and Schmidt, N. (2022). "*EU member states exported weapons to Russia after the 2014 embargo.*" Published March 17, 2022. Accessed November 11, 2024. https://www.investigate-europe.eu/en/posts/eu-states-exported-weapons-to-russia.

British Broadcasting Corporation (2024). "*Bitesize: Paris Peace Treaties and the League of Nations, to 1933: Terms of the Paris Peace Treaties.*" Accessed June 25, 2024. https://www.bbc.co.uk/bitesize/guides/zbg4t39/revision/4.

Cambridge Dictionary (2024a). "*BC adverb.*" Accessed August 27, 2024. https://dictionary.cambridge.org/dictionary/english/bc.

Cambridge Dictionary (2024b). "*BCE adverb.*" Accessed August 27, 2024. https://dictionary.cambridge.org/dictionary/english/bce.

Carozza, P., Glendon, M., Hazard, J., Jolowicz, H., Kiralfy, A., Millner, M., Powell, R., Rheinstein, M., and Stein, P. (1998). "*Roman law.*" Published July 24, 1998. Last updated February 16, 2024. Accessed August 27, 2024. https://www.britannica.com/topic/Roman-law.

Carroll, E., and Hepler, R. (2024). "*Bosnian Crisis of 1908: Overview, History & Effect.*" Accessed June 24, 2024. https://study.com/academy/lesson/the-bosnian-crisis-of-1908-annexation-by-austria-hungary.html.

CFR Education (2023). "*Why Did World War II Happen?*" Last updated July 25, 2023. Accessed July 16, 2024. https://education.cfr.org/learn/reading/why-did-world-war-ii-happen.

Chmielewski, K. (2023). "*Casualties of World War II.*" Published August 31, 2023. Updated May 15, 2024. Accessed July 18, 2024. https://www.britannica.com/event/casualties-of-World-War-II-2231003.

Cica, A. (2014). The Principle of *Iura Novit Curia.* University of Miami School of Law: Young Scholars in International Arbitration – A collection of essays prepared for the ICCA 2014 Congress, 105-124.

Colorio, M. (2024). The *Aut Dedere Aut Judicare System* for Crimes Against Humanity: A Critical but Missing Tool in the Fight Against Impunity, *Journal of International Criminal Justice*, 22(1), 1-17.

Conquest, R., Dewdney, J., McCauley, M., Pipes, R., and Dobrianskyi, Y. (1999). "*Soviet Union.*" Published July 26, 1999. Last updated June 7, 2024. Accessed June 8, 2024. https://www.britannica.com/place/Soviet-Union.

Cooper, J. (2008). The burden and standard of proof. Courts and Tribunals Judiciary: Principles in Practice, Spring 2008. London: Judicial Office.

Cornell University (2022). "*Cornell Law School: Legal Information Institute – inter se.*" Last updated in April 2022. Accessed September 3, 2024. https://www.law.cornell.edu/wex/inter_se.

Court, E. (2023). Lukashenko admits Russian troops invaded Ukraine through Belarus in 2022, *The Kyiv Independent*, Friday 18 August 2023.

Courts and Tribunals Judiciary (2024). "*An Introduction to the Chancery Division.*" Accessed November 28, 2024. https://www.judiciary.uk/courts-and-tribunals/business-and-property-courts/chancery-division/the-work-of-the-chancery-division/introduction-to-the-chancery-division/.

Demeter, D., and Nasirova, Z. (2018). International legal harmonisation in theory and practice. Universitatea Spiru Haret: Facultatea de Ştiinţe Juridice, Politice şi Administrative Bucureşti – Centrul de Cercetări Juridice: Legal and Administrative Studies – Proceedings of Conference Legal, Political and Administrative Consequences of Romania's Accession to the European Union, Bucureşti, 17-18 Mai 2018, 66-76.

Demirci, S. (1997). *The Lausanne Conference: The Evolution of Turkish and British Diplomatic Strategies 1922-1923.* Dissertation for the Degree of Doctor of Philosophy in International History at the London School of Economics and Political Science, March 1997. Ann Arbor: ProQuest LLC.

Derecho Internacional Público (2024). Dumbarton Oaks – Washington Conversations on International Peace and Security Organization, October 7, 1944: Proposals for the Establishment of a General International Organization.

Draycott Browne Solicitors (2024). "*What is the definition of evidence in UK criminal law?*" Accessed October 28, 2024, https://www.draycottbrowne.co.uk/investigations/types-evidence.

Duke University (2024). "*Duke Law School: International Legal Research Tutorial – General Principles of Law.*" Accessed October 20, 2024. https://law.duke.edu/ilrt/cust_law_10.htm.

Dumbarton Oaks Archives (2015). "*The Dumbarton Oaks Conversations, 1944.*" Published June 15, 2017. Accessed July 11, 2024. https://www.doaks.org/newsletter/news-archives/2015/the-dumbarton-oaks-conversations-1944.

Encyclopaedia Britannica (1998a). "*Ambrogio Lorenzetti.*" Published July 20, 1998. Last updated March 22, 2024. Accessed December 7, 2024. https://www.britannica.com/biography/Ambrogio-Lorenzetti.

Encyclopaedia Britannica (1998b). "*Armistice of Mudros: Turkish history [1918].*" Published July 20, 1998. Last updated October 23, 2023. Accessed June 25, 2024. https://www.britannica.com/event/Armistice-of-Mudros.

Encyclopaedia Britannica (1998c). "*Atlantic Charter.*" Published July 20, 1998. Last updated March 11, 2024. Accessed July 22, 2024. https://www.britannica.com/event/Atlantic-Charter.

Encyclopaedia Britannica (1998d). "*Dumbarton Oaks Conference.*" Published July 20, 1998. Last updated August 14, 2023. Accessed July 11 and 23, 2024. https://www.britannica.com/event/Dumbarton-Oaks-Conference.

Encyclopaedia Britannica (1998e). "*History of Crimea.*" Published July 20, 1998. Last updated June 14, 2024. Accessed June 14, 2024. https://www.britannica.com/place/Crimea/History.

Encyclopaedia Britannica (1998f). "*Hundred.*" Published July 20, 1998. Last updated February 24, 2012. Accessed November 28, 2024. https://www.britannica.com/topic/hundred-English-government.

Encyclopaedia Britannica (1998g). "*Paris Peace Conference 1919-1920.*" Published July 20, 1998. Last updated April 19, 2024. Accessed June 25, 2024. https://www.britannica.com/event/Paris-Peace-Conference.

Encyclopaedia Britannica (1998h). "*Treaty of Lausanne: Allies-Turkey [1923].*" Published July 20, 1998. Last updated June 7, 2024. Accessed June 25, 2024. https://www.britannica.com/event/Treaty-of-Lausanne-1923.

Encyclopaedia Britannica (1999). "*Yalta Conference.*" Published May 4, 1999. Last updated July 24, 2024. Accessed July 26, 2024. https://www.britannica.com/event/Yalta-Conference.

Encyclopaedia Britannica (2009). "*Council of Foreign Ministers.*" Published March 18, 2009. Last updated September 25, 2013. Accessed July 21, 2024. https://www.britannica.com/topic/Council-of-Foreign-Ministers.

Encyclopaedia Britannica (2018a). "*Potsdam Declaration.*" Published January 31, 2018. Last updated July 19, 2024. Accessed July 19, 2024. https://www.britannica.com/topic/Potsdam-Declaration.

Encyclopaedia Britannica (2018b). "*Tripartite Pact.*" Published February 27, 2018. Last updated September 20, 2023. Accessed July 18, 2024. https://www.britannica.com/topic/Tripartite-Pact.

Encyclopaedia Britannica (2021). "*Atomic bombings of Hiroshima and Nagasaki.*" Published May 3, 2021. Last updated June 21, 2024. Accessed July 19, 2024. https://www.britannica.com/event/atomic-bombings-of-Hiroshima-and-Nagasaki.

Encyclopaedia Britannica (2024a). "*How did World War II end?*" Accessed July 19, 2024. https://www.britannica.com/question/How-did-World-War-II-end.

Encyclopaedia Britannica (2024b). "*How many people died during World War II?*" Accessed July 18, 2024. https://www.britannica.com/question/How-many-people-died-during-World-War-II.

Encyclopaedia Britannica (2024c). "*pacta sunt servanda: law principle.*" Accessed October 25, 2024. https://www.britannica.com/topic/pacta-sunt-servanda.

Encyclopaedia Britannica (2024d). "*rebus sic stantibus: law principle.*" Accessed October 27, 2024. https://www.britannica.com/topic/rebus-sic-stantibus.

Encyclopaedia Britannica (2024e). "*The Effects of Good Government in the City.*" Accessed December 7, 2024. https://www.britannica.com/art/The-Effects-of-Good-Government-in-the-City#/media/1/2235274/291140Access%20Date.

Erpelding, M. (2019). 'Introduction: Versailles and the Broadening of 'Peace Through Law' *in* Erpelding, M., Hess, B., and Ruiz Fabri, H. (eds.) (2019), *Peace Through Law: The Versailles Peace Treaty and Dispute Settlement After World War I*, First edition. Baden-Baden: Nomos Verlagsgesellschaft.

Gouvernement de France (2024). "*Chemins de Mémoire: An ordinary red-brick school.*" Accessed July 19, 2024. https://www.cheminsdememoire.gouv.fr/en/ordinary-red-brick-school-0.

Government of the United States of America (1919). *Treaty of Peace with Germany (Treaty of Versailles).* Treaty and protocol signed at Versailles June 28, 1919; protocol signed by Germany at Paris January 10, 1920. Entered into force January 10, 1920, 4.15 p.m., as between contracting parties (the United States was not a party). 1919 For. Rel. (Paris Peace Conference, XIII) 55, 740, 743; 66th Congress, 1st Session, Senate Document 51, 43-240.

Government of the United States of America (1944). *Events leading up to World War II: Chronological history of certain major international events leading up to and during World War II with the ostensible reasons advanced for their occurrence, 1931-1944*, 78th Congress, 2nd Session, House Document No.541. Washington: United States Government Printing Office.

Government of the United States of America (2009). "*U.S. Department of State Archive: The Potsdam Conference, 1945.*" Published January 20, 2009. Accessed July 20, 2024. https://2001-2009.state.gov/r/pa/ho/time/wwii/93275.htm.

Government of the United States of America (2024a). "*Department of State – Office of the Historian: Foreign Relations of the United States, 1946, Paris Peace Conference: Proceedings, Volume III.*" Accessed July 20, 2024. https://history.state.gov/historicaldocuments/frus1946v03/introduction.

Government of the United States of America (2024b). "*Department of State – Office of the Historian: Foreign Relations of the United States, Diplomatic Papers, 1945, General – The United Nations, Volume I: Guide to discussions of Dumbarton Oaks proposals and corresponding articles of the Charter of the United Nations, 1944-1945.*" Accessed July 25 and 26, 2024. https://history.state.gov/historicaldocuments/frus1945v01/guide.

Government of the United States of America (2024c). "*Department of State – Office of the Historian: The Formation of the United Nations, 1945.*" Accessed July 26, 2024. https://history.state.gov/milestones/1937-1945/un.

Government of the United States of America (2024d). "*Department of State – Office of the Historian: The Tehran Conference, 1943.*" Accessed July 23, 2024. https://history.state.gov/milestones/1937-1945/tehran-conf.

Government of the United States of America (2024e). "*U.S. Department of Defense: Victory over Japan Day End of WWII.*" Accessed July 19, 2024. https://www.defense.gov/Multimedia/Experience/VJ-Day/.

Grant, T. (2019). 'Chapter 2 – The League of Nations as a Universal Organization' *in* Erpelding, M., Hess, B., and Ruiz Fabri, H. (eds.) (2019), *Peace Through Law: The Versailles Peace Treaty and Dispute Settlement After World War I*, First edition. Baden-Baden: Nomos Verlagsgesellschaft.

Guterres, A. (2022a). "*Readout of the Secretary-General's meeting with H.E. Mr. Vladimir Putin, President of the Russian Federation.*" Published April 26, 2022. Accessed June 13, 2024. https://www.un.org/sg/en/content/sg/readout/2022-04-26/readout-of-the-secretary-general%E2%80%99s-meeting-he-mr-vladimir-putin-president-of-the-russian-federation?_gl=1*1fmukpc*_ga*MzI1NTMwMjU0LjE3MTgyMTA0OTc.*_ga_TK9BQL5X7Z*MTcxODI3NzU3MC40LjAuMTcxODI3NzU3MC4wLjAuMA..

Guterres, A. (2022b). "*Secretary-General's remarks at press encounter with Russian Foreign Minister, Sergey V. Lavrov.*" Published April 26, 2022. Accessed June 13, 2024. https://www.un.org/sg/en/content/sg/press-encounter/2022-04-26/secretary-generals-remarks-press-encounter-russian-foreign-minister-sergey-v-lavrov?_gl=1*26o48x*_ga*MzI1NTMwMjU0LjE3MTgyMTA0OTc.*_ga_TK9BQL5X7Z*MTcxODI4MTk1My41LjEuMTcxODI4MjIzNC4wLjAuMA..

Harry S. Truman Presidential Library and Museum (2024). "*Invasion of Manchuria.*" Accessed July 18, 2024. https://www.trumanlibrary.gov/education/presidential-inquiries/invasion-manchuria.

Hertogen, A. (2015). Letting *Lotus* Bloom, *The European Journal of International Law*, 26(4), 901-926.

History.com Staff. (2020). "*Outbreak of World War I.*" Published August 24, 2018. Updated November 10, 2020. Accessed June 24, 2024. https://www.history.com/topics/world-war-i/outbreak-of-world-war-i.

Honniball, A. (2020). "*ICJ Amendments to the Rules of Court.*" Published June 29, 2020. Accessed August 13, 2024. https://demaribus.net/2020/06/29/icj-amendments-to-the-rules-of-court-2/.

Houthoff (2024). "*Eleven international publishing: Excess of Powers in International Commercial Arbitration – Compliance with the Arbitral Tribunal's Mandate in a Comparative Perspective: Piotr Wiliński.*" Accessed October 28, 2024. https://www.houthoff.com/-/media/houthoff/publications/pwilinski/flyer----excess-of-powers-in-international-commercial-arbitration.pdf.

Howell, J. (2024). "*Which kontris dey supply weapons give Russia?*" Published October 16, 2024. Accessed November 11, 2024. https://www.bbc.com/pidgin/articles/cevywyxlxvjo.

Hughes, T., and Royde-Smith, J. (1998). "*World War II: 1939-1945.*" Published August 23, 1998. Last updated July 13, 2024. Accessed July 18, 2024. https://www.britannica.com/event/World-War-II.

Human Rights Watch (2022). Russia, Ukraine & International Law: On Occupation, Armed Conflict and Human Rights: Questions and Answers, *Human Rights Watch*, Wednesday 23 February 2022.

Imperial War Museums (2024). "*The Peace Treaties that Ended The First World War.*" Accessed June 25, 2024. https://www.iwm.org.uk/history/the-peace-treaties-that-ended-the-first-world-war.

International Committee of the Red Cross (2024). "*How does law protect in war? Lex specialis.*" Accessed October 25, 2024. https://casebook.icrc.org/a_to_z/glossary/lex-specialis.

International Court of Justice (1951). *Reservations to the Convention on the Prevention and Punishment of the Crime of Genocide*, Advisory Opinion of 28 May 1951, *I.C.J. Reports 1951*, 15-30.

International Court of Justice (1971). *Legal Consequences for States of the Continued Presence of South Africa in Namibia (South West Africa) notwithstanding Security Council Resolution 276 (1970)*, Advisory Opinion of 21 June 1971, *I.C.J. Reports 1971*, 16-66.

International Court of Justice (1986). *Case concerning Military and Paramilitary Activities in and against Nicaragua (Nicaragua v. United States of America), The Merits*, Judgment of 27 June 1986, *I.C.J. Reports 1986*, 14-150.

International Court of Justice (2012). *Questions relating to the Obligation to Prosecute or to Extradite*, Judgment of 20 July 2012, *I.C.J. Reports 2012*, 422-463.

International Court of Justice (2022). *Allegations of Genocide under the Convention on the Prevention and Punishment of the Crime of Genocide (Ukraine v. Russian Federation), Provisional Measures*, Order of 16 March 2002, *I.C.J. Reports 2022*, 211-231.

International Court of Justice (2024a). *Application of the International Convention on the Elimination of All Forms of Racial Discrimination (Armenia v. Azerbaijan), Preliminary Objections*, Judgment of 12 November 2024, *2024 12 November General List No. 180.*

International Court of Justice (2024b). *Application of the International Convention on the Elimination of All Forms of Racial Discrimination (Azerbaijan v. Armenia), Preliminary Objections*, Judgment of 12 November 2024, *2024 12 November General List No. 181.*

International Court of Justice (2024c). "*Basic Documents.*" Accessed August 12, 2024. https://www.icj-cij.org/basic-documents.

International Court of Justice (2024d). "*Current Members.*" Accessed September 10, 2024. https://www.icj-cij.org/index.php/current-members.

International Court of Justice (2024e). "*Declarations recognizing the jurisdiction of the Court as compulsory.*" Accessed November 20, 2024. https://www.icj-cij.org/declarations/.

International Court of Justice (2024f). "*History.*" Accessed July 4, 9, 11, 12 and 15, 2024, and August 9 and 10, 2024. https://www.icj-cij.org/history.

International Court of Justice (2024g). "*Judge Georg Nolte.*" Accessed September 8, 2024. https://www.icj-cij.org/index.php/node/4058.

International Court of Justice (2024h). "*Pending cases.*" Accessed December 10, 2024. https://www.icj-cij.org/pending-cases.

International Court of Justice (2024i). "*Permanent Court of International Justice.*" Accessed July 4, 2024. https://www.icj-cij.org/pcij.

International Court of Justice (2024j). "*States not members of the United Nations parties to the Statute.*" Accessed August 17, 2024. https://www.icj-cij.org/states-not-members.

International Criminal Court (2009). *Situation in Uganda in the case of the Prosecutor v. Joseph Kony, Vincent Otti, Okot Odhiambo, Dominic Ongwen*, Judgment of 23 February 2009, The Appeals Chamber of the International Criminal Court, ICC-02/04 OA and ICC-02/04-01/05 OA2.

International Criminal Court (ICC) Legal Tools Database (2008). "*Covenant of the League of Nations.*" Published November 10, 2008. Accessed June 28, 2024. https://legal-tools.org/doc/106a5f.

International Criminal Court (ICC) Legal Tools Database (2024). Covenant of the League of Nations, 1919, as amended. The Hague: International Criminal Court.

International Labour Office – Official Bulletin (1923). Chapter VI: Part XIII of the Treaty of Peace of Versailles. *International Labour Office – Official Bulletin*, Volume I, April 1919 – August 1920, 332-345.

International Law Commission (1951). Report of the International Law Commission 1951: Reservations to Multilateral Conventions, *Yearbook of the International Law Commission*, 1951, Volume II, 125-131.

International Law Commission (1963). Report of the International Law Commission 1963: Questions of extended participation in general multilateral treaties concluded under the auspices of the League of Nations, *Yearbook of the International Law Commission*, 1963, Volume II, 217-223.

International Law Commission (1979). Review of the Multilateral Treaty-Making Process (Paragraph 2 of General Assembly Resolution 32/48), Document A/CN.4/325, Report of the Working Group on review of the multilateral treaty-making process, *Yearbook of the International Law Commission*, 1979, Volume II, Part One, 183-212.

International Law Commission (2006). Report of the International Law Commission on the work of its fifty-eighth session (1 May – 9 June and 3 July – 11 August 2006), Document A/61/10, Chapter IX. Unilateral acts of states, D.2. Text of the guiding principles with commentaries thereto adopted by the Commission at its fifty-eighth session, *Yearbook of the International Law Commission*, 2006, Volume II, Part Two, 161-166.

International Law Commission (2011a). Report of the International Law Commission on the work of its sixty-third session (26 April – 3 June and 4 July – 12 August 2011), Document A/66/10, Chapter IV. Reservations to treaties, F.1. Text of the guidelines constituting the Guide to Practice, followed by an annex on the reservations dialogue, *Yearbook of the International Law Commission*, 2011, Volume II, Part Two, 26-38.

International Law Commission (2011b). Report of the International Law Commission on the work of its sixty-third session (26 April – 3 June and 4 July – 12 August 2011), Document A/66/10, Chapter VI. Effects of armed conflicts on treaties, E.1. Text of the draft articles, *Yearbook of the International Law Commission*, 2011, Volume II, Part Two, 107-108.

International Law Commission (2013). First report on formation and evidence of customary international law, by Sir Michael Wood, Special Rapporteur, Document A/CN.4/663, *Yearbook of the International Law Commission*, 2013, Volume II, Part One, 109-144.

International Law Commission (2014). Second report on identification of customary international law, by Sir Michael Wood, Special Rapporteur, Document A/CN.4/672, *Yearbook of the International Law Commission*, 2014, Volume II, Part One, 163-203.

International Law Commission (2015a). "*Summaries of the Work of the International Law Commission: Extended participation in general multilateral treaties concluded under the auspices of the League of Nations.*" Last updated July 15, 2015. Accessed August 31, 2024. https://legal.un.org/ilc/summaries/1_5.shtml.

International Law Commission (2015b). "*Summaries of the Work of the International Law Commission: Review of the multilateral treaty-making process.*" Last updated July 15, 2015. Accessed September 5, 2024. https://legal.un.org/ilc/summaries/1_7.shtml.

International Law Commission (2015c). Third report on identification of customary international law, by Sir Michael Wood, Special Rapporteur, Document A/CN.4/682, *Yearbook of the International Law Commission*, 2015, Volume II, Part One, 93-134.

International Law Commission (2016). Fourth report on identification of customary international law, by Sir Michael Wood, Special Rapporteur, Document A/CN.4/695 and Addendum 1, *Yearbook of the International Law Commission*, 2016, Volume II, Part One, 215-249.

International Law Commission (2017). "*Summaries of the Work of the International Law Commission: Question of treaties concluded between States and international organizations or between two or more international organizations.*" Last updated December 4, 2017. Accessed August 29, 2024. https://legal.un.org/ilc/summaries/1_2.shtml.

International Law Commission (2018a). Report of the International Law Commission on the work of its seventieth session (30 April – 1 June and 2 July – 10 August 2018), Document A/73/10, Chapter IV. Subsequent agreements and subsequent practice in relation to the interpretation of treaties, E.1. Text of the draft conclusions, *Yearbook of the International Law Commission*, 2018, Volume II, Part Two, 24-25.

International Law Commission (2018b). Report of the International Law Commission on the work of its seventieth session (30 April – 1 June and 2 July – 10 August 2018), Document A/73/10, Chapter V. Identification of customary international law, E.2. Text of the draft conclusions and commentaries thereto, *Yearbook of the International Law Commission*, 2018, Volume II, Part Two, 91-113.

International Law Commission (2023a). "*Membership: 2021 Election of the International Law Commission.*" Last updated August 4, 2023. Accessed August 23, 2024. https://legal.un.org/ilc/elections/2021election_outcome.shtml.

International Law Commission (2023b). "*Summaries of the Work of the International Law Commission.*" Last updated August 9, 2023. Accessed August 26, 2024. https://legal.un.org/ilc/summaries/summaries.shtml.

International Law Commission (2023c). "*Summaries of the Work of the International Law Commission: Effects of armed conflicts on treaties.*" Last updated November 6, 2023. Accessed September 6 and 7, 2024. https://legal.un.org/ilc/summaries/1_10.shtml.

International Law Commission (2023d). "*Summaries of the Work of the International Law Commission: Law of treaties.*" Last updated June 23, 2023. Accessed August 29, 2024. https://legal.un.org/ilc/summaries/1_1.shtml.

International Law Commission (2023e). "*Summaries of the Work of the International Law Commission: Reservations to multilateral conventions.*" Last updated June 22, 2023. Accessed August 31, 2024, and September 1, 2024. https://legal.un.org/ilc/summaries/1_6.shtml.

International Law Commission (2023f). "*Summaries of the Work of the International Law Commission: Reservations to treaties.*" Last updated June 29, 2023. Accessed September 4, 2024. https://legal.un.org/ilc/summaries/1_8.shtml.

International Law Commission (2023g). "*Summaries of the Work of the International Law Commission: Succession of States in respect of treaties.*" Last updated June 30, 2023. Accessed September 11, 2024. https://legal.un.org/ilc/summaries/3_2.shtml.

International Law Commission (2024a). "*About the Commission: Organization, programme and methods of work.*" Accessed August 22, 2024. https://legal.un.org/ilc/methods.shtml.

International Law Commission (2024b). "*About the Commission: Origin and background – Drafting and implementation of Article 13, paragraph 1, of the Charter of the United Nations.*" Accessed August 21 and 22, 2024. https://legal.un.org/ilc/drafting.shtml.

International Law Commission (2024c). "*B. Formation and evidence of customary law.*" Accessed September 23, 2024. https://legal.un.org/ilc/sessions/66/pdfs/english/ icil_czech_republic.pdf.

International Law Commission (2024d). "*Current status of the work of the Commission and forthcoming deadlines.*" Last updated September 18, 2024. Accessed December 10, 2024. https://legal.un.org/ilc/status.shtml.

International Law Commission (2024e). "*Summaries of the Work of the International Law Commission: General principles of law.*" Last updated October 8, 2024. Accessed October 20, 2024. https://legal.un.org/ilc/summaries/1_15.shtml.

International Law Commission (2024f). "*Summaries of the Work of the International Law Commission: Identification of customary international law.*" Last updated July 18, 2024. Accessed September 23 and 24, 2024. https://legal.un.org/ilc/summaries/1_13.shtml.

International Law Commission (2024g). "*Summaries of the Work of the International Law Commission: Peremptory norms of general international law (Jus cogens).*" Last updated July 16, 2024. Accessed October 6 and 7, 2024. https://legal.un.org/ilc/summaries/1_14.shtml.

International Law Commission (2024h). "*Summaries of the Work of the International Law Commission: Provisional application of treaties.*" Last updated July 18, 2024. Accessed September 10 and 11, 2024. https://legal.un.org/ilc/summaries/1_12.shtml.

International Law Commission (2024i). "*Summaries of the Work of the International Law Commission: Subsequent agreements and subsequent practice in relation to interpretation of treaties.*" Last updated July 18, 2024. Accessed September 8 and 9, 2024. https://legal.un.org/ilc/summaries/1_11.shtml.

International Law Commission (2024j). "*Summaries of the Work of the International Law Commission: Subsidiary means for the determination of rules of international law.*" Last updated September 27, 2024. Accessed October 31, 2024. https://legal.un.org/ilc/summaries/1_16.shtml.

International Tribunal for the Law of the Sea (2023). Press Release 335, 2 May 2023. Hamburg: International Tribunal for the Law of the Sea.

International Tribunal for the Law of the Sea (2024a). "*Cases: Docket – List of pending cases and current status.*" Accessed December 11, 2024. https://www.itlos.org/en/main/cases/docket/.

International Tribunal for the Law of the Sea (2024b). Press Release 351, 4 June 2024. Hamburg: International Tribunal for the Law of the Sea.

International Tribunal for the Law of the Sea (2024c). Press Release 352, 10 June 2024. Hamburg: International Tribunal for the Law of the Sea.

International Tribunal for the Law of the Sea (2024d). Press Release 354, 13 June 2024. Hamburg: International Tribunal for the Law of the Sea.

International Tribunal for the Law of the Sea (2024e). "*The M/T "Heroic Idun" (No. 2) Case (Marshall Islands/Equatorial Guinea).*" Accessed December 11, 2024. https://www.itlos.org/en/main/cases/list-of-cases/the-m/t-heroic-idun-no-2-case-marshall-islands/equatorial-guinea/.

International Tribunal for the Law of the Sea (2024f). *The M/T "Heroic Idun" (No. 2) Case (Marshall Islands/Equatorial Guinea)*, Order of 25 July 2024, *List of Cases No. 32 Order 2024/2.*

International Tribunal for the Law of the Sea (2024g). *The "Zheng He" Case (Luxembourg v. Mexico)*, Order of 13 June 2024, *List of Cases No. 33 Order 2024/1.*

International Tribunal for the Law of the Sea (2024h). *The "Zheng He" Case (Luxembourg v. Mexico)*, Order of 27 July 2024, *List of Cases No. 33 Order 2024/2.*

International Tribunal for the Law of the Sea (2024i). *The "Zheng He" Case (Luxembourg v. Mexico)*, Order of 8 August 2024, *List of Cases No. 33 Order 2024/3.*

Jones, D. (2009). Competence-Competence, *The International Journal of Arbitration, Mediation and Dispute Management*, 75(1), 56-64.

Keegan, J. (1998). "*Normandy Invasion.*" Published July 20, 1998. Last updated June 8, 2024. Accessed July 19, 2024. https://www.britannica.com/event/Normandy-Invasion.

Kelsen, H. (1944). The Principle of Sovereign Equality of States as a Basis for International Organization, *The Yale Law Journal*, 53(2), 207-220.

Kostenko, M., Marquardt, A., and McCluskey, M. (2024). Large group of Russian and North Korean forces prepared to retake Russia's Kursk region from Ukraine, *CNN*, Monday 11 November 2024.

Krol, G. (2022). "*Memoir | The Shushkevich I knew.*" Published May 12, 2022. Accessed November 7, 2024. https://eurasianet.org/memoir-the-shushkevich-i-knew.

Lagerwall, A. (2015). "*Jus Cogens.*" Last updated May 29, 2015. Accessed August 27, 2024. https://www.oxfordbibliographies.com/display/document/obo-9780199796953/obo-9780199796953-0124.xml.

Lampe, J., Malcolm, N., and Pickering P. (1999). "*Bosnia and Herzegovina under Austro-Hungarian rule.*" Published June 1, 1999. Last updated June 23, 2024. Accessed June 24, 2024. https://www.britannica.com/place/Bosnia-and-Herzegovina/Bosnia-and-Herzegovina-under-Austro-Hungarian-rule.

Latin Dictionary (2024). "*Latin – English Dictionary.*" Accessed August 27, 2024. https://www.online-latin-dictionary.com/.

League of Nations – Official Journal (1920). The Covenant of the League of Nations. *League of Nations – Official Journal*, February 2020, 3-11.

Lexis Nexis (2024a). "*Ratio decidendi definition.*" Accessed November 21, 2024. https://www.lexisnexis.co.uk/legal/glossary/ratio-decidendi.

LexisNexis (2024b). "*Stare decisis definition.*" Accessed November 21, 2024. https://www.lexisnexis.co.uk/legal/glossary/stare-decisis.

Libreria Editrice Vaticana (2008). "*Benedict XVI General Audience: Paul VI Audience Hall – Wednesday, 9 January 2008.*" Accessed December 7 and 8, 2024. https://www.vatican.va/content/benedict-xvi/en/audiences/2008/documents/hf_ben-xvi_aud_20080109.html.

Lone, F. (2012). "*Uti Possidetis Iuris.*" Last updated March 23, 2012. Accessed October 27, 2024. https://www.oxfordbibliographies.com/display/document/obo-9780199796953/obo-9780199796953-0065.xml.

Lowe, K. (2020). "*How and when did WW2 end?*" Published September 1, 2020. Accessed July 19, 2024. https://www.historyextra.com/period/second-world-war/how-when-ww2-end-ve-day-vj-day-fighting-atomic-bombs-japan-world-europe/.

Lowe, K. (2021). "*A brief guide to VE Day.*" Published May 8, 2021. Accessed July 19, 2024. https://www.historyextra.com/period/second-world-war/brief-guide-ve-day-victory-europe-ww2/.

Marriott, H. (2020). "*Admissibility of evidence in civil proceedings: An overview and case law update.*" Published July 13, 2020. Last updated September 1, 2020. Accessed October 28, 2024. https://www.stiveschambers.co.uk/content/uploads/2020/09/HM-Admissibility-of-evidence-in-civil-proceedings.pdf.

Massimino, I. (2024). The ICC and in-absentia proceedings: Finding a response to the difficulties of executing arrest warrants, *ESIL Reflections*, 13(9).

McIntyre, J. (2019). "*The International Court of Justice Releases New Rules of Court.*" Published November 4, 2019. Accessed August 13, 2024. https://www.ejiltalk.org/the-international-court-of-justice-releases-new-rules-of-court/.

McIntyre J. (2024). "*The ICJ Changes the Rules for Intervention.*" Published March 11, 2024. Accessed August 13, 2024. https://www.ejiltalk.org/the-icj-changes-the-rules-for-intervention/.

Mémorial de l'Armistice (2018). "*The Armistice of 1918.*" Accessed June 25, 2024. https://armistice-museum.com/understanding-the-history/the-armistice-of-1918/.

Merriam-Webster (2024). "*force majeure.*" Accessed October 27, 2024. https://www.merriam-webster.com/dictionary/force%20majeure.

Milners (2023). "*A (very) brief history of the legal system in England and Wales.*" Published March 24, 2023. Accessed November 28, 2024. https://www.milnerslaw.co.uk/a-very-brief-history-of-the-legal-system-in-england-and-wales/.

Mirage News (2022). "*Full Text of Putin State of Nation Speech 21 Feb 2022.*" Published February 22, 2022. Accessed November 13, 2024. https://www.miragenews.com/full-text-of-putin-state-of-nation-speech-21-951701/.

Mullen, M., Onion, A., Sullivan, M., and Zapata, C. (2009a). "*World War II.*" Published October 29, 2009. Updated March 13, 2024. Accessed July 18 and 20, 2024. https://www.history.com/topics/world-war-ii/world-war-ii-history.

Mullen, M., Onion, A., Sullivan, M., and Zapata, C. (2009b). "*Yalta Conference.*" Published October 29, 2009. Updated November 1, 2022. Accessed July 26, 2024. https://www.history.com/topics/world-war-ii/yalta-conference.

Munez, E. (2023). "*Paris Peace Treaties 1947.*" Published May 1, 2023. Accessed July 20, 2024. https://www.britannica.com/topic/Paris-Peace-Treaties-1947.

Municipality of Siena Culture and Tourism Directorate (2024a). "*visitsiena: Allegory and Effects of Good and Bad Government.*" Accessed December 7, 2024. https://visitsienaofficial.it/en/allegory-and-effects-of-good-and-bad-government/.

Municipality of Siena Culture and Tourism Directorate (2024b). "*visitsiena: Civic Museum of Siena.*" Accessed December 7, 2024. https://visitsienaofficial.it/en/civic-museum-of-siena/.

National Archives (2022). "*Milestone Documents: President Woodrow Wilson's 14 Points (1918).*" Last reviewed February 8, 2022. Accessed June 27, 2024. https://www.archives.gov/milestone-documents/president-woodrow-wilsons-14-points.

National Archives (2023). "*Milestone Documents: Surrender of Germany (1945).*" Last reviewed January 10, 2023. Accessed July 19 and 20, 2024. https://www.archives.gov/milestone-documents/surrender-of-germany.

National Security Archive (2021). Record of Dinner Conversation between Gorbachev, Bush, Gonzalez and King Juan Carlos of Spain, Madrid, October 29, 1991, Savranskaya, S. (tr.).

Nikolskaya, P., and Osborn, A. (2022). Russia's Putin authorises 'special military operation' against Ukraine, *Reuters*, Thursday 24 February 2022.

North Atlantic Treaty Organization (2024a). "*Relations with Ukraine.*" Last updated May 10, 2024. Accessed June 12, 2024. https://www.nato.int/cps/en/natohq/topics_37750.htm.

North Atlantic Treaty Organization (2024b). "*What is NATO?*" Accessed June 12, 2024. https://www.nato.int/nato-welcome/.

Oxford Reference (2024a). "*Lex posterior derogat (legi) priori.*" Accessed October 25, 2024. https://www.oxfordreference.com/display/10.1093/acref/9780195369380.001.0001/acref-9780195369380-e-1282.

Oxford Reference (2024b). "*Overview: erga omnes obligations.*" Accessed October 6, 2024. https://www.oxfordreference.com/display/10.1093/oi/authority.20110803095756413.

Oxford Reference (2024c). "*Overview: pacta sunt servanda.*" Accessed October 25, 2024. https://www.oxfordreference.com/display/10.1093/oi/authority.20110803100300496.

Oxford Reference (2024d). "*Overview: Paris Peace Treaties.*" Accessed July 20, 2024. https://www.oxfordreference.com/display/10.1093/oi/authority.20110803100306594.

Pearsall, J. (editor) (1998). *The New Oxford Dictionary of English.* Oxford: Oxford University Press.

Permanent Court of Arbitration (2016a). 1899 Convention for the Pacific Settlement of International Disputes. The Hague: Permanent Court of Arbitration.

Permanent Court of Arbitration (2016b). 1907 Convention for the Pacific Settlement of International Disputes. The Hague: Permanent Court of Arbitration.

Permanent Court of International Justice (1926a). Protocol of Signature for the Permanent Court of International Justice provided for by Article 14 of the Covenant of the League of Nations. *P.C.I.J. Series D No.1*, 5-6.

Permanent Court of International Justice (1926b). Resolution concerning the establishment of a Permanent Court of International Justice passed by the Assembly of the League of Nations, Geneva, December 13th, 1920. Statute of the Court. *P.C.I.J. Series D No.1*, 4.

Permanent Court of International Justice (1926c). Statute of the Court. *P.C.I.J. Series D No.1*, 7-27.

Permanent Court of International Justice (1927). *The Case of the S.S. "Lotus"*, Judgment of 7 September 1927, *P.C.I.J. Series A No. 10 (1927)*, 4-33.

Permanent Court of International Justice (1940). Statute of the Court, as amended. *P.C.I.J. Series D No. 1*, 13-28.

Peters, A. (2014). '*The Principle of Uti Possidetis Juris: How Relevant is it for Issues of Secession?*' *in* Walter, C., von Ungern-Sternberg, A., and Abushov, K. (eds.) (2014), *Self-Determination and Secession in International Law*, First edition. Oxford: Oxford University Press.

Reuters (2014). Timeline: Political crisis in Ukraine and Russia's occupation of Crimea, *Reuters*, Saturday 8 March 2014.

Rotelle, J. (ed.) (1994). *The Works of Saint Augustine: A Translation for the 21st Century, Part III – Sermons, Volume 9: Sermons 306-340A.* Hill, E. (tr.). New York: New City Press.

RTÉ (2018). "*WWI: Scale and horror of the conflict.*" Published November 7, 2018. Accessed June 24, 2024. https://www.rte.ie/news/2018/1107/1008936-world-war-one-numbers/.

Rucker, H., and Wiese, K. (2024). Clear the Stage for J. S. Bach – Act 1: Church Music in Praise of God. Leipzig: Bach-Museum Leipzig.

Salem, H., and Walker, S. (2014). Russian parliament approves troop deployment in Ukraine, *The Observer*, Saturday 1 March 2014.

Salenko, A. (2015). Legal Aspects of the Dissolution of the Soviet Union in 1991 and Its Implications for the Reunification of Crimea with Russia in 2014. *Heidelberg Journal of International Law*, Volume 15, 141-166.

Scowcroft, B. (1991). Information: Memorandum for the President – Developments in the USSR, 6506, September 5, 1991.

Security Council Report (2015). Research Report: The Veto. New York: Security Council Report.

Security Council Report (2024a). "*About Security Council Report.*" Accessed November 15, 2024. https://www.securitycouncilreport.org/about-security-council-report.

Security Council Report (2024b). The Security Council Veto. New York: Security Council Report.

Security Council Report (2024c). "*UN Security Council Working Methods: The Veto.*" Published February 13, 2024. Accessed November 16 and 18, 2024. https://www.securitycouncilreport.org/un-security-council-working-methods/the-veto.php.

Shakespeare, W. (1599). 'The Tragedy of Julius Caesar' *in* Jowett, J., Montgomery, W., Taylor, G., and Wells, S. (eds.) (1986), *William Shakespeare: The Complete Works* (Oxford: Oxford University Press), 675-703.

Shaw, M. (1999). "*International law: Historical development.*" Published July 26, 1999, Last updated July 30, 2024. Accessed August 27, 2024. https://www.britannica.com/topic/international-law/Historical-development.

Siegelbaum, L. (2024). "*Seventeen Moments in Soviet History: The Gift of Crimea.*" Accessed November 7, 2024. https://soviethistory.msu.edu/1954-2/the-gift-of-crimea/.

Tams, C. (2019). 'Chapter 10 – Peace Through International Adjudication: The Permanent Court of International Justice and the Post-War Order' *in* Erpelding, M., Hess, B., and Ruiz Fabri, H. (eds.) (2019), *Peace Through Law: The Versailles Peace Treaty and Dispute Settlement After World War I*, First edition. Baden-Baden: Nomos Verlagsgesellschaft.

Tennessee Virtual Archive (2024). "*League to Enforce Peace convention invitation to Governor Rye.*" Accessed June 26, 2024. https://teva.contentdm.oclc.org/digital/collection/p15138coll18/id/2590/.

The British Army (2020). "*Marking the 75 Anniversary of the Luneberg Surrender.*" Published May 4, 2020. Accessed July 19, 2024. https://www.army.mod.uk/news-and-events/news/2020/05/veday-lueneberg-surrender/.

The National WWII Museum New Orleans (2024a). "*Research Starters: Worldwide Deaths in World War II.*" Accessed July 18, 2024. https://www.nationalww2museum.org/students-teachers/student-resources/research-starters/research-starters-worldwide-deaths-world-war.

The National WWII Museum New Orleans (2024b). "*The End of World War II 1945.*" Accessed July 19, 2024. https://www.nationalww2museum.org/war/topics/end-world-war-ii-1945.

The Nobel Prize (2024a). "*Woodrow Wilson: Biographical.*" Accessed June 27, 2024. https://www.nobelprize.org/prizes/peace/1919/wilson/biographical/.

The Nobel Prize (2024b). "*Woodrow Wilson: Facts.*" Accessed June 26, 2024. https://www.nobelprize.org/prizes/peace/1919/wilson/facts/.

United Nations (1945a). "Charter of the United Nations," *United Nations Treaty Series* Registration Number N/A.
United Nations (1945b). "Statute of the International Court of Justice," *United Nations Treaty Series* Registration Number N/A.
United Nations (1946). Resolution 94 (I) adopted by the General Assembly on 11th December 1946.
United Nations (1948). "Convention on the Prevention and Punishment of the Crime of Genocide," *United Nations Treaty Series* Registration Number 1021.
United Nations (1950). Resolution 478 (V) adopted by the General Assembly on 16th November 1950.
United Nations (1952). Resolution 598 (VI) adopted by the General Assembly on 12th January 1952.
United Nations (1958). "Convention on the High Seas," *United Nations Treaty Series* Registration Number 6465.
United Nations (1959). Resolution 1452 (XIV) adopted by the General Assembly on 7th December 1959.
United Nations (1962). Resolution 1766 (XVII) adopted by the General Assembly on 20th November 1962.
United Nations (1963). Resolution 1903 (XVIII) adopted by the General Assembly on 18th November 1963.
United Nations (1966). "International Convention on the Elimination of All Forms of Racial Discrimination," *United Nations Treaty Series* Registration Number 9464.
United Nations (1969a). Resolution 2501 (XXIV) adopted by the General Assembly on 12th November 1969.
United Nations (1969b). Resolution 2520 (XXIV) adopted by the General Assembly on 4th December 1969.
United Nations (1969c). "Vienna Convention on the Law of Treaties," *United Nations Treaty Series* Registration Number 18232.
United Nations (1972). Resolution 2926 (XXVII) adopted by the General Assembly on 28th November 1972.
United Nations (1973). Resolution 3071 (XXVIII) adopted by the General Assembly on 30th November 1973.
United Nations (1974). Resolution 3314 (XXIX) adopted by the General Assembly on 14th December 1974.
United Nations (1975). Resolution 3496 (XXX) adopted by the General Assembly on 15th December 1975.
United Nations (1977a). Resolution 32/47 adopted by the General Assembly on 8th December 1977.
United Nations (1977b). Resolution 32/48 adopted by the General Assembly on 8th December 1977.
United Nations (1978). "Vienna Convention on the Succession of States in respect of Treaties," *United Nations Treaty Series* Registration Number 33356.
United Nations (1981). Resolution 36/39 adopted by the General Assembly on 18th November 1981.
United Nations (1982). "United Nations Convention on the Law of the Sea," *United Nations Treaty Series* Registration Number 31363.
United Nations (1984). Resolution 39/86 adopted by the General Assembly on 13th December 1984.
United Nations (1986). "Vienna Convention on the Law of Treaties between States and International Organizations or between International Organizations," A/CONF.129/15, Official Records of the United Nations Conference on the Law of Treaties between States and International Organizations or between International Organizations, Volume II, 93-109.
United Nations (1991a). General Assembly: Forty-sixth session – Agenda items 22, 68, 98, 127, 131 and 135, Letter dated 12 December 1991 from the Permanent Representative of Belarus to the United Nations addressed to the Secretary-General, A/46/771, 13 December 1991.
United Nations (1991b). General Assembly: Forty-seventh session, Security Council: Forty-sixth year, Letter dated 27 December 1991 from the Permanent Representative of Belarus to the United Nations addressed to the Secretary-General, A/47/60 and S/23329, 30 December 1991.
United Nations (1993). Resolution 48/31 adopted by the General Assembly on 9th December 1993.
United Nations (1995). General Assembly Official Records Forty-seventh Session Supplement No.2 (A/47/2): Report of the Security Council 16 June 1991-15 June 1992. New York: United Nations.
United Nations (1998). "Rome Statute of the International Criminal Court," *United Nations Treaty Series* Registration Number 38544.
United Nations (2001). Resolution 56/83 adopted by the General Assembly on 12th December 2001.
United Nations (2011a). Resolution 66/98 adopted by the General Assembly on 9th December 2011.
United Nations (2011b). Resolution 66/99 adopted by the General Assembly on 9th December 2011.
United Nations (2011c). Resolution 66/100 adopted by the General Assembly on 9th December 2011.

United Nations (2012a). Alabama claims of the United States of America against Great Britain: Award rendered on 14 September 1872 by the tribunal of arbitration established by Article I of the Treaty of Washington of 8 May 1871. *Reports of International Arbitral Awards*, Volume XXIX, 125-134.

United Nations (2012b). United Nations Audiovisual Library of International Law: Statute of the International Court of Justice. New York: United Nations.

United Nations (2013). Resolution 68/111 adopted by the General Assembly on 16th December 2013.

United Nations (2014a). "*Digital Library: Territorial integrity of Ukraine: resolution / adopted by the General Assembly – 2014.*" Published March 27, 2014. Accessed November 9, 2024. https://digitallibrary.un.org/record/767565?ln=en.

United Nations (2014b). Resolution 68/262 adopted by the General Assembly on 27th March 2014.

United Nations (2017). Resolution 72/121 adopted by the General Assembly on 7th December 2017.

United Nations (2018). Resolution 73/202 adopted by the General Assembly on 20th December 2018.

United Nations (2018). Resolution 73/203 adopted by the General Assembly on 20th December 2018.

United Nations (2021a). Report of the International Law Commission: Seventy-second session (26 April – 4 June and 5 July – 6 August 2021), Document A/76/10, Chapter V. Provisional application of treaties, E.1. Text of the draft guidelines and the draft annex constituting the Guide to Provisional Application of Treaties, General Assembly Official Records, Seventy-sixth Session, Supplement No.10 (A/76/10), 54-55.

United Nations (2021b). Resolution 76/113 adopted by the General Assembly on 9th December 2021.

United Nations (2022a). "*Activities of Secretary-General in Russian Federation, 25-26 April: SG/T/3309.*" Published May 6 2022. Accessed June 13, 2024. https://press.un.org/en/2022/sgt3309.doc.htm.

United Nations (2022b). "*Digital Library: Aggression against Ukraine: resolution / adopted by the General Assembly – 2022.*" Published March 2, 2022. Accessed November 10, 2024. https://digitallibrary.un.org/record/3959039.

United Nations (2022c). "*Digital Library: Furtherance of remedy and reparation for aggression against Ukraine: resolution / adopted by the General Assembly – 2022.*" Published November 14, 2022. Accessed November 10, 2024. https://digitallibrary.un.org/record/3994052?ln=en.

United Nations (2022d). "*Digital Library: Humanitarian consequences of the aggression against Ukraine: resolution / adopted by the General Assembly – 2022.*" Published March 24, 2022. Accessed November 10, 2024. https://digitallibrary.un.org/record/3965954?ln=en.

United Nations (2022e). "*Digital Library: Territorial integrity of Ukraine: defending the principles of the Charter of the United Nations: resolution / adopted by the General Assembly – 2022.*" Published October 12, 2022. Accessed November 10, 2024. https://digitallibrary.un.org/record/3990400?ln=en.

United Nations (2022f). Report of the International Law Commission: Seventy-third session (18 April – 3 June and 4 July – 5 August 2022), Document A/77/10, Chapter IV. Peremptory norms of general international law (*jus cogens*), E.2. Text of the draft conclusions and commentaries thereto, General Assembly Official Records, Seventy-seventh Session, Supplement No.10 (A/77/10), 16-89.

United Nations (2022g). Resolution 77/103 adopted by the General Assembly on 7th December 2022.

United Nations (2022h). Resolution ES-11/1 (LXXVI) adopted by the General Assembly on 2nd March 2022.

United Nations (2022i). Resolution ES-11/2 (LXXVI) adopted by the General Assembly on 24th March 2022.

United Nations (2022j). Resolution ES-11/4 (LXXVII) adopted by the General Assembly on 12th October 2022.

United Nations (2022k). Resolution ES-11/5 (LXXVII) adopted by the General Assembly on 14th November 2022.

United Nations (2022l). United Nations Audiovisual Library of International Law: Mr. Juan Manuel Gómez-Robledo. New York: United Nations.

United Nations (2023a). "*Dag Hammarskjöld Library: Ask DAG – UN Trusteeship Council Documentation: Trust Territories Introduction.*" Last updated December 29, 2023. Accessed August 7, 2024. https://research.un.org/en/docs/tc/territories.

United Nations (2023b). "*Digital Library: Principles of the Charter of the United Nations underlying a comprehensive, just and lasting peace in Ukraine: resolution / adopted by the General Assembly – 2023.*" Published February 23, 2023. Accessed November 10, 2024. https://digitallibrary.un.org/record/4003921?ln=en.

United Nations (2023c). Report of the International Law Commission: Seventy-fourth session (24 April – 2 June and 3 July – 4 August 2023), Document A/78/10, Chapter IV. General principles of law, C.2. Text of the draft conclusions and commentaries thereto, General Assembly Official Records, Seventy-eighth Session, Supplement No.10 (A/78/10), 13-35.

United Nations (2023d). Resolution ES-11/6 (LXXVII) adopted by the General Assembly on 23rd February 2023.

United Nations (2024a). 4. Declarations recognizing as compulsory the jurisdiction of the International Court of Justice under Article 36, paragraph 2, of the Statute of the Court, I4. Charter of the United Nations and Statute of the International Court of Justice. New York: United Nations.

United Nations (2024b). "*About Us.*" Accessed November 19, 2024. https://www.un.org/en/about-us.

United Nations (2024c). "*Amendments to Articles 23, 27, 61, 109.*" Accessed August 9, 2025. https://www.un.org/en/about-us/un-charter/amendments.

United Nations (2024d). "*Dag Hammarskjöld Library: Ask DAG – Where can I find the letters of 24 December 1991 regarding the continuation of the membership of the USSR by the Russian Federation?*" Last updated April 25, 2024. Accessed June 10, 2024. https://ask.un.org/faq/378083.

United Nations (2024e). "*Dag Hammarskjöld Library: UN Membership – Founding Member States.*" Last updated November 11, 2024. Accessed November 22, 2024. https://research.un.org/en/unmembers/founders.

United Nations (2024f). "*General Assembly of the United Nations: Sixth Committee (Legal).*" Accessed August 31, 2024. https://www.un.org/en/ga/sixth/.

United Nations (2024g). "*Member States.*" Accessed June 8, 2024, and November 19, 2024. https://www.un.org/en/about-us/member-states.

United Nations (2024h). "*Model United Nations: The History of the UN.*" Accessed July 23 and 26, 2024. https://www.un.org/en/model-united-nations/history-united-nations.

United Nations (2024i). "*Predecessor: The League of Nations.*" Accessed July 2, 2024. https://www.un.org/en/about-us/history-of-the-un/predecessor.

United Nations (2024j). Report of the International Law Commission: Seventy-fifth session (29 April – 31 May and 1 July – 2 August 2024), Document A/79/10, Annex I. Compensation for the damage caused by internationally wrongful acts, General Assembly Official Records, Seventy-ninth Session, Supplement No.10 (A/79/10), 125-145.

United Nations (2024k). Report of the International Law Commission: Seventy-fifth session (29 April – 31 May and 1 July – 2 August 2024), Document A/79/10, Annex II. Due Diligence in International Law, General Assembly Official Records, Seventy-ninth Session, Supplement No.10 (A/79/10), 146-162.

United Nations (2024l). Report of the International Law Commission: Seventy-fifth session (29 April – 31 May and 1 July – 2 August 2024), Document A/79/10, Chapter V. Subsidiary means for the determination of rules of international law, C. Text of the draft conclusions on subsidiary means for the determination of rules of international law provisionally adopted thus far by the Commission, General Assembly Official Records, Seventy-ninth Session, Supplement No.10 (A/79/10), 30-53.

United Nations (2024m). "*Russian Federation.*" Accessed June 8, 2024. https://www.un.org/en/about-us/member-states/russian-federation.

United Nations (2024n). "*The League of Nations.*" Accessed June 29, 2024. https://www.ungeneva.org/en/about/league-of-nations/overview.

United Nations (2024o). "*The San Francisco Conference.*" Accessed July 26, 2024. https://www.un.org/en/about-us/history-of-the-un/san-francisco-conference.

United Nations (2024p). "*The United Nations and Decolonization: International Trusteeship System.*" Accessed August 7, 2024. https://www.un.org/dppa/decolonization/en/history/international-trusteeship-system-and-trust-territories.

United Nations (2024q). "*The United Nations and Decolonization: Non-Self-Governing Territories.*" Accessed August 6, 2024. https://www.un.org/dppa/decolonization/en/nsgt.

United Nations (2024r). "*Transition to the United Nations.*" Accessed July 2, 2024. https://www.ungeneva.org/en/about/league-of-nations/transition.

United Nations (2024s). "*Türkiye.*" Accessed June 25, 2024. https://www.un.org/en/about-us/member-states/turkiye.

United Nations (2024t). "*Ukraine.*" Accessed June 8, 2024, and November 19, 2024. https://www.un.org/en/about-us/member-states/ukraine.

United Nations (2024u). "*United Nations Treaty Collection: Chapter XVIII Penal Matters – 10. Rome Statute of the International Criminal Court.*" Last updated June 13, 2024. Accessed June 13, 2024. https://treaties.un.org/Pages/ViewDetails.aspx?src=TREATY&mtdsg_no=XVIII-10&chapter=18&clang=_en.

United Nations (2024v). "*United Nations Treaty Collection: Chapter XXI Law of the Sea – 6. United Nations Convention on the Law of the Sea.*" Last updated November 25, 2024. Accessed November 21, 22, 23 24 and 25, 2024. https://treaties.un.org/pages/ViewDetailsIII.aspx?src=TREATY&mtdsg_no=XXI-6&chapter=21&Temp=mtdsg3&lang=en.

United Nations (2024w). "*United Nations Treaty Collection: Chapter XXIII Law of Treaties – 3. Vienna Convention on the Law of Treaties between States and International Organizations or between International Organizations.*" Last updated August 29, 2024. Accessed August 29, 2024. https://treaties.un.org/Pages/ViewDetails.aspx?src=TREATY&mtdsg_no=XXIII-3&chapter=23&clang=_en.

United Nations (2024x). "*United Nations Treaty Collection: Definitions – Definition of key terms used in the UN Treaty Collection.*" Accessed August 28, 2024. https://treaties.un.org/Pages/overview.aspx?path=overview/definition/page1_en.xml.

United Nations (2024y). "*UN News: Global perspective Human stories – Palestine's status at the UN explained.*" Published April 18, 2024. Accessed December 1, 2024. https://news.un.org/en/story/2024/04/1148351.

United States Senate (2024). "*Senate Rejects the Treaty of Versailles.*" Accessed June 29, 2024. https://www.senate.gov/about/powers-procedures/treaties/senate-rejects-treaty-of-versailles.htm.

Walker, N. (2024). "*Research Briefing: Conflict in Ukraine: A timeline (current conflict, 2022 – present).*" Published September 16, 2024. Accessed November 8, 2024 https://.commonslibrary.parliament.uk/research-briefings/cbp-9847/.

Watling, T. (2024). G7 leaders strike deal on $50bn funding for Ukraine using Russian assets. *The Independent*, Thursday 13 June 2024.

Wilson Center (2024). "*About Woodrow Wilson.*" Accessed June 26, 2024. https://www.wilsoncenter.org/about-woodrow-wilson.

Wilson, W. (1917). "Peace Without Victory" speech, January 22, 1917. 64th Cong., 23 Sess., Senate Document No.685: "A League for Peace".

Worldometer (2024a). "*Countries in the world by population (2024).*" Accessed December 1, 2024. https://www.worldometers.info/world-population/population-by-country/.

Worldometer (2024b). "*World Population: Top 20 Largest Countries by Population (Live)*". Accessed December 1, 2024. https://www.worldometers.info/world-population/#top20.

World Population Review (2024). "*Countries Sending Troops to Ukraine 2024." Accessed November 11, 2024.*" https://worldpopulationreview.com/country-rankings/countries-sending-troops-to-ukraine.

Yale University (2008a). Yale Law School Lillian Goldman Law Library The Avalon Project – Atlantic Charter: August 14, 1941.

Yale University (2008b). Yale Law School Lillian Goldman Law Library The Avalon Project – Declaration by the United Nations: January 1, 1942.

Yale University (2008c). Yale Law School Lillian Goldman Law Library The Avalon Project – Inter-Allied Meeting Held in London at St. James's Palace on June 12, 1941: Resolution.

Yale University (2008d). Yale Law School Lillian Goldman Law Library The Avalon Project – The Moscow Conference Joint Four-Nation Declaration: October, 1943.

Index

A

African Union, 134
Allegations of Genocide under the Convention on the Prevention and Punishment of the Crime of Genocide (Ukraine v. Russian Federation), Provisional Measures, 8, 227, 263
Assembly of the League of Nations, 13, 20, 25, 28, 36, 230, 267

C

Case concerning Military and Paramilitary Activities in and against Nicaragua (Nicaragua v. United States of America), The Merits, 7, 227, 262
Case of the S.S. "Wimbeldon", 26
Charter of the United Nations (UN Charter), xi, xiii, 1, 3, 4, 5, 6, 7, 8, 9, 10, 11, 23, 33, 35, 36, 42, 43, 44, 45, 46, 47, 48, 49, 50, 51, 52, 53, 54, 55, 56, 57, 59, 62, 63, 65, 66, 73, 88, 100, 102, 134, 137, 140, 141, 154, 158, 159, 161, 166, 167, 168, 169, 173, 174, 175, 176, 177, 182, 183, 184, 185, 186, 201, 202, 203, 204, 205, 206, 219, 227, 234, 235, 236, 237, 238, 255, 256, 261, 265, 269, 270, 271
Conclusions on subsequent agreements and subsequent practice in relation to the interpretation of treaties, 92
Conclusions on identification of customary international law, 111, 132
conflict resolution, 153
Consistency of Certain Danzig Legislative Decrees with the Constitution of the Free City, 29
Convention on Fishing and Conservation of the Living Resources of the High Seas 1958, 197
Convention on the Continental Shelf 1958, 197
Convention on the High Seas 1958, 197
Convention on the Prevention and Punishment of the Crime of Genocide 1948, 78
Convention on the Territorial Sea and the Contiguous Zone 1958, 197
Council of the League of Nations, 13, 22, 25, 27, 28, 77, 175, 176
Covenant of the League of Nations, 13, 16, 17, 19, 20, 21, 22, 23, 24, 25, 26, 27, 28, 175, 176, 196, 229, 230, 263, 266, 267

D

Designation of the Workers' Delegate for the Netherlands at the Third Session of the International Labour Conference, 26
dispute resolution, 6, 142, 152, 173, 174, 183, 186, 195, 201, 203, 215, 219, 223
dispute settlement, 31, 33, 142, 152, 173, 174, 184, 185, 186, 193, 199, 213
Draft conclusions on general principles of law, 144, 148
Draft conclusions on identification and legal consequences of peremptory norms of general international law (*jus cogens*), 65, 70, 72, 108, 119, 120, 121, 122, 123, 124, 125, 126, 127, 128, 129, 130, 131, 132, 133, 134, 135, 136, 137, 138, 139, 140, 141, 142, 143, 154, 158, 161, 166, 167, 169, 171, 219, 246, 247, 248, 249, 250, 251, 252, 270
Draft conclusions on subsidiary means for the determination of rules of international law, 156, 158, 201, 254, 271

E

Economic and Social Council of the United Nations (ECOSOC), xiii, 48, 49, 52, 55, 69, 177
erga omnes, 65, 120, 121, 134, 135, 143, 154, 167, 267
European Union (EU), xiii, 11, 134, 153, 170, 190, 225, 259, 260

G

General Assembly, 4, 5, 7, 8, 9, 44, 46, 47, 48, 49, 52, 54, 55, 57, 58, 62, 65, 66, 67, 68, 69, 70, 72, 75, 76, 77, 78, 79, 84, 85, 88, 89, 92, 93, 94, 95, 107, 110, 117, 121, 127, 134, 136, 137, 138, 139, 140, 154, 158, 159, 162, 166, 167, 168, 169, 176,

177, 205, 206, 207, 227, 238, 243, 244, 245, 246, 247, 248, 249, 250, 251, 252, 253, 254, 255, 257, 263, 269, 270, 271
general principles of law, 30, 60, 65, 66, 72, 123, 124, 125, 143, 144, 145, 146, 147, 148, 149, 150, 151, 152, 153, 154, 155, 158

I

Inter-Allied Committee on the Future of the Permanent Court of International Justice, 57
International Atomic Energy Agency, 76
International Civil Aviation Organization, 76, 134
International Commission on Intervention and State Sovereignty (ICISS), 182
International Court of Justice (ICJ), xiii, 5, 7, 8, 11, 13, 14, 25, 26, 30, 32, 33, 34, 35, 36, 47, 48, 50, 54, 56, 57, 58, 59, 60, 61, 62, 63, 65, 66, 69, 72, 73, 74, 78, 79, 89, 93, 98, 107, 118, 121, 124, 126, 127, 135, 140, 141, 142, 143, 144, 145, 147, 148, 153, 154, 157,159, 173, 183, 184, 185, 186, 187, 193, 194, 199, 201, 202, 204, 205, 213, 214, 215, 219, 220, 221, 222, 223, 224, 225, 227, 230, 237, 239, 246, 248, 255, 256, 257, 262, 263, 266, 271
International Criminal Police Organization, 76
International Labour Conference, 75
International Labour Conventions, 33
International Labour Organization, 22, 23, 33, 76, 96, 98
International Law Commission (ILC), xi, xiii, 63, 65, 67, 68, 69, 70, 72, 73, 75, 77, 78, 79, 84, 85, 87, 88, 89, 91, 92, 94, 95, 107, 108, 109, 110, 120, 121, 127, 130, 131, 132, 134, 135, 139, 140, 142, 143, 144, 147, 148, 153, 154, 155, 156, 158, 159, 161, 166, 171, 173, 195, 199, 201, 202, 214, 215, 220, 221, 223, 224, 238, 239, 240, 242, 243, 244, 245, 246, 247, 248, 249, 250, 251, 252, 253, 254, 256, 257, 263, 264, 265, 270, 271
International Maritime Organization, 76
International Tribunal for the Law of the Sea (ITLOS), xiii, 118, 183, 184, 186, 193, 215, 220, 222, 223, 224, 257, 258, 265

J

jus cogens, 65, 70, 72, 108, 119, 120, 121, 122, 123, 124, 125, 126, 127, 128, 129, 130, 131, 132, 133, 134, 135, 136, 137, 138, 139, 140, 141, 142, 143, 154, 158, 161, 166, 167, 169, 171, 219, 246, 247, 248, 249, 250, 251, 252, 270

L

League of Nations, 13, 14, 16, 17, 19, 20, 21, 22, 23, 24, 25, 26, 27, 28, 33, 36, 60, 70, 77, 159, 176, 196, 228, 229, 230, 239, 259, 262, 263, 264, 266, 271
Legal Consequences for States of the Continued Presence of South Africa in Namibia (South West Africa) notwithstanding Security Council Resolution 276 (1970), 6
Lighthouses in Crete and Samos, 29

M

Member(s) of the League of Nations, 13, 19, 20, 21, 22, 23, 24, 26, 29, 31

O

Organisation for the Prohibition of Chemical Weapons, 76

P

Permanent Court of International Justice (PCIJ), xiii, 13, 14, 17, 24, 25, 26, 27, 28, 29, 30, 31, 32, 33, 35, 36, 56, 57, 59, 60, 61, 63, 107, 118, 148, 187, 196, 197, 201, 214, 228, 230, 231, 256, 263, 267, 268
Phosphates in Morocco, Preliminary Objections, 29
Preparatory Commission for the Comprehensive Nuclear-Test-Ban Treaty Organization, 76
Protocol concerning the Revision of the Statute of the Permanent Court of International Justice, 25, 28, 31
Protocol of Signature of the Statute for the Permanent Court of International Justice, 13, 26

Q

Questions relating to the Obligation to Prosecute or to Extradite (Belgium v. Senegal), 126, 127, 248, 262

R

Reservations to the Convention on the Prevention and Punishment of the Crime of Genocide, 78, 79, 262
Resolution concerning the establishment of a Permanent Court of International Justice, 230, 267
Resolution concerning the Revision of the Statute of the Permanent Court of International Justice, 28
resolution(s), xi, 4, 6, 7, 8, 9, 11, 13, 25, 33, 46, 50, 51, 62, 66, 70, 75, 77, 79, 85, 88, 89, 92, 93, 94,

98, 108, 109, 110, 113, 115, 117, 126, 127, 133, 134, 139, 140, 147, 149, 161, 165, 166, 167, 168, 169, 182, 184, 186, 193, 201, 203, 206, 207, 210, 255, 270
Rules of Court of the Permanent Court of International Justice (PCIJ), xiii, 13, 14, 17, 24, 25, 26, 27, 28, 29, 30, 31, 32, 33, 35, 36, 56, 57, 59, 60, 61, 63, 107, 118, 148, 187, 196, 197, 201

S

Seat of the League of Nations, 21
Secretary-General, 1, 5, 9, 10, 16, 21, 25, 31, 49, 53, 54, 59, 61, 63, 68, 69, 76, 77, 78, 79, 85, 87, 90, 93, 110, 121, 144, 162, 177, 185, 186, 190, 203, 204, 219, 262, 269, 270
Security Council (UNSC), xi, xiii, 1, 3, 4, 5, 6, 7, 8, 9, 10, 11, 35, 42, 43, 44, 45, 46, 47, 48, 49, 50, 51, 52, 54, 55, 56, 57, 58, 59, 62, 63, 69, 88, 134, 139, 163, 173, 174, 175, 176, 177, 178, 179, 180, 182, 183, 199, 201, 203, 205, 215, 219, 224, 255, 262, 268, 269
Security Council Report, 177, 179, 255, 268
Statute of the International Court of Justice (ICJ), 8, 33, 58, 59, 60, 61, 62, 74, 77, 148, 184, 185, 186, 194, 227, 230, 237, 238, 256, 269, 270, 271
Statute of the International Law Commission (ILC), 68, 69, 238, 254
Statute of the Permanent Court of International Justice (PCIJ), 25

T

The Borchgrave Case, Preliminary Objections, 29
The Case of the S.S. "Lotus", 256, 267
The Diversion of Water from the Meuse, 29
The Electricity Company of Sofia and Bulgaria, Preliminary Objection, 29
The M/T "Heroic Idun" (No. 2) Case (Marshall Islands/Equatorial Guinea), 215, 222, 257, 258, 265
The Pajzs, Czáky, Esterházy Case, 29
The Panevezys-Saldutiskis Railway Case, 29
The "Société Commerciale de Belgique", 29
The "Zheng He" Case (Luxembourg v. Mexico), 215, 222, 223, 258, 265

U

United Nations Convention on the Law of the Sea 1982 (UNCLOS), xiii, 173, 183, 184, 186, 188, 189, 190, 191, 192, 193, 194, 195, 197, 222, 223
United Nations Industrial Development Organization, 76
Universal Postal Union, 19, 76

V

veto(es), xi, 1, 3, 4, 5, 6, 9, 10, 11, 43, 45, 46, 47, 49, 56, 150, 173, 175, 176, 177, 178, 179, 180, 181, 182, 199, 201, 205, 215, 224, 255, 268
Vienna Convention on the Law of Treaties 1969, 65, 73, 75, 80, 83, 84, 90, 94, 98, 99, 100, 101, 102, 103, 104, 105, 106, 123, 127, 128, 129, 130, 131, 132, 133, 142, 143, 154, 158, 188
Vienna Convention on the Law of Treaties between States and International Organizations or between International Organizations 1986, 65, 73, 76, 80, 83, 84, 105, 106, 158, 188
Vienna Convention on the Succession of States in respect of Treaties 1978, 65, 84, 95, 97, 107, 158

W

World Health Organization, 76
World Intellectual Property Organization, 76
World Trade Organization, 118, 134
World Trade Organization Dispute Settlement Body, 118